ARTHURIAN STU

CW00554983

A COMPANION T

ARTHURIAN STUDIES

General Editor: Norris J. Lacy

ISSN 0261–9814

Previously published volumes in the series
are listed at the back of this book

A COMPANION TO CHRÉTIEN DE TROYES

Edited by Norris J. Lacy and Joan Tasker Grimbert

D. S. BREWER

First published 2005
D. S. Brewer, Cambridge
Reprinted in paperback 2008

ISBN 978 1 84384 161 6

D. S. Brewer is an imprint of Boydell & Brewer Ltd
PO Box 9, Woodbridge, Suffolk IP12 3DF, UK
and of Boydell & Brewer Inc.
668 Mt Hope Avenue, Rochester, NY 14620, USA
website: www.boydellandbrewer.com

A CIP catalogue record for this book is available
from the British Library

Library of Congress Catalog Card Number: 2005009926

This publication is printed on acid-free paper

Contents

PART III: MEDIEVAL RECEPTION AND INFLUENCE

The Contributors

JOHN W. BALDWIN is the Charles Homer Haskins Professor Emeritus of History at Johns Hopkins University. He was president of the Medieval Academy and is presently Membre de l'Institut de France as Associé étranger of the Académie des Inscriptions et Belles Lettres. He was decorated with the Légion d'Honneur. His writings include *Masters, Princes and Merchants* (1970), *The Government of Philip Augustus* (1986), *The Language of Sex* (1994), and *Aristocratic Life in Medieval France* (2000). A new volume, *Paris, 1200*, will appear shortly in France.

EMMANUÈLE BAUMGARTNER is Professor of Medieval French Literature at the Université de la Sorbonne nouvelle. President of the French Branch of the International Arthurian Society, she has written extensively on Chrétien de Troyes, prose Arthurian romances, Tristan and Yseut, and Villon and has published editions of medieval texts. She has also published a history of medieval literature and a study of 'Le récit médiéval'. At present, she is preparing a bilingual edition of *La Mort le roi Artu*.

MATILDA TOMARYN BRUCKNER is Professor of French at Boston College. She has published numerous books and articles in the fields of French romance and troubadour lyric, including *Shaping Romance: Interpretation, Truth, and Closure in Twelfth-Century French Fictions* and *Songs of the Women Troubadours*. Her current book project, focused on Chrétien's grail romance and its four verse continuations, explores how their contradictions, intertwined heroes, and collective authorship raise unresolved questions about violence, sexuality and religion.

KEITH BUSBY is Professor of French at the University of Wisconsin-Madison. He has published widely on medieval French literature, including a study of the figure of Gauvain in French Arthurian romance (1980) and a critical edition of Chrétien de Troyes's *Perceval* (1993). His most recent book is *Codex and Context* (2002). Among his current projects is a study of manuscripts of Old French copied in Italy.

ANNIE COMBES is Maître de Conférences in Medieval Literature at the Université de Nantes. In her research on Arthurian literature, she has published a book on the romance of *Lancelot*, titled *Les Voies de l'aventure*, as well as a study of the Grail motif, *Ecritures du Graal*, written in collaboration with Annie Bertin. She has co-edited *Floriant et Florete* with Richard Trachsler, and she is currently completing an edition of a prose version of the *Chevalier de la charrette*.

PETER F. DEMBOWSKI is the Distinguished Service Professor of French Emeritus at the University of Chicago. He is the author of *La Chronique de Robert de*

Clari: Etude de la langue et du style and *Jean Froissart and his Meliador*. He has edited *Ami et Amile, Jourdain de Blaye, La Vie de sainte Marie l'Egyptienne, Erec et Enide, Estrif de Fortune et Vertu* and *Le Paradis d'Amour et L'Orloge amoureus*. He is a member of the editorial board of *Romance Philology*.

JOAN TASKER GRIMBERT, Professor of French and Chair of Modern Languages & Literatures at Catholic University of America, is the International Treasurer of the International Arthurian Society. Her books include *'Yvain' dans le miroir: une poétique de la réflexion dans le 'Chevalier au lion' de Chrétien de Troyes* (1988), *Tristan and Isolde: A Casebook* (1995), *Songs of the Women Trouvères* (2001) and *Philologies Old and New: Essays in Honor of Peter Florian Dembowski* (2001). Her current project concerns the conjuncture of lyric and romance.

TONY HUNT, Besse Fellow at St Peter's College, Oxford, is a Fellow of the British Academy and a Foreign Member of the Norwegian Academy of Science and Letters. He has worked and published largely in the fields of medieval vernacular medicine, Anglo-Norman, Chrétien de Troyes, François Villon, editing medieval texts, the study of Latin in medieval England, and commentaries on the *Song of Songs*.

LAURENCE HARF-LANCNER, Professor of Medieval French Literature at the Université de la Sorbonne nouvelle (Paris III), has published several studies on medieval imagination, notably *Les Fées au Moyen Age. Morgane et Mélusine ou la naissance des fées* (Paris, 1984 et 1991) and *Le Monde des fées dans l'Occident médiéval* (Paris, 2003), as well as bilingual editions of medieval narratives. She is particularly interested in the reception of classical mythology, historiography, and the relationships between text and image.

DOUGLAS KELLY is Professor Emeritus of French and Medieval Studies at the University of Wisconsin-Madison. He has written extensively on medieval literature and poetics, rhetoric, and the *Roman de la rose*; he has also published a bibliography on Chrétien de Troyes. His most recent book is *The Conspiracy of Allusion: Description, Rewriting, and Authorship from Macrobius to Medieval Romance*; he is completing a book on Opinion in the writings of Christine de Pizan.

ROBERTA L. KRUEGER is Professor of French at Hamilton College. She is the author of *Women Readers and the Ideology of Gender in Old French Verse Romance* (1993) and editor of *The Cambridge Companion to Medieval Romance* (2000). She has also published numerous articles on medieval romance and didactic literature.

NORRIS J. LACY is Edwin Erle Sparks Professor of French and Medieval Studies at the Pennsylvania State University. He is Honorary President of the International Arthurian Society and holds the rank of Officier in the Ordre des Palmes Académiques. His publications include *The Craft of Chrétien de Troyes, The New Arthurian Encyclopedia, Reading Fabliaux, The Arthurian Handbook* and, as general editor and one of the translators, *Lancelot-Grail: The Old French Arthurian Vulgate and Post-Vulgate in Translation*.

DONALD MADDOX, Professor of French and Italian Studies at the University of Massachusetts, Amherst, is Honorary President of the International Courtly

Literature Society. Among his books are *The Arthurian Romances of Chrétien de Troyes* (1991) and *Fictions of Identity in Medieval France* (2000). Some seventy of his articles address topics in Medieval Studies, and recent co-edited collective volumes include *The Medieval French Alexander* (2002), *Froissart Across the Genres* (1998), *Melusine of Lusignan: Founding Fiction in Medieval France* (1996), *Transtextualities: Of Cycles and Cyclicity in Medieval French Literature* (1996) and *Literary Aspects of Courtly Culture* (1994). He is currently working on Latin and vernacular hagiography.

JUNE HALL MCCASH is Professor Emerita of French at Middle Tennessee State University. She is President of the International Courtly Literature Society and past president of the Southeastern Medieval Association. Her recent publications are on the works of Marie de France and patronage in medieval literature, including *The Cultural Patronage of Medieval Women*. She is currently working as co-editor of an edition and translation of a hagiographical text, *La Vie Seinte Audree*.

RUPERT T. PICKENS is Professor of French at the University of Kentucky. He has published books and articles on a variety of topics, including Chrétien de Troyes, Grail literature, Marie de France, Wace, poetry from the troubadours and Villon to the French poems of Thomas Merton, and French and francophone culture of the twelfth century. He is completing a book on *translatio* and the monstrous in the four works attributed to Marie de France.

SARA STURM-MADDOX is Professor Emerita of French and Italian Studies at the University of Massachusetts, Amherst. Her work explores medieval and Renaissance lyric, epic and romance. In addition to collaborative volumes in Medieval Studies edited with Donald Maddox, her books include *Petrarch's Metamorphoses* (1985), *Petrarch's Laurels* (1992) and *Ronsard, Petrarch, and the Amours* (1999). Her current project is a study of the collaboration of Ronsard and Catherine de' Medici.

MICHELLE SZKILNIK is Professor of Medieval French Literature at the Université de Nantes. Her research focuses on Arthurian and non-Arthurian narratives from the twelfth to the fifteenth centuries. Her latest titles include *Jean de Saintré, une carrière chevaleresque au XVe siècle* and the edition of *Meraugis de Portlesguez*, a thirteenth-century verse romance by Raoul de Houdenc. She is currently editing the *Jouvencel*, a fifteenth-century narrative by Jean de Bueil.

The publishers are grateful to the Vinaver Trust for generously
providing a subvention towards the original
production costs of this volume

The paperback edition was published with generous financial support
from the Catholic University of America
and Penn State University

Introduction

NORRIS J. LACY and JOAN TASKER GRIMBERT

Chrétien de Troyes is justly considered to be the creator of Arthurian romance. Although important Arthurian texts and perhaps oral tales as well pre-dated his works, he used that material and his imagination to produce something entirely new. The episodic romance, as he developed it, was a composition centered on the Arthurian court but primarily focused on the adventures of one (or two) of Arthur's knights, generally over a limited period of time. Chrétien also emphasized the nature of adventure – its uses and abuses – and examined the efficacy of chivalry and of the Arthurian ethic. The problems treated in his romances range from the connections and often the conflicts between love and prowess, between private pleasures v. public duties, between the couple and society and, in his final romance, between spiritual and secular quests.

Owing to his artistry, his prestige and the interest held by his themes, Chrétien proved to be a remarkably influential author, as the final section of this book indicates. His influence did not by any means end with medieval authors, though, and the modern recognition of his importance has led to the publication of many dozens of scholarly books and many hundreds, indeed thousands, of articles. In fact, during recent decades, Chrétien has been the most extensively studied of all Arthurian authors, and the bibliography is vast.

Even Chrétien specialists surely find the volume of critical studies on Chrétien daunting, and students, however diligent, will find it virtually impossible to select the most useful scholarship and to read and master even a small part of it. That very difficulty is the compelling justification for the present volume. Although we hope and expect that even Chrétien scholars will find a good deal of useful information and provocative criticism here, we are directing our chapters in particular to advanced students – to those who may have read Chrétien but wish now to undertake more serious study of his methods and accomplishment – and even to scholars in other disciplines, such as English or German Arthurian literature, who may wish to re-examine their literature's Arthurian antecedents and the current state of Chrétien scholarship. For those readers we offer initial chapters devoted to important subjects preliminary to a study of his romances, and the volume concludes with considerations of his influence. The heart of the book, though, consists of six major chapters, treating the works themselves.

A word is in order about the corpus of works we study in this volume. Obviously, we devote a major chapter to each of the five Arthurian romances that

Chrétien is known to have composed. Beyond those texts, however, questions of attribution become complicated. Two *chansons* (lyrics) are assumed to be his work, and he may have composed others, now lost or without attribution. The two poems are often neglected in discussions of Chétien, but his activity as a lyric poet or *trouvère* is both intrinsically significant and pertinent to his treatment of themes and motifs within his romances. We therefore include discussion of the *chansons* in the chapter devoted to *Cligés*. There is more controversy surrounding the authorship of *Philomena* (an adaptation of the Philomela story from Ovid) and the non-Arthurian composition *Guillaume d'Angleterre*. Although not all scholars agree with the attribution of the former to Chrétien, the majority of them now accept it as his work, as do we and the majority of our contributors. We thus include a chapter devoted to that text. The authorship of *Guillaume d'Angleterre*, however, is rendered more problematic not only by the subject (similar in form and tone to a saint's life) but also by the relatively limited artistry it displays, and we consider it unlikely, though not impossible, that the author is Chrétien de Troyes. We thus exclude it, for practical purposes, from our corpus.

The dating and, in one instance, even the chronology of Chrétien's compositions remain a subject of controversy, and rather than ask contributors to discuss this matter in their chapters, we can quickly summarize here the little we know about it. Some scholars have argued that Chrétien wrote in the 1160s and 1170s; others that his works date from the 1170s and 1180s. The only certainties, or near certainties, about dates are in fact negative ones. He could not have begun his *Lancelot*, dedicated to Marie, Countess of Champagne, earlier than 1159, the probable date when she acquired that title by marrying Henry the Liberal, Count of Champagne. Moreover, because Philip of Flanders, the patron of his final romance (*Perceval*) left for the Third Crusade in 1190 and died in 1191, Chrétien necessarily undertook that composition before the second of those dates and most likely before the first. Within those limits, there is little or no agreement about the dating of his works.

As noted, there is one instance of chronological uncertainty. Traditionally, most scholars assumed that, after *Erec* and *Cligés*, Chrétien composed *Lancelot* and then *Yvain* before undertaking *Perceval*. Because *Yvain* contains three allusions to plot elements we find in *Lancelot*, it was accepted that the latter romance had already been written. However, a number of scholars contend that the composition of these two romances overlapped. Moreover, it could even be argued, and sometimes has been, that *Yvain* was written first and that Chrétien then developed fully in *Lancelot* those elements merely referred to in his previous work. This question, like that of the dates of Chrétien's activity, remains unsettled and appears insoluble in the present state of our knowledge. Fortunately, although such questions are important in the assessment of Chrétien's influence on authors writing at about the same time, they are not major impediments to the evaluation of his artistic accomplishment.

Having left our contributors largely free to develop their subjects as they wished, we have not produced in this volume any systematic accounting of the variety or evolution of Chrétien scholarship. That scholarship is so rich and so diverse that it is impossible to characterize it in a brief space; nor can our own very selective bibliography do more than offer a useful guide to further reading. We still regularly have studies of Chrétien's influence on other romance authors, and considerations of his narrative technique and artistic innovations are varied and numerous. Other subjects prominently represented in the literature include his uses of irony, the systematic marks of fictionality in his work, and questions of patronage. In addition, the manuscripts of Chrétien's work have been productively studied of late. Both the volume and the variety of scholarship frustrate efforts to convey a sense of critical trends. We might suggest, though, that the evolution of Chrétien scholarship has followed a trajectory leading from the early search for sources and analogues to a greater concentration on textual analysis and, more recently, to a broadening of focus that serves to place Chrétien's works in the context of what we might categorize as cultural studies, such as consideration of sociological, anthropological or gender questions. The best indication of evolving critical practice may be found by perusing the Chrétien bibliographies compiled by Douglas Kelly (see the bibliography to the present volume). We do not have in English a thorough survey of historical trends in Chrétien scholarship, but Kelly's bibliography (especially pp. 62–70) lists broader reviews of scholarship: Grail studies, Arthurian scholarship in general and work on the courtly romance form. Readers of French can also find a concise but helpful survey of critical trends in Per Nykrog's study (also listed in our bibliography).

Readers of this book will note occasional disagreements among the authors of chapters. Differences may involve the interpretation of a passage or an entire text, or they may reflect variant views of Chrétien's source material or of the extent to which that material influenced his composition. We are fully aware of such conflicting views but have thought it neither necessary nor desirable to homogenize chapters. Such a process would conceal legitimate differences of opinion rather than give an accurate impression of the vigorous debates that often occur among Chrétien scholars. We have therefore made comparatively little effort to harmonize views, though we have in some instances inserted notes directing readers of a chapter to divergent judgments offered by another of our authors.

We should add a note about the editions of Chrétien's works and about our own editorial approach. Even in the twenty-first century we still have full and proper critical editions of only two of the Arthurian romances, *Cligés* by Claude Luttrell and Stewart Gregory and *Perceval* by Keith Busby. Those are the editions used for those two texts. For the other three Arthurian romances and the lyrics, our references are to the editions published in the Pochothèque series, of which Michel Zink is general editor. *Philomena* is cited in the edition by Emmanuèle Baumgartner. Specific bibliographical information is given in each chapter's first reference to any of Chrétien's compositions.

Some discrepant spellings of names and titles occur in our chapters. Our general policy has been to spell names as they would be given in a modern critical edition, even when those forms differ from more traditional spellings. Thus, in referring to the character, we write Cligés rather than Cligès. However, when we cite titles or quote from critical studies, we naturally follow the form given therein. This practice never leads to confusion but does, on rare occasions, produce some spellings that depart from convention. Finally, and purely for the sake of convenience in discussing Chrétien's romances, we and our contributors often refer to them, as we have in this introduction, by the briefest customary titles rather than by the full titles provided by the author himself. Thus, for example, the reader will encounter the title *Perceval* more frequently than *Le Conte du Graal*.

PART I
BACKGROUND

1

Chrétien in History

JOHN W. BALDWIN

A genius in creating fictional worlds, Chrétien was remarkably insulated from his own historical context.* Even his name presents a problem. Was he from Troyes in Champagne as he asserts in his first romance, *Erec et Enide* (vs. 9) – and this was probably the case – or was his name an ironic oxymoron, a Christian from the pagan Greek city of Troy from which the Frankish peoples claimed their mythological descent, in imitation of Vergil's account of the origins of the Romans? His five canonical romances are relatively free of markers of place and time that point outside the text. Only *Cligés*, his second romance, unfolds in a contemporary geographic setting. The story shifts back and forth between the eastern Greek empire designated by the cities of Athens and Constantinople and King Arthur's realm in England, punctuated by the sites of London, Windsor and Oxford-Wallingford. The ports of entry and departure are appropriately Southampton and Shoreham on the Sussex coast. The German empire occupies a middle space, designated by the cities of Regensburg and Cologne. The action in *Erec et Enide*, however, is limited to the Celtic fringe signified by Cardigan in Wales, York and Tenebroc on the Scottish borders and Nantes in Brittany, but without connecting itineraries or the crossing of seas. Space in the three remaining romances is Arthurian and mythological of Chrétien's invention. *Lancelot* and *Perceval* feature the fictive kingdom of Logres and romantic place names such as Noauz and Beaurepaire. *Yvain* and *Perceval* purport to take place in Wales. Caerleon, where Arthur stays, is actually in Wales, but the place name 'Carduel', which Chrétien specifies as Arthur's chief seat in Wales in *Yvain* and *Perceval*, may be a confusion for Cardigan in Wales, but it is the normal spelling in French for Carlisle on the borders of Scotland. Other identifiable places occur in connection with minor characters; such as a certain David and a Tiebaut of Tintagel; or allusions to valued products known from their place of origin, as, for example, silks from Thessaly, Constantinople and Alexandria and horses from Gascony, Arabia, Spain and especially Norway. Except for *Cligés*, time is invariably marked by the calendar of the great ecclesiastical feasts, particularly Pentecost, when the weather usually promises to be fine. The feast of the birth of

---

* The primary sources that undergird this chapter are so numerous and complex that it would be impossible to acknowledge them in full. They have been used and summarized in standard secondary works that I have included in a bibliographic note at the end of the chapter. This plan appears preferable to citing them repetitiously in footnotes.

St John the Baptist (24 June) figures prominently in *Yvain*, where deadlines govern the plot.

Chrétien exhibits no need to evoke contemporary historical events or person-ages. Modern critics have long amused themselves by linking episodes like Erec's wedding at Nantes and the maidens in the sweatshop of the castle of Pesme Aventure (*Yvain*) with historical referents, but the connections are not Chrétien's. Amidst a galaxy of fictional Celtic kings, the chief political personage is, of course, Arthur, whom Chrétien encountered, if not in the Latin pages of Geoffrey of Monmouth, at least in the French translation of the Anglo-Norman poet Wace. The great Breton hero was doubtlessly a powerful ideological image for the Plantagenet court of King Henry II, further historicized by the alleged discovery of Arthur's tomb at Glastonbury in 1191, but whether Chrétien himself equated Arthur with the English king is highly doubtful. In all events, our author studiously avoids explicit connections between Arthur (or any other of his characters) and historical personages.

The closest Chrétien comes to acknowledging his contemporary world lies in the recurrence of certain aristocratic amusements that accurately correspond to current practice. For example, the frequent tournaments where knights fight both in single combat and as teams appear to approximate the contemporary contests revealed in the slightly later but historically orientated *Histoire de Guillaume le Maréchal*. The numerous festivities are replete with games, jongleurs, songs, dances and banquets; the enticing descriptions of food and clothing not only express alimentary and vestimentary codes but also the actual commodities themselves, although explicit historical referents are absent. It is also true, however, that the paucity of testimony on these matters outside the literary accounts has forced historians to rely heavily on authors like Chrétien for details that, in turn, add circularity to their arguments.

Only two, perhaps three, exceptions puncture this hermetic bubble of Chrétien's fictional universe. Never claiming to have invented his stories himself, but always attributing their origin to someone else, our author announces that the story of *Cligés* (vss 18–21) was found in a book located at the actual cathedral of Saint-Pierre de Beauvais. More important, two other romances were based on material supplied by two historical personages to whom the works were addressed. These two can be authenticated without doubt from the historical record. *Lancelot* (vss 1–23) was addressed to Marie, countess of Champagne, who held court at Troyes. The romance's preoccupation with adultery was likewise attributed to the countess in a Latin treatise on love by Andreas Capellanus, who also spent time at Troyes. Eight of the surviving thirty-four thirteenth-century manuscripts were written in the Champenois dialect, including the earliest copy (Guiot) of all the romances that was preserved in the countal library at Troyes. Chrétien's last romance, *Perceval* (vss 1–64), was sent to Philip of Alsace, count of Flanders, whose pious virtues celebrated in the dedication correspond to the religious orientation of the narra-tive. Fifteen of all the thirteenth-century manuscripts were in the Picard dialect, suggesting that north-east France, where the count ruled, provided a large and appreciative audience for Chrétien's writing. (Of this number, seven of the fifteen *Perceval* manuscripts were in Picard). Although Chrétien isolated himself from his political world, the names of Countess Marie and Count Philip associate him with two influential contemporary courts and provide points of orientation within the historical world as he might have experienced it. To the Flemish and the Champenois we must, of course, add two other courts, the Anglo-Norman-Angevin and the French Capetian, to complete Chrétien's political context.

If we accept the dates of 1160 to 1191 as the time period during which Chrétien wrote, the court of Champagne is framed by the careers of Count Henry the Liberal (1152–81), his wife Countess Marie (1164–98) and their son Count Henry II (1187–97). They inherited a vast feudal complex of fragmented and dispersed lands lying both to the east and west of Paris. To the east the broad open country was known as Champagne (*campania*) and consisted chiefly of regions surrounding the towns of Troyes, Provins and Meaux. To the south and west were the fiefs of Sancerre, Blois, Châteaudun and Chartres. Henry the Liberal took the county of Troyes for himself, assigning Sancerre to his brother Stephen, and Blois and Chartres to his brother Theobald. The feudal complexity of this conglomeration was remarkable. Only Meaux was held from the king of France, with Troyes from the duke of Burgundy, and important lands in the east from the archbishop of Reims and even the German emperor. The poor soil to the east was compensated by the commercial wealth that came from the famous fairs of Champagne located at Troyes, Provins, Lagny and Bar-sur-Aube that had become centres of international trade.

Count Philip of Alsace (1157–91) presided over the court of Flanders and held a compact, fertile and populous fief situated in north-eastern France and present-day Belgium. It profited from manufacturing cities like Ghent, Bruges, Douai, Lille, Ypres, Saint-Omer and Arras. Specializing in the production of woollen cloth, they depended on raw materials shipped from England. The southern regions of Flanders were held in fief from the French king, but the eastern parts from the German emperor. (Chrétien ignores Philip's French vassalage by addressing him as 'the most worthy man in the empire of Rome', *Perceval*, vss 11–15.) Through strategic marriages Philip expanded his influence south into Vermandois and Artois and to the east into Hainaut.

In Chrétien's day the Anglo-Norman-Angevin court was ruled by the great King Henry II of England (1154–89). In two breathtaking years Henry assembled through family ties the largest collection of fiefs in western Europe. In 1154 he inherited from his mother the English crown (which included Wales and Cornwall as well) and the duchy of Normandy (with overlordship of Brittany) and from his father the county of Anjou (which also comprised Maine and Touraine). In 1153 he had married Eleanor, the heiress of Aquitaine, freshly separated from the king of France. This vast duchy extended from Poitou in the north to Gascony and Toulouse in the south. Whereas Henry the Liberal chose his brothers, Henry Plantagenet enlisted his sons to help him rule his vast continental holdings. His eldest, the young King Henry, was associated with his father to rule the heartland of England, Normandy and Anjou. Geoffrey was assigned Brittany; Richard, Aquitaine; and the infant John was left out for the time, hence his surname 'Lackland'. In addition to his insular British kingdom, King Henry was therefore lord over the western half of France extending from

Normandy to Gascony, for all of which he was the nominal vassal of the French king. Since Henry had assembled his vast lands through feudal inheritance, he and his sons remained scrupulous in observing fealty and homage to their suzerain, the Capetian king, despite their disagreements and open hostilities. At the time the French king was Louis VII (1137–79), who was then succeeded by his son Philip Augustus (1179–1223). Although feudal suzerain of the entire kingdom of France, Louis in fact ruled directly only a small conglomeration of territories centred upon the cities of Paris, Compiègne, Orléans and Bourges. Known as the Ile-de-France, these miniscule lands were the 'France' of romance parlance, but they were overshadowed by the powerful Flemish to the north (Vermandois lay only twenty-five kilometres from Paris), the Champagne family to the east and south and the vast Anglo-Norman-Angevin fiefs to the northwest and west.

From early times the courts of Champagne, Flanders, the Anglo-Norman-Angevins and the French kings were essentially itinerant and consisted of household officers bearing the titles of seneschal who procured the provisions, of butler who dispensed the drink, of chamberlain who guarded the sleeping quarters, of constable or marshal who cared for the horses and of chancellor who oversaw the chapel and the secretariat. Except for the chancellor these domestic officials usually held their positions by hereditary right. As this primitive but omni-competent court peregrinated throughout the dispersed lands, it discharged the elemental functions of record-keeping, justice and finance. During the twelfth century, however, new centralized institutions were established at fixed places that began to transform the primitive courts into structured principalities. To these focal points new local officials were summoned periodically to give account for their duties. Champagne, for example, was governed chiefly from the towns of Troyes, Provins and Meaux. In 1157 Henry the Liberal founded Saint-Etienne at Troyes, a collegiate church of canons attached to the count's palace that not only housed Henry's personal library but also supplied him with chancellors, a secretariat of clerics for drafting his letters, future storage for his archives, and most likely an accounting bureau for his finances. Throughout the county of Troyes his lands were organized around castles held in fief by local castellans. Although it is not clear what control the count exercised over these officials, in 1172 he did record a survey of all of the knights (some 1900) who owed service in these castellanies. This was a fitting inventory for the most feudalized of all the principalities in France.

In Flanders the counts boasted of one of the earliest chanceries in France that was presided over by a chancellor chosen from the church of Saint-Donatian at Bruges. By the time of Philip of Alsace, this official generally supervised the count's administration. Another official from Saint-Donatian, the prévôt, presided over a central accounting bureau at the church that recorded both the count's revenues and his expenses. Like Champagne, the knights of the county of Flanders were organized into castellanies where they owed the service of castle-guard as vassals. The castellan was normally responsible for justice in the locality, but Philip of Alsace created a new local official, the bailli, who encroached on the castellan's duties. A salaried officer, the bailli was directly responsible to the count, administered justice, collected revenues and accounted for them periodically at the central bureau. A surviving account from 1187 demonstrates not only sophisticated accounting techniques, but also governmental institutions staffed by efficient officials. As a developing principality, Flanders was a step ahead of Champagne.

The most precocious, however, were the Anglo-Norman-Angevin fiefs. Inheriting the reforms of his grandfather King Henry I in the early twelfth century, Henry II profited from this English legacy to introduce the most advanced governmental techniques to the Continent. The chancery remained with the king's court, thus providing continuity as it travelled incessantly throughout the dispersed lands. Treasuries were established at Poitiers, Angers, Chinon, Falaise and especially Caen to provide administrative focal points within the respective fiefs. Henry relied on the seneschals at the courts of Anjou, Brittany and Poitou to serve as his chief agents. Directly held by the king, Anjou was firmly governed, but in Brittany and Poitou the seneschals assisted Henry's sons, Geoffrey and Richard, to manage their respective fiefs. Closely attached to England since the early twelfth century, Normandy was the important exception to the essentially feudal structure of Henry's French lands. In this duchy Henry inherited a system of local officers called vicomtes who, like the royal sheriffs in England, collected the duke's revenues and administered justice in the localities. Twice a year they travelled to the ducal exchequer at Caen to render account of their finances just as the sheriffs came to Westminster. The resulting financial rolls were the earliest on the Continent. A central court of justice was established at the exchequer to hear pleas from the entire duchy. It was staffed by permanent justices, among whom certain were detached to travel in pairs throughout the duchy to make the duke's justice more widely accessible. In 1172, like the count of Champagne, Henry also recorded an inquest into the service he was owed by all of the knights in the duchy just as he done in England in 1166. As the other French fiefs, Normandy was thoroughly feudalized, but it was closely supervised and managed by officials who were directly responsible to the duke-king.

The least developed of these courts was that of the Capetians. Although theoretically suzerain over the above fiefs, Kings Louis VII and Philip Augustus were satisfied with a rudimentary court and local officials to govern their small domain in the Ile-de-France that had only recently been pacified for safe travel by Louis and his father. The royal court consisted of the traditional household officers, seneschal, butler, chamberlain, constable and chancellor, who performed the necessary governmental functions along with their domestic duties. In particular the seneschal assisted with justice, the chamberlain with finances and the chancellor with record-keeping. The domain was administered by local officials called prévôts who, like the Norman vicomtes, manned the castles, held justice and collected revenues. They were supervised by the peregrinating court that could cross the small domain in a few days. It was easier to bring the court to the countryside than the reverse. Paris emerged gradually as the preferred residence of the itinerant king. Only after Chrétien stopped writing (around 1190) did Philip Augustus begin to modernize his government to accommodate his absence on the Third Crusade. At that moment the Capetians caught up with and even surpassed the governmental institutions of their vassal principalities.

If Chrétien attended the courts of Champagne and Flanders, he paid no attention to their developing governmental institutions. Whether or not he personally knew Count Henry the Liberal at Troyes, he explicitly acknowledged Countess Marie who ruled the county from 1179 to 1187 during Henry's absence in the Holy Land followed by his death and her regency for her son Henry II and again from 1190 to 1198 during Henry II's absence in the Holy Land until her own death. King Arthur, the sole political focal point of Chrétien's romances, remains unsuccessful in battle, helpless in keeping the peace, has no interest in governing, not even in assuring his succession. Queen Guinevere remains inexplicably barren. His court is constantly on the move as befitted the traditional and primitive feudal court, but it contains no household officers, except for the Seneschal Kay who is distinguished by his sharp tongue, not by the duties of provisioning the court or dispensing justice. All that concerns Chrétien is the celebrated Round Table that assembles the best knights of the realm, whose prime function is to depart on adventures and return with reports of glorious exploits. Kingship for Arthur consisted of the martial renown of his companion warriors. The Ile-de-France, the central domain of the Capetian kingdom, is virtually ignored except as the centre of learning and chivalry in the West (*Cligés*, vss 24–44), the place of elegant clothes (*Cligés*, vss 4968–70) and of women who speak French well (*Lancelot*, vss 39–40).

The contemporary chroniclers writing in Latin were not especially interested in the governmental developments within the French principalities except for the English historians who, conditioned by the precocity of their kings, took cognizance of political activities. Being monks and clerics, the contemporary chroniclers naturally favoured ecclesiastical affairs, like the assassination of Thomas Becket, archbishop of Canterbury, in 1169. When they turned to the lay world, they noticed the ebb and flow of intermittent warfare and the accompanying treaties and alliances sealed by innumerable political marriages among the royalty and nobility. If the chroniclers reflected common knowledge shared by the clerics, knights and ladies at the courts of Champagne and Flanders, these would be the events known to Chrétien if he frequented these assemblies. Because of the French king's suzerainty, if not his effectiveness, contemporary politics therefore revolved around the royal court.

One of the principal foundations of the Capetian monarchy was dynastic continuity. For six generations the kings had succeeded in producing a male heir and persuading the barons to accept him as king without the disputed successions that had plagued the contemporary royal houses in England and Germany. A crisis occurred under Louis VII, however, when, after three wives and nearly thirty years of marriage, only daughters had been engendered. A birth of a son, Philip, to the aged king in 1165 was therefore greeted by the inhabitants of the Ile-de-France with understandable jubilation and relief, and the infant prince was endowed with the sobriquet *dieudonné*. We shall see, however, that the many daughters were to prove politically useful. Chrétien's political world was framed by the Second and Third Crusades (1147–90). These four decades witnessed a three-cornered competition among the families of Champagne, Flanders, and the Anglo-Norman-Angevins that revolved around the Capetian court. Amidst the bewildering confusion of political, marital and military events, four major stages can be discerned. At the outset the traditional rivalries consisted of the Capetians against the house of Blois-Troyes (the future Champagne complex) that encircled them and the rivalry between Blois and Anjou in the Loire Valley over Tours. Normally the Capetians sided with the Angevins against Blois, but Henry II's accession to the Norman and Angevin dominions in 1154 provoked a diplomatic revolution that may be seen as opening the first stage. This, we remember, had been preceded by Henry's marriage in 1153 to Eleanor, heiress of Aquitaine. Decades earlier, in 1137, Louis VII had married Eleanor, thereby acquiring Aquitaine which he had attached to the French crown without integrating the domains. The incompatibility of the royal couple, reinforced by a lack of sons required by the royal succession, provoked Louis to separate from the queen and seek a second wife, Constance of Castile. The motivation for the decision is plausible, but Louis's subsequent inability to prevent Eleanor from marrying the future King Henry is perplexing. Thus emboldened, Henry forced Louis to cede the Vexin (the strategic borderland between Normandy and the Ile-de-France) as the dowry of Margaret, Louis's eldest daughter by Constance of Castile, as the price of her marriage to the young King Henry in 1160. (Later the king was obliged to affiance Adelaide, his second daughter by Constance, to Henry's third son, Richard, in 1169.) Overpowered by the Anglo-Norman-Angevin lands on at least two sides, the French king was forced to scrap former alliances and seek new allies. His choice fell on the Champagne family, newly formed from Blois and Troyes. Theobald of Blois had been named seneschal of the royal court in 1154. Immediately after Constance's death in 1160 Louis himself espoused Adèle of Champagne and in rapid succession in 1160 proposed his two daughters by Eleanor of Aquitaine to the Champagne brothers: Marie (Chrétien's addressee) to Henry the Liberal and Alix to Theobald of Blois. When William, the youngest of the Champagne brothers, was finally elevated to the archbishopric of Reims, the bonds between the king and the Champagne family were complete. Reinforced by this support, Louis attempted to withstand Henry's domination by lending support to Thomas Becket, the estranged archbishop of Canterbury and finally to aid Henry's sons as they rebelled against their father with the encouragement of Eleanor, now estranged from Henry as well. When the uprising was suppressed in 1174, Henry forgave his sons and made a truce with Louis at Nonencourt in 1177.

The second epoch in the conflict opened at Reims on 1 November 1179 with the coronation of Philip Augustus, son of Louis VII and Adèle of Champagne, which provided a stage for the three major contenders. Most visible was Philip of Alsace (Chrétien's addressee), who carried the king's sword in the opening procession and performed the duties of seneschal at the concluding banquet. King Henry of England was absent but was represented by his sons, the young King Henry, who carried the crown and placed it on Philip's head, and counts Geoffrey and Richard, who brought conspicuous gifts. The family of Champagne was likewise represented by William, archbishop of Reims, who officiated over the ceremonies. Queen Adèle was doubtless absent with the bedridden Louis, who soon succumbed to a stroke. Her brothers Henry and Theobald were either abroad in the Holy Land or disaffected by the prominence of the count of Flanders who was intent on dominating the fourteen-year-old Capetian.

Not only had Philip of Alsace frequented the royal court, but he also had reinforced his territorial base in Flanders with a series of strategic marriages. In 1159 he himself had married the heiress to the county of Vermandois, thus advancing his borders close to the royal domain, and later he gave his sister Margaret to Baldwin V, count of Hainaut, thus protecting his eastern lands. But the climax of his marital politics was achieved in 1180 when he succeeded in proposing his niece, Isabelle, daughter of Count Baldwin and Margaret of Hainaut, as wife for the new king. This move threatened the position of the Champagne house at court, because Isabelle as the new queen now supplanted the queen mother, Adèle of Champagne. (Isabelle, moreover, had been previously betrothed to the eldest son of Henry the Liberal and Marie of Champagne.) Adèle responded by fortifying her own lands and calling upon the intervention of King Henry of England, who appeared on the scene but refused to profit from the disturbance at court and mediated a peace between the contending factions at Gisors in 1180.

Frustrated at court, Philip of Alsace opened the third phase of the three-cornered conflict by openly defying the king. He further reinforced his position by arranging marriages between two of his sisters' children from Hainaut with the house of Champagne. He even considered matrimony with Marie of Champagne herself, now widowed by the death of Count Henry the Liberal in 1181. The support of Stephen, count of Sancerre, was enlisted as well. Philip Augustus responded by threatening to divorce Queen Isabelle of the Hainaut-Flemish house and seeking to split the alliance between her father Count Baldwin and the count of Flanders. These marital and diplomatic manoeuvres were accompanied by overt hostilities as the king attacked Flanders, and Philip of Alsace threatened to plant his banner on the Petit-Pont at Paris. The two armies finally confronted each other across the river Somme, but with the mediation of the Champagne family they agreed on a peace at Boves in 1185. Throughout this third phase, King Henry of England was remarkably restrained from profiting from the French king's discomfiture. Since 1180 he had renewed the traditional arrangement with the count of Flanders that paid the count a rent of 1,000 pounds sterling in exchange for 500 knights. Had he chosen to join forces with the Flemish, the young Capetian would have been helpless.

Whatever the reasons for King Henry's neutrality, Philip Augustus never forgot his father's advice learned from the diplomatic revolution of 1154 – that the chief threat to the Capetians was the encirclement of the royal lands by the Anglo-Norman-Angevins. After Flanders was neutralized in 1185, Philip initiated the fourth phase of the conflict by returning to his father's policy of pitting the sons of Henry against their father. We remember the marriage agreements of the 1160s that had united Henry's sons with Philip's half-sisters by Queen Constance: the young King Henry wedded Margaret and Richard, duke of Aquitaine, affianced Adelaide. (This last wedding, constantly postponed by Richard, became the unfinished business of the decade.) The young King Henry's unexpected death in 1183, however, not only removed him from Philip's machinations but also disturbed the father's plan for succession. King Henry's solution was to replace Henry with Richard as the young king and to set John in Richard's place as duke of Aquitaine. When Richard steadfastly resisted relinquishing a real fief for an undefined position under the shadow of his father,

Henry, in turn, refused to confirm Richard's place in the royal succession. With the disappearance of the young Henry, Philip Augustus turned his attention to Geoffrey, count of Brittany, to whom he offered, it was rumoured, the royal seneschalcy. But Geoffrey himself also disappeared from the scene in 1186, the victim of a tournament accident. With this opportunity also gone, the Capetian's grief was doubtlessly genuine as he buried the count in the cathedral of Notre-Dame at Paris.

While the French king gained little against the Anglo-Norman-Angevins during the fighting on the Norman borders and in the Berry that followed these negotiations, Philip finally found a receptive response to his attentions from the discontented Richard. By 1187 the two had become fast friends, which gave Philip opportunity to nourish Richard's fears that his father intended to disinherit him in favour of John. When in 1188 at Bonmoulins the English king refused to confirm Richard's place in the succession, Richard turned his back, knelt in homage to King Philip, and left the court in anger. Thereafter, in league with the Capetian, he pursued and harried his father until the old man died heartbroken near Tours in 1189. Throughout this last phase of the Capetians versus King Henry, the Champagne and Flemish parties remained in attendance at the royal court. Like the Anglo-Norman-Angevins during the previous stages, they did not attempt to take advantage of Philip Augustus's difficulties. By 1189 the archbishop of Reims and the count of Flanders sought to negotiate peace among the warring parties. Whatever the former opposition of the families of Champagne and Flanders, they became loyal vassals by the end of the decade.

As the 1180s revolved, the tempo of armed conflict in skirmishes and sieges of castles increased until it reached a crescendo in the final stage against the Anglo-Norman-Angevins that extended from Normandy into the Loire Valley. These hostilities were brought to a sudden halt, however, by the intrusion of an outside event, the defeat of a Christian army in the Holy Land and the fall of Jerusalem to the Saracen general Saladin in 1187. The papacy summoned the royalty and nobility of western Christendom to participate in the Third Crusade and condemned as scandalous the fighting among Christians in France while the Holy City was in the hands of the infidel. With characteristic spontaneity Count Richard took the cross immediately, but his father and the French king were wary about the strategic and political implications of their mutual departures. With Henry's death in 1189, Richard thereby inherited his father's position and concerns, and he too was obliged to make careful agreements with Philip before they could take leave of their lands. Both assumed the cross on the same day in 1190, Philip at Saint-Denis outside of Paris, and Richard at Tours. They met briefly at the abbey of Vézelay and then took separate routes, Philip to Genoa and Richard to Marseilles, and thence by sea to the Holy Land. To protect the Capetians against rebellion during the king's absence, Philip made sure that all of his major barons accompanied him, including Philip of Alsace, count of Flanders, and Counts Theobald of Blois and Stephen of Sancerre of the Champagne family. (On the death of Count Henry the Liberal in 1181 his son Henry II had made his own way to Palestine.) When Philip Augustus returned eighteen months later, he left these old men of his father's generation, Philip, Theobald and Stephen, buried in the Palestinian sands. Henry II remained in the East until his death in 1197. Arriving at Paris in 1191, the Capetian revived his campaign against his major rivals, the Anglo-Norman-Angevins, now headed by his former friend, Richard. A brutal attack was planned against the lands of the newly-crowned Richard, who had remained in the Holy Land. The Third Crusade, however, not only brought a brief respite to France from the warring factions, but also brought to a close Chrétien's political world. His acknowledged addressee from the court of Flanders was dead; his male patrons at the court of Champagne were likewise dead or absent; and Marie was left regent once again in the place of her son, Henry II, until her own death in 1198.

The period between the two crusades is the best-chronicled epoch of French history of the high Middle Ages. The politics, alliances, treaties, and marriages that have just been rehearsed were reported in vivid detail in the pages of historians like Rigord, the royal historiographer at the Capetian court, Robert, canon of Auxerre, for the Champenois region, Gislebert of Mons, canon of Namur, for the Flemish-Hainaut area, but most especially the English chroniclers, such as 'Benedict' of Peterborough, Roger of Howden and Ralph de Diceto. Stimulated by the brilliant court of King Henry II and his political and governmental achievements, these English historians attained what can rightfully be called the golden age of medieval English historiography. To these Latin treatises may also be added the unusual occurrence in French verse of the *Histoire de Guillaume le Maréchal*, which details the career and tournaments of a historical English knight in France during the period under consideration. Even if situated at the courts of Troyes and Flanders, Chrétien nonetheless wrote romances that remained totally oblivious to the political, matrimonial and martial events of his day, just as they ignored the governmental achievements within the three surrounding principalities and the king's domain. The knights who depart from and return to King Arthur's court are primarily interested in the affairs of chivalric prowess, romantic love, and especially their interaction. Prowess is displayed largely in tournaments, single combats, and the relief of castles under siege. While the reader might perceive similarities to these activities in the historical world, never does Chrétien call attention to them. When knights and kings fall in love, most often they marry the women whom they love; rarely are their unions motivated by politics as we have witnessed in scores of royal and aristocratic marriages in the chronicles. Never did Chrétien let slip an explicit allusion to an event that can be identified from contextual sources. His *monde événementiel* remains that of his own imagination.

Chrétien's creative genius, however, generated a truly impressive literary sequel. Not only was he quickly translated, notably into German, Norse and English, but his impact on French continued for centuries. Whether the *Perceval* was left unfinished by design or not, it attracted at least four continuations in verse and many other versions in prose, culminating in the monumental Vulgate (*Lancelot-Grail*) and Post-Vulgate Cycles. Chrétien also provoked another kind of reaction, if less spectacular, in the next generation of French romances. From about 1200 to 1230 Jean Renart (certainly an obfuscating name) and his imitator Gerbert de Montreuil composed three romances, *Escoufle, Roman de la rose ou Guillaume de Dole* and *Roman de la violette*, that they, like Chrétien, sent to historical personages: Count Baldwin VI of Hainaut and IX of Flanders (the son of

Count Baldwin V of Hainaut and the nephew of Count Philip of Alsace and of Flanders), Milon of Nanteuil, prévôt of the archbishopric of Reims ('in Champagne' as Jean Renart specifies) and Marie, countess of Ponthieu (daughter of Adelaide of France, granddaughter of Louis VII and Constance of Castile, and therefore half-sister of Philip Augustus). Although professing to echo Chrétien, the three romances, in direct contrast to his, are set in historical time and place. The narrative of *Escoufle* starts in Normandy, follows the crusading route to the Holy Land, returns to Italy and back to Normandy, and then south again to Montpellier and Saint-Gilles, with the chief action taking place in the middle space of Lorraine, particularly around Toul. The *Roman de la rose* takes place largely among the imperial cities and castles of the Rhine and Meuse valleys with much of the action centering on Saint-Trond near Liège where a tournament is held. The *Roman de la violette*, like *Escoufle*, travels through the middle space between the French kingdom and the Empire, especially Metz and Cologne, before terminating at the tournament of Montargis in the Gâtinais. At each spot in the narrative the place can be located and the itinerary verified. With one possible exception, the principal heroes and heroines of the three romances are fictional, but most of the secondary characters can be readily identified with historical personages found in the contemporary chronicles. Count Richard of Montivilliers (in Normandy), for example, who departs on a crusade, is easily recognized as Richard, son of King Henry II of England. The participants in the tournament of Saint-Trond divide into French and imperial camps with the former all identified as partisans of Philip Augustus and the latter of the contemporary German emperor, Otto of Brunswick. Similarly, the tournament at Montargis pits knights loyal to the Capetians against turbulent knights from the Massif Central. Numerous details are supplied to add contextual 'reality effects' to the essentially fictional plots. Although Jean's and Gerbert's debt to Chrétien is patent, they reject the never-never land of Arthurian space, the remoteness of time, and the fantasy of their predecessor's cast of characters. They invite their audiences to identify directly with their own time and history. Their insistence on specific events and well-known politics testifies, by their opposition, to the unavoidable influence of the mighty but unhistorical Chrétien de Troyes.

Bibliographic Note

The basic authority on the feudal origins of Champagne is Michel Bur, *La Formation du comté de Champagne, v. 950 – v. 1150* (Nancy, 1977). Recent work on the politics and government of Count Henry the Liberal and Marie of Champagne is found in the studies of Theodore Evergates: *Feudal Society in the Baillage of Troyes under the Counts of Champagne, 1152–1284* (Baltimore, 1975), *Feudal Society in Medieval France: Documents from the County of Champagne* (Philadelphia, 1993), 'Aristocratic Women in the County of Champagne', *Aristocratic Women in Medieval France*, ed. Theodore Evergates (Philadelphia, 1999), pp. 72–82, and 'The Chancery Archives of the Counts of Champagne: Codicology and History of the Cartulary-Registers', *Viator*, 16 (1985), 159–79.

The rich bibliography on the politics and government of Philip of Alsace, count of Flanders, can be approached through David Nicholas, *Medieval Flanders* (London, 1992). The standard study of King Henry II's continental politics and government remains Jacques Boussard, *Le Gouvernement d'Henri II Plantagenêt* (Paris, 1956). Yves Sassier's *Louis VII* (Paris, 1991) is a recent introduction to the king's reign. The most authoritative work on the politics of Philip Augustus is Alexander Cartellieri, *Philipp II. August, König von Frankreich*, 4 vols (Leipzig, 1899–1922). His politics are introduced and his government studied in John W. Baldwin, *The Government of Philip Augustus: Foundations of French Royal Power in the Middle Ages* (Berkeley, 1986).

Examples of attempts by modern critics to identify contemporary events in the works of Chrétien include Carleton Carroll, 'Quelques observations sur les reflets de la cour d'Henri II dans l'œuvre de Chrétien de Troyes', *Cahiers de civilisation médiévale*, 37 (1994), 33–39, and Krijnie Ciggar, 'Chrétien de Troyes et la "matière byzantine": les demoiselles de Pesme Aventure', *Cahiers de civilisation médiévale*, 32 (1989), 325–31. For Chrétien as an exponent of Plantagenet ideology, see Amaury Chauou, *L'Idéologie Plantagenêt (XIIe–XIIIe siècles)* (Rennes, 2001), 97–109, 203–30. For Chrétien's depiction of tournaments, festivities, food, and clothing see John W. Baldwin, 'Jean Renart et le tournoi de Saint Trond: Une conjonction de l'histoire et de la littérature', *Annales: économies, sociétés, civilisations*, 45 (1990), 565–88, and *Aristocratic Life in Medieval France: The Romances of Jean Renart and Gerbert de Montreuil, 1190–1230* (Baltimore, 2000), pp. 68–86.

Statistics on Chrétien's manuscripts are drawn from Terry Nixon, 'Catalogue of Manuscripts', in *Les Manuscrits de Chrétien de Troyes*, ed. Keith Busby, Terry Nixon, Alison Stones and Lori Walters (Amsterdam, 1993), II, pp. 1–85. *Andreas Capellanus on Love*, ed. P.G. Walsh (London, 1986), and *Histoire de Guillaume le Maréchal*, ed. Paul Meyer, 3 vols, Société de l'histoire de France [255, 268, 304] (Paris, 1891–1901), contain the editions of the works of Andreas Capellanus and William the Marshal. Antonia Gransden, *Historical Writing in England c. 550 to 1307* (Ithaca, 1974), pp. 219–68, surveys the English chroniclers of the 'golden age'.

John W. Baldwin, *Aristocratic Life* (cited above) introduces the romances of Jean Renart and Gerbert de Montreuil.

2

Chrétien's Patrons

JUNE HALL McCASH

Chrétien de Troyes, whose contribution to twelfth-century literature is unsur-
passed, wrote for two of the most notable cultural patrons of his time. Like all
literary patronage in the Middle Ages, the respective roles of Chrétien and his
patrons represented a reciprocal and mutually beneficial relationship. As a rule,
a poet composed at the request of a patron, who in turn provided him with a
reward that could take the form of gifts, monetary payment, a position within
the court (e.g. clerk, scribe), or the lending of the patron's influence to his work.
Although in some instances poets dedicated works to a lord or lady merely in
hope of a reward, Chrétien clearly received commissions for the two romances
he wrote for identified patrons – *Le Chevalier de la Charrette* for Marie, Countess
of Champagne, and *Le Conte du Graal* for Philippe d'Alsace, Count of Flanders
(hereafter referred to as Philip of Flanders). Marie, he tells us, supplied him with
the *matiere* [material or plot] and *san* [interpretation] for the *Lancelot*, while
Philip provided the *livre* [source text] for the *Perceval*. Chrétien undertook the
requested works presumably in exchange for their generosity (or the promise of
it).

Chrétien was fortunate to have found such remarkable and educated patrons.
Scholars remember Marie de Champagne as one who held a brilliant literary
court in the north of France during the last quarter of the twelfth century. The
elder of two daughters of the French king, Louis VII, and his first wife, Eleanor
of Aquitaine, Marie was born in 1145. Eleanor's two marriages, the second to
King Henry II of England, produced ten children, many of whom, particularly
the daughters, were responsible for the dissemination of Arthurian materials
and the concept of *fin'amors* [ennobling love] throughout western Europe. In
1153, the year following King Louis's divorce from Eleanor, he betrothed his two
daughters, Marie and Alix, to the brother counts of Champagne, Henri the
Liberal and Thibaut of Blois. Marie married Count Henri in 1159, when she was
fourteen.[1] By birth and by marriage she became a wealthy and powerful
woman.

---

[1] An 1159 charter refers to Marie as 'Trecensis comitissa', evidence that the marriage of Henri
and Marie had already taken place (John Benton, 'The Court of Champagne', *Speculum*, 36
[1961], 554). Some scholars still cite the date of 1164, proposed by Henri d'Arbois de
Jubainville (*Histoire des ducs et des comtes de Champagne* [Paris, 1861], III, p. 96), who bases it on
'a late and unreliable document' ('Court of Champagne', 554).

Marie's husband, Henri the Liberal, was a literate and intelligent man who also sponsored much literature before his death, but his tastes, distinctly different from those of his wife, included primarily religious texts written in Latin. Unlike her husband, Marie apparently did not read Latin well and preferred texts in the vernacular. Her requests for biblical translations are among the earliest in French. Marie's independent patronage seems to have occurred primarily during her husband's absence from court on crusade and during her widowhood, that is, from 1179 until her death in 1198. A number of authors wrote about the Countess, including such well-known poets as Gautier d'Arras, Richard the Lion Hearted (her half-brother) and Rigaut de Barbezieux.[2] Andreas Capellanus, author of the treatise on courtly love known as the *De Amore*, included the Countess as a character in his book, where she rules over courts of love with her mother and other noble ladies.[3] An Andreas Capellanus witnessed nine charters at Marie's court between 1182 and 1186, but since the author of the *De Amore* wrote in Latin, his work was most likely not composed for her but rather for another audience. Other poets, however, suggested that she encouraged them to write or actually commissioned their works. Gace Brulé, for example, noted that 'la contesse de Brie . . . m'a commandé a chanter' [the Countess of Brie . . . has commanded me to sing].[4] An unnamed author, tentatively identified by T. Atkinson Jenkins as Marie's chaplain and counsellor Adam de Perseigne, composed for Marie the *Eructavit*, a rhymed paraphrase and commentary on psalm forty-four of the Vulgate Bible.[5] One of her clerks, who gives his name as Evrat, prepared for Marie a heavily-glossed translation of *Genesis*. Her tastes, as characterized by John Benton, were decidedly avant-garde, including the works of one of the first lyric poets writing in French (Gace Brulé); the earliest poet in France to use Arthurian materials in conjunction with the concept of *fin'amors* (Chrétien de Troyes); and finally the two authors mentioned above who engaged in the bold new phenomenon of biblical translation.

Chrétien's other known patron, Philip, Count of Flanders from 1168 to 1191, was the son of Thierry d'Alsace and Sybilla, daughter of Foulques V of Anjou, King of Jerusalem. Born in 1142, Philip was twice married, first to Elisabeth of Vermandois (1159) and second to Matilda, the daughter of Alfonso I, King of Portugal (1184). Philip's lengthy rule and his widespread fame as the 'flower of chivalry' gave him a particular distinction in Flemish history. Many knights

---

2   Benton suggested that Rigaut de Barbezieux should 'be dropped from the list' ('Court of Champagne', 585). Others disagree. See Alberto Vàrvaro, *Rigaut de Berbezilh: Liriche* (Bari, 1960), p. 206; June Hall Martin McCash, 'Eleanor of Aquitaine and Marie de Champagne: A Relationship Revisited', *Speculum*, 54 (1979), 702–3.
3   Andreas Capellanus, *De Amore libri tres*, ed. E[mil] Trojel (Copenhagen, 1892; repr. Munich,1964).
4   Holger Peterson Dyggve, *Gace Brulé* (Helsinki, 1951), song 45, vss 3–5. Brie was a part of Marie's dower. One manuscript attributes this poem to Aubouin de Sézanne. See Benton, 'Court of Champagne', 585.
5   *Eructavit*, ed. T. Atkinson Jenkins (Dresden, 1909), pp. xiii–xviii. For commentary on this work, see June Hall McCash, '*Eructavit cor meum*; Sacred Love in a Secular Context at the Court of Marie de Champagne', in *Earthly Love, Spiritual Love, Love of the Saints*, ed. Susan J. Ridyard (Sewanee, TN, 1999), pp. 159–78.

flocked to his side, among them Henry the Young King of England and Philip Augustus, both half-brothers of Marie de Champagne. Walter Map writes of one of his youthful relatives who sought out the Count of Flanders for instruction in the art of chivalry, and chose him as his lord.[6] And William Marshal, a special devotee of the Young King of England, also learned combat strategies from Philip.[7]

Considered by some as 'the most important legal innovator ever to be count of Flanders', Philip had considerable experience ruling the county even before his father's death.[8] In 1157 his father went to Palestine accompanied by his wife Sybilla. Because he was considering the possibility of remaining there, he had his fourteen-year-old son installed as count before his departure.[9] But Thierry returned in 1159 without his wife, who had entered a Jerusalem convent, and Philip would never see his mother again.[10] Although his father resumed his role as count upon his return, Philip continued to handle many administrative duties. Thierry returned once more to Palestine from 1164 to 1166 and died in 1168, shortly after his return. Thus from a very young age, Philip of Flanders wielded significant authority.

Philip has been described as 'the first Count of Flanders known to have taken an active part in encouraging literary production'.[11] His patronage, however, seems somewhat more limited than Marie's. Only two authors have openly and undisputedly proclaimed the Count as their patron. Other writers sometimes associated with his court include Gautier d'Arras and Conon de Béthune (both of whom wrote for Marie de Champagne), but neither lists Philip among his patrons, although Gautier, during his most productive years, witnessed more than one hundred charters for the court of Flanders between 1160 and 1185.[12] Scholars have cited three other names in connection with Philip – Gautier d'Epinal, the Châtelain de Coucy, and Guiot de Provins – but they have been unable to prove these links. Lacking clear evidence of the artistic role played by these various writers at the court of Flanders is as disappointing as knowing that, although the chronicler Villehardouin was a member of Marie's court from 1185 until her death, he left no account of its activities.

We know with certainty of only one writer besides Chrétien de Troyes who wrote for Philip and who claimed to live for a time on his benefactions – the anonymous compiler in about 1175 of a collection of proverbs, *Li Proverbe au vilain*, which survives in a number of manuscripts and was first edited in 1895

---

6   Walter Map, *De Nugis Curialium: Courtier's Trifles*, ed. and trans. M.R. James; rev. C.N.L. Brooke and R.A.B. Mynors (Oxford, 1983), pp. 278–79.
7   See *Histoire de Guillaume le Maréchal*, ed. Paul Meyer (Paris: 1891), I, vss 2723–35.
8   David Nicholas, *Medieval Flanders* (London, 1992), p. 85.
9   Nicholas, *Medieval Flanders*, p. 71. See Helen Adolf, 'A Historical Background for Chrétien's *Perceval*', *PMLA*, 58 (1943), 601.
10   Sybilla died between 1163 and 1167.
11   Mary D. Stanger, 'Literary Patronage at the Medieval Court of Flanders', *French Studies*, 11 (1957), 214.
12   F.A.G. Cowper, 'More Data on Gautier d'Arras', *PMLA*, 64 (1949), 302–16.
13   Adolf Tobler, *Li Proverbe au vilain* (Leipzig, 1895).

by Adolf Tobler.[13] Interestingly, Chrétien de Troyes uses in his works fourteen of the proverbs included in this collection.[14]

Rarely do we know more about the interaction between a poet's patrons than we do about those of Chrétien – Marie de Champagne and Philip of Flanders. Their association may explain not only how Gautier d'Arras came to write for the Countess, but also how Count Philip first took notice of Chrétien. Initially the relationship between the two patrons was adversarial. Long before his departure on crusade, Marie's husband, Henri of Champagne, betrothed his eldest son to Isabelle, daughter of Baudouin of Hainaut and niece of Count Philip. However, the political scene changed dramatically during Count Henri's absence. As King Louis grew weaker, he arranged for the coronation of his son, Philip Augustus, and entrusted to Philip of Flanders the role of counsellor to the young King. The Count took advantage of Henri's absence to nullify the betrothal of young Henri to Isabelle and arrange instead for her marriage to the new King, thus tying himself to the crown by marriage. To sweeten the attraction for the King, Count Philip even provided his niece with a dowry that included Artois, 'on condition that he be allowed its use during his own lifetime'.[15] To add insult to injury, at the second coronation of the young King with his bride, the crown was placed on the royal heads by the Bishop of Sens at Saint-Denis, usurping a privilege that had previously belonged to the Bishop of Reims, Count Henri's brother. Finally, Philip Augustus seized the dower lands of his mother (Count Henri's sister), forcing her to flee into the arms of her Champenois brothers. Thus, through his counsel and manipulation, Count Philip earned for the King the enmity of his sister Marie and her brothers-in-law, Thibaut of Blois and Etienne of Sancerre.

It was not long, however, before the young King grew weary of the constant advice and interference of Philip of Flanders and began to form other alliances. As a consequence, Count Philip found himself better served by joining the Champenois coalition in a war against Philip Augustus. The Count made every effort to patch up his relationship with Marie, arranging for Yolande, the younger sister of Isabelle of Hainaut, to replace her in the broken marriage agreement between Hainaut and Champagne. And following the death of his wife in 1182, Philip became the suitor of Marie de Champagne, seeking her hand in marriage.

Why the relationship came to naught is a matter of conjecture. Benton suggested that the proposal probably stemmed from political motives, which, after the Countess made peace with the King, were no longer relevant. Jean Frappier states, without providing evidence, that the decision to end the relationship was that of Marie, who 'refusa d'épouser le prétendant' [refused to marry the suitor].[16] The only medieval source that provides any reason for its being broken off was a later chronicler who reported gossip that cast aspersions

14 William A. Nitze, ' "Or est venuz qui aunera": A Medieval Dictum', *Modern Language Notes*, 56 (1941), 408. For biographical comments, see *Li Proverbe*, stanza 97.
15 John W. Baldwin, *The Government of Philip Augustus: Foundations of French Royal Power in the Middle Ages* (Berkeley, 1986), p. 16.
16 Benton, 'Court of Champagne', 588; Jean Frappier, *Chrétien de Troyes et le mythe du graal: étude sur Perceval ou le conte du graal* (Paris, 1979), p. 50.

on the morals of the Countess, but even the chronicler was not convinced of the rumour's validity.[17] The more likely reason the marriage negotiations ceased abruptly is that the 'horrible war' between the King and his Champenois vassals ended in 1183, thus eliminating the need for Marie to strengthen the alliance between Flanders and Champagne.[18] No doubt Philip Augustus, still at odds with Count Philip, used whatever influence he had as Marie's brother and liege lord to thwart the marriage plans, seeing only danger to the crown from such an alliance.[19] Her aborted betrothal to Philip of Flanders represented the only marriage that Marie would ever consider during her seventeen years of widowhood. In fact, she probably had little desire for another husband for, as a widow, she had considerably more autonomy than she would have had as Count Philip's wife.[20] The following year, Philip married a Portuguese princess. Nonetheless, the relationship between Marie and the Count of Flanders was productive in that it provided an opportunity for Philip to meet and eventually engage the services of Chrétien de Troyes.

Marie, as Chrétien's first patron, had every reason to have confidence in the poet she chose for the task of infusing the Arthurian story of Lancelot and Guenevere with the concept of fin'amors. Prior to her commission of the Lancelot, he had already written works based on classical and Celtic sources. As he listed them in the prologue to the Cligés, they include his first Arthurian romance, Erec et Enide; four Ovidian texts and finally a version of the Tristan legend.[21] Having worked with both Ovidian and Arthurian materials, Chrétien would seem an excellent choice to compose the tale that Countess Marie wanted of Lancelot and Guenevere.

The writing of the Lancelot may have been the result of coincidences that brought together poet, patron and inspiration at a serendipitous moment. The work could have been composed any time between 1159 and 1191, while Marie was Countess of Champagne and before the probable date of Chrétien's death, but the most persuasive and repeatedly proposed period has been that between 1177 and 1181.[22] I find even more likely the period between 1179 and 1181. Two things happened in 1179 that may have served as catalysts for the work. Henri the Liberal set out for his personal crusade to the Holy Land, leaving the Countess to assume for the first time an active political role. Her new independ-

---

[17] See William of Ardres, *Monumenta Germaniae historica, Scriptores*, XXIV, p. 715; Benton, 'Court of Champagne', 554, n. 11.

[18] This date is attested by a note by Johanne Monoculo attached to a manuscript of Pierre Comestor in the Abbey of Arouaise. See *Art de vérifier les dates* (Paris, 1818–44), XXIII, p. 313. See also Edmond Martène et Ursin Durand, *Voyage Littéraire de deux religieux bénédictins de la Congrégation de Saint-Maur* (Paris, 1717), p. 61. Peace was not reached between Philip Augustus and Philip of Flanders until July 1185. See Baldwin, *Government of Philip Augustus*, p. 18.

[19] Philip Augustus would also block any future marriage for Marie's widowed daughter-in-law, Blanche of Navarre.

[20] On the advantages of widowhood for wealthy noblewomen, see Louise Mirrer, 'Introduction', in *Upon My Husband's Death: Widows in the Literature and Histories of Medieval Europe*, ed. Louise Mirrer (Ann Arbor, 1992), pp. 1–4.

[21] For a discussion of the prologue, see the essay on *Cligés* in this volume.

[22] See, for example, Karl D. Uitti and Michelle A. Freeman, *Chrétien de Troyes Revisited* (New York, 1995), p. 61.

ence may have emboldened her to consider, perhaps also for the first time, the role of literary patron. Earlier works written for the court had always reflected Henri's conservative tastes. But now Marie was in charge and could request whatever she chose.

Shortly before her husband's departure, the Count and Countess had received at their château in Troyes a prominent visitor fresh from the English court of Henry II – Walter Map. Well known as a witty raconteur and writer, Walter accepted their hospitality en route to the Lateran Council called by Pope Alexander III, where he was to serve as King Henry's representative. Walter was a secular canon and royal clerk who functioned as secretary at the English court, but he was also a Welshman who must have known the Celtic legends on which much Arthurian material was based.[23] Thus, along with news of Countess Marie's mother, it is likely that he also brought a repertoire of Arthurian tales. Walter's name has long been associated with the prose cycle of the *Lancelot*, which claims to be 'translations of a Latin original preserved at the abbey of Salisbury, made "by Walter Map at the request of King Henry his lord" '.[24] Some scholars argue that Walter had little interest in these matters and that it was merely customary for authors to claim such sources. However, given the persistence with which Walter's name was associated with these materials from the thirteenth through the nineteenth centuries, coupled with the known interest of the Plantagenet court in Arthurian legends, it is logical that Walter may indeed have collected such tales for the court. Whether he ever wrote them down is another matter, but, as a well-known teller of tales, he may have been partly responsible for their dissemination.

The only text definitively attributed to him today is *De Nugis Curialium*. That he composed other types of literature seems probable, however, from such comments as that of Walter's compatriot, Gerald of Wales, who urged him to stop wasting his time on such childish things as the songs of poets, which he compared to the croaking of frogs.[25] Another contemporary of Walter Map, Hue de Rotelande, who wrote the romance *Ipomedon* sometime between 1170 and 1191, seems to suggest that Walter was, like himself, a writer of romances, sometimes called 'lies' by authors of more serious works: 'Sul ne sai pas de mentir l'art, / Walter Map reset bien sa part' [I am not the only one who knows the art of lying, Walter Map does his share of it well].[26] Map avows in *De Nugis Curialium* that he is indeed 'a foolish and dull poet', but not a writer of lies, 'ineptum me fateor et insulsum poetam, at non falsigrafum; non enim mentitur qui recitat, sed qui fingit' [for *he does not lie who repeats a tale*, but he who makes it].[27] The statement suggests that some of his work consisted of collecting tales

---

[23] For information on the life of Walter Map, see *De Nugis Curialium*, pp. xiii–xlv. In this work, Walter comments on his visit to the court of Troyes (pp. 450–53).

[24] *De Nugis Curialium*, p. xx. Webster argues that Walter Map is the author of much French verse and a French romance of *Lancelot* ('Walter Map's French Things', *Speculum*, 15 [1940], 272). See also Jessie Weston, *The Three Days Tournament* (London, 1902).

[25] *The Historical Works of Giraldus Cambrensis*, ed. Thomas Wright, 2 vols (London, 1894), I, pp. 271–89.

[26] *Ipomedon: poème de Hue de Rotelande, fin du XIIe siècle*, ed. A.J. Holden (Paris, 1979), vss 7183–84.

[27] *De Nugis Curialium*, pp. 112–13. Italics mine.

and retelling them in some form. Though he denies knowing 'the caves of the Muses', he also notes that 'it is not hard *to gather* or write something which the goodness of the good may turn to their profit (for to the good all things work together for good) or to commit to good ground seed that may prosper' (non difficile legere uel scribere quod bonis sua faciat utile bonitas [cum omnia bonis cooperentur in bonum] nec terre bone mandare semina que proficient).[28] The image of the writer as a sower of seeds that he hopes will fall on good ground is an image well familiar to scholars of Chrétien, who would later use this same image in the prologue to the *Perceval*.

The timing of Walter Map's visit to the court of Troyes and its proximity to the writing of the *Lancelot* is certainly noteworthy. Chrétien, who had already revealed his interest in Arthurian materials, may have met Walter during his stay and perhaps heard his stories along with the Countess. If so, the seeds of Walter's tales evidently fell on fertile ground.

What little we know about Chrétien and his relationship with the Countess we learn from his prologue to the *Lancelot*, where he opens the text by emphasizing that Marie had a greater role than he in its creation. Assuming a subservient role, he positions himself like Lancelot in the text, as obedient to her every command: 'Puis que ma dame de Chanpaigne / Vialt que romans a feire anpraigne, / Je l'anprendrai *molt volentiers* / *Come cil qui est suens antiers*'[29] [Since my lady of Champagne wishes me to undertake a romance, I shall do so *most willingly, as one who is entirely hers*]. It is surely not mere coincidence that he uses precisely the same wording in describing Lancelot's actions at the tournament at Noauz when his lady orders him to do his worst: 'Quant cil l'öi, / Si li dist que *molt volantiers,* / *Come cil qui est suens antiers*', vss 5654–56 [When he heard it (her command), he answered that he would do so *most willingly, as one who is entirely hers*].

Keeping the reader (and perhaps the Countess) somewhat off balance, he follows this deferential introduction of his patron by coyly refusing to flatter her, though he does concede slyly that such flattery from others, whom he characterizes as *losengiers* [sycophants], may well be deserved:

> Mes tex s'an poïst antremetre
> Qui i volsist losenge metre,
> Si deïst, et jel tesmoignasse,
> Que ce est la dame qui passe
> Totes celes qui sont vivanz.   (vss 7–11)

> [But another might begin by wishing to flatter her. He might say, and I would bear witness to it, that she is the lady who surpasses all women who are living.]

Throughout the prologue he is careful to avoid any personal or direct declara-

---

28 *De Nugis Curialium*, pp. 210–11.
29 Chrétien de Troyes, *Le Chevalier de la Charrette ou Le Roman de Lancelot*, ed. and trans. Charles Méla, in *Romans suivis des Chansons avec, en appendice, Philomena*, genl ed. Michel Zink (Paris, 1994), vss 1–4; translations and italics are mine.

tion of the Countess's worth. He seems to be teasing his reader and his patron, as though he knows what she wants to hear, yet withholds it from her.[30]

Even more significant in the prologue is a passage, important in the history of courtly patronage, that outlines their respective roles in the text, noting that 'Ses comandemanz an ceste oevre', vs. 22 [her command in this work] accomplishes more 'Que sans ne painne que g'i mete', vs. 23 [than any meaning or labour I put into it]. He goes on to specify their respective contributions to the text:

> Del *Chevalier de la charrete*
> Comance Crestïens son livre,
> Matiere et san li done et livre
> La contesse et il s'antremet
> De panser, que gueres n'i met
> Fors sa painne et s'antancïon.   (vss 24–29)
>
> [Chrétien begins his book about the *Knight of the Cart*. The Countess is providing him with the plot and interpretation, and he is undertaking it thoughtfully, so that he puts nothing into it except his labour and (mental) effort.]

In these final lines Chrétien seems to disavow any substantive responsibility for the work and its content.

It has become a widely accepted view that Chrétien was unenthusiastic about writing the *Lancelot*. According to Frappier, Chrétien, who is often viewed as an apologist for love within marriage, worked on the tale of the adulterous relationship between Lancelot and the queen against his own moral convictions and in the end refused to complete the work.[31] However, Chrétien knew from the outset the *matière* that he was to use, and he seemed to have had no problem writing about their single night of passion. Why would he have been able to tolerate the subject matter for more than six thousand lines, only to abandon the project less than a thousand lines from its conclusion? And why would he have encouraged another poet to finish the text, if he disapproved of it? It is possible, of course, that he fell ill and required the assistance of another poet or, as Moshé Lazar suggests, that he felt he had written the essence of the text, which another could complete. It is far more probable that the timing of the work and the wishes of the Countess were, once again, the determining factors in the decision to leave the work unfinished. In 1181 Count Henri returned ill from his crusade and died a week after his arrival. The Countess in mourning might well have brought to an end the project about adultery, so that it would not be gossiped about during her widowhood.

---

30 Scholars have suggested that Chrétien may be contrasting his work to the hyperbole that Gautier d'Arras heaped upon his patron Beatrix in *Ille et Galeron*. See Matilda Tomaryn Bruckner, '*Le Chevalier de la Charrette (Lancelot)*', in *The Romances of Chrétien de Troyes: A Symposium*, ed. Douglas Kelly (Lexington, KY, 1985), p. 134.

31 See Jean Frappier, 'Vues sur les conceptions courtoises dans les littératures d'oc et d'oïl au XIIe siècle', *Cahiers de civilisation médiévale*, 2 (1959), 135–56. See Moshé Lazar, *Amour courtois et 'Fin'amors' dans la littérature du XIIe siècle* (Paris, 1964), especially pp. 199–243. Although Lazar sees Chrétien as 'contre l'amour adultère' (p. 233) [against adulterous love], he does not accept that as sufficient reason for his abandoning the work.

The text was eventually completed by Godefroi de Leigni, but, according to the epilogue, only with Chrétien's (not Marie's) 'boen gré': 'Mes nus home blasme ne l'an mete / Se sor Crestïen a ovré, / Car ç'a il fet par le boen gré / Crestïen qui le comança', vss 7104–7 [Let no one blame him (Godefroy de Leigni) if he worked on Chrétien's text, for he did it with the willingness of Chrétien who began it]. Godefroi neither renews the dedication to the Countess nor indicates that he has *her* permission or command to complete the romance. Since he is a different poet from that of the prologue, his failure to acknowledge her patronage in the epilogue of the romance suggests strongly that Marie had withdrawn her support from the project.

Chrétien undertook his second patronage project, *Le Conte du Graal*, for Count Philip sometime between 14 May 1181, the date of the latter's military alliance with Countess Marie and her brothers-in-law, and September 1190,[32] when Count Philip left on Crusade. Chrétien would not finish this romance either, but this time we have a clearer explanation. According to Gerbert de Montreuil, writing, around 1220, one of the four continuations of the *Perceval*, Chrétien died before completing his last poem.[33] His patron also died of fever at Acre on 1 June 1191. Here again, as in the prologue to the *Lancelot*, Chrétien stresses the *painne* [physical labor] and *antancion* [mental effort] he intends to put into the work.[34] In the *Perceval*, however, he recasts them in a more active mode, transforming the nouns into verbs: 'Crestïens . . . *entant et paine* / Par le commandement le conte / A rimoier le meillor conte / Qui soit contez a cort roial' [Therefore, Chrétien . . . strives and works by command of the Count to put into rhyme the best story that has ever been told in a royal court].[35]

But there the similarity ends. In *Le Conte du Graal*, Chrétien begins his prologue by speaking of himself and taking credit for his work, in contrast to the *Lancelot* where he attributed full responsibility to his patron. While he acknowledges in formal and formulaic terms that he is writing his Grail romance for Philip, 'le plus preudome', vs. 11 [the noblest of men], who provided him with the book on which the text will be based, he underscores that he, as author, is its essential creator. He begins by commenting not on his patron's contribution, but on his own role as the sower of seeds on fertile ground: 'Crestïens semme et fait semence / D'un romans que il encomence, / Et si le seme en si bon leu / Qu'il ne puet [ester] sanz gran preu', vss 7–10 [Chrétien sows and spreads the seed of a romance that he is beginning, and he sows it in such a good place that it cannot be without great profit]. Such variations, subtle as they are, suggest a significant shift in approach on the part of the author. Chrétien seems more enthusiastic about his work for Count Philip and expresses greater freedom in bringing

---

32 Jean Frappier, *Chrétien de Troyes* (Paris, 1968), p. 1.

33 See Gerbert de Montreuil, *La Continuation de Perceval*, ed. Mary Williams (Paris, 1922), vss 6984–87.

34 These terms have been variously interpreted. See, for example, Douglas Kelly, 'Chrétien de Troyes: The Narrator and His Art', in *The Romances of Chrétien de Troyes: A Symposium*, ed. Douglas Kelly (Lexington, KY,1985), p. 22, and, in the same volume, see Bruckner, '*Le Chevalier de la Charrette*', p. 141.

35 Chrétien de Troyes, *Le Roman de Perceval ou Le Conte du Graal*, ed. Keith Busby (Tübingen, 1993), vss 62–65.

something of his own to it. Thus, he positions himself quite differently as Philip's poet than he had, earlier, as Marie's.

He is also more generous and less coy in his exordial praise of Philip than he was in regard to the Countess. Chrétien underscores Philip's *largesse*, noting that 'S'est plus larges que l'en ne set, / Qu'il done selonc l'Evangille, / Sanz ypocrisie et sanz gille', vss 28–30 [He is more generous than anyone knows, for he gives according to the Gospel, without hypocrisy or deceit], so that his left hand does not know the good his right hand does, and only God knows 'toz les secrez', vs. 34 [all the secrets] of his good works.

Although Chrétien conceded that others might say that Marie surpassed all other *living* women, he depicts Philip, by contrast, as surpassing even the *dead* Alexander the Great, recognized as the medieval model of *largesse*. But, Alexander had 'Toz les visces et toz les maus', vs. 19 [all the vices and all the evils] from which the Count is free. Chrétien is precise and lavish in his praise of Philip, who does not listen to 'Vilain gap ne parole', vs. 22 [base mockery or words] but who loves 'droite justise / Et loiauté et Sainte Eglise', vss 25–26 [true justice and loyalty and Holy Church]. Either he truly admires his patron or he is flattering him in hope of greater reward, something he refused to do (explicitly, at least) in the text composed for Marie. In either case, his praise of Philip is direct, expansive and unequivocal.

Given the nature of *Le Conte du Graal*, Chrétien's admiration may well be genuine. Certainly, no other text could better combine Philip's interests in chivalry and the spiritual, and if this were the only work he ever requested, it would be sufficient to make him an important medieval patron. Why Count Philip requested the *Conte du Graal* has been a matter of speculation, yet an interest in the Grail legend would continue through later generations of Flemish rulers. Jeanne, Countess of Flanders, would sponsor the continuation of Chrétien's work by Manessier in the thirteenth century. One interest that Philip may have had in the story of Perceval was the evolution of an ignorant lad into an accomplished knight. Given Philip's interests in knightly training, that aspect of the work, and particularly the role of Gornemant de Goort, Perceval's first male mentor, no doubt strongly appealed to him.[36] Helen Adolf has speculated that Philip may have perceived a special connection between the story of the Grail knight Perceval and that of his own family, for his mother was connected to a royal line in a sacred city (Jerusalem) where the leper king Baldwin, Philip's cousin, had to be carried about, like the Fisher King of the *Perceval*, on a litter. A phial of holy blood brought back to Flanders by Philip's father during the Second Crusade, she suggested, may further 'account for the interest in the House of Flanders in the Grail Literature'.[37] William A. Nitze added that the recovery of Longinus's lance at Antioch might also have piqued the interest of a relic collector like Count Philip in the Grail story.[38] When Philip went to Palestine in 1177, partly on a private crusade and partly to visit the tomb of his dead mother, he was offered the regency and command of the army (which

---

[36] See Stanger, 'Literary Patronage', 216.
[37] Adolf, 'Historical Background', p. 601.
[38] William A. Nitze 'The Bleeding Lance and Philip of Flanders', *Speculum*, 21 (1946), p. 306.

Adolf sees as parallel to the sword as a gift to Perceval at the Grail castle). But he refused, failing the court as Perceval had failed when he did not ask the necessary questions. Certainly, we have no evidence that Philip's taking up the cross again to go to Jerusalem in 1190 had any connection to the Grail story. Nevertheless, the parallels are intriguing.

In the final analysis, why is the patronage of these two twelfth-century nobles important? Douglas Kelly has described the texts that Chrétien wrote for his patrons as the 'two most remarkable *matières* in his romances'.[39] Certainly, they are the two most powerful and influential works he ever produced. The story of Lancelot and Guenevere and that of the Grail knight Perceval have been retold countless times, in many variations, even into our own day, while the romances that he completed and wrote apparently without patronage, though they may be artistically superior, have remained largely within their medieval context and have not caught the world's imagination as these two have. The story of the lover's obedient service to his lady is the quintessential story of selfless abnegation to love (however Chrétien may sometimes have injected humour into the situation), and it is a tale that takes on renewed life in every retelling. That of Perceval (and his later permutations) in search of the Grail captures the essence of the spiritual quest, of the goal greater than self and the material world, which Chrétien's death left for later continuators to interpret. Both tales still fascinate modern readers, writers and even film-makers. The two works portray knights in service to something universal and greater than themselves, more important than their own reputations, their personal honour or even their social responsibility. They resonate within the modern world in ways more compelling than the stories of characters like Erec and Yvain, who seek primarily to find a way to reconcile their roles as knights, who must constantly prove themselves in chivalric contexts, with their social responsibilities as husband and ruler. Without the influence of patrons who provided the materials for the texts and set him to work, Chrétien might never have undertaken to write either the *Lancelot* or the *Perceval*. Thus, Chrétien's patrons challenged him, making him reach beyond his own personal visions, to incorporate theirs as well, and to give us today two legends that show no signs of waning in importance.

[39] Kelly, 'Chrétien de Troyes', p. 17.

3

Chrétien's Literary Background

LAURENCE HARF-LANCNER

[Translated by Amy L. Ingram]

In 1170, the date commonly accepted for the composition of *Erec et Enide* (the first Arthurian romance), French literature began to rival literature from the Latin tradition. The defining cultural trait of the Middle Ages was, in fact, bilingualism, the coexistence of Latin and the vernacular languages. But until the end of the eleventh century, the only written language was Latin. It was the privilege of clerics to have access to learned culture, essentially represented by apologetics and literature from Latin Antiquity. And let us not forget that, during the Carolingian cultural renaissance, the growth of literature in the eighth and ninth centuries was limited to Latin texts.

The first written trace of the development of vernacular languages was offered by the famous Strasbourg Oaths, sworn in 842 by Charlemagne's grandsons – one, by Charles II (the Bald), in French, the other, by Louis the German, in German – in the presence of their troops (of course, this document is not a literary text). Next came several texts – Latin religious poems translated into French – intended for the edification of the faithful. Among them are hagiographic poems such as *La Cantilene de sainte Eulalie* (c. 880) and *La Vie de saint Alexis* (eleventh century).

But the second medieval cultural renaissance, the true birth of French literature, began around 1100 with the rise to power of the chivalric class. The nobility represented the dominant class, unified by the relationship of one man to another (the feudal system) around a common ideology. Courts were developing during this era as well. The court of the King of France was not yet an important cultural centre, unlike those of his great vassals, particularly the court of London.[1] Henry Plantagenet, Count of Anjou and Duke of Normandy, extended his power over Aquitaine by his marriage to Eleanor in 1152 (following her repudiation by her first husband, Louis VII of France) and became king of England in 1154. A new aristocratic and secular culture began to express itself through a new form of literature, destined for laymen, the 'illiterati' (those who did not know Latin), and thus composed in the vernacular, which became both a written and literary language. Clerics in the service of

---

1 Reto R. Bezzola, *Les Origines et la formation de la littérature courtoise en Occident (500–1200)*, 3 vols (Paris, 1963), Part Three, vol. I.

princes were to express in their texts the aspirations of the chivalric class, and of the three orders of society – the priesthood or *oratores*, the nobility or *bellatores* and the peasantry or *laboratores* – they would glorify the martial. Thus, martial values hold a dominant place in this literature, along with the values of courtly society, which developed at the same time. It was definitely a literature intended for a certain class: clerics and knights shared the same distaste for the third order, that of the *laboratores*, the *vilains*, as the prologue of *Le Roman de Thebes*, written about 1150, makes clear:

> Or s'en tesent de cest mestier,
> se ne sont clerc ou chevalier,
> car aussi pueent escouter
> conme li asnes a harper.

> [Let those who are not clerics or knights spare themselves the trouble of listening to me, because they are as likely to understand me as the donkey is to understand the art of the harp.][2]

The twelfth century marked the birth of romance. Originally an adverb (from the Latin *romanice*), *romanz* came to signify 'en roman', that is, written in a romance language rather than in Latin. The adverb then became a noun, *li romanz* (*romans*), designating a work written in French and often adapted – *translaté* – from a Latin text. These narratives were situated on the boundary between legend and history. They promote, for example, the glorification of England's Breton past in *Le Roman de Brut* (a chronicle of the kings of Britain starting with the eponymous Brutus), by Wace, who, in 1155, transposed Geoffrey of Monmouth's *Historia regum Britanniae* (1138) into the romance tongue.[3] At the same time, Wace's *Roman de Rou* and the *Chronique des ducs de Normandie* by Benoît de Sainte-Maure prolonged the prehistory of the kingdom of England along with the history of the Norman dukes and the conquest of England.[4]

The final stage in the evolution of romance in the twelfth century was the identification of a French text presenting certain characteristics that constitute a new literary form.[5] These two meanings already appear in the prologue to Benoît de Sainte-Maure's *Roman de Troie* (c. 1165):

> Et por ce me vuell travailler
> En une estoire conmencer
> Que, de latin ou je la truis,
> Se j'ai le sens e se ge puis,
> Le voudrai si en *romanz* metre

---

[2] *Le Roman de Thèbes*, ed. Guy Raynaud de Lage (Paris, 1966; trans. Aimé Petit, Paris, 1991), ms. C, vss 13–16. See also the bilingual edition by Francine Mora-Lebrun (Paris, 1995), ms. S.

[3] Geoffrey of Monmouth, *Historia regum Britanniae*, ed. Edmond Faral, in *La Légende arthurienne*, 3 vols (Paris, 1929), vol. 3; trans. Laurence Mathey-Maille, *Histoire des rois de Bretagne* (Paris, 1992); Wace, *Brut*, ed. Judith Weiss (Exeter, 1998). See below, ch. 4, 'The Arthurian Legend Before Chrétien'.

[4] Wace, *Le Roman de Rou*, ed. A.J. Holden, 3 vols (Paris, 1970–73); Benoît de Sainte-Maure, *Chronique des ducs de Normandie*, ed. C. Fahlin and O. Södergard, 4 vols (Uppsala, 1951–79).

[5] Emmanuèle Baumgartner, *Le Récit médiéval* (Paris, 1995).

Que cil qui n'entendront la letre
Se puissent deduire el *romanz*.

[This is why I want to put all my effort into beginning a story, and my
intention, if I have the capacity and the force, is to translate from Latin
where I find it into French, so that those who do not understand Latin
can take pleasure in the French text.][6]

There would be no more effective way to play on the polysemy of the term
'romanz'. The cleric, wanting to share his knowledge with the layman, translates
the text 'en roman' (in French) with the explicit purpose of combining the enjoy-
able and the useful, in order to provide his readers with pleasure, a notion that is
inseparable from this newly developing form of 'le roman' – that is, the French
text.

Romance adopted the octosyllabic couplet, the most neutral metre, the closest
to prose: it is thus in radical opposition to the *chanson de geste,* composed in
chanted decasyllabic or alexandrine stanzas (*laisses*). Romance was meant to be
read aloud before a number of listeners or quietly by a single reader. Often cited
in support of the latter is the scene from *Le Chevalier au lion* in which a young girl
is reading to her parents:

Apuyé voit deseur son coute
Un prodomme qui se gisoit
Seur .i. drap de soie, et lisoit
Une puchele devant li
En un rommans, ne sai de cui.
Et por le rommans escouter
S'i estoit venue acouter
Une dame, et estoit sa mere.

[He sees a gentleman reclining on a silk cloth, leaning on his elbow;
and before him, a young girl was reading a romance aloud, I do not
know of whom, and a lady had also come and sat down to hear the
romance; and it was her mother.][7]

We also see the beginnings of a new dynamic between the narrator and his
public: the jongleur's address to his listeners in the *chanson de geste* is replaced by
the relationship between the 'I' of the author-narrator and the reader. This relationship is made explicit in the prologue that generally opens the romance.[8] In
the epic prologue, the speaker is the jongleur, who insists on the superiority of
the version that he is presenting, which far surpasses the other versions sung by
other jongleurs. In the romance text, on the other hand, the speaker is also the
author, who justifies the value of his work as a writer.[9] *Le Roman de Thebes,* the

---

6   Benoît de Sainte-Maure, *Le Roman de Troie,* ed. Léopold Constans, 6 vols (Paris, 1904–12); ed.
     and trans. Emmanuèle Baumgartner and Françoise Vielliard (Paris, 1998), vss 33–39.
7   Chrétien de Troyes, *Le Chevalier au lion (Yvain),* ed. and trans. David F. Hult, in *Romans suivis
     des Chansons, avec, en appendice, Philomena,* genl. ed. Michel Zink (Paris, 1994), vss 5358–65.
8   Two well-known exceptions are *Le Roman d'Eneas* and *Le Chevalier au lion,* both of which begin
     in medias res.
9   Emmanuèle Baumgartner, 'Texte de prologue et statut de texte', in *Essor et fortune de la chanson*

first romance (c. 1150) in every sense of the word, also offers the first romance prologue, bringing together elements that would become the *topoi* of later romances. The author intends to make the readers profit from his knowledge and prevent the past from being forgotten (committing *histoire* to *mémoire*, with a rhyme that will become standard).[10] He situates himself in the traditions of Homer, Plato, Virgil and Cicero.[11] Thus is glorified the work of the writer, who, as Benoît proclaims, 'o sa main les moz escrit, / Ensi taillez e si curez / E si asis e si posez / Que plus ne meinz n'i a mester' [He writes the words with his own hand. He has shaped, polished, arranged and placed them so well that nothing could be added or excised].[12] Benoît proudly signs his name at the end of his prologue; Alexandre de Paris names himself in the epilogue of his romance. In the tradition of the earlier romances, Chrétien will insist on the value of his work as a writer and will systematically name himself in the prologue and/or epilogue of his romances.[13]

At the beginning of the twelfth century in the south of France, there also appeared a new art of love, *fin'amor* [true love], linked to a new aristocratic ideal of life and poetry that blossomed in the southern courts: courtliness, *la courtoisie*. This ideal is expressed in the lyric poetry of the troubadours, initiated by Guillaume IX of Aquitaine around 1100, then, beginning in the 1150s, in the north of France with the *trouvères*. Courtliness comprises, first and foremost, the qualities of those who live at the court, that is to say a combination of refined qualities: the adjective *courtois* and the noun *courtoisie* made their first appearance around 1150, in Wace's *Brut* and in *Le Roman de Thebes*. But this refinement goes hand in hand with a new representation of love. The *canso* of the Occitan troubadours, soon recast by the northern *trouvères*, spread this doctrine of *fin'amor*, which glorified amorous passion. Only one who loves with *fin'amor* can be courtly, because love induces the poet/lover to transcend himself, leading to the full realization of his entire being. This is the creative power of poetry. One must love in order to write. But the key to this love is unfulfilled desire, where satisfaction is constantly sought after and always out of reach, since love feeds on desire, and consummation kills both desire and love. The beloved is the *dompna*, the lady, the suzerain of the vassal in love, in a relationship modelled on the feudal one. Love is thus frequently incompatible with marriage, which implies the quenching of desire and man's domination of woman. *Fin'amor* is adulterous.[14] This exacting doctrine contrasts courtly love with the passionate love of Tristan and Iseut, even if suffering is their common fate. One is a vital force, pushing the lover to a constant quest for perfection, with the goal of becoming more worthy of his lady. The other is a force of exclusion, continually

de geste dans l'Europe et l'Orient latin, Actes du IXe Congrès International de la Société Rencesvals (Modena, 1984), pp. 465–73.

10   'Conter vous voel d'antive estore / Que li clerc tiennent en memore' [I want to tell you an old story, / preserved in the memory of the clerks], *Le Roman de Thèbes*, ed. Léopold Constans, 2 vols (Paris, 1890; repr. New York, 1968); prologue from the long version (mss A and P), vss 18–19.

11   *Le Roman de Thèbes*, ed. Raynaud de Lage, vss 5–6.

12   Benoît de Sainte-Maure, *Le Roman de Troie*, vss 134–37.

13   *Erec*, vss 9, 26; *Cligés*, vss 23, 6702; *Lancelot*, vs. 25; *Yvain*, vs. 6805; *Perceval*, vs. 7.

14   René Nelli, *L'Erotique des troubadours* (Paris, 1974).

requiring the lovers to defy their social values in a tragic crescendo that can only end in death.

It is undeniable that this doctrine deeply influenced the court of Troyes. Gace Brulé, one of the first *trouvères* to sing about courtly love, frequented this court. Andreas Capellanus wrote his *De Amore* for Countess Marie, probably between 1181 and 1186. The first of its three books treats the nature of love; the second recounts the judgments concerning love, handed down by the noblest women in the realm, among them the Countess of Champagne and her mother, Eleanor of Aquitaine; the courtly casuistry revealed therein is disconcerting for its contrast with the third book, an antifeminist text that condemns love, following in the tradition of Ovid's *Remedia amoris* [Remedies of Love]. This ambiguous text attests in any case that the Countess of Champagne's social circle was responsive to *fin'amor*.[15] Chrétien provides new evidence with his two courtly songs. And with the legendary couple Lancelot and Guenevere, introduced into literature by *Le Chevalier de la charrette*, the lyric model of the courtly lover and his haughty lady is recast in a narrative mould. The love that led the poet/lover to record his joy and suffering in verse now inspires the chivalric lover to triumph in the most perilous tests, in order to make himself worthy of his lady.[16]

If the opening lines of Jean Bodel's *La Chanson des Saisnes* [of the Saxons], composed around 1200, are often cited, it is because they offer a valuable typology of secular narrative literature at the end of the twelfth century:

> Ne sont que III matieres a nul home antandant,
> De France et de Bretagne et de Rome la grant
> Et de ces III matieres n'i a nule samblant.
> Li conte de Bretaigne sont si vain et plaisant,
> Cil de Rome sont sage et de san aprenant,
> Cil de France de voir chascun jor apparent.

> [For any man of understanding, there are only three subject matters: those of France, Britain and illustrious Rome. And each of these three subjects is distinct from the others. The stories from Britain are fictitious but engaging; those of Rome are wise and educational; those of France appear truer every day.][17]

These three subjects are distinguished by their specificity:

– the epic matter, characterized by historical truth: the history of France;
– the classical matter, defined by its didactic and scholarly character;
– the Brittonic matter, 'vaine et plaisante' in contrast to the other two, does not reconstruct a glorious past and is the source not of knowledge but of pleasure, owing to its fictions.

---

[15] Andreas Capellanus, *De Amore libri tres*, ed. E[mil] Trojel (Copenhagen, 1892; repr. Munich, 1964); *The Art of Courtly Love*, trans. John Jay Parry (New York, 1941, 1959).

[16] Emmanuèle Baumgartner, *Yvain et Lancelot* (Paris, 1992).

[17] Jean Bodel, *La Chanson des Saisnes*, ed. Annette Brasseur, 6 vols (Geneva, 1989; trans., Paris, 1992).

The birth of romance is inseparable, as we have seen, from the recasting of Latin material in French: the first romancers drew their inspiration from classical literature. The intellectuals from the twelfth century considered themselves new, modern men, but modern ones who imitated the ancients and were nourished by them; they were 'nains juchés sur les épaules de géants' [dwarves standing on the shoulders of giants], as Bernard de Chartres famously put it.[18] In its ambiguity, this statement reveals the relationship between medieval culture and antiquity. It affirms the superiority of the earlier giants over the modern dwarves, but also expresses faith in the progress of knowledge and culture. *Le Roman de Thebes* can coexist with Statius's *Thebaidos*, *Eneas* with Virgil's *Aeneid*, since, in rewriting the epic for a courtly public of the twelfth century, the medieval romancer integrates into this model the culture of his time and thus allows it to span the centuries by winning over a new public.

This rewriting of classical matter in romance form was first linked to the figure of Alexander the Great. As early as the third century in Alexandria, the first fictional biography of Alexander emerged, falsely attributed to Callisthenes, his companion. The Pseudo-Callisthène recounts successively Alexander's childhood, his conquest of the Persian Empire and his exploration of the fabulous faraway places of India.[19] This Greek text, which combines historical and legendary sources of Greek and Egyptian origin, was more widely circulated than the Bible. In the fourth century, Julius Valerius translated the Pseudo-Callisthène into Latin, and his translation was summarized in the ninth century in the *Epitome Julii Valerii*.[20] This text was the primary source of the French narratives that multiplied from the twelfth century onward. In the first third of the century, Alberic de Pisançon wrote the 'enfances' [first exploits] of the hero in a dialect from the south of France, in monorhymed octosyllabic *laisses*, of which 105 lines survive. Around 1160, a cleric from Poitou transposed Alberic's work into decasyllabic *laisses*. Then, in the 1170s, three new poems in dodecasyllabic verse appeared: *Le Fuerre de Gadres* (*Le Fourrage de Gaza*) by a certain Eustache, recounting the confrontation between Alexander's men and the army of Duke Betis de Gadres. Lambert le Tort of Chateaudun tells of the expedition in India against King Porus and the discoveries of the marvels of the East. A third poem reports Alexander's death in Babylon. It was left to Alexandre de Paris, around 1180, to combine these separate stories into a complete romance that constitutes the vulgate version of *Le Roman d'Alexandre*, in laisses consisting of the dodecasyllabic lines that would later be named alexandrines.[21] At the same time were composed the Anglo-Norman romance *Le Roman de toute chevalerie* (written by Thomas de Kent between 1174 and 1200) and *Alexandreis*, a Latin epic by

---

[18] Laurence Harf-Lancner, 'L'Idée de progrès dans l'Occident médiéval: un paradoxe?', in *Progrès, réaction, décadence dans l'Occident médiéval*, ed. Emmanuèle Baumgartner and Laurence Harf-Lancner (Geneva, 2003), pp. 7–22.

[19] Pseudo-Callisthène, *Le Roman d'Alexandre*, trans. Gilles Bounore and Blandine Serret (Paris, 1992).

[20] Julius Valerius, *Res gestae Alexandri Macedonis*, ed. M. Rosellini (Stuttgart, 1993); *Epitome Julii Valerii*, ed. J. Zacher (Halle, 1867).

[21] *The Medieval French Roman d'Alexandre*, ed. E.C. Armstrong et al., 7 vols (Princeton, 1937–76); Alexandre de Paris, *Le Roman d'Alexandre*, ed. and trans. Laurence Harf-Lancner (Paris, 1994).

Gautier de Chastillon, based on the biography of Alexander by Quinte-Curce.[22] The romances of Alexander grew out of the epic aesthetic and rhetoric, but Alexander's personal adventure and his quest for transcendence make him quite simply one of the first romance heroes of the western world.[23] He is also considered to be the incarnation of generosity, a reputation recalled by Chrétien when, in his prologue to Le Conte du Graal, he contrasts Alexander's refined generosity with the charity of the Count of Flanders.

Beginning in the 1150s, in the court of Henry Plantagenet, a trilogy of romances – of Thebes, Eneas and Troie – took shape. The London court was, in fact, a school for the imitation of Antiquity. Around 1150, a cleric from Poitou adapted Statius's Thebaidos as Le Roman de Thebes, which recounts the fratricidal conflict between Eteocles and Polynice, sons of Œdipus, haunted by their father's curse. This first romance clearly illustrates the process of rewriting undertaken by the translator.[24] Despite the use of the octosyllabic couplet, the influence of epic poetics is still evident in the presence of stanzas related to the laisse and to epic formulas and motifs. Yet the story has been reinterpreted in an original way through the use of narrative additions: the story opens and closes with the summary of the legend of Œdipus, absent from the Thebaidos; thus the entire romance is coloured by accounts of misdeeds and maledictions. Invented episodes, such as the siege of Monflor or the treason of Daire le Roux, introduce problems of feudal casuistry into the narrative. The prominence of female characters and their hopeless loves introduces a courtly dimension. Finally, the Thebes of the medieval romance goes up in flames, as if to denounce kingdoms founded on sin and to prefigure the burning of Troy.

The Eneas was probably composed (by a Norman cleric) around 1155–60, shortly before Le Roman de Troie (c. 1160–65).[25] However, the manuscripts group the three romances in an order that does not follow that of their composition, but rather one determined by a different logic, that of narrative chronology – Thebes, Troie, Eneas – evidence of the scribes' awareness that they were constructing a cycle. Benoît de Sainte-Maure (curial cleric for Henry II) tells the history of Troy from its foundation to its destruction. He uses two Latin prose narratives as sources: De excidio Troiae, which dates from the sixth century and is attributed to Dares Phrygius, a supposed witness to the war, and Ephemeris belli Troianni, attributed to Dictys Cretensis. The war consists of twenty-three battles, interrupted by truces that allow love interests to develop. The fall of the city is followed by the story of the often tragic returns of the Greek leaders to their kingdoms. Benoît makes Troy the symbol of civilization and culture, both of which will be destroyed with the city but transferred to the West with Aeneas and transmitted to Rome. The trilogy is unified by reflections on the city, on the

---

22 Thomas de Kent, Le Roman d'Alexandre ou Le Roman de toute chevalerie, trans. Catherine Gaullier-Bougassas and Laurence Harf-Lancner; text ed. Brian Foster and Ian Short (Paris, 2003); Gautier de Châtillon, Alexandreis, ed. Marvin L. Colker (Padua, 1978); trans. R.Telfryn Pritchard (Toronto, 1986).

23 Catherine Gaullier-Bougassas, Les Romans d'Alexandre (Paris, 1998).

24 Aimé Petit, Naissances du roman (Paris, 1985).

25 Le Roman d'Enéas, ed. J.J. Salverda de Grave (Paris, 1929); Francine Mora-Lebrun, L'Enéas: la naissance du roman (Paris, 1994).

foundation and destruction of kingdoms, on the life and death of human societies.[26]

Similarly, *Le Roman d'Eneas* constitutes the continuation of *Le Roman de Troie*, since, unlike the *Aeneid*, it begins with the fall of Troy and the flight of Eneas and ends with the announcement of the founding of Rome. Its narrative framework remains very faithful to that of the *Aeneid*, but the author pauses to describe at length Eneas's loves – with Dido and particularly with Lavine – revelling in the depiction of the pangs of awakening passion.

Finally, Wace's *Roman de Brut* (1155), a transposition into French of Geoffrey of Monmouth's *Historia regum Britanniae* (1138), closes the cycle, bridging the gap between the subject matter of antiquity and that of Britain. Proposing to clarify the story of the first British kings, the romance summarizes Eneas's voyages before turning to the adventures of Brutus, his great-grandson, the eponymous King of Britain, who will found a new Troy with the city of London.

The authors of the romances of antiquity, in an effort both to embellish the narratives and to give them an appropriate length, include extended descriptions of objects of art (in the style of the *ekphrasis* of classical antiquity), portraits of heroes and heroines (such as we find in Chrétien's works) and, particularly in the *Eneas*, the development of a discourse on love expressed through the monologues, dialogues, and inner debates that reappear, for example, in *Cligés*.

The trilogy also helped anchor in the medieval imagination the myth of cultural continuity across time and space, the idea of the simultaneous transfer of power and knowledge (*translatio imperii et studii*), from one civilization to another, from East to West, as the prologue to *Cligés* affirms:

> Ce nos ont nostre livre apris
> Qu'an Grece ot de chevalerie
> Le premier los et de clergie.
> Puis vint chevalerie a Rome
> Et de la clergie la some
> Qui or est an France venue.
> Dex doint qu'ele i soit maintenue
> Et que li leus li abelisse
> Tant que ja mes de France n'isse
> L'enors qui s'i est arestee.

> [This is what our books have taught us: Greece was first in chivalry and knowledge; then chivalry proceeded to Rome, in company of the highest learning. Now it has come to France. May God grant that it be sustained here and its stay so pleasing that the honour that has arrived here in France may never depart.][27]

Power and knowledge followed the same path from East to West, from Greece to Rome, ending up in the medieval West – that is, in France, according to the clerk

---

[26] Catherine Croizy-Naquet, *Thèbes, Troie et Carthage: poétique de la ville dans le roman antique au XIIe siècle* (Paris, 1994).

[27] Chrétien de Troyes, *Cligés*, ed. Claude Luttrell and Stewart Gregory (Cambridge, 1993), vss 30–39.

of Marie de Champagne; in England, according to Henry II's clerks, who, in their writings, make the King of England the descendant of Brutus the Trojan and make Arthur the king of Logres.

The influence of Ovid in the twelfth century is conveyed by the composition (among others) of three works taken from *Metamorphoses* – three tales of love and death: *Piramus et Tisbé* (c. 1160), the *Lai de Narcisus* (1165–75) and *Philomena*, all marking the appearance of the short narrative form in French literature.[28] These three *Ovidiana* share as a common theme the prominent expression of the suffering of lovesickness (in the style of *Eneas*, with long introspective monologues).

As forerunners of Romeo and Juliet, Pyrame and Thisbé flee their feuding families and, because of a misunderstanding, commit suicide. Thisbé, the first to arrive at the site of their rendezvous, sees a lion and flees, leaving behind her scarf, which the lion stains with blood. Pyrame thinks her dead and stabs himself. Thisbé returns and, seeing her lover dead, kills herself, and the mulberry, which was white, becomes the colour of the lovers' blood. In order to embellish the lamentations on love, the poet interlaces the octosyllabic couplets with lyric stanzas.

In the *Lai de Narcisus*, the Ovidian scenario is profoundly modified: the nymph Echo, a disembodied being, is transformed into Dané, a young girl in love, and the hero's metamorphosis into a flower is deleted, replaced by the death of both lovers. Narcisus falls in love with his own reflection and dies; Dané, like Iseut, dies of love, collapsing over her dead lover's body.

The cruel tale of *Philomena* has been preserved in the fourteenth-century *Ovide moralisé*, which retells and annotates Ovid's *Metamorphoses*. The work is attributed to a certain 'Crestïens li Gois', whom it is tempting to identify as Chrétien de Troyes, since a work dealing with the same subject is included in the list that opens the prologue of *Cligés*:

> Cil qui fist *D'Erec et d'Enide*
> Et *Les comandemanz d'Ovide*
> Et *L'art d'amors* an romans mist
> Et *Le mors de l'espaule* fist,
> Del roi Marc et d'Ysalt la blonde
> Et *De la hupe et de l'aronde*
> Et *Del rossignol la muance*,
> Un novel conte recomance
> D'un vaslet qui an Grece fu
> Del linage le roi Artu.   (vss 1–10; editors' italics)

> [He who wrote *Erec et Enide* and translated Ovid's *Commandments* and the *Art of Love* into French, who composed *The Shoulder Bite*, and told of King Mark and Iseut the Blonde and *of the metamorphosis of the hoopoe, swallow and nightingale*, begins a new story of a young man in Greece who was of Arthur's lineage.][29]

---

28 *Pyrame et Thisbé, Narcisse, Philomena*, ed. and trans. Emmanuèle Baumgartner (Paris, 2000).
29 See, below, the chapters devoted to *Philomena, Erec et Enide* and *Cligés*.

Tereüs, in love with his sister-in-law, Philomena, rapes her and holds her captive in the forest, after having cut out her tongue. She weaves the story of her calamities on cloth to convey them to her sister, Progné. The two sisters, once reunited, kill the son of Progne and Tereüs and serve him as a meal to his father. The three central figures of this dreadful story are transformed into a swallow, a hoopoe, and a nightingale. In the prologue to *Cligés*, references to the Breton romances *Erec et Enide* and *Marc et Ysalt* (why not Tristan?) are thus interlaced with a whole series of stories taken from Ovid's work: *The Remedies of Love*, *The Art of Love* and two tales from the *Metamorphoses*: the story of Pelops's shoulder, eaten by Demeter and replaced by a shoulder made of marble, and the legend of Philomena. Chrétien made extensive use of subjects from antiquity before creating the Breton romance.

Chrétien initiated this new form of romance with his *Erec et Enide* in 1170. But the matter of Britain was already established in literature before that. The Arthurian myth gradually attained literary status with several scattered texts written between the sixth and twelfth centuries, and especially with the two founding texts, Geoffrey of Monmouth's *Historia regum Britanniae* (1138) and its 'mise en roman' [translation into French] in Wace's *Brut* (1155), which Chrétien seemed to know as well as he knew the *Eneas*.[30] In *Le Roman de Brut*, the Arthurian framework is already in place: the Round Table, the court and its principal figures, King Arthur as the incarnation of courtliness, Queen Guenevere, Gauvain the faithful nephew, and Keu the seneschal.

Already in the *Brut*, Wace notes the flourishing of the legends that storytellers were circulating about the glorious reign of Arthur:

> Que par amur de sa largesce,
> Que pur pöur de sa prüesce,
> En cele pais que jo di
> (Ne sai si vus l'avez oï)
> Furent les merveilles provees
> E les aventures trovees
> Que d'Arthur sunt tant recuntees
> Que a fable sunt aturnees:
> Ne tut mençunge ne tut veir,
> Ne tut folie ne tut saveir.
> Tant unt li cuntëur cunté
> E li fablëur tant fablé
> Pur lur cuntes enbeleter,
> Unt tut fait fables sembler.

> [It was during this period of peace – I do not know if you have heard about it – when his generosity was admired as much as his prowess was feared, that there occurred the wondrous events and the adventures that have been recounted so often about Arthur that they seem to be fabrications – neither all lies nor all truth, neither entirely foolish nor entirely wise. So long have the storytellers spun tales and the

---

[30] See below, ch. 4, 'The Arthurian Legend Before Chrétien'.

writers of fables lied in order to embellish their stories that, in the
end, they have made them appear to be fiction].[31]

This mention of 'cunteür' and 'cuntes' brings us necessarily to Marie de
France, who referred to 'Les contes . . . dunt li Breton unt fait les lais'.[32] The
origin of the term *lai* is uncertain: is it Latin or Celtic? Some have suggested that
it is related to the Latin *laicus*; it would thus refer to the opposition between
learned Latin culture and popular lay culture and would designate, like the
word *roman*, the common language of the people and thus the texts written in
this language. However, some have also linked *lai* to the Celtic *laid*, 'song'. The
first use of the term (in Wace's *Roman de Brut*, in 1155) seems to designate, in fact,
a melody. Arthur's court resounded with lays performed on all sorts of
instruments:

> Mult out a la curt jugleürs,
> Chanteürs, estrumenteürs:
> Mult peüssiez oïr chançuns,
> Rotrüenges e novels suns,
> vïeleüres, lais de note,
> lais de vïeles, lais de rotes,
> lais de harpes, lais de frestels. . .
>
> [The court was full of jongleurs, singers and instrumentalists, and, all
> around, you could have heard songs, lovesongs and new composi-
> tions, *viele* music, lays with melodies, lays played on the harp or flute
> . . .][33]

The narrative lay is a short text (between one hundred and one thousand lines)
composed in octosyllabic couplets. There are about thirty of these texts, written
in the last third of the twelfth or the first half of the thirteenth century and identified as *lais* by the authors or scribes. The most famous are the *Lais* of Marie de
France (around 1180), which are steeped in the supernatural universe of Celtic
lore. Marie attributes their origin to a legendary adventure (situated in Britain,
in a mythic past) that supposedly engendered an oral tale and a musical composition described as a *lai*. The lay is characterized by its commemorative value – it
preserves the memory of a prodigious adventure – and by its connection to
instrumental music or song. But the narrative element became the dominant
one, and the term came to designate the verse tale derived from the legend,
which had itself given birth to the musical composition. That explains the great
importance attributed to the titles of these tales. Their titles are often given in
several languages: the story of *Bisclavret*, the werewolf, is called *Garwaf* in
Anglo-Norman; *Chievrefoil*, which relates a brief encounter between Tristan and
Iseut, is also *Gotelef* in English; *Laostic* is the Briton term for the French *Rossignol*
and the English *Nihtegale*. The importance attached to the title is clear if the tale

---

[31] Wace, *Le Roman de Brut*, in *La Geste d'Arthur*, ed. and trans. Emmanuèle Baumgartner and Ian
     Short (Paris, 1993), vss 1057–70.
[32] *Guigemar*, in *Lais de Marie de France*, ed. Jean Rychner (Paris, 1966), vss 19–20: 'The stories . . .
     from which the Bretons made their lays'.
[33] *Brut*, ed. Baumgartner and Short, vss 1717–23.

refers to a musical composition whose words are not necessarily known to everyone. The title thus incorporates the very essence of the story: in two lays, we find a debate intended to determine the title that best corresponds to the meaning of the narratives. *Eliduc* tells the story of a man torn between two women and saved by his wife's sacrifice. Marie was firmly opposed to the title corresponding to the name of the hero (Elidus): she favoured the one that emphasizes the two heroines (Guildeluëc and Guilliadon). In response to a woman who laments the death of three of the knights devoted to her and the wounds of the fourth one, and who wants to preserve the memory of her adventure in a lay titled *Les Quatre Deuls* ('The Four Sorrows'), the surviving knight persuades her to acknowledge his greater misfortune by choosing another title, *Chaitivel* ('The Unhappy One').

In the lays of Marie de France, as in the anonymous lays that are products of the same folklore sources, we find the themes and structure of popular tales. The adventure marks the division between the real and the surreal. Guigemar, who wounded a mythical doe endowed with the antlers of a stag, hears the animal reveal his destiny to him; the prophecy begins to come true when he boards a mysterious boat with no pilot, which leads him to the woman who will make him discover love, a woman who, in a supernatural tale, would no doubt be the incarnation of the doe. The hero, 'emerveillé' [filled with wonder] at the prodigious richness of the vessel, which he suddenly realizes is on the open sea, understands that he must accept the adventure, which will allow him to discover love and will separate him from his lady before returning her to him, once he has suffered sufficiently. The lays of *Graelent* and *Guingamor*, inseparable from Marie de France's lay *Lanval*, recount the love of a mortal and a fairy: Graelent and Guingamor are lured into the other world by a wondrous animal, a white doe or a white boar, reminiscent of the white doe from *Guigemar* and, of course, the hunt for the white stag in *Erec et Enide*. Like Lanval, they disappear into the other world, the only homeland that favours perfect loves.

But the stories' plots are integrated into an original poetic universe. In their diversity, the narratives provide the material for a veritable reflection on love. Guigemar would be a perfect knight if he did not scorn love; at the end of his painful trials, he will find happiness in the union of love and prowess (like the heroes of Chrétien de Troyes). Love is inseparable from suffering – a purifying suffering that enables the lovers from *Guigemar*, *Fresne* and *Milun* to be united in this world. The lovers from *Deus Amanz* will be reunited in death, and *Chievrefoil* recalls the fate of Tristan and Iseut: 'de lur amur ki tant fu fine, / dunt il ourent meinte dolur; / puis en mururent en un jur' [of their perfect love that caused them so much suffering; and then they both died on the same day].[34] As for *Chaitivel*, the story is constructed around the thorny question of who should be pitied most. Whether it is the woman who lost her four lovers all at once or the surviving knight, whose wounds prevent him from enjoying the love of his lady, this lay seems to parody the judgments passed by Eleanor of Aquitaine or Marie

---

34 *Chievrefoil*, in *Lais*, ed. Rychner, vss 77–78.

de Champagne on the vicissitudes of love and reported by Andreas Capellanus in his *De amore* or *The Art of Courtly Love*.

Stories of the marvellous exerted a determining influence on the structure of romances. Did they not allow Chrétien to draw 'd'un conte d'avanture / Une mout bele conjunture', *Erec*, vss 13–14 [a very pleasing composition from a story of adventure]? These tales frequently revolve around the love between a mortal and a fairy. We see a fairy fall in love with a human being and follow him into the world of mortals, in order to provide him with a lineage: such is the story of the fairy Mélusine. We also see a fairy fall in love with a mortal and lure him into the other world, where she attempts to keep him, as does the fairy Morgan in the prose romances of the thirteenth century.

This setting is already present in *Erec et Enide*, underlying the story of the hunt for the white stag, leading the hero far from court to a castle where he will win Enide. But Enide no longer has any of the characteristics of a fairy other than her supernatural beauty, as does the heroine of *Guigemar*, where Marie similarly 'rationalizes' the text. In several of Chrétien's romances we also find the same narrative structure, offering a variant of the 'Morganian' tales – the story of the giant and the fairy, a veritable *leitmotiv* of the Breton romances of the twelfth and thirteenth centuries. Here the hero travels to a supernatural place and conquers the mistress of the land by fighting the giant, the guardian of the other world, and defeating him.[35] The first romance setting of this motif is the 'Joie de la cour' episode in *Erec*. Within the magical castle, Brandigan, there is a beautiful lady protected by a great knight, Mabonagrain. All those who have previously accepted the challenge have lost their heads in the enchanted orchard. But Erec will overturn the evil custom and restore joy to the court. The same scenario reappears at the beginning of *Le Chevalier au lion*. In the forest of Brocéliande, both Calogrenant and, later, Yvain confront the giant Esclados le Ros, guardian of the fountain of Barenton. Yvain's victory will liberate the castle and will win for him the hand of the defeated knight's widow. Finally, we find the same adventure in *Le Conte du Graal*, in Gauvain's encounter with the Orgueilleuse de Logres and the great knight. But the quest of the romance hero is not the same as that of the heroes of fairy tales. If all of Chrétien's romances are proof of the integration of tales of the marvellous into the romance mythology of the Middle Ages, the mythic themes are used to support the chivalric ideal of romance, in a perfect osmosis.

In addition to the Arthurian matter, Breton tales provided Chrétien with the main theme for his reflection on the conflicts encountered between the demands of love and society: Tristan and the myth of passionate love. Not only did he compose the romance 'del roi Marc et d'Ysalt la blonde' mentioned in the prologue to *Cligés*, but he also wrote his four 'worldly' romances (*Erec et Enide*, *Cligés*, *Lancelot*, *Yvain*) as a response to the story of the love and death of Tristan and Iseut.

The first Tristan romances have been completely or partially lost. Of the twelfth-century French verse romances, there remain half of Béroul's romance

---

[35] Laurence Harf-Lancner, *Les Fées au Moyen Age* (Paris, 1984; 1991) et *Le Monde des fées dans l'Occident médiéval* (Paris, 2003).

(in the 1170s), a sixth of Thomas's romance (1172–75) and three short narratives. The Bern *Folie Tristan* and The Oxford *Folie Tristan* both recount the same episode of the legend: Tristan disguised as a fool, in an attempt to enter Marc's court, and his manipulation of the fool's mask, making him recognizable only to Iseut.[36] Marie de France's lay *Chievrefoil* evokes a furtive encounter between Tristan and Iseut. Tristan reveals himself to Iseut by a message carved on a hazel branch, which thus symbolizes the very essence of their love, similar to the force that unites the honeysuckle and the hazel tree: they can live only if intertwined, one with the other, and their separation condemns them to death: ' "Bele amie, si est de nus; / Ne vuz sanz mei, ne jeo sanz vus" ' ['Dear friend, so it is with us: neither you without me, nor I without you'].[37] All versions of the sombre story of Tristan and Iseut inspire the same fascination and the same fear in narrators. It is hardly surprising, then, that Tristan's shadow hovers over all of Chrétien's romances (except *Le Conte du Graal*).

Béroul's so-called common version of the Tristan legend has often been contrasted with Thomas's, called the courtly version, and it is true that Thomas's text bears the mark of the new model of the hero proposed by romance, and of the new conception of love that blossomed in lyric poetry from the south. It would therefore be more just to contrast Béroul's epic version with Thomas's lyric one.[38] Béroul's text is ambiguous at every turn. The lovers live a guilty passion but do so innocently, since they are under the influence of an all-powerful potion (even if its power weakens, in a seeming contradiction, after three years). Guilty in fact but innocent in intention, the lovers are therefore justified in all the ruses they use against the snares of their enemies. Iseut can thus implement a Machiavellian scheme to exonerate herself of the accusation of adultery by swearing an oath on relics: never was any man between her thighs except King Marc and the poor leper (Tristan's new disguise) on whose shoulders she chose to cross Mal Pas. She is thus cleared of all suspicion in the eyes of men, whereas God's judgment remains hidden.

On the other hand, in the version of the episode offered by Gottfried von Strassburg and the Old Norse saga (drawing from a missing part of Thomas's text), God performs an astonishing miracle for the lovers, since Iseut, after her ambiguous oath, firmly grasps the hot iron without being burned. But the subtle analyses that Thomas creates for the long monologues ascribed to the lovers and his own subsequent commentary are all related to suffering and lead inescapably to a conclusion that can only be the death of the lovers. And the epilogue of the romance, dedicated to all lovers, presents itself as a warning against the infinite torments of love, which lead to death. For Thomas, as for Béroul, the legend admits of no other interpretation. It is the Oxford *Folie* that offers the most beau-

---

36 *Tristan et Iseut, Les Poèmes français, La Saga norroise*, ed. and trans. Philippe Walter and Daniel Lacroix (Paris, 1989); Thomas, *Le Roman de Tristan* suivi de *La Folie Tristan* de Berne et *La Folie Tristan* d'Oxford, trans. Emmanuèle Baumgartner and Ian Short, texts ed. Félix Lecoy (Paris, 2003).

37 *Le Chèvrefeuille*, in *Lais*, ed. Rychner, vss 77–78.

38 As Jean-Charles Payen proposes in his edition of the text, *Tristan et Yseut* (Paris, 1974). See also Payen's 'Le Palais de verre dans la *Folie d'Oxford*: De la folie métaphorique à la folie vécue', *Tristania*, 5.2 (1980), 17–27.

tiful image of this impossible love, when Tristan, in his disguise as fool, proposes to lead the queen into a glass palace suspended in the air, the only refuge for a forbidden love.[39] 'Il est évident que la réponse que donne le *Tristan*, réponse que ne modifient pas en profondeur ni la version de Béroul ni la version *courtoise* de Thomas, est en total désaccord avec le culte du désir que propose la lyrique occitane puis avec l'image positive et optimiste de l'amour qu'à partir de 1160 Chrétien de Troyes met en place, d'un roman à l'autre' [It is obvious that the response given by the *Tristan* – a response that neither Béroul's version nor Thomas's *courtly* version alters significantly – is in total disagreement both with the cult of desire that the Occitan lyrics proposed and with the positive and optimistic image of love that, beginning in 1160, Chrétien de Troyes elaborated in one romance after another].[40]

The Tristan legend, however, exerted such an influence on Chrétien's work that it seems to constitute one of the primary underpinnings of his reflection on the place of love in his heroes' quest and on its relation to social values. In *D'Amors, qui m'a tolu a moi*, the poet/lover contrasts the mortal passion of Tristan, poisoned by the potion, to the *fin'amor* to which he is devoted:

> Onques du buvrage ne bui
> Dont Tristan fu enpoisonnez;
> Mes plus me fet amer que lui
> Fins cuers et bone volentez.

> [I never drank the potion that poisoned Tristan; but a noble heart and good will make me love better than he.][41]

The same denial is expressed in the words of Fenice, who finds herself in the same situation as Iseut:

> 'Mialz voldroie estre desmanbree
> Que de nos .II. fust remanbree
> L'amors d'Ysolt et de Tristran,
> Don tantes folies dit an
> Que honte m'est a recorder'.   (*Cligés*, vss 3125–29)

> ['I would prefer to be drawn and quartered rather than have anyone mention in regard to us the loves of Iseut and Tristan, about whom so much foolishness is told that I am ashamed even to mention'.][42]

This is why *Cligés* has been characterized as an anti-Tristan or a neo-Tristan, in the sense that Chrétien, in a valiant effort, transforms the elements of the Tristanian legend in his attempt to neutralize their subversive character.[43]

---

[39] *La Folie d'Oxford*, ed. and trans. Baumgartner and Short, vss 301–10.
[40] Emmanuèle Baumgartner, *Tristan et Iseut* (Paris, 1987).
[41] *Chansons*, ed. Marie-Claire Zai, in Chrétien de Troyes, *Romans suivis des Chansons*, genl ed. Zink, p. 1220.
[42] *Cligés*, vss 3125–29.
[43] For a sharply contrasting view of Chrétien's attitude toward the Tristan legend, especially as evidenced in the Chansons and *Cligés*, see the essay by Joan Tasker Grimbert in this volume and the articles cited in notes 27 and 35 of that chapter.

Similarly, even if *Le Chevalier de la Charrette* sets the elements of lyric into the framework of romance, and if the relationship between the lady and the lover/poet is applied to that between Lancelot and Guenevere, the influence of the Tristan legend is nevertheless present in the love scene where a wounded Lancelot, like Tristan in Béroul's romance, leaves bloodstains on the queen's bedsheets.

The *topos* of the transference of power and knowledge from East to West over the course of the centuries, illustrated by the prologue to *Cligés*, should not make us forget that the western component of romance thematics (the matter of Britain) coexists with a series of romances dominated by the marvels of the East, centred on the mythic Byzantium. *Le Conte de Floire et Blancheflor* (c. 1150), whose premise is based on an Arabian tale, illustrates this perfectly, while also founding the genre of the idyllic romance (the thwarted love of two heroes who have loved each other since childhood).[44] The adventures of Floire, a pagan, and Blancheflor, a Christian, unfold in an Eastern setting that is both magical and real (Babylon, Cairo, Baghdad). They also evoke the same confrontation of East and West found in *Cligés*.

The Anglo-Norman writer Hue de Rotelande sets the adventures of his hero, Ipomedon, in southern Italy and Sicily at the end of the twelfth century. Ipomedon, son of the King of Puglia, falls in love with the Duchess of Calabria. Their son, the eponymous hero of *Protheselaus*, is the Duke of Calabria and King of Puglia, and he marries Medea, Queen of Crete, after numerous adventures.[45] *Florimont*, by Aimon de Varennes (1188), is an adventure story in a Mediterranean setting: its hero, Florimont, son of Mataquas, Duke of Albania, confronts the giant Garganeüs at Mount Gargan in Puglia and becomes the ally of Risus, Prince of Calabria, in order to come to the aid of Philippe, King of Greece. He marries Philippe's daughter, Romadanaple, frees her father from prison in Carthage and succeeds his father-in-law on the Greek throne.[46] Alexander the Great will be his grandson. *Partonopeu de Blois* (c. 1185) is a retelling of the story of Cupid and Psyche, as Apuleius recounts it in *The Golden Ass*, but here, the roles are reversed: it is the male hero (Partonopeu) who is kidnapped by a fairy who is in love with him and who turns out to be the Empress of Byzantium.[47] Between 1176 and 1181, another cleric, Gautier d'Arras, who was Chrétien's contemporary and perhaps even his rival, composed *Eracle* for Marie de Champagne and Count Thibaut de Blois. The prologue to this romance announces that it is a biography of Heraclius, Emperor of Byzantium from 610 to 641; at the conclusion of his adventures, the Emperor Eracle removes the Holy Cross from the Persian, Cosroé, and returns it to Jerusalem.[48]

---

44 *Le Conte de Floire et Blanchefleur*, ed. and trans. Jean-Luc Leclanche (Paris, 2003).
45 Hue de Rotelande, *Ipomédon*, ed. A.J. Holden (Paris, 1979); *Protheselaus*, ed. A.J. Holden (London, 1993).
46 Aimon de Varennes, *Florimont*, ed. Alfons Hilka (Göttingen, 1932).
47 *Partonopeu de Blois*, ed. Joseph Gildea (Villanova, PA, 1967–70).
48 Gautier d'Arras, *Eracle*, ed. G. Raynaud de Lage (Paris, 1976); Gautier is also the author of *Ille et Galeron* (ed. Y. Lefèvre, Paris, 1988), which retells the story of the lay of *Eliduc* by Marie de France. See Corinne Pierreville, *Gautier d'Arras, l'autre Chrétien* (Paris, 2001).

The second half of the twelfth century witnessed the birth of a romance literature of extraordinary richness. But only Chrétien had the genius to create,
around the tutelary figure of Arthur, a fictional universe forged from the matter
of Britain, a universe in which to meditate both on the mysteries of literary
creation and on the complex relations that humankind entertains with love and
with society.[49]

---

49 Emmanuèle Baumgartner, *Romans de Chrétien de Troyes* (Paris, 2003), p. 16.

4

The Arthurian Legend Before Chrétien de Troyes

NORRIS J. LACY

It is both traditional and correct to identify Chrétien de Troyes as the creator of Arthurian romance and as the writer who inaugurated a number of Arthurian motifs and themes. Those include Camelot, Lancelot, the Grail; the nature of the court and of a good many Arthurian characters; and above all, the complex quest structure resting on the opposition of public v. private responsibilities, of the individual (or couple) v. society, occasionally of love v. chivalry itself.

However, preliminary to a study of Chrétien's accomplishment is a review of the Arthurian legend before his time. Much of the material concerning that legend, though, is necessarily irrecuperable, since there must have been a great many Arthurian stories that circulated orally, in Celtic and other languages, but either were never written or were recorded in texts that have not survived. That such stories existed within oral tradition cannot be in doubt, but neither can the information about them be corroborated with confidence, and authors' statements to the effect that 'the story says . . .' or that 'I have heard it said . . .' may often be nothing more than commonplaces or efforts to support their texts with the authority of pre-existing narratives.

The following census of early Arthuriana will not tell us what sources Chrétien may have known and drawn upon directly, with the single exception of Wace's *Roman de Brut*, written in 1155. Because Wace was the first to speak of the Round Table, and because he first put into French the narrative of Arthur's life and career – though without many of the characters and events that were later to become a regular part of the story – Chrétien clearly knew and used Wace's work (for which see below). He may also have known Wace's source, Geoffrey of Monmouth's *Historia regum Britannie*,[1] but that is not certain.

Chrétien himself speaks of sources but gives us little information about what they may have been. In all five of his Arthurian romances, he makes tantalizing but frustrating allusions to pre-existing material that he is adapting for the public. In his first romance, *Erec et Enide*, he refers to the story of his hero and contends that the storytellers who have recounted it previously 'depecier et corrompre suelent' [habitually mangle and corrupt it].[2] His second Arthurian

---

[1] The title has traditionally been spelled 'Britanniae', though without manuscript authority, and following Wright's edition (see below), many scholars are adopting the spelling of his manuscript.

[2] Chrétien de Troyes, *Erec et Enide*, ed. and trans. Jean-Marie Fritz, in *Romans suivis des chansons,*

composition, *Cligés*, opens with a list of Chrétien's previous works (including some that may or may not have existed) and then announces that the story he is now going to tell is found in a book from the library of St Peter's Church in Beauvais.[3] However, that book, if it existed, has not been found and indeed could not be found, since the church, presumably with all its books, burned in 1180. In the famous prologue to the *Chevalier de la charrette*, Chrétien informs us that the story was commissioned by Marie de Champagne – 'Matiere et san li done et livre / La contesse' [the Countess has given him (i.e. to Chrétien) the subject matter and meaning],[4] and she had no doubt heard it from other sources. In his conclusion to *Yvain*, the author alludes obliquely to a source, insisting that the story he has just narrated is complete, that 'Onques plus dire n'en oï' [I never heard any more about it].[5] The final romance, *Perceval*, refers again, as had *Cligés*, to a book preserving the story he is adapting. That book, we are told, was given to him by his patron Philippe de Flandre: 'li quens li bailla le livre' [the Count gave him the book].[6]

All these passages hint at Chrétien's access to Arthurian sources, but they do not convincingly demonstrate it, nor do they give us enough information to draw more than the most tentative conclusions about it. Three of his comments presumably refer to oral sources – we cannot know from where Marie took her story, but her commission to Chrétien was delivered orally – whereas the two others refer to a book that we do not have and that may or may not have existed (though their existence is not implausible). In all these cases, it is impossible to know the precise content or form of Chrétien's putative sources. And finally, if we do take Chrétien at his word and accept his reliance on particular texts or tales, we still cannot be certain that those sources were Arthurian. It is clearly possible that one or all three were non-Arthurian narratives that Chrétien, by choice or by patronal command, set into an Arthurian context.[7]

If we broaden our focus, moving from what Chrétien may have known to what *we* now know about the pre-Chrétien development of the Arthurian

---

    avec, en appendice, Philomena, genl ed. Michel Zink (Paris, 1994), vs. 21. Except where otherwise indicated, translations in this chapter are my own.

3   Chrétien de Troyes, *Cligés*, ed. Claude Luttrell and Stewart Gregory (Cambridge, 1993), vss 18–26. In vss 24–26 Chrétien offers the observation that 'Li livres est molt anciens / Qui tesmoingne l'estoire a voire; / Por ce fet ele mialz a croire' [The book is very old, which indicates that the story is true; for this reason it is more believable]. This statement is both a claim of authority for Chrétien's story and an illustration of *translatio studii*, the belief in the transfer of older (usually classical) learning to 'modern' France.

4   Chrétien de Troyes, *Le Chevalier de la charrette ou le roman de Lancelot*, ed. and trans. Charles Méla, in *Romans suivis des Chansons*, genl ed. Michel Zink (Paris, 1994), vss 26–27.

5   Chrétien de Troyes, *Le Chevalier au lion (Yvain)*, ed. and trans. David Hult, in *Romans suivis des Chansons*, genl ed. Michel Zink (Paris, 1994), vs. 6806.

6   Chrétien de Troyes, *Le Roman de Perceval, ou le conte du Graal*, ed. Keith Busby (Tübingen, 1993), vs. 67.

7   Particularly in the case of the *Charrette*, the conventional assumption is that the Countess commissioned a narrative featuring Guenevere and an extramarital love. However, we cannot categorically exclude the possibility that in its earlier incarnation it was set in a non-Arthurian context. Conceivably, an element of Chrétien's commission (or perhaps his own choice) was to provide an Arthurian setting for the non-Arthurian tale of a knight subservient to his lady's wishes and whims. This conjecture seems unlikely but cannot be dismissed out of hand, and it indicates how little we actually know about the sources of Chrétien's works and the proportion of adaptation to original creation in his art.

legend, we find ourselves with three kinds of material. One involves Arthurian artefacts: depictions in the visual arts. The other two are in written form, but they divide into early and usually fragmentary references in lists or chronicles, on the one hand, and to imaginative expansions of Arthuriana, on the other.

A number of artefacts offer evidence of the early circulation of Arthurian tales, and in some cases they predate the appearance of romances. The earliest sculptural depiction of a scene that may well be Arthurian, though the identification is uncertain, is the Perros Relief, on a pier in the church of St Efflam (Brittany). This sculpture, dating from around 1100, depicts three figures, one of them lying prone between the two others. One of the standing figures, holding a crozier, is doubtless St Efflam. One of the two other persons may be Arthur, perhaps lying exhausted from a battle in which St Efflam assisted him through prayer.[8]

The most famous of the early artefacts is undoubtedly the Modena archivolt in Italy.[9] Now dated, though not without dissent from some quarters, between 1120 and 1140,[10] the archivolt, on the north portal, the Porta della Pescheria, depicts several Arthurian figures attacking a castle in which a woman is held captive. Names carved above or alongside some of the figures identify them: Artus de Bretania, Che (Kay), Galvagin (Gauvain) and others. Within the castle is Winlogee, often assumed to be Guenevere, though that identification is clearly open to question. The scene has sometimes been taken as a visual allusion to the queen's abduction and eventual liberation in the *Chevalier de la charrette*, but the Modena sculpture does not enable us to draw that conclusion with confidence. Nonetheless, the archivolt offers irrefutable evidence of the existence and probable popularity of an Arthurian tradition in Italy prior to the composition of the first Arthurian romances by Chrétien and most likely prior even to Geoffrey of Monmouth's *Historia regum Britannie* (c. 1138).

The cathedral of Otranto, Italy, contains a mosaic floor illustrating prominent figures and themes from biblical and profane history. Commissioned in 1165, and thus roughly contemporaneous with the first French Arthurian romances, the mosaic depicts Arthur astride a goat. Shown nearby is a large cat, perhaps a reference to Arthur's battle with Palug's Cat (a feline monster that reputedly lived, depending on the version of the story, either near Lausanne or on Anglesey), though in an early Welsh text, it was killed by Cei rather than Arthur. But if the narrative elements are uncertain, the identification of the human figure is not, as his name, Rex Arturus, is preserved within the mosaic.[11]

---

8   Michel Renouard, *Art roman en Bretagne* (Rennes, 1978).
9   The presence of Arthurian art in Italy at such an early date may be attributable to the dissemination of stories taken to Italy and beyond by knights in the First Crusade. See Christopher Snyder, *The World of King Arthur* (London, 2000), p. 128. Muriel Whitaker offers a different, but compatible, suggestion: that Arthurian tales were brought to Italy as a result of the Normans' conquest of Apulia, Calabria and Sicily in the eleventh century. See Whitaker's *The Legends of King Arthur in Art* (Cambridge, 1990), pp. 52–53. For more thematic and art historical information on the archivolt, see Whitaker, pp. 86–88.
10   Concerning the dating and interpretation of the sculpture, see Jacques Stiennon and Rita Lejeune, 'La Légende arthurienne dans la sculpture de la cathédrale de Modène', *Cahiers de civilisation médiévale*, 6 (1963), 281–96.
11   Whitaker, *Legends of King Arthur in Art*, pp. 88–89; Roger Sherman Loomis and Laura Hibbard Loomis, *Arthurian Legends in Medieval Art* (London, 1938), p. 36, fig. 9, 9a.

By the time Chrétien was writing, Arthurian material had been recorded, if only sporadically, for some six centuries.[12] Although virtually none of it would have been known to Chrétien (unless remnants of it were also preserved in oral form), this survey enables us better to evaluate Chrétien's creation by measuring it against what had come or, more often, had not come before him.

Discussions of early Arthurian documents generally begin with Gildas's *De excidio Britanniae*, a sixth-century work that is in fact not explicitly Arthurian at all.[13] The 'ruin of Britain' discussed by Gildas is the Saxon invasion of Britain after the Romans' departure. Gildas points out that the Saxon wars culminated in the 'siege of Mount Badon', but he makes no reference to Arthur. Nevertheless, Gildas's work is generally regarded as the first stage in the chronicle account of Arthur simply because Badon was soon identified explicitly in other documents as one of the King's battles. Gildas alludes also to several themes that would become inextricably associated with the Arthurian legend; those themes include the removal of the Roman garrison and invasions by Picts, Scots and others (all of whom will soon come to be designated by a generic term 'Saxons').

It may well be that the earliest explicit mention of Arthur occurs in *Y Gododdin*, attributed to Aneirin. This work, presenting a series of laments, may date from around the year 600 and is thus relatively close to the so-called 'Arthurian era' (that is, the fifth and sixth centuries). One section of this Welsh composition praises a warrior but immediately qualifies the praise by adding, 'but he was no Arthur'. This reference seems to prove that Arthur was already, at a comparatively early date, reputed as an extraordinary, if not legendary, military figure. It also indicates that, at the time of its composition, Arthur was sufficiently well known that no explanation of that reference was required. It must be added that the *Gododdin* appears to have undergone revision at a later period, and a number of scholars have concluded that the reference to Arthur is an interpolation, perhaps from the ninth or tenth century.[14] However, Koch has argued that the allusion is in fact early and that Arthur's reputation was established, at least in the north, by about 600 CE.[15] In either case, not only Arthur's name but his illustrious reputation as well was set long before the appearance of romances.

---

[12] The most succinct account of the references and texts mentioned here may well be that of Geoffrey Ashe in ch. 1 of Norris J. Lacy and Geoffrey Ashe, with Debra Mancoff, *The Arthurian Handbook*, 2nd ed. (New York, 1997). More detailed accounts of Welsh material, most of it early despite its preservation in post-Chrétien manuscripts, can be found in Rachel Bromwich, A.O.H. Jarman and Brynley F. Roberts, eds, *The Arthur of the Welsh* (Cardiff, 1991), passim. An important examination of Welsh sources and related research problems is provided by John T. Koch, 'The Celtic Lands', in Norris J. Lacy, *Medieval Arthurian Literature: A Guide to Recent Research* (New York, 1996), pp. 239–322. Still standard, though seriously outdated in many points, is R.S. Loomis, ed., *Arthurian Literature in the Middle Ages* (Oxford, 1959); see particularly chaps 1, 'The Arthur of History', by Kenneth Hurlstone Jackson (pp. 1–11), and 2, 'Arthur in Early Welsh Verse', also by Jackson (pp. 12–19).

[13] Koch, 'The Celtic Lands', pp. 241–42.

[14] See, for example, Thomas Charles-Edwards, 'The Arthur of History', in Bromwich, Jarman and Roberts, eds, *The Arthur of the Welsh*, p. 15.

[15] Koch, 'The Celtic Lands', pp. 244–45. Koch's *The Gododdin of Aneirin: Text and Context from Dark-Age North Britain* (Andover, MA, 1997) includes a historical study, a 'reconstructed' text and a translation of the *Gododdin*.

Arthur's name occurs as well in the *Historia Brittonum*, sometimes attributed to Nennius, a Welsh cleric.[16] In this text, from the ninth century, we find Arthur praised but described as a *dux bellorum* [a leader of battles, a military leader] rather than as a king. (It was not until the twelfth century that Arthur was regularly identified as king.) Arthur's twelve battles are enumerated, and Nennius notes that in the last of them, the battle of Mount Badon, Arthur himself defeated 960 of the enemy, a fact that confirms his legendary status. (If the *Gododdin* reference to Arthur is in fact a later interpolation, this passage from the *Historia Brittonum* could well be the earliest mention of his name.)

Between the tenth and twelfth centuries, a number of other texts add information about Arthur and contribute further to the expansion of his legendary status. Two of them date from the tenth century: the *Annales Cambriae* and *Preiddeu Annwn*. The former records Arthur's death, referring to 'the strife of Camlann in which Arthur and Medraut fell' but without indicating whether Medraut [Mordred] and Arthur were adversaries or allies. The Welsh *Preiddeu Annwn* recounts a voyage taken by Arthur and his followers to the other world.

Other events and texts prior to Chrétien confirm the belief, widespread but certainly not universal, in Arthur's immortality, in the fact that he was still alive or that he would return in due course. One of the dramatic incidents related to this belief was recorded by Hermann of Tournai in 1113 and involved a group of French canons travelling with relics. As Geoffrey Ashe summarizes the account,

> A Cornishman with a withered arm approached in hope of a cure. Something brought up the topic of Arthur, and he assured one of the party that the King was alive. The Frenchmen laughed, but the bystanders supported him and a fight broke out. The withered arm remained withered. . . . Hermann, giving his account of this fracas, remarks that the French have the same problem with the Bretons, who insist that Arthur has never died, and seem to think he will come back to help them.[17]

The chronicler William of Malmesbury, around 1125, also treats this subject in his *Gesta regum Anglorum*, pointing out that ancient songs predict Arthur's return.[18] In the same work, William laments the fact that so many fictional details had been added to the reality of Arthur:

> This is the Arthur concerning whom the idle tales of the Britons rave wildly even today – a man certainly worthy to be celebrated, not in the foolish dreams of deceitful fables, but in truthful histories; since for a long time he sustained the declining fortunes of his native land and incited the uncrushed courage of the people to war.[19]

---

[16] That attribution, once generally accepted (though not without hesitation), has more recently been challenged or rejected by increasing numbers of scholars.

[17] Geoffrey Ashe, *The Discovery of King Arthur* (New York, 1985), p. 151.

[18] Ashe, *Discovery*, p. 152.

[19] The translation is taken from Robert Huntington Fletcher, *The Arthurian Material in the Chronicles* (New York, 1965), p. 40. Fletcher's volume is an invaluable presentation of the chronicle material from Gildas through Geoffrey and Wace and on through the sixteenth century.

His statement confirms his belief in Arthur's historicity but also documents further the legendary – now almost mythic – status of the King.

This brief discussion of early Arthurian documents is very far from exhaustive.[20] Omitting a good many texts in Welsh or Latin (and all in Cornish, Breton and other languages), it is offered merely as an indication of the rich tradition of Arthurian lore developing from the sixth into the twelfth century. As noted, there is no suggestion that Chrétien de Troyes would have known any of these works.[21] However, as we approach the decades during which he wrote, we come also to two of the crucial Arthurian compositions of the period. Chrétien may have known the first; he indisputably knew the second.

The former is one of the great medieval monuments of Arthuriana: the *Historia regum Britannie*, by Geoffrey of Monmouth. Geoffrey also composed the *Prophetiae Merlini*, which introduced the prophet and mage as a vivid and developed character,[22] but he is of most interest here for the Arthurian section of the *Historia*, which, composed around 1138, is the first comparatively full biography of Arthur. It attained remarkable popularity, as is indicated by the survival of over 200 manuscripts in Latin and Welsh.[23]

Geoffrey's purpose was to fill, insofar as was possible, the gaps in early British history.[24] He informs us that his work was translated from a 'very ancient book' given him by Walter, Archdeacon of Oxford.[25] Whether such a book existed is uncertain; basing a claim of historical or literary authority on an earlier book is a medieval commonplace (cf. Chrétien's statement concerning the source

---

[20] Deserving of a fuller presentation are important works such as *Culhwch ac Olwen*, an early and archaic text in which Arthur and his men assist Culhwch in accomplishing tasks required in order to win the hand of Olwen; and *Pa gur*, a fragmentary text in which Arthur recounts the accomplishments to a gatekeeper. For a more thorough discussion of pre-Chrétien Welsh Arthurian material, see among others Patrick Sims-Williams, 'The Early Welsh Arthurian Poems', in Bromwich, Jarman and Roberts, eds, *The Arthur of the Welsh*, pp. 33–71; O.J. Padel, *Arthur in Medieval Welsh Literature* (Cardiff, 2000); Koch, 'The Celtic Lands', pp. 239–322.

[21] There remains some controversy, though now comparatively little, over the so-called *Y Tair Rhamant*, three Welsh romances that are obvious analogues of three of Chrétien's romances. The three are *Owein* (or *The Lady of the Fountain*), which shares narrative elements with *Yvain*; *Peredur*, parts of which closely resemble *Perceval*; and *Gereint uab Erbin*, resembling portions of *Erec and Enide*. A good many earlier scholars considered the Three Romances to be sources for Chrétien's works, but they almost certainly post-date Chrétien, and it has been noted that they appear to have been subject to Continental linguistic and cultural influences (the latter including courtly themes). It is probable either that the Welsh romances drew on Chrétien's romances or that both Welsh and French descend from a common source. If the latter, the loss of that source (whether it was oral or, most likely, written) complicates the task of defining the state of the Arthurian legend prior to Chrétien. For a survey of the problem and of competing theories concerning transmission, see Koch, 'The Celtic Lands', pp. 280–88.

[22] Important as Merlin is in the Arthurian tradition in general, he is not a prominent figure in Chrétien, and thus I do not offer detail concerning Geoffrey's presentation of him.

[23] For a full list of manuscripts see Julia C. Crick, *The Historia Regum Britannie of Geoffrey of Monmouth, III: A Summary Catalogue of the Manuscripts* (Cambridge, 1989). Among available editions, see in particular that of Neil Wright, *The Historia Regum Britannie of Geoffrey of Monmouth, I: Bern Burgerbibliothek MS 568* (Cambridge, 1985).

[24] Brynley F. Roberts, 'Geoffrey of Monmouth, *Historia regum Britanniae* and *Brut y Brenhinedd*', in Bromwich, Jarman and Roberts, eds, *The Arthur of the Welsh*, pp. 99–100.

[25] Although Geoffrey's own origins are open to question – he may have been of Welsh parentage, though Breton is more likely – it is known that he spent a good part of his life in Oxford. For the little that is known or conjectured about his life, see Roberts, 'Geoffrey of Monmouth', in Bromwich, Jarman and Roberts, eds, *The Arthur of the Welsh*, pp. 97–99.

of *Perceval*), and most often we are unable to distinguish a fictitious source from a real one. In any event, Geoffrey provides a coherent if fanciful account of the Britons. Roberts notes that Geoffrey created 'a spurious body of evidence but in so doing put on the mantle of a real historian'.[26] Ashe alters the emphasis, pointing out that Geoffrey clearly makes use of older materials but that 'there is no doubt that Geoffrey is a writer of fiction'.[27]

The *Historia* opens with a narrative of the founding of Britain and then proceeds through accounts of a number of early kings, the majority of them imaginary, before coming to the story of Arthur, which occupies about one-fourth of the whole. Here we find many of the familiar elements of the Arthurian legend, beginning with Merlin's aid to Uther, who begets Arthur. The latter becomes king while still a teenager, and soon he defeats the Saxons, most notably at the battle of Bath (Geoffrey's interpretation of Badon). After a pause during which he marries Guenevere, he conquers Ireland and Iceland, and those exploits are followed by a twelve-year period of peace, during which he founds a new chivalric order (but does not refer, here or elsewhere, to a Round Table).

Following that peace, Arthur sets out on another round of conquests, beginning with Norway and Denmark. He then crosses into Gaul and captures that country by defeating its governor, Frollo. When Arthur appears to be at the height of his power, Rome demands that he pay tribute and return conquered lands to the Empire. Rejecting these demands, he returns to Gaul, preparing to battle the Romans. However, word comes that he has been betrayed by Mordred, whom he had left in charge in Britain. Mordred has usurped the crown. The King returns and defeats Mordred's army but is mortally wounded in the battle. He is then taken to 'the Isle of Avalon' to have his wounds cared for. Geoffrey neither predicts Arthur's eventual return nor denies its possibility.

In addition to the predicted return of Arthur from Avalon, the familiar motifs and names that are missing from Geoffrey's account include Camelot, Lancelot, the Grail and the Round Table. The first three of these occur in fact in Chrétien de Troyes and may be his own innovations. The Round Table, though, is added in a crucial text intermediary between Geoffrey and Chrétien. That work is the *Roman de Brut*, written in 1155 by the Norman author Wace. This text is important both for its quality and for the fact that Wace made the Arthurian biography, as presented by Geoffrey, available in the vernacular and thus accessible to a far wider public.

If Geoffrey wrote pseudo-history (or an imaginative chronicle), Wace offered, particularly in the Arthurian portion of his work, what we can only call a chronicle-romance. He tells much of the story as found in Geoffrey's *Historia*, but he rearranges some events, expands or compresses episodes, invents some new characters and, of particular interest, generally shows more concern for human reaction and emotion than had his source. However, his most important innovation was the concept of the Round Table. He explains it as follows:

---

[26] Roberts, 'Geoffrey of Monmouth', in Bromwich, Jarman and Roberts, eds, *The Arthur of the Welsh*, p. 103.
[27] Geoffrey Ashe, 'Geoffrey of Monmouth', in *The New Arthurian Encyclopedia*, ed. Norris J. Lacy et al. (New York, 1991, 1996), p. 181.

Fist Artur la Runde Table
Dunt Bretun dient mainte fable.
Illuec seeient li vassal
Tuit chevalment e tuit egal;
A la table egalment seeient
E egalment servi esteient;
Nul d'els ne se poeit vanter
Qu'il seïst plus halt de sun per,
Tuit esteient assis meain,
Ne n'i aveit nul de forain.   (vss 9750–61)

[Arthur established the Round Table, concerning which the Bretons
tell many a tale. There the vassals sit, all at the head table and all
equal. They sit equally at the table and are served equally; none of
them can boast that he is seated higher than another. All were seated
near the place of honour and none at the far end.][28]

The Round Table – both the object and its powerful symbolism – quickly became
inextricably associated with the Arthurian ideal.

And then came Chrétien, who by his genius profoundly transformed the
Arthurian legend. He took from Wace the idea of the Round Table, but in
Chrétien's works and afterward the Table generally represented less a specific
endorsement of equality than a social (and often religious) ideal of adventure,
quest and service. Despite his dependence on numerous sources,[29] Chrétien was
a remarkable innovator. Not only did he first mention Camelot by name, but he
featured the story of a young French knight, Lancelot, who was not only among
the very greatest of them but also, owing to his love affair with the queen, a
direct contributor to the downfall (recounted in romances of the thirteenth
century) of the Arthurian world. In those later romances, too, the destruction of
the Arthurian ideal of chivalry was related to, indeed virtually required by, a
new and ultimately incompatible ideal, that of the Grail. And here again,
Chrétien stands at the head of a long literary and artistic tradition, for the Grail,
as the marvellous object of a quest, though not yet the Holy Grail of the Last
Supper, first appears in Chrétien's final romance.

Concluding, we should not overlook Chrétien's 'invention' of romance itself.[30]
What preceded him most immediately was a body of Arthurian chronicles –

---

28 Wace, *Wace's Roman de Brut: A History of the British*, ed. and trans. Judith Weiss (Exeter, 1999),
    vss 9751–60. I cite the Old French text from Weiss, but the translation is mine. However, for the
    elucidation of difficulties in this passage, both Weiss and I rely on suggestions made by Beate
    Schmolke-Hasselmann in 'The Round Table: Ideal, Fiction, Reality', *Arthurian Literature*, 2
    (1982), p. 48.
29 In addition to folktales and early chronicles (as well as genealogical lists, etc.), it should be
    noted that Chrétien undoubtedly drew upon a large store of Celtic motifs and images that
    were not Arthurian, but were 'arthurianized' by Chrétien. The principal proponent of Celtic
    sources for Arthurian romance was Roger Sherman Loomis. Though Loomis was at times too
    diligent – too creative? – in his quest for Celtic sources, his work remains both important and
    very controversial. See especially *Arthurian Tradition and Chrétien de Troyes* (New York, 1949).
30 In purely chronological terms, this assertion is open to challenge if not simply wrong, for the
    romances of antiquity preceded him, and other romances (e.g., *romans d'aventure* [romances of
    adventure]) were composed at about the same time as his earliest works. But in terms of inno-
    vation, of influence, of acknowledged literary status, Chrétien devised and launched the form
    that we recognize as romance.

themselves growing out of anecdotes, fragmentary narratives, and lists of names and battles – and an elusive and indefinable store of narratives that circulated orally. It was Chrétien, though, who, out of this mass of material, set the paradigm of the episodic romance, shifted the primary focus from Arthur himself to one or more of his knights, and created a fictional world and a body of work that would inspire imitators (and sometimes intimidate would-be rivals) and that would stand among the greatest and most influential literary monuments of the Middle Ages.

5

Narrative Poetics: Rhetoric, Orality and Performance

DOUGLAS KELLY

Poetics, or the art of poetry, is traditionally viewed in the Middle Ages as ancillary to rhetoric. Rhetoric in Chrétien's times was the art of persuasion by eloquence. The rhetorical mode was used in Chrétien's romances.[1] They were written for reading aloud, using embellishment that enhances such reading while effectively communicating a story and its lessons and setting out opposing views on issues of interest to aristocratic audiences in Chrétien's time.[2] Reading aloud can, of course, be highly diversified,[3] ranging from private settings like that illustrated in *Yvain* where a maiden reads a romance to her parents (*Yvain*, vss 5358–68), to public readings illustrated in many medieval manuscripts; mimes could act out what a reader related. All such readings are performances and include interpretation.[4] They are common in societies like Chrétien's in which most members of the aristocratic audiences he addresses cannot read.[5] Chrétien's romances also include 'intrusions' by a narrator reading aloud.[6]

The octosyllabic rhyming couplet is characteristic of medieval French verse romance. Chrétien contributed to innovations in French versification, notably couplet breaking and rich rhyme.[7] Rhetorical colours also characterize his verse, including tropes, or language that is not merely literal, and figures of thought and speech, or figurative language.[8] This is 'rhetoric' in the sense of the word common today.

---

1   References are to Chrétien de Troyes, *Romans suivis des chansons, avec, en appendice, Philomena*, genl ed. Michel Zink (Paris, 1994); *Cligés*, ed. Stewart Gregory and Claude Luttrell (Cambridge, 1993); and *Perceval*, ed. Keith Busby (Tübingen, 1993); and, for translations, *Arthurian Romances*, trans. William W. Kibler, with Carleton W. Carroll (London, 1991).
2   Eugène Vinaver, 'From Epic to Romance', *Bulletin of the John Rylands Library*, 46 (1964), 495–98.
3   Paul Zumthor, *La lettre et la voix: de la 'littérature' médiévale* (Paris, 1987), especially ch. 13; Joseph J. Duggan, 'Oral Performance of Romance in Medieval France', in Norris J. Lacy and Gloria Torrini-Roblin, eds, *Continuations: Essays in Honor of John L. Grigsby* (Birmingham, AL, 1989), pp. 51–61; and (with caution) Evelyn Birge Vitz, *Orality and Performance in Early French Romance* (Cambridge, 1999).
4   Paul Zumthor, '*Litteratus / illitteratus*: remarques sur le contexte vocal de l'écriture médiévale', *Romania*, 106 (1985), 1–18.
5   On this issue, see Brian Stock, *The Implications of Literacy: Written Language and Models of Interpretation in the Eleventh and Twelfth Centuries* (Princeton, 1983), ch. 1.
6   Norris J. Lacy, *The Craft of Chrétien de Troyes: An Essay on Narrative Art* (Leiden, 1980), pp. 34–38.
7   Jean Frappier, 'La Brisure du couplet dans *Erec et Enide*', *Romania*, 86 (1965), 1–21.
8   Representative studies: Valeria Bertolucci, 'Commento retorico all'*Erec* e al *Cligés*', *Studi*

Such embellishment is not hard to find in Chrétien's romances. Insistent *Tu* pronouns expressing a knight's scorn for Lancelot because he rode in the cart illustrate *annominatio*, or play with form or meaning of words.[9]

> '*Tu*? *Tu*? Comant l'osas panser?
> Einz *te* deüsses apanser
> Que *tu* anpreïsses tel chose
> A quel fin et a quel parclose
> *Tu* an porroies parvenir,
> Si *te* deüst resovenir
> De la charrete ou *tu* montas'. (*Lancelot*, vss 2589–95)

> ['You! You? Whatever gave you that idea? Before undertaking such a thing you should have thought of how you might end up; and you should have recalled the cart you climbed into'.]

Elsewhere, alliteration, assonance and internal rhyme evoke a maiden's distress while alone in the woods during a stormy night: 'Et la nuis et li bos li font / Grant anuy, mais plus li anuie / Que li bos ne la nuis la pluie', *Yvain*, vss 4838–40 [the night and the forest frightened her, but she was more upset by the rain than either the night or the forest]. Identifying these features as *annominatio* is useful only if one notes the special effects sought by such speech, effects that would be obvious to a listening audience, especially if the reader is talented and the audience attentive.

Elsewhere, metaphor engages audience reflection on emotions while, perhaps, eliciting comparisons with other works that use analogous metaphors. In *Cligés* (vss 541–63), Chrétien adapts the traditional *amer* (love), *amer* (bitter), *la mer* (sea) metaphor to explain how love sickness can appear to be seasickness.[10] Lacking the science and terminology of modern psychology, Chrétien relied on metaphorical and figurative language to explain emotions and states of mind.

Personification is prominent in such explanations. For example, Lancelot's hesitation to mount the cart elicits a debate in his mind between Reason and Love (*Lancelot*, vss 365–77). In *Cligés* (vss 475–523, 897–1046), Soredamors too relies on internal debate until, as with Lancelot before the cart, she decides to take the leap and surrender herself to love. Such internal debate is a kind of interpretation that also engages audiences during oral recitation.[11] Personifying her eyes and heart, Soredamors questions their responsibility for her distress. This interrogation by question and answer leads to the *amer la mer* metaphor. For

---

mediolatini e volgari, 8 (1960), 9–51; Pierre Gallais, 'Métonymie et métaphore dans le "Conte du Graal"', in *Mélanges de littérature offerts à Jeanne Lods*, 2 vols (Paris, 1978), I, pp. 213–48; Emmanuèle Baumgartner, 'Jeux de rimes et roman arthurien', *Romania*, 103 (1982), 550–60; Don A. Monson, 'La "surenchère" chez Chrétien de Troyes', *Poétique*, 70 (1987), 231–46; SunHee Kim Gertz, 'Rhetoric and the Prologue to Chrétien de Troyes' *Erec et Enide*', *Essays in French Literature*, 25 (1988), 1–8.

9   Edmond Faral, *Les Arts poétiques du XIIe et du XIIIe siècle: recherches et documents sur la technique littéraire du moyen âge* (Paris, 1924), pp. 93–97.

10 The *amer la mer* metaphor occurs in Thomas d'Angleterre's *Tristan*, a work to which Chrétien relates *Cligés* by contrasting Iseut's love with Fenice's; see as well his poem 'D'Amors, qui m'a tolu a moi', vss 28–36; and Hubert Weber, *Chrestien und die Tristandichtung* (Bern, 1976).

11 Faral, *Arts poétiques*, pp. 63–67.

his part Alexandre analyzes his love for Soredamors by probing the eyes-heart conflict using comparisons to fire and illness, lanterns and candles; he amplifies on sight as an arrow that bears the image of his beloved and lodges it in his heart without harming his eyes (vss 770–860).[12]

In her second monologue, Soredamors parses her name using paranomasia, or play on words, to take apart and rearrange the syllables in her name in new configurations that justify her love.[13] 'Por neant n'ai ge pas cest non / Que Soredamors sui clamee. / Amer doi, si doi estre amee, / Si le vuel par mon non prover', vss 962–65 ['I have not been given the name Soredamors for nothing. I must love and I must be loved, and I wish to prove this by my name, if I can reason it out']. She notes that the word love *amor* is part of her name, as is the word for the most refined gold – *sor* – as in *fine amors*. *Nomen est omen* in this kind of medieval etymology.[14]

> Car qui par mon droit non m'apele
> Toz jorz *Amors* me renovele.
> Et l'une mitiez l'autre *dore*
> De *doreüre* clere et *sore*,
> Qu'autretant dit *Soredamors*
> Come *sororee d'Amors*.   (vss 975–80)

> [For whoever calls me by my right name evokes Love's tint within me. One half of my name gilds the other with the bright yellow hue of gold, for 'Soredamors' means 'gilded over with Love'.]

Medieval audiences admired Chrétien's 'bel françois' (*Tournoiement* vs. 3539). Although French was not yet the literary language it became in the thirteenth and fourteenth centuries,[15] Chrétien used metaphorical and figurative language to invent a new genre, romance.[16] Such language enhanced oral storytelling, sometimes in amusing ways, as when Chrétien evokes the bone-crunching lions that threaten to eat Lancelot alive after he crosses the Sword Bridge (*Lancelot*, vss 3060–65) – amusing because the lions are an illusion. More ominous are the sounds and colours of swordplay in combat in *Yvain* (vss 6113–20). Such devices

---

12 See Douglas Kelly, 'The Art of Description', in *The Legacy of Chrétien de Troyes*, ed. Norris J. Lacy, Douglas Kelly and Keith Busby, 2 vols (Amsterdam, 1987), I, p. 217. This comparison seems to have been especially admired; see Huon de Mery, *Li Tornoiemenz Antecrit*, ed. Georg Wimmer (Marburg, 1888), vss 2601–03. Like the first-person voice in Chrétien's lyrics that addresses various audiences, Alexandre addresses an audience: 'Or vos reparlerai del dart', vs. 770 ['Now I shall tell you (about) the arrow'].

13 Simonetta Bianchini, '*Interpretatio nominis* e *pronominatio* nel *Cligès* di Chrétien de Troyes', *Vox Romanica*, 61 (2002), 186–88.

14 On 'etymology' as a trope, see Ernst Robert Curtius, *Europäische Literatur und lateinisches Mittelalter* (Bern, 1954), pp. 486–90; R. Howard Bloch, *Etymologies and Genealogies: A Literary Anthropology of the French Middle Ages* (Chicago, 1983), pp. 54–58.

15 Michel Zink, 'Héritage rhétorique et nouveauté littéraire dans le "roman antique" en France au moyen âge: remarques sur l'expression de l'amour dans le roman d'*Eneas*', *Romania*, 105 (1984), 248–69; however, it was progressing in Chrétien's verse; see Jean Frappier, *Chrétien de Troyes* (Paris, 1968), pp. 119–21.

16 Zink, 'Une Mutation de la conscience littéraire: le langage romanesque à travers des exemples français du XIIe siècle', *Cahiers de civilisation médiévale*, 24 (1981), 3–27.

are dramatically effective in oral recitation when they enliven verse, sentence or other small units of discourse such as monologues.[17]

Tropical and figurative devices may also colour the audience's perception of the narrative and articulate narrative structures.[18] *Erec et Enide* offers a good example. The first part of this romance ends with the marriage of Erec and Enide. A striking metaphor mirrors the passionate consummation of their marriage.

> Cers chaciez qui de soif alainne
> Ne desirre tant la fontainne,
> N'espreviers ne vient au reclain
> Si volentiers con il a fain,
> Que plus volentiers n'i venissent,
> Ainçois que il s'entretenissent.   (vss 2077–82)

> [The hunted stag who pants from thirst does not so yearn for the fountain, nor does the hungry sparrowhawk return so willingly when called, that they did not come into each other's arms more eagerly.]

The consummation is a *conjointure*, a word for sexual intercourse in Old French.

Similarly, the first part of *Erec et Enide* relates two narratives devoted to the stag and sparrowhawk of the metaphor: the Hunt for the White Stag and the Sparrowhawk Duel. The former customarily concludes when the winner of the Hunt bestows a kiss on the most beautiful woman at court; the latter identifies which combatant champions the most beautiful woman.[19] Enide's beauty conjoins the two events. Chrétien effects this *conjointure* when Erec wins the Sparrowhawk duel and brings Enide to Arthur's court where all agree that she is the most beautiful. Thereupon the narrator announces the end of the 'premerains vers' (vs. 1840). That is to say, here ends the first tale – '*vers*' means not only 'verse', but also 'tale' in Old French – about the Hunt for the White Stag. The second tale on the Sparrowhawk duel is incomplete until Erec marries Enide. Two tales, or *vers*, conjoin in a whole and complete plot. The union of husband and wife and the union of these two tales effect each a *bele conjointure*, a term Chrétien introduces in the prologue to *Erec et Enide*. Chrétien there favourably contrasts his *bele conjointure*[20] with antecedent versions of *Erec et Enide* that storytellers are wont to shred or leave incomplete ('depecier et corrompre', vs. 21).

> . . . raisons est que totes voies
> Doit chascuns penser et entendre
> A bien dire et a bien aprendre,

---

[17] Philippe Ménard, *Le Rire et le sourire dans le roman courtois en France au moyen âge (1150–1250)* (Geneva, 1969), pp. 522–680; Ménard, 'Rires et sourires dans le roman du *Chevalier au lion*', in '*Le Chevalier au lion': approches d'un chef-d'œuvre*, ed. Jean Dufournet (Paris, 1988), pp. 23–29.

[18] Douglas Kelly, *The Art of Medieval French Romance* (Madison, 1992), pp. 272–304.

[19] On these and other 'customs' in Chrétien's romances, see Donald Maddox, *The Arthurian Romances of Chrétien de Troyes: Once and Future Fictions* (Cambridge, 1991).

[20] On *conjointure*, see Gerold Hilty, 'Zum *Erec*-Prolog von Chrétien de Troyes', in *Philologica Romanica Erhard Lommatzsch* (Munich, 1975), pp. 245–56; Kelly, *Art*, pp. 15–31, 318–20.

Et trait d'un conte d'aventure
Une mout bele conjointure.   (vss 10–14)

[It is reasonable for everyone to think and strive in every way to
speak well and teach well, and from a tale of adventure to draw a
beautifully ordered composition.]

Chrétien refers to his narrative poetics in prologues, epilogues and other
interventions to his romances. Scholarship has focused on the terminology
Chrétien uses to describe his art of narrative composition.[21] The terms are well
known and often referred to in discussing the composition of his and other
romances in French and other vernaculars. There are four principal sets of terms:
bele conjointure; matiere and *san; pensers* as *painne* and *sens* or *antancion*; and *oltre la
matire*.[22]

According to the prologue to *Erec et Enide*, a *bele conjointure* can be instructive.
The *Lancelot* prologue claims that a patron, Marie de Champagne, commissioned
the romance and that she provided its source material: 'Matiere et san li done et
livre / La contesse', vss 26–27[23] [The subject matter and meaning are furnished
and given him by the Countess]. Her commission, including both matter and
meaning of the romance, precedes the author's effort to conjoin them in a narrative that is whole, complete and instructive. Chrétien allows, perhaps in confor-
mity with medieval views on the primacy of the idea over execution, that the
Countess's commission is more effective in the realization of her project 'Que
sans ne painne que g'i mete', vs. 23 [than any thought or effort I might put into
it]. He concludes by stating that 'il s'antremet / De panser, que gueres n'i met /
Fors sa painne et s'antancïon', vss 27–29 [he strives carefully to add nothing but
his effort and careful attention]. This 'effort' to conjoin *matiere* and *san* is his
contribution to the new *Lancelot*'s *bele conjointure*.

The patron or patroness is obviously significant in Chrétien's narrative
poetics. Besides Marie's commission to write *Lancelot*, Philippe de Flandre gave
Chrétien the 'book' that he put into verse as *Perceval* (vss 61–67). His patrons
gave him two of the richest subjects of medieval romance: the love of Lancelot
and Guenevere for *Lancelot* and the Grail for *Perceval*. The one romance conjoins
the Queen and her knight, the other rewrites *graal*, which meant an ordinary
platter or dish in Old French, so that it means henceforth 'Grail' and, indeed, a
'Holy Grail' (*Perceval*, vs. 6425).

Another description mirrors a romance's composition.[24] The Perilous Fountain in *Yvain* reflects the cycle of love and hate characteristic of Yvain's relation to
Laudine. Its boiling water is colder than marble; when the water is poured on a

---

21 Pierre Gallais, 'Recherches sur la mentalité des romanciers français du moyen âge', *Cahiers de
     civilisation médiévale*, 7 (1964), 479–93 and 13 (1970), 333–47; Pierre-Yves Badel, 'Rhétorique et
     polémique dans les prologues de romans au moyen âge', *Littérature*, 20 (1975), 81–94; SunHee
     Kim Gertz, *Poetic Prologues: Medieval Conversations with the Literary Past* (Frankfurt/M., 1996).
22 I have kept medieval orthography in order to preclude reading modern meanings into these
     terms, especially when they survive without their earlier meanings into modern French.
23 Kelly, *Art*, pp. 106–10.
24 Baumgartner, 'La Fontaine au pin', in *Chevalier au lion: approches*, pp. 31–46; Joan Tasker
     Grimbert, *'Yvain' dans le miroir: une poétique de la réflexion dans le 'Chevalier au lion' de Chrétien de
     Troyes* (Amsterdam, 1988), pp. 75–83.

stone next to it, a violent storm breaks out, followed by a great calm rendered more beautiful by birdsong. Is this not analogous to Laudine's own feelings? Widowed when Yvain kills her husband, she soon becomes his loving wife; later, angered by his prolonged absence, she remains an estranged, even violent spouse. Much as the sweet song of birds, a commonplace of courtly love lyric, follows on the destructive storms that the Fountain produces when it is dashed with water, Laudine finally becomes again a loving wife after her husband unleashes violent storms on her lands. This *bele conjointure* of hot and cold, love and hatred, is a description.

In Chrétien's narrative poetics, description shows a person, thing or action in a manner useful for narrative meaning.[25] Enide is very beautiful, but also poor, her father having lost his wealth in wars. Her shabby clothing does not become her. Beautiful people should not be poor, nor should they, as members of the nobility, dress as Enide must. In *Yvain*, three hundred noble maidens must do sweatshop work in the Pesme Aventure episode. Noble beauty should not be subject to physical labour,[26] nor to sexual abuse like that Harpin de la Montagne intends in abandoning a lord's daughter to gang rape by his kitchen scullions (*Yvain*, vss 3867–71); nor even to self-mutilation, as when Laudine lacerates her face while mourning her husband's death (*Yvain*, vss 1146–65). These comparisons show how a static description like that of the Perilous Fountain, when projected into narrative, produces adventures that can move an audience, yet perplex it by conjoining seemingly irreconcilable antitheses like storm and calm, love and hate, violence and order, that conjoin intriguing, even provocative narratives.

For example, when Calogrenant relates the story of his shame (*Yvain*, vss 57–60), it produces disagreement, debate and action. Yvain's decision to avenge his cousin Calogrenant provokes Kay's mockery and Arthur's own plan to go to the Perilous Fountain. Chrétien therefore rewrites Calogrenant's tale as a tale of honour in which Yvain succeeds where Calogrenant fails by defeating the defender of the Fountain. Nor does Yvain's story stop there. He also falls in love with the Lady of the Fountain, wife and now widow of the defender of the Fountain, whom Yvain killed.

Yvain's plot conjoins two versions of the same tale, a tale of shame and a tale of honour. Standing alone, Calogrenant's version is incomplete because, as Yvain notes, there has been no vengeance (vss 582–87). Shame requires vengeance, a commonplace that provides a plan for Yvain's story. By exacting vengeance, Yvain completes the tale properly. Similarly, in *Erec et Enide*, Yder shames Erec by allowing his dwarf to strike him and a maiden. Erec avenges his shame in the sparrowhawk duel.

These interlaced and interlocking tales of shame, honour and vengeance illustrate the principle of the *bele conjointure* that Chrétien lauds in his version of the Erec and Enide story, a *conjointure* he contrasts with the piecemeal, incomplete versions of their story told by storytellers in high courts. Such storytellers are

[25] Kelly, *Legacy*, I, pp. 191–221; *Art*, pp. 291–305.
[26] Antonio Pioletti, 'Lettura dell'episodio del "Chastel de Pesme Aventure" ("Yvain", vv. 5101–5805)', *Medioevo Romanzo*, 6 (1979), pp. 227–46.

like Calogrenant because their stories are incomplete – they leave out important parts of the tale. Calogrenant's own story is 'corrupt' because it lacks vengeance. Yvain's version completes the scheme by re-enacting the Fountain adventure.

The *Erec et Enide* prologue underscores the value of *bele conjointure* not only in getting the story right, but also in communicating knowledge. Calogrenant's story reveals shame. In Yvain's version, a tale of vengeance metamorphoses into a tale of honour and love. Yvain's love triumphs over the widow's vengeance when he becomes her new husband and, *ipso facto*, the defender of the Fountain. But a turnabout occurs when Yvain fails to keep his promise to return to Laudine after a year of tourneying. His conduct mirrors Erec's denying his love to Enide when she questions his honour for not tourneying. This apparent conflict in judgments has raised a question in modern scholarship: do Erec and Yvain balance the respective demands of love and knighthood, or do they fail to do so, the former by his uxoriousness, the latter by his devotion to tournaments?

The dilemma comes to a head in *Lancelot*. Here Meleagant's abduction of Guenevere permits Chrétien to introduce a new character, her lover. Lancelot's role in this, perhaps Chrétien's most controversial romance today, is marked by contrasting evaluations of his actions and intentions by characters in the plot. His shame brings ridicule while his achievements honour him. Guenevere underscores the dilemma by rejecting Lancelot's quest to liberate her; but then, blaming herself for this light-hearted act, she atones for her rebuff by receiving him into her bed. These opposing reactions to the quest by the Queen's lover inform the tournament at Noauz, where Lancelot fights alternately his best *au mialz*, then his worst *au noauz* at her command and once again *au mialz* when she requests it.[27]

Guenevere rebuffs Lancelot because he hesitated before the cart. This episode appears to have been drawn from the *matiere* Chrétien received from Marie de Champagne. It introduces Guenevere's knight as her lover in terms analogous to those Calogrenant uses to explain his tale of shame:[28] voice and heart. Calogrenant claims that his words must be understood in the heart, 'Car parole oïe est perdue / S'ele n'est de cuer entendue', vss 151–52 ['for words that are not understood by the heart are lost completely']. Just so, Lancelot's hesitation before mounting the cart contrasts *Raison* with *Cœur*, or language[29] with understanding and, therefore in his case, Reason with Love. After a brief hesitation Lancelot follows his heart and springs into the cart. Chrétien thus confronts two standards for evaluating Lancelot's action: Reason's based on chivalric honour and Love's based on amorous devotion. The contrast is underscored by the different responses to the cart by Lancelot and Gauvain. The former springs into the cart for the sake of love, whereas the latter refuses to do so because he has a good horse, a reminder that he is a knight (*cheval-ier*) and that knights ride horses, not carts. Gauvain believes he can reach Guenevere by following the cart on his horse. He is wrong.

---

27 Matilda Tomaryn Bruckner, *Shaping Romance: Interpretation, Truth, and Closure in Twelfth-Century French Fictions* (Philadelphia, 1993), pp. 60–70.

28 On the meaning of *honte* in Chrétien, see David F. Hult, 'Lancelot's Shame', *Romance Philology*, 42 (1988), pp. 30–50.

29 *Raison* in Old French can signify either 'language' or 'reason'.

Chrétien explains why the cart is shameful using two comparisons. First, a current proverb links the cart to misfortune; to avoid misfortune, those who encounter a cart should cross themselves. Second, the cart in Lancelot's time functions like a pillory: each publicly shames criminals convicted of serious crimes. This *conjointure* of explanations gives meaning (*san*) to the cart adventure while leaving open the evaluation of Lancelot's actions. Yet Chrétien's *conjointure* of Marie's *matiere* and *san* prompts debate about the significance of the romance *conjointure* he fashioned. Lancelot's cart ride raises a more general issue: is any act performed for love's sake justifiable (vss 4348–60), even adultery with a queen?

Description represents a person, thing or action that is both exemplary and verisimilar in the context of the work. In the cart episode, for example, the knight Lancelot exemplifies the lover by jumping into the cart, a shameful act for him as a knight. The antithetical conduct of a knight and a lover becomes a matter of debate for those who observe him in the cart or hear about it, including Guenevere herself. The plot seems to support Lancelot's decision since he rescues the Queen. His acts performed for the sake of love are honourable, despite other standards that are inapplicable in his case. He is lover before he is knight. This standard holds whenever love and knighthood conflict.

Lancelot contrasts *san* like that attributed to Marie de Champagne with artistic *sens* like Chrétien's that weaves her meaning and her matter into whole cloth. In Lancelot's case the combination both exemplifies the *san* and problematizes it in a way that might elicit audience debate as to its validity.[30] Such problems are evident in opposing views on the relation between love and tournaments in *Erec* and *Yvain*, between conjugal and adulterous love in *Cligés* and *Lancelot*, and between individual consent and parental choice in contracting marriage. We observe this last issue in Erec's failure to consult his parents before marrying Enide, Fenice's internal resistance to marriage and consummation with anyone other than the man she loves, Laudine's fluctuating feelings regarding Yvain, first as prospective husband and, later, as false husband, and the especially heinous religious and social sin of adultery with a queen. Similar issues emerge elsewhere, notably forced marriage (Allier episode in *Yvain*), 'permissible' rape (the custom of Logres),[31] the tournament when it conflicts with religious or feudal standards (Tintagel tournament in *Perceval*) and conduct exemplifying or violating maxims, or *sens* (*Perceval*, vs. 527) for chivalry like those Perceval learns from his mother, Gornemant de Gohort and his hermit uncle (vss 533–72, 1639–70, 6440–73), and that he has such a difficult time following. By treating problems, Chrétien constructs meaningful narratives using 'cultural and historical codes that operate outside as well as inside literature'.[32] Such composition

---

30 Per Nykrog, *Chrétien de Troyes, romancier discutable* (Geneva, 1996).
31 On this astonishing chivalric custom, see Kathryn Gravdal, *Ravishing Maidens: Writing Rape in French Literature and Law* (Philadelphia, 1991), pp. 43–67; Maddox, *The Arthurian Romances*, pp. 35–53.
32 Matilda Tomaryn Bruckner, 'Intertextuality', *Legacy*, I, p. 223; see also Lacy, *Craft*, pp. 15–33; Marie-Luce Chênerie, *Le Chevalier errant dans les romans arthuriens en vers des XIIe et XIIIe siècles* (Geneva, 1986), pp. 216–17.

was habitual for school-trained writers like Chrétien.[33] Yet by articulating the meaning or *san* of *matiere*, Chrétien also raises controversial issues like those discussed above. Chrétien's romances are indeed problem romances.[34]

Pensers, the author's contribution, determines which features reveal a person's, thing's or action's significance in the plot.[35] These features are common places, that is, 'places' common to such persons, things or actions.[36] Traditionally, they include name, nature (mental and physical attributes such as nationality, language, gender, age, genius and talent), way of life, fortune, character, goals, appetites, judgment, luck, exploits and speech.[37] Chrétien describes such 'places' and, in so doing, reveals both *san* and his artistry or purpose (*antancion*) as the *conjointure* of *matiere* and *san*.

The naming 'place' is a good example.[38] In *Lancelot* Lancelot is at first anonymous.[39] He then acquires the pseudonym Knight of the Cart, a constant reminder of the act that opposes honour and shame in the dual, yet conflicting contexts of knighthood and love. When the goal of his quest and of his love, Guenevere, reveals his given name: 'Lanceloz del Lac a a non', vs. 3660 ['the knight is called Lancelot of the Lake'], the audience realizes what it means to be a Lancelot – the lover of a queen whose chivalric excellence derives from that love – an adulterous love.[40]

Guenevere too is described with similar attention to common places. To be sure, her emotions correspond to Lancelot's: 'Certes, fet ele, jel voel bien, / Mes voloirs pas ne vos detient', *Lancelot*, vss 4616–17 ['Of course I want you with me', she replied. 'My wishes will never keep you back']. Yet she is also arbiter. She must preserve her honour as queen despite the love she feels for Lancelot. The end of the romance illustrates this when Reason (the 'judgment place') restrains her foolish heart (the 'emotion place') (vss 6846–53). One perceives here the debate between Reason and Heart that Lancelot experienced before mounting the cart, as well as the difference it makes when a knight or a lady – the 'gender place' – confronts the *qu'en dira-t-on* problem [gossip or 'what will people say?']. The 'cultural code' does not grant a lady virtually free ride in carts for the sake of love.

Descriptions can be deceptive, even malicious. When Lunete sets out to convince Laudine that Yvain would be a good match, she first asks her mistress who is the better knight, the one who wins or the one who loses (vss 1696–99). That is, she replaces the description of one type, the killer of Laudine's husband,

33 Vinaver, 'From Epic', p. 493; cf. Roberta L. Krueger, 'The Author's Voice: Narrators, Audiences and the Problem of Interpretation', *Legacy*, I, pp. 115–21 on the 'elusive author'.
34 Vinaver, 'From Epic', pp. 497–503.
35 Kelly, *Art*, pp. 99–105.
36 Douglas Kelly, *The Arts of Poetry and Prose* (Turnhout, 1991), pp. 71–78; for more on topical invention in Chrétien's romances, see Eugene Vance, *From Topic to Tale: Logic and Narrativity in the Middle Ages* (Minneapolis, 1987); ch. 9 in *The Arthur of the French* (Cardiff, forthcoming).
37 Kelly, *Art*, pp. 49–61.
38 Bianchini 2002, pp. 181–221.
39 On Lancelot's other common places, see Douglas Kelly, 'Les Fées et les arts dans la représentation du Chevalier de la charrette', in *Lancelot: Actes du colloque*, ed. Danielle Buschinger (Göppingen, 1984), pp. 85–97.
40 Peggy McCracken, *The Romance of Adultery: Queenship and Sexual Transgression in Old French Literature* (Philadelphia, 1998).

with another, the victor in combat. She uses the naming topos at the end of the romance in what Chrétien calls a *jeu de verité* (*Yvain*, vs. 6624).[41] From the Fountain Yvain is unleashing destructive storms on Laudine's land and castle. Laudine can stop him with the help of the Knight of the Lion. By substituting surname for proper name, Lunete dupes Laudine, who agrees to reconcile the Knight of the Lion with his beloved because she is unaware that the surname is her husband's and that she is the beloved.

Earlier scholarship often treated each of Chrétien's romances as promoting a moral or social lesson that sets a standard for chivalric, amorous or moral conduct that their heroes and heroines strive to achieve. To be sure, there are conflicts, even contradictions, as when Guenevere praises love in marriage in *Cligés*, a view her actions seem to contradict in *Lancelot*. Yet each romance suggests a view that can provoke debate regarding diverse standards for action. Such debate moves Chrétien's romances from the fable with a moral to the problem romance. In problem romances, the narrator's point of view looms large, as do the points of view of characters in the plot.[42] They provoke audiences, eliciting reactions from a personal point of view as well.

The foregoing analysis of Chrétien's critical terminology seeks to show how his narrative poetics can help us interpret his romances. However, since 'applications' of poetic imitation 'have almost always been subtler than the doctrines enunciated by grammarians, rhetoricians' and 'literary critics and theorists',[43] each of Chrétien's romances and each retelling of them is an original performance of transmitted matter. The art he enunciates in prologues and elsewhere tells us how he invented romance plots. Yet problems remain that preclude facile judgments about the compositions illustrating that art. The issues they raise invite study and debate. Two such problems have emerged in recent scholarship. They arise from interventions in Chrétien's last two romances.

The epilogue to *Yvain* claims that this romance is the definitive version of the Knight of the Lion's story. 'Onques plus dire n'en oï, / Ne ja plus n'en orés conter / S'on n'i velt mençogne ajoster', *Yvain*, vss 6806–8 [I've not heard any more about it, and you'll never hear anything more unless one adds lies to it]. The paradox that one cannot add lies to fiction is intriguing.[44] We may well ask: what is this romance to which nothing more should be added? The *Yvain* plot relates that Gauvain is absent from court because of his unsuccessful quest for Guenevere in *Lancelot*. As a result, Arthur's nephew cannot come to the defence of his *amie* Lunete nor his relatives besieged by Harpin de la Montagne. Yvain takes his place. Since we need to know the *Lancelot* plot in order to understand events in *Yvain*, does not the epilogue's reference to 'this romance' include the *Lancelot* as a 'premerains vers' in its *conjointure*?[45] Although scholarship traditionally separates the *Lancelot* from *Yvain*, Chrétien does not appear to do so.

---

41 On this expression, see Kelly, 'Le Jeu de la vérité', in *Chevalier au lion: approches*, pp. 105–17.

42 Lacy, *Craft*, pp. 38–66.

43 Jan Ziolkowski, 'The Highest Form of Compliment: *Imitatio* in Medieval Latin Culture', *Poetry and Philosophy in the Middle Ages: Festschrift Peter Dronke* (Leiden, 2001), p. 295.

44 Cf. Michel Zink, 'Chrétien et ses contemporains', *Legacy*, I, pp. 15–19.

45 Barbara N. Sargent-Baur, 'The Missing Prologue of Chrétien's *Chevalier au lion*', *French Studies*, 41 (1987), 385–94; cf. Emmanuèle Baumgartner, *Chrétien de Troyes: Yvain, Lancelot, la charrette et le lion* (Paris, 1992).

By conjoining the plots of *Lancelot* and *Yvain*, Chrétien obliges us to rethink Godefroi de Lagny's assertion that he would go 'oltre la matire' (vs. 7099) if he added more to it: 'n'i vialt plus metre / Ne moins, por le conte malmetre', vss 7111–12 [he wishes to add nothing further, nor omit anything, for this would harm the story]. Does not Chrétien do precisely that by adding *Lancelot* to *Yvain*? But then, is he not also adding lies to the *Yvain* fiction? This query leads to further questions. Godefroi and Chrétien both leave out the continuation of the Lancelot-Guenevere affair. Guenevere alludes to a continuation when she decides to put off her embraces 'Jusque tant que voie et espit / Un boen leu et un plus privé', vss 6850–51 [until she could find a better and more private place]. But neither *Lancelot* nor *Yvain* relates this continuation. Would telling it go 'oltre la matire'? Or, by failing to do so, does the *Lancelot depecier et corronpre* its *conjointure*, like the stories Chrétien criticizes in the *Erec* prologue?

Similar questions crop up with *Perceval*. To be sure, Chrétien's Grail romance seems incomplete.[46] But Gauvain's role compounds the problem. His story even appears to unravel. During the crisis at Arthur's court precipitated by the Hideous Damsel's call to adventure, Gauvain vows to relieve the siege of the Demoiselle de Mont Esclaire. Then he must respond to the accusation that he murdered Guinganbresil's suzerain, the king of Escavalon. Setting aside the aid promised the Demoiselle, he hastens to Escavalon to answer the challenge to his honour. Yet when he arrives there incognito, the demands of the hospitality custom prevent the trial by combat. Moreover, Gauvain is offered the possibility to redeem his honour if he can bring the Bleeding Lance to Escavalon. Perceval is also seeking this lance that, Chrétien mentions mysteriously, is destined to destroy Logres, Arthur's realm (*Perceval*, vss 6166–71). Gauvain sets out on this new quest. But once again his goal of this new quest vanishes from the plot as Gauvain confronts new adventures with new challenges. By repeatedly exchanging one goal for another, is Chrétien not going *oltre sa matire*?

But there are other ways to view the issue. For example, Matilda Tomaryn Bruckner has noted what she terms the centripetal tendency of Chrétien's plots before *Perceval*, a movement that fits the quest motif and its fixation on a goal that, once achieved, makes the narrative whole and complete while elucidating the problems it raises.[47] Yet *Perceval* seems centrifugal, especially the Gauvain narrative: a plot made up of incomplete parts loses its direction and flies off, as it were, into new directions. Indeed, the apparently disjointed whole, or *disjointure*, characterizes some post-Chrétien romances.[48] Has Chrétien de Troyes invented a new poetics, one based on a *bele disjointure* and a new kind of romance composition?

In the last analysis the marvellous adventures Chrétien's narratives bring together will always surprise and even perplex his audiences. This is especially obvious in the extraordinary denouements he invents. *Perceval* of course remains

---

[46] Although this has been questioned; see, for example, Roger Dragonetti, *La Vie de la lettre au moyen âge: Le Conte du Graal* (Paris, 1980); Roel Zemel, 'Perceval en geen einde', *Voortgang*, 16 (1996), 7–26.

[47] Bruckner, 'Intertextuality', I, pp. 226, 250–53.

[48] Cf. Richard Trachsler, *Disjointures—conjointures: étude sur l'interférence des matières narratives dans la littérature française du Moyen Age* (Tübingen, 2000).

a problem because it appears incomplete. But the problems in its *conjointure/disjointure* mirror anomalous features in his other romances – for example, the Perilous Fountain in *Yvain* and the knight as lover in *Lancelot* – anomalies appropriate to adventures as the unexpected intervention of fortune, chance or the irrational (the fortune or luck common places). Who would have predicted the denouement to *Lancelot* if we lacked the thousand lines Godefroi de Lagni says he penned? Who could have foreseen the outcome of the duel between Yvain and Gauvain for the Noire Espine sisters and Yvain's reconciliation with Laudine by bombarding her castle with storms from the Fountain, were *Yvain's* last thousand lines missing? Yet these *conjointures* of unexpected adventures in problematic plots make Chrétien's narratives intriguing romances that, by their concatenation of marvellous adventures, achieve extraordinary denouements. As *faits accomplis* they are also *beles conjointures* aesthetically satisfying because of their marvellous qualities.[49] Whole and complete, Chrétien's romances hold in balance their centrifugal and centripetal movements, all the while remaining ever open to the sudden intrusion of new and unexpected adventures that do not, in Godefroi's words, 'malmetre' the story. They maintain this balance until Chrétien added Gauvain's adventures to Perceval's. Does *bele disjointure* replace *bele conjointure* in this case?

---

[49] Daniel Poirion, 'Théorie et pratique du style au Moyen Age: le sublime et la merveille', *Revue d'histoire littéraire de la France*, 86 (1986), 15–32.

6

The Manuscripts of Chrétien's Romances

KEITH BUSBY

Any examination of a medieval text should begin with the examination of the manuscripts in which it is preserved. The manuscript is our only means of direct access to the reality of the medieval text and is its only indisputably medieval witness. While we cannot with any measure of certainty reconstruct Chrétien de Troyes's *ipsissima verba* on the basis of the extant manuscripts of his romances, we can at least be sure that each manuscript was for a period of time in the Middle Ages *the* text of Chrétien for its owners, readers and listeners. It is unlikely that these individuals (and groups) could have availed themselves of more than one manuscript, and there is little evidence, outside of monastic circles, that medieval readers would have been at all concerned with variants or redactions or establishing a definitive text in anything like the modern sense. The manuscripts of medieval vernacular literature have generally been regarded by modern scholars, however, precisely as material for a critical edition, as Peter Dembowski demonstrates in the following chapter. My aim in this chapter is therefore not to anticipate Dembowski's discussion of the theory and practice of editing as it relates to Chrétien's romances, but rather to give an overview of the physical appearance of the Chrétien manuscript corpus and to suggest what close examination of it can reveal.

I cannot offer an exhaustive survey of the Chrétien manuscripts here, and for that refer readers to *The Manuscripts of Chrétien de Troyes*.[1] However, by looking at the transmission and codicological context of the individual romances, I hope to discuss most of the significant issues, and treat most of the principal witnesses. With the notable exception of *Perceval* (fifteen more or less complete manuscripts and some fragments), most of Chrétien's romances are preserved in seven or eight copies and a few fragments. For works which enjoyed the kind of respect they apparently did in the Middle Ages, this is about average. Many texts well known to modern readers are poorly attested (*Aucassin et Nicolette*, for example in one copy only), while others have come down to us in larger numbers (dozens of the Arthurian prose cycles, and over two hundred of *Le Roman de la rose*, although this last is rather exceptional). The apparent lack of

---

[1] *Les Manuscrits de Chrétien de Troyes/The Manuscripts of Chrétien de Troyes*, ed. Keith Busby, Terry Nixon, Alison Stones and Lori Walters, 2 vols (Amsterdam, 1993). All known manuscripts and fragments of Chrétien's romances are described and studied, with accompanying photographs, in these volumes.

first-generation manuscripts may be due partly to historical accident and partly to the fact that few ever existed in the first place. It would correspond well to Beate Schmolke-Hasselmann's contention that Chrétien's first audiences in Anglo-Angevin court circles were probably enthusiastic but quite small.[2] The increasing numbers of copies surviving from the later thirteenth and fourteenth centuries go hand in hand with a dissemination, geographical as well as chronological, outside of these narrowly circumscribed initial parameters. The entire corpus of Chrétien manuscripts suggests a continued popularity and reception over many generations. This itself urges us to be cautious in our 'interpretations' of Chrétien's romances, for what Chrétien himself may have had in mind when writing for a quite specific audience may not have been what the owners and readers of the later manuscripts saw or appreciated in his works.

As is usually the case with Old French texts of the earlier period, no manuscripts survive from Chrétien's own time. Of the more than forty manuscripts and fragments containing one or more of Chrétien's romances, the earliest copies are the Tours *Cligés*, the Clermont-Ferrand *Perceval*, and the so-called Annonay fragments (of all the romances except *Lancelot*). Tours, BM 742 dates from around the end of the twelfth century, possibly within thirty years of the romance's composition. Clermont-Ferrand, BMI 248 and Annonay appear to be from the first quarter of the thirteenth century, and may not be much further removed chronologically from Chrétien's time than Tours 742. Although it is dangerous to generalize on the basis of two or three manuscripts, one can infer by looking at the transmission of other works that the romances circulated individually in the early stages and that they were gathered into larger collections of different kinds as time passed. If Annonay, as it appears, is an *œuvres complètes,* it demonstrates an early awareness of Chrétien as an author.[3] The later manuscript transmission of the romances both consolidates the notion of Chrétien's authorship of a body of work and illustrates the manner in which the individual romances could be worked into other types of codicological structure.

In the rest of this chapter, I shall pass in review the romances in their generally accepted order of composition (*Erec et Enide, Cligés, Yvain, Lancelot* – or the last two vice versa – and *Perceval,* leaving out of consideration *Guillaume d'Angleterre* and *Philomena*), pointing out any distinctive features of their manuscript transmission. Space does not permit discussion or even mention of all extant manuscripts and fragments, although I shall treat the major codices and make representative choices for the others. Since some manuscripts contain several romances, the principal discussion of those particular manuscripts will be found in connection with the first romance they contain.

Although one cannot normally deduce the contents of a whole codex from surviving fragments of one text (and there are three such fragmentary manuscripts of *Erec et Enide*), the transmission of Chrétien's first romance is domi-

---

[2] Beate Schmolke-Hasselmann, *Der arthurische Versroman von Chrestien bis Froissart: zur Geschichte einer Gattung* (Tübingen, 1980), pp. 178–248; English version, *The Evolution of Arthurian Romance: The Verse Tradition from Chrétien to Froissart,* trans. Margaret and Roger Middleton (Cambridge, 1998), pp. 219–94.

[3] Some of the Annonay fragments have been reproduced by Albert Pauphilet, *Chrétien de Troyes. Le manuscrit d'Annonay* (Paris, 1934).

nated by narrative collections of various kinds. The Annonay fragments, as mentioned above, appear to have been from an *œuvres complètes* of Chrétien, while Paris, BnF, fr. 794 (the celebrated, or rather, notorious, copy made by the scribe Guiot),[4] fr. 1450, and Chantilly, Musée Condé 472 (all from around the middle of the thirteenth century) are sizeable romance collections. Fr. 794 and 1450 place all of Chrétien's romances in the context of *translatio studii et imperii*[5] by situating them in the wake of one or more *romans antiques*, and in the case of fr. 1450 by intercalating them into the text of the *Brut* at the point where Wace talks of the marvellous happenings that took place during a peaceful period of Arthur's reign.[6] BnF, fr. 1420, from the same period, includes *Erec et Enide*, *Cligés* and *Le Roman de Troie*, and although the context of classical antiquity is clear here and in general, the structure of fr. 1420, with the romances ending at the ends of quires, raises the possibility of post-medieval rebinding and the questions of whether the present state of manuscript is its original, medieval, one. Such matters should always be taken into account when considering the manuscript context of a work and the structure of the codices which contain it. A later manuscript, Paris, BnF, fr. 1376 (from the late thirteenth or early fourteenth century) precedes *Erec et Enide* by the *Florimont* of Aimon de Varennes, a romance 'prequel' to *Le Roman d'Alexandre*, inviting thematic comparison between the two texts; here again, however, the two works have an independent quire structure.

Chantilly 472, likewise from the mid-thirteenth century, has been much discussed. With the exception of one branch of *Le Roman de Renart*, it is a collection of Arthurian romances, including a number of the so-called 'epigonal romances',[7] as well as *Erec et Enide*, with *Yvain* and *Lancelot* as a pair, and its contents are probably determined by some notion of genre. Whether it is a 'Gauvain-cycle' or not is arguable in my view, but it is clearly not an author-based manuscript, as Annonay most likely was, nor does it contain large or dominant Chrétien sections, as do BnF, fr. 794 and 1450. Indeed, by opening the book with one of the very last Arthurian romances in verse, *Les Merveilles de Rigomer*, its compiler seems to be playing down the importance of Chrétien as an author and 'inventor' of the genre. This manuscript is also important as the unique surviving copy of the *Merveilles*, *Hunbaut* and Renaut de Beaujeu's *Le Bel inconnu*.[8]

Romance is not the only context of collections which include *Erec et Enide*. In BnF, fr. 24403 (last quarter of the fourteenth century), it is accompanied by two *chansons de geste*, *Garin de Monglane* and *Ogier le Danois*. Whether it is possible to argue in favour of a thematic structure for this manuscript ot not, it at least illus-

---

4   On Guiot, see Keith Busby, *Codex and Context: Reading Old French Verse Narrative in Manuscript*, 2 vols (Amsterdam, 2002), I, pp. 93–108, and the literature referred to there.
5   Essentially the movement of learning and the seat of power from east to west (in this case, from ancient Greece to France and Britain).
6   On fr. 1450, see Lori Walters, 'Le Rôle du scribe dans l'organisation des manuscrits de Chrétien de Troyes', *Romania*, 106 (1985), 303–25.
7   Epigones are authors writing in the wake and tradition of a master, imitating or emulating in various ways. This is the subject of Schmolke-Hasselmann's book referred to in n. 2 above.
8   See Lori Walters, 'The Formation of a Gauvain Cycle in Chantilly, MS 472', *Neophilologus*, 78 (1994), 29–43, and *Codex and Context*, I, pp. 405–13.

trates the compatibility of epic and romance in the view of manuscript makers (and presumably owners) of the period. It may be that this is an indication of a kind of levelling taking place in the manner in which genres were perceived. And from the turn of the thirteenth and fourteenth centuries, BnF, fr. 375 is a large narrative collection from Arras, which includes *Cligés* and *Erec et Enide* among many other romances (*Thebes, Troie, Athis et Prophilias, Alexandre, Rou, Guillaume d'Angleterre, Floire et Blancheflor, Blancandin, Ille et Galeron* by Gautier d'Arras, *Amadas et Ydoine*, some shorter tales, humorous, courtly and edifying. Although this important manuscript might seem to be a random assortment of popular works with no apparent connection, a contemporary or near contemporary table of contents by Perrot de Nesle argues in favour of planning and the necessity for users to be able to locate individual texts within what is a very large book.[9] Given the literary activity in Arras at the time, this manuscript may well have been the property of some kind of *confrérie* [brotherhood, here of *jongleurs* or minstrels] and in any case demonstrates by its contents the varied tastes of readers and listeners in the north-east.

The distinctly Artesian identity of fr. 375 (by virtue of some of its contents and dialect) raises the question of geographical provenance of the manuscripts of *Erec et Enide* and of Chrétien's *œuvre* as a whole. Despite Chrétien's apparent origins in Troyes and the fact that one of his known patrons (Marie de Champagne) is located securely in central France, the manuscripts of his romances have a wide regional distribution. As regards *Erec et Enide*, only the Guiot manuscript and the Annonay fragments can be safely attributed to central France (Champagne); fr. 1420 may be from the Île-de-France, while fr. 1376 is very markedly Burgundian. The other four complete copies are in fact north-eastern: fr. 375, fr. 1450, fr. 24403 (probably Arras itself), and Chantilly 472 (Flanders-Hainaut). The fragments from the same manuscript split between Amsterdam (UB 446) and Brussels (KBR, IV 837) are likewise north-eastern, while the Ste-Geneviève fragment (1269, now lost) and the L'Aigle fragments are too short to be localized linguistically; the list of knights copied in London, BL, Harley 4971 is Anglo-Norman, and precious witness to the circulation of *Erec et Enide* in England.[10]

Cligés, the second of Chrétien's romances, is preserved in exactly the same number of whole manuscripts and fragments (twelve) as *Erec et Enide*, suggesting that it was as widely known, this in contrast with its relative neglect at the hands of modern scholars. Conspicuously absent from Chantilly 472 (perhaps because of its less 'Arthurian' nature), *Cligés* is also to be found in some of the same large collections as *Erec et Enide* (fr. 375, fr. 794, and fr. 1450) and one smaller one (fr. 1420). BnF, fr. 12560, which also contains *Yvain* and *Lancelot* and dates from about the middle of the thirteenth century, is probably from Champagne, and may have been an author collection. Probably the most significant feature of the manuscript transmission of *Cligés*, however, is that Tours, BM 942 is the earliest of all the Chrétien manuscripts. It contains *Cligés* alone (although

---

9   Charles François, 'Perrot de Neele, Jehan Madot et le ms. BN fr. 375', *Revue Belge de Philologie et d'Histoire*, 41 (1963), 761–79.
10   I treat what I term 'The Geography of the Codex' in my *Codex and Context*, II, pp. 485–635.

incomplete, codicological examination confirms that it was always a single-item codex), dates from the turn of the twelfth and thirteenth centuries, and comes from western France, possibly Anjou. Even though this is not a first-generation copy, it may be an indication of the nature of the early transmission of Chrétien's romances: in the Anglo-Angevin domains and in single-item codices. Another interesting feature of the corpus of *Cligés* manuscripts is the fourteenth-century paper copy (now largely destroyed) in Turin, BNU, L. I. 13, where it was preceded by Gautier d'Arras's *Eracle*, two poems by Jean de Condé and *Sone de Nansai*, and followed by *Richars li biaus*. We see Gautier d'Arras in Chrétien's company elsewhere, *Sone de Nansai* is marginally Arthurian, and *Richars li biaus* is a conventional enough romance, but Jean de Condé's two short narratives are unique in the Chrétien manuscript corpus. The Turin manuscript is markedly north-eastern by virtue of its dialect and other contents (probably Flanders-Hainaut), confirming the importance of this region as a literary centre. Typical by virtue of its contents (the *chansons de geste* of *Parise la duchesse* and *Girart de Vienne*, a life of St Eustace, the religious 'epic', *La Venjance Nostre Seigneur*, Gerbert de Montreuil's *Le Roman de la violette*, and Aimon de Varennes's *Florimont*, with *Cligés* placed between *Parise la duchesse* and the Eustace life at the beginning of the manuscript), BnF, fr. 1374 is atypical because of its southern provenance, possibly from the Dauphiné. As the Harley 4971 excerpt from *Erec et Enide* proves knowledge of that romance in England, an excerpt from the beginning of *Cligés* (Alexandre's arrival at Arthur's court) copied as filler in Florence, Riccardiana 2756 (fourth quarter of the thirteenth century) is invaluable testimony to knowledge of Chrétien in Italy.

There is some obscurity concerning the order of composition of *Lancelot* and *Yvain*, but Chrétien may have begun work on *Lancelot* first. With the possible exception of *Perceval* (which owes its enduring fame in part to the introduction of the Grail theme into western literature), *Lancelot* is probably the best known of Chrétien's romances. It is paradoxically the least well-attested codicologically, being preserved in a total of eight manuscripts and fragments. Preserved in the larger romance collections (fr. 794, fr. 1450, and Chantilly 472), *Lancelot* is also associated with *Yvain* in what looks like a pairing in fr. 12560 (*Yvain*, *Lancelot*, and *Cligés*), Princeton, University Library, Garrett 125 (fourth quarter of the thirteenth century) and Vatican City, Reg. Lat. 1725 (turn of the thirteenth and fourteenth centuries), in both of which it precedes *Yvain*. This may not necessarily be an indication of the order of composition of the two romances, but almost certainly proceeds from some notion of a conjuncture between them, textually authorized. Extending this notion, we may then legitimately consider the structure of the larger codices and the way in which the individual romances inform each other by inviting comparisons of various kinds (thematic, evolutionary and so on). The Vatican manuscript also contains Jean Renart's *Guillaume de Dole* and Raoul de Houdenc's *Meraugis de Portlesguez*, in what may be a prolonged exploration of male companionship. Garrett 125 is fragmentary and also contains *La Chevalerie Judas Machabee* and *Garin de Monglane* (also alongside *Erec et Enide* in fr. 24403); its present state makes specific conclusions about its composition hazardous, except to reiterate that such religious and epic texts were not regarded as incompatible with Arthurian romance by medieval audiences. The epic context is further underlined in the case of *Lancelot* by Escorial, RBM, M. III. 21 (third quarter of the thirteenth century), where it is accompanied by a text of *Fierabras*. The Escorial manuscript may come from western France (possibly the eastern edge of Normandy, although analysis of its dialectal features is not conclusive), but the Vatican and Princeton texts are clearly north-eastern once more. *Lancelot*'s absence from the Annonay fragments is probably accidental, as the surviving parts from all the other romances suggest it was an *œuvres complètes*.

Yvain is preserved in the same number of manuscripts, fragments and excerpts as *Erec et Enide* and *Cligés*, namely twelve (not counting the sixteenth-century adaptation by Pierre Sala in BnF, fr. 1638). There are two basic contexts for *Yvain*: the large author and genre collections (Annonay, fr. 794, fr. 1450, and Chantilly 472) and manuscripts in which, as we have seen, it is paired with *Lancelot* (fr. 12560, Garrett 125 and Reg. Lat. 1725). I shall discuss the illuminated manuscripts of Chrétien's romances shortly, but it would be remiss not to mention in passing here that Garrett 125 is quite nicely illustrated, although not as luxuriously as BnF, fr. 1433 (north-eastern France, second quarter of the fourteenth century), where *Yvain* is preceded by the anonymous *L'Atre perilleux* (also in Chantilly 472). Fr. 1433 is another example of a manuscript of moderate size in which one of Chrétien's romances is joined to an epigonal romance, inviting structural and thematic comparison.[11] BnF, fr. 12603 (turn of the thirteenth and fourteenth centuries) is a large collection in many ways resembling fr. 375. *Yvain* is its only Chrétien romance, but it is the unique copy of a long and late Arthurian text, *Le Chevalier as deus espees*, which opens the book and immediately precedes *Yvain*. It preserves the antique and British context with *Le Roman d'Enéas* and Wace's *Brut* (to which pair *Yvain* is linked by a scribal addition), and epic associations with Adenet le Roi's *Enfances Ogier* and *Fierabras*. A section of shorter works, including Marie de France's *Ysopet* and some *fabliaux* at the end of the manuscript, has a separate quire structure but is probably in its original position in this large book, like fr. 375 from Arras.[12] Again, the varied nature of its contents may suggest ownership and use in professional classes. Fragments in Bruges and Modena (the latter currently missing) have little to tell us, but the first ten lines of *Yvain* are copied, curiously, at the beginning of the text of *La Chanson de Roland* in Lyon, BM 743 (probably southern France, first quarter of the fourteenth century). While it confirms Chrétien's presence in the south (cf. fr. 1374 of *Cligés*), this manuscript remains something of a puzzle, although the *Yvain* excerpt introducing a version of the *Roland* which emphasizes the hero's martyrdom may be no more than a piece of scribal whimsy.

Of all Chrétien's romances, *Perceval* is the best attested, with a total of eighteen complete manuscripts and fragments; additionally, several fragments of the various continuations were almost certainly from manuscripts which originally

---

[11] See Lori Walters, 'Paris, Bibliothèque nationale, fonds français 1433: The Creation of a "Super Romance" ', *The Arthurian Yearbook*, 1 (1991), 3–25.

[12] See my *Codex and Context*, 1, pp. 434–36 and 455–57, and Richard Trachsler, 'Le Recueil Paris, BNF, fr. 12603', *Cultura Neolatina*, 54 (1994), 189–211.

contained Chrétien's text, bringing the total known to have existed to more than twenty. The context of this last romance is the most varied, not simply because of the larger number of extant copies but primarily because of the nature of the text itself. Two copies, Clermont-Ferrand, BMI 248, and Florence, Riccardiana 2943, are among the earliest of all the Chrétien manuscripts (first and second quarter of the thirteenth century respectively), modest in appearance, and frankly scruffy in the case of the Florence copy, which cannot possibly have been intended for sale. Later, *Perceval* is included in the usual author and genre collections (fr. 794, fr. 1450, the Annonay fragments), and in a large Burgundian manuscript best known for its fabliaux and short tales, Bern, Burgerbibl. 354 (second quarter of the thirteenth century), also containing the prose *Sept sages de Rome*.[13] There is, however, another context for *Perceval*, created by the unfinished nature of Chrétien's text, which generated up to four continuations, transforming *Perceval* into a Grail romance of sometimes more than 30,000 lines. The traditional editing of Chrétien's part of the compilation or cycle therefore does violence to the cohesive nature of the codicological whole. There are nine such manuscripts ranging in date from the first quarter of the thirteenth century (London, BL, Add. 36614, which must have been copied shortly after the last continuation was composed) through the middle of the century (Paris, BnF, fr. 1420), the third quarter (Edinburgh, NLS, Advocates 19. 1. 5) peaking with four copies in the last quarter (Paris, BnF, fr. 1429, fr. 12576, Montpellier, BI, Sect. Méd. H 249, and Mons, BPU 331/206), and the last two (BnF, fr. 1453 and fr. 12577) from the second quarter of the fourteenth. *Perceval* is the most frequently and richly illustrated of Chrétien's romances, and it is among the Grail compilation manuscripts that its illuminations are to be found. Geographically, the most interesting features of the *Perceval* corpus are its general range (the usual high number from the North-east), the early London copy from Champagne, four central copies, at least two of which are distinctly Parisian (fr. 1453 and fr. 12577), and the only Anglo-Norman copy of a complete Chrétien romance, London, College of Arms, Arundel XIV (middle of the fourteenth century). This last manuscript is also notable as one of the latest of all Chrétien manuscripts and for its preservation of the British context (Wace's *Brut*, Gaimar's *Estorie des Engleis*, *Le Lai d'Haveloc*, Langtoft's *Chronicle*, and *La Lignee des Bretons et des Engleis*, all of which precede *Perceval*). Moreover, it shows traces of being copied from a model that once contained the Continuations, and may be proof that these texts also circulated in England.[14]

Given the celebrity of Chrétien's romances in France and in western Europe generally (through circulation of manuscripts, adaptations, and so on), it is perhaps rather surprising to learn that only a few of the manuscripts are illuminated (although there are also some illustrations in the form of wall paintings, ivory caskets, church sculpture and misericords). It is unlikely that illustrations were part of the Chrétien manuscript tradition from the beginning, and those

---

13 On Bern 354, see Luciano Rossi, 'À propos de l'histoire de quelques recueils de fabliaux. 1: Le code de Berne', *Le Moyen Français*, 13 (1983), 58–94, and my *Codex and Context*, I, pp. 443–47.
14 See Keith Busby, 'The Text of Chrétien's *Perceval* in MS London, College of Arms, Arundel XIV', in *Anglo-Norman Anniversary Essays*, ed. Ian Short (London, 1993), pp. 75–85.

that exist represent a form of secondary reception, perhaps interpretation, of the romances, from the time that the individual manuscripts were manufactured. Alison Stones's tally of historiated illumination (which term covers both historiated initials and miniatures) comes to eleven manuscripts and some 250 illustrations.[15] This number includes the *Perceval* Continuations and Pierre Sala's *Yvain*, and represents approximately one quarter of the total corpus of manuscripts. The unillustrated manuscripts may have as much to tell us about the reception of Chrétien's romances as the illustrated ones, for despite the universal association of courtly romance with wealth, the modest nature of some of the copies suggests owners of modest means and the likelihood (as I will suggest below) that the romances were performed aloud, luxurious illustration being superfluous in such a situation. The nature of the illuminations, moreover, suggests that subjects for illustration were chosen only after the romances became sufficiently well known and certain scenes emblematic.

The earliest illuminated manuscripts date from the last quarter of the thirteenth century, close to a century after the composition of *Perceval*, Chrétien's last romance. The earliest illustrations are, in fact, of *Perceval*, in Montpellier H 249, BnF, fr. 12576, and Mons 331/206, illustrated across the whole compilation in varying degrees of density, but with miniatures and historiated capitals of very modest size and accomplishment. Montpellier H 249 is difficult to localize, but fr. 12576 is very clearly from Arras, and the Mons copy most likely from Tournai. The other two illustrated *Perceval* manuscripts (BnF, fr. 1453 and fr. 12577) are both Parisian and probably from the second quarter of the fourteenth century, the work of artists closely associated with some of the most important figures of the Paris book trade. These last two books are relatively speaking luxurious, rare among the Chrétien manuscripts, but run-of-the-mill for the time and place. They are part of a commercial enterprise of considerable proportions.[16] Examination of the scenes chosen for illustration and of the interplay between text, image and rubric (where present) tells us much about the way in which the manuscripts were planned and made, and sometimes about how the planners understood the text and how well. Occasionally, the illustrations are frequent enough to offer a kind of commentary on the text, but more often than not, they accompany what are clearly regarded as favourite scenes, the ones by which a romance is fixed in the mind of readers. With twenty-five, the Montpellier manuscript has the largest number of miniatures for Chrétien's romances and comes closest to offering a visual commentary. The other illustrated copies are more selective in their choice of scenes: fr. 12576 has six illustrations (including one four-part miniature), Mons has seven, fr. 12577 has eight, and fr. 1453, fifteen (the missing first folio probably also contained one or more illustrations). Planners often choose spectacular or symbolic episodes (Perceval leaving home and his first adventures, Gauvain on the Lit de la Merveille, etc.)

---

[15] Alison Stones, 'The Illustrated Chrétien Manuscripts and Their Artistic Context', in *Les Manuscrits de Chrétien de Troyes*, I, pp. 227–322.

[16] On the Paris book trade, see Richard H. Rouse and Mary A. Rouse, *Illiterati et Uxorati. Manuscripts and Their Makers: Commercial Book Producers in Medieval Paris, 1200–1500*, 2 vols (London, 2000).

and the artistic representation in the manuscripts mirrors that on other media and allusions in other literary texts. Although there are some scenes common to all of the illuminated copies of *Perceval*, there appears to have been no standard programme of illustration, and planners and artists appear to have enjoyed and exercised considerable freedom in their presentation, organization and portrayal of Chrétien's romance and its Continuations.[17]

Also from Paris, perhaps dating from a couple of decades earlier than fr. 1453 and fr. 12577, is BnF, fr. 1433 of *Yvain*, preceded by *L'Atre perilleux*.[18] This is arguably the most accomplished artistically of the illustrated Chrétien manuscripts, with two full-page multi-compartment miniatures at the head of *L'Atre perilleux*, an historiated initial at the beginning of the text itself and two further miniatures. *Yvain* has one historiated initial at the beginning of the text and nine miniatures, six of which are multi-compartment (including one full-page). The classic scenes from the text are chosen for illustration (list not exhaustive): Calogrenant at the fountain, the combat of both Calogrenant and Yvain with Esclados, Yvain and Lunete, the funeral of Esclados, Yvain naked in the woods, Yvain's rescue of the lion, the defeat of Harpin de la Montagne, Lunete at the stake, Pesme Aventure, the combat of Yvain and Gauvain, the reconciliation of Yvain and Laudine; conspicuously absent is Calogrenant's encounter with the Giant Herdsman. The illustrations accompanying *L'Atre perilleux* add a visual level to the comparison between it and *Yvain* invited by the simple juxtaposition of the two romances in a single codex.

A little earlier still (end of the thirteenth century) is Princeton, UL, Garrett 125, the remains of a manuscript containing *Yvain*, *Lancelot*, the epic poem of *Garin de Monglane* and *La Chevalerie Judas Machabee*. This manuscript was almost certainly made in Amiens. The remaining part of *Yvain* contains seven miniatures, some of which treat the same subjects as those in fr. 1433 (for example, the defeat of Harpin de la Montagne, the rescue of Lunete from the stake and the combat of Yvain and Gauvain).[19] It is difficult to draw firm conclusions about this manuscript, given its fragmentary state (some 6200 lines of *Yvain* [over 90%] and about 1600 [over 20%] of *Lancelot*), but as with all of the other illustrated Chrétien manuscripts considered so far, there seems to be an attempt to capture some of the crucial and memorable scenes and to offer a kind of visual punctuation, dividing the narrative up into segments, perhaps functioning as bookmarks. Although these segments may not correspond to the articulation of the narrative perceived by modern scholars, they may represent a medieval view of the structure of the romances and are worthy of consideration as such. They may also suggest that romances were not necessarily read integrally episode-by-episode in narrative order, but that owners may have read and re-read certain

---

17 Cf. Keith Busby, 'The Illustrated Manuscripts of Chrétien de Troyes', *Zeitschrift für französische Sprache und Literatur*, 98 (1998), 41–52, repr. in *Les Manuscrits de Chrétien de Troyes*, I, pp. 351–63, and 'Text, Miniature, and Rubric in the Manuscripts of the *Perceval* Continuations', in *Les Manuscrits de Chrétien de Troyes*, I, pp. 365–76.
18 See Lori Walters, 'Paris, Bibliothèque nationale, fonds français 1433' (n. 8).
19 Garrett 125 became widely known only after the publication of Robert L. McGrath, 'A Newly Discovered Illustrated Manuscript of Chrétien de Troyes's *Yvain* and *Lancelot* in the Princeton University Library', *Speculum*, 38 (1963), 583–94.

favourite passages, which the illustrations helped them find and visualize. The two miniatures illustrating the fragments of *Lancelot* would have functioned in similar fashion: one of the two represents the arrival of Meleagant at Arthur's court towards the beginning of the romance, and the other, Lancelot talking to the two sons of a vavassor at the entrance to the castle. Although unillustrated, Montpellier, BIU, Sect. Méd. H 252 (middle of the fourteenth century) has eight *tituli* for its 1921 lines of *Yvain*; these may have been copied from a manuscript which was illuminated. Four of the eight *tituli* refer to scenes illuminated in fr. 1433 and/or the Princeton manuscript.[20]

There are no illustrations in any of the manuscripts of *Cligés*, and a total of four only in two manuscripts of *Erec et Enide*. In both fr. 1376 and fr. 24403, there are historiated capitals at the very beginning of the text (the 'L' of 'Li Vilains dist') representing Arthur's hunt of the white stag. In fr. 24403, two further miniatures show Erec attacking one of the robber knights (with Enide looking on) and rescuing Cadoc from the giants. Clearly, there can be no question here of a programme of illustration in any sense of the term, at best a selection of scenes the planner may have considered significant or an attempt to divide the romance up into sections, although these would have been of somewhat unequal length.[21]

Nothing is more familiar to students of manuscripts (of most kinds and in most languages) than red and blue pen-flourished initials (sometimes called lombards or filigree initials). These are usually formed by a large red capital with blue pen-flourishing or by a blue capital with red flourishing. Red and blue alternate with blue and red. More expensive manuscripts may have painted capitals (usually in red, blue and gold, with or without flourishing), often called 'champie' initials, and all forms (pen-flourished and champie) can be of different sizes within a single manuscript. Although these initials are obviously decorative, they also, perhaps principally, act as a form of punctuation, drawing attention to movements and pauses in the narrative. The larger ones share with some miniatures the function of indicating major divisions of a story, while the smaller ones often indicate the beginning and end of reported speech, the arrival or departure of characters, and temporal movement. As such they make a vital contribution to the experience of reading a Chrétien romance in manuscript, but are rarely reproduced or commented on in critical editions; some editions may indicate their location in the base manuscript by a capital letter.[22]

The consideration of the manuscript context of Chrétien's romances, the physical nature of the books in which they are transmitted, and the relationship between word and image in the illustrated copies, can tell us a good deal about the ways in which the texts were viewed over a period of almost two centuries following their composition (the last manuscripts date from the middle of the fourteenth century). Such matters are important and are finally beginning to

---

[20] See Keith Busby, 'Absence de l'image dans le ms. Montpellier, BIU, Sect. Méd. H 252', in *Actes du colloque Mobilité*, ed. Milena Mikhaïlova (Orléans, forthcoming).

[21] On the *Erec* illustrations, see Carleton W. Carroll, 'Text and Image: The Case of *Erec et Enide*', in *Word and Image in Arthurian Literature*, ed. Keith Busby (New York, 1996), pp. 78–98.

[22] See my *Codex and Context*, I, pp. 184–95, and the literature cited there.

attract the attention they have long deserved from scholars. Equally important, however, may be the minutiæ of the *mise en texte* of Old French literary manuscripts, by which I mean the manner in which the words are disposed on the line and the lines on the page, the nature and use of abbreviations, and the significance of punctuation, where present. My suggestions in this regard will be valid, *mutatis mutandis*, of course, for all manuscripts containing Old French texts in octosyllabic rhyming couplets. I make this proviso as some elements of the *mise en texte* are dependent on verse form.

One of the first features that students remark on when attempting to read a medieval manuscript for the first time is the frequent lack of traditional spacing between words. This varies quite a lot from one manuscript to the next, and there are some manuscripts which do not exhibit the feature at all, but often words will appear to be grouped or clustered, with spaces between the clusters. For example: 'lirois' ('li rois'), 'lareine', 'asadevise', 'desadame', 'quansaiche', 'lias', 'siloumenaca', 'ilnesepoist' and so on. Some clusters represent enclisis and other grammatical and morphological features, but all of them seem to correspond to rhythmical patterns within the octosyllable, and may indicate the correct delivery to a performer. Moreover, if such clustering appears confusing at first sight and makes a text difficult to decipher, when read aloud the meaning becomes perfectly clear. Another so-called 'obstacle' to the fluent reading of Old French texts in manuscript is the use of abbreviation. This is in fact only a temporary hindrance, as practice makes perfect when readers become familiar with the abbreviative system and the particular text or kinds of text they are reading. A high incidence of abbreviation in a manuscript may indicate ownership or use in the ranks of professional performers, and, like word-clustering, any ambiguities or obscurities are generally resolved on reading aloud. Beginning students also often remark that there is no punctuation in medieval manuscripts. This is not the case, although it is less frequent than in modern texts, and the individual marks are quite different. The use of marks such as the *punctus*, *punctus interrogativus*, *punctus elevatus* or *comma* and *virgula*, where present, generally seems to indicate rhythm and voicing (falling and rising intonation, serial enumeration, enjambement), requiring, like a high density of abbreviation, close knowledge of a system, the lexicon and conventions of the material. Many of the Chrétien manuscripts may therefore have served as performance copies for jongleurs or reference copies for professional organizations. Oral performance on one occasion, of course, does not preclude individual reading on another, and the possibility that manuscripts served a double function. Some of the later, illuminated, manuscripts were almost certainly intended for individual private reading (after all, one can hardly read miniatures aloud), but the modesty and various features of the *mise en page* and *mise en texte* of many of the copies suggests the likelihood that they were at one time read aloud.[23]

Study of the manuscripts of Chrétien de Troyes's romances puts us in direct contact with the reality of medieval texts as experienced by their owners, readers and those who listened to readings from them. It can teach us much

---

[23] On word-clustering, punctuation and abbreviation, see my *Codex and Context*, I, pp. 127–82.

about the place of Chrétien's *œuvre* within the larger corpus of Old French literature and its manner of reception across the centuries. Close codicological and palæographical examination provides fascinating insights into the mechanics of book production, scribal behaviour, attitudes to language and the modalities of reading and performance. A basic familarity with the material transmission of the literature we claim to know and love – in this case, the romances of Chrétien de Troyes – would therefore seem to be a *sine qua non*.

7

Editing Chrétien

PETER F. DEMBOWSKI

The works of Chrétien de Troyes have challenged editors for well over a century and a half, and the first to recognize the merit of medieval France's most famous *romancier* were not actually French. The honour of producing the first edition of any work by Chrétien belongs to a British woman: Lady Charlotte Guest, who produced, in 1838, *The Mabinogion, Llyfr Coch o Hergest and Other Ancient Welsh Manuscripts*; it contains a quite inaccurate transcription of *Yvain* taken from the manuscript Paris, B.N. fr. 12560.[1] Shortly thereafter, in 1841, Adalbert Keller published fragments of *Yvain* and, three years later, of both *Lancelot* and *Yvain*.[2]

The first French edition of Chrétien was Prosper Tarbé's *Le Roman du chevalier de la Charrette*.[3] According to Alexandre Micha,[4] Tarbé followed B.N. fr. 12560, believing it to be B.N. fr. 794 (hereinafter referred to as 'Guiot' from the name of the scribe). Soon afterward, Willem J.A. Jonckbloet published a further edition, which contains the *Roman de Lancelot du Lac* by Gauthier Map and a quite faithful rendering of the Guiot text, with some variants taken from Keller.[5] The *editio princeps* of *Erec et Enide* was published by Immanuel Bekker using a transcription of B.N. fr. 1376 made by Francisque Michel.[6]

Among Chrétien's five romances, *Perceval* has always represented the greatest editorial challenge. This immensely popular romance, left unfinished by Chrétien, has come to us preserved in more numerous and divergent manuscripts than the other romances. In more than half of them, *Perceval le Vieil* (i.e., Chrétien's romance)[7] is followed consecutively by the Continuations of *Perceval*. The first editor was Charles Potvin, who published the initial volume in 1866.[8]

---

1 Vol. 1 (London, 1838).
2 *Li romans dou chevalier au leon. Bruchstücke aus einer Vaticanischen Handschrift* (Tübingen, 1841); *Romvart: Beiträge zur Kunde mittelalterlicher Dichtung aus italienischen Bibliotheken* (Mannheim, 1844).
3 *Le Roman du chevalier de la Charrette par Chrétien de Troyes et Godefroy de Laigny* (Reims, 1849).
4 *La Tradition manuscrite des romans de Chrétien de Troyes* (Paris, 1939; repr. 1966), p. 14.
5 *Le Roman de la Charrette d'après Gauthier Map et Chrestiens de Troies* (The Hague, 1850).
6 'Der Christian von Troyes Erec und Enide', *Zeitschrift für deutsches Altertum*, 10 (1856), 373–550.
7 Guiot, 385v, offers *Explycyt Percevax le Viel*.
8 *Perceval le Gallois, ou, le Conte du Graal . . . publié d'après les manuscrits originaux . . .*, 6 vols (Mons, 1866–71; repr. Geneva, 1977). Poitvin's edition also contains two anonymous prologues, the *Elucidation* and *Bliocadran*. See Albert Wilder Thompson, ed., *The Élucidation, a Prologue to the Conte del Graal* (New York, 1931) and Lenora D. Wolfgang, ed., *Bliocadran: a Prologue to the Perceval of Chrétien de Troyes: Edition and Critical Study* (Tübingen, 1976).

The whole of vol. 2 (1866) and the beginning of vol. 3 (1868) contain *Perceval le Vieil*, ending with vs. 10,601. The editor used chiefly the manuscript Mons, Bibliothèque Universitaire 331/206.

Potvin's *Perceval* marks the end of what could well be called the 'early' period of editorial activities. It was characterized by a virtual absence of discussions pertaining to the theory and practice of the editorial craft.

Although it was published a little before Potvin, Wilhelm Ludwig Holland's edition of *Yvain* could be considered as the first satisfactory modern edition of Chrétien.[9] The importance of Holland's work lies in a clearly stated and followed editorial principle (I translate): 'The text of *Yvain* which I offer here is based on my own transcription of the excellent Paris manuscript Cangé 73 [= our Guiot]'. The editor offers some variants from B.N. fr. 12560 and B.N. fr. 1450. He also consulted Lady Guest's edition and Keller's fragments.

With Wendelin Foerster we enter the period in which, as Douglas Kelly has it, '. . . modern critical positions have tended to become impositions by their exclusivity. They reflect the standards and credos of given decades of Chrétien scholarship, or of the nationalities of different scholars'.[10] Kelly's view certainly applies to the editions of Chrétien. Between 1884 and 1899, Foerster edited four of Chrétien's romances: *Cligés*, *Yvain*, *Erec et Enide* and *Lancelot*. His original plan also included *Perceval*. The general title of each volume reads: Christian von Troyes, *Sämtliche erhaltene Werke, nach allen bekannten Handschriften*. Each volume also bears an individual title.[11] Foerster attempted to explain his editorial policy in the introduction to each volume. In theory, he was a 'Lachmannian': he did not follow a base manuscript, for he was convinced, like Karl Lachmann (1793–1851), that a critical edition should establish a filiation between the existing manuscripts in order to arrive at a *critical text*, that is, a text that reconstructs the archetype for the given tradition – close, ideally, to the author's original. Foerster used all the available manuscripts: sometimes a single line is composed of readings from three different manuscripts. He did not hesitate to correct many readings by his own intuition without manuscript support, and his literary taste in choosing what readings should belong to Chrétien was often excellent. Although his variants are certainly not exhaustive and often incorrectly recorded, Foerster was nevertheless responsible for the introduction of scientific rigour to the edition of Chrétien, even if his actual *practice* did not always achieve the intended rigour.[12]

Each of the four romances published by Foerster was later to be known as the *grosse Ausgabe* (large edition). The first three were also individually recast as a *kleine Ausgabe* (small edition) in the Romanische Bibliothek series. These 'small' editions were constantly revised by Foerster (and after his death, in 1915, by

---

9 *Li Romans dou Chevalier au lyon* . . . (Hanover and Paris 1862, 1880², 1886³; repr. 1982).
10 *Chrétien de Troyes, An Analytic Bibliography* (London, 1976), p. 11.
11 Thus: vol. 1: *Cliges, zum ersten Male herausgegeben* . . ., Halle 1884; vol. 2: *Der Löwenritter (Yvain)* . . . (Halle, 1887); vol. 3: *Erec und Enide* . . . (Halle, 1890; repr. Amsterdam, 1965); vol. 4: *Der Karrenritter (Lancelot) und Das Wilhelmsleben (Guillaume d'Angleterre)* . . . (Halle, 1899).
12 For a detailed critique of Foerster's editorial theory and practice, see Micha, *Tradition manuscrite*, pp. 18–27.

Alfons Hilka). They contained but a modicum of variants.[13] The 1926 Foerster/ Hilka text of *Yvain* was re-edited by T.B.W. Reid in 1942.[14]

Foerster's editorial theory and practice were followed by C. de Boer in his edition of *Philomena* (1909), a short work attributed to Chrétien.[15] The 1470 octosyllables of *Philomena* in de Boer's edition represent a solid attempt at a reconstitution of the original poem. It is, therefore, a *critical*, or Lachmannian edition. De Boer republished *Philomena* in vss 2217–3684 of his edition of *Ovide moralisé* (1920).[16] In 1986, Raymond Cormier published the text of *Philomena* in the 1920 edition along with two other Ovidian tales, accompanied by an English translation.[17] More recently, Emmanuèle Baumgartner has published the same tales with a modern French translation.[18] (For the manuscript utilized, see below, n. 33.)

Foerster, in collaboration with Hermann Breuer, also prepared a dictionary of Chrétien's romances.[19] The index of names and the glossary is preceded by a 237–page study of Chrétien's work and his language, as well as an edition of Chrétien's lyric poems. The *Glossary* was gleaned from the four romances edited by Foerster (plus *Guillaume d'Angleterre*) and with only an occasional reference to *Perceval* as edited by Potvin.

Foerster had never found the time to produce a 'large' edition of *Perceval*. In 1909, Gottfried Baist, wishing to offer a text to the students in his seminar, published, anonymously and privately, an edition based on one manuscript.[20] Baist worked on a 'large' edition of *Perceval* for some twenty years but could not finish the task before his death in 1920. Alfons Hilka continued the work, and the edition appeared in Foerster's series as vol. 5: *Der Percevalroman (Li Contes del Graal), unter Benutzung des von Gottfried Baist nachgelassenen handschriftlichen Materials* (Halle, 1932). Initially, the editor tried to follow the general principles adopted by Foerster, but in vain. As he put it (I translate): 'Despite years of work on the text of *Perceval*, I also have not been successful in arriving at a definitive judgment concerning the relations of the manuscripts of this work . . . ' (p. ix).

---

13 *Cligés: Textausgabe mit Einleitung, Anmerkungen und Glossar . . .*, Rom. Bibl. 1 (Halle, 1888, 1901[2], 1910[3], 1921[4]); *Yvain (der Löwenritter): Textausgabe mit Einleitung und Glossar . . .*, Rom. Bibl. 5 (Halle 1891, 1902[2], 1906[3], 1912[4], 1926 – same as 1912[4], with an Afterword by Hilka; repr. Geneva, 1977); *Erec und Enide: Textausgabe mit Variantenauswahl . . .*, Rom. Bibl. 13 (Halle, 1896, 1909[2], 1934[3]; repr. Amsterdam, 1965).

14 *Yvain (Le Chevalier au Lion). The Critical Text of Wendelin Foerster with Introduction, Notes and Glossary* (Manchester, 1942; repr. 1948, 1952, 1961, 1967 and 1984).

15 *Philomena: conte raconté d'après Ovide par Chrétien de Troyes publié d'après tous les manuscrits de l'Ovide moralisé . . .* (Paris, 1909).

16 *Ovide moralisé: Poème du commencement du XIVe siècle . . .* (Amsterdam, 1920; repr. Wiesbaden, 1966).

17 *Three Ovidian Tales of Love: Piramus et Tisbé, Narcisus et Dané, and Philomena et Procné* (New York, 1986).

18 *Pyrame et Tisbé, Narcisse, Philomena. Trois contes du XIIe siècle français imités d'Ovide . . . édition bilingue* (Paris, 2000).

19 *Kristian von Troyes. Wörterbuch zu seinen sämtlichen Werken . . .*, Rom. Bibl. 21 (Halle, 1914). It was corrected and re-edited with the index of proper names, but without the introduction by Hermann Breuer, *Wörterbuch zu Kristian von Troyes sämtlichen Werken von Wendelin Foerster, zweite veränderte Ausgabe . . .*, Rom. Bibl. 21 (Halle, 1933).

20 *Contes del Graal (Percevaus li galois). Abdruck des Handschrift Paris, français 794 . . .* (Freiburg i. B., 1911). There exists a corrected second edition, signed by Baist and accompanied by a Glossary (1912).

Hilka chose Guiot for his base manuscript, which he corrected freely. His edition contains a long introduction, followed by the text, with an account of rejected readings and an exhaustive presentation of variants from the thirteen manuscripts known to the editor. The apparatus is arranged in a two-tier fashion: the upper register of notes lists the rejected readings, the lower one all the meaningful variants. Hilka's text is followed by the *Elucidation* and *Bliocadran* (see above, n. 8), seven interpolations of the romance and copious, detailed notes. He also appended the lyric poems by Chrétien published by Foerster in his *Wörterbuch* and an Index of Proper Names. Curiously, there is no glossary. Hilka's edition would become a model – if not of a *critical* edition, in the Lachmannian sense – at least of a *complete* edition of Chrétien.

While passing in review the editions of Chrétien's romances, one would have the impression that French scholarship before World War I paid little attention to textual philology. This was not the case. In 1875, the Société des Anciens Textes Français (SATF) came into being and had published some seventy editions by 1914. A special commission of the Société saw to it that its editions met all the specific standards demanded by the editorial commission. It is fair to state that the rigour and completeness of the SATF editions made them comparable to the 'large' editions by Foerster, but the Société did not publish Chrétien in its series.[21]

In 1910, Mario Roques founded Classiques Français du Moyen Age (CFMA) and remained its director until his death. CFMA texts were to be less exhaustive than those published in the SATF series, and these 'small' editions were in no way to replace the 'large' SATF. When the directorship of the SATF became vacant (with Joseph Bédier's death in 1938), Roques became also the *Commissaire responsable* of the SATF.

In 1952, Roques made the crucial decision to publish Chrétien's romances in CFMA.[22] *Cligés* was edited by Micha, but Roques was responsible for the remaining three texts. Each of the volumes has been reprinted several times. What is important about the CFMA volumes is clearly stated on the title page of each romance and in vol. VI published later by Félix Lecoy in the same series (see below). The editorial policy reflects the serious objections made at the beginning of the twentieth century by many scholars to eclectic and/or composite editions, i.e., editions loosely based on Lachmann's method. The objections led to the (re-)establishment of the 'best-', or 'good-', or 'one-manu-

---

[21] However, such editions were planned in France. Micha's *Tradition manuscrite* (1939) was a preliminary for a series of 'large' editions. He himself wished to edit *Cligés*; see his *Prolégomènes à une édition de Cligés* (Paris, 1938). Pierre Jonin, for his part, clearly intended at one point to edit *Yvain*; see his *Prolégomènes à une édition d'Yvain* (Aix en Provence, 1958). I believe that neither Micha nor Jonin could have published these editions, chiefly because of the strong ideological position taken by Mario Roques against 'large' editions. After Bédier's death in 1938, Roques controlled both the SATF and the CFMA. His successor, Félix Lecoy, was equally averse to 'Lachmannianism'.

[22] *Les Romans de Chrétien de Troyes édités d'après la copie de Guiot (Bibl. nat. fr. 794)* . . .: vol. I, *Erec et Enide*, CFMA 80 (Paris, 1952); vol. II, *Cligés*, CFMA 84 (Paris, 1957); vol. III, *Le Chevalier de la Charrete* . . ., CFMA 86 (Paris, 1958); vol. IV, *Le Chevalier au lion (Yvain)* . . ., CFMA 89 (Paris, 1960). The reader should ignore the dates printed on the title page, for the publisher, Champion, prints the date of the last reprint as if it were the date of the edition.

script' method, usually called the 'Bédier method' (after Joseph Bédier, 1864–1938).[23] German scholars tended to be traditionalists or Lachmannians, and the French to be 'Bédierists'.

As far as I can ascertain, none of the Bédierists dealing with Chrétien has ever mentioned the fact that Holland (1862) and Baist (1912), while conscious of the allurement of Lachmannism, or better, 'Foersterism', reproduced the text of the Guiot manuscript of *Yvain* and *Perceval*. However, Roques (*Yvain*, p. iv) mentioned the first American one-manuscript edition of Chrétien, Robert White Linker's edition of *Yvain*.[24] Linker presented a good text with corrections, a choice of variants and an index of all the forms glossed in English. This privately printed text is difficult to find.

The three romances edited by Roques not only reproduced the Guiot manuscript in a conservative fashion, but, more important, they greatly reduced the critical apparatus. Roques does mention on rare occasions his abandoning or correcting his 'best' manuscript, and lists variants chiefly to demonstrate the superiority of Guiot. Micha (in his *Cligés*) followed the general principles espoused by the director of the CFMA.[25]

While Roques was publishing Chrétien in CFMA, William Roach edited *Perceval*.[26] Roach accepted the single manuscript principle, but contrary to Roques and Lecoy he did not become a 'slave' to the chosen copyist. He corrects his manuscript when readings present serious difficulties, explaining that (I translate): 'Anyone who has worked on medieval manuscripts knows perfectly well that no copyist is free from making errors and that a literal reproduction of a single manuscript, be it amongst the best, can only be justified if it is a diplomatic transcription'.[27] Roach offers only a limited number of variants in his Notes.

The real test of the Guiot manuscript as a base came with Félix Lecoy's edition of *Perceval*.[28] Lecoy – director of the CFMA after Roques's death in 1961 – was as convinced a Bédierist as was Roques, but his most persuasive argument against the best manuscript method applied to *Perceval* is his insertion of the *décompte des vers* [calculation of verses]. He lists here the lines that seem to be missing from Guiot and are to be found in other manuscripts. The *décompte* contains more than 300 lines, most of which should have been incorporated in the text.

The inexpensive CFMA volumes were very successful, and for some twenty years bilingual editions have been the only competition. In Germany, a new

---

23 This is not the place to discuss the protracted conflict between the Lachmannians and the Bédierists. For a general discussion of this conflict, see my 'The "French" Tradition of Textual Philology and Its Relevance to the Editing of Medieval Text', *Modern Philology*, 90 (1993), 512–32.
24 *Li Chevaliers au lyon, or Yvain, edited from BN. fr. 794* (Chapel Hill, NC, 1940).
25 *Erec et Enide, Cligés* and *Yvain* also contain lengthy Indexes of Words concerning civilization.
26 *Le Roman de Perceval, ou le Conte du Graal, publié d'après le MS fr. 12.576 de la Bibliothèque nationale* (Geneva-Paris 1956, 1958[2], revised and enlarged).
27 Roach, *Perceval*, p. xi.
28 *Le Conte du Graal (Perceval)*, vols V–VI, CFMA 100 and 103 (Paris, 1973 and 1975). The 1973 volume contains vss 1–6008, the 1975 volume, vss 6009–8900 and Introduction, Notes, Variants (taken from Hilka's edition), Table of Proper Names, and a Glossary.

series, Klassische Texte des romanischen Mittelalters in zweisprachigen Ausgaben, directed by Hans Robert Jauss and Erich Köhler, has published all of Chrétien's romances (1962–91), except *Cligés*.[29] These editions utilize the occasionally modified Foerster text of the 'small' edition. They offer no variants.

Several bilingual editions have also appeared in the Garland Library of Medieval Literature, Series A (1981–90): William W. Kibler's edition/translation of both *Lancelot* and *Yvain*; Carleton W. Carroll's edition/translation of *Erec et Enide*; and Rupert T. Pickens's edition (with translation by Kibler) of *Perceval*.[30] These editions are accompanied by a line-by-line English translation. All of them use the Guiot manuscript as base, but, contrary to their French predecessors, they are less conservative, i.e., they correct more freely and list all the rejected readings, while offering only a modicum of variants.

Alfred Foulet and Karl D. Uitti prepared, in 1989, a careful edition of *Lancelot* with a linear translation into modern French.[31] The text is based on the Guiot manuscript, but it is corrected intelligently and prudently. Only occasional variants are offered, but there is a complete list of rejected readings and an account of the manuscripts from which the emendations are taken (most often from B.N. fr. 12560).

In 1989, Michel Zink founded the bilingual Lettres Gothiques series, which has published all of Chrétien's romances: *Perceval* (Charles Méla); *Lancelot* (Méla); *Erec et Enide* (Jean-Marie Fritz); *Cligés* (Méla and Olivier Collet); and *Yvain* (David F. Hult).[32] Contrary to the CFMA editions, which followed the Guiot manuscript as a matter of principle, the Lettres Gothiques series uses other manuscripts, as well as the translation of *Lancelot* by Jean Frappier. Méla appreciates many readings chosen by Foerster.

In 1994, all the editions of Chrétien in the Lettres Gothiques series were gathered in one volume by Michel Zink and republished as: *Chrétien de Troyes, Romans, suivies des Chansons, avec, en appendice, Philomena* (Paris). There is a general introduction by Jean-Marie Fritz. The introductions to individual romances were shortened and their critical apparatus slightly modified. The volume ends with the *Chansons*, edited by Marie-Claire Zai, and *Philomena* in the de Boer edition with a translation by Olivier Collet. There is a general Index of Proper Names.

[29] Ilse Nolting-Hauff, *Yvain* . . . (Munich, 1962); Helga Jauss-Meyer, *Lancelot* . . . (Munich, 1974); Ingrid Kasten, *Erec und Enide* . . . (Munich, 1979); Monica Schöler-Beinhauer, *Der Percevalroman* . . . (Munich, 1991).

[30] *Lancelot, or the Knight of the Cart (Le Chevalier de la Charrete)* (New York, 1981); *The Knight with the Lion or Yvain (Le Chevalier au lion)* (New York, 1985); *Erec and Enide* (New York, 1987); *The Story of the Grail (Li Contes del Graal, or, Perceval)* (New York, 1990).

[31] *Le Chevalier de la Charrette (Lancelot). Texte établi, traduit, annoté et présenté avec variantes. Avant-propos de D. Poirion* (Paris, 1989).

[32] Charles Méla, ed., *Chrétien de Troyes, Perceval le Gallois. Edition du manuscrit 354 de Berne, traduction critique, présentation et notes* (Paris 1990); Charles Méla, ed., *Chrétien de Troyes, Le Chevalier de la Charrette ou le Roman de Lancelot, d'après tous les manuscrits existants, traduction et notes* (Paris 1992); Jean-Marie Fritz, ed., *Chrétien de Troyes, Erec et Enide. Edition critique d'après le manuscrit B.N. 1376, traduction. présentation et notes* (Paris 1992); Charles Méla and Olivier Collet, eds, *Chrétien de Troyes, Cligés. Edition critique du manuscrit B.N. 12560 . . . Suivi des Chansons courtoises de Chrétien de Troyes, présentation, édition critique et traduction par Marie-Claire Gérard-Zai* (Paris 1994); David F. Hult, ed., *Le Chevalier au lion, ou le Roman d'Yvain. Edition critique d'après le manuscrit B.N. fr. 1433, traduction, présentation et notes* (Paris, 1994).

Roughly at the same time as Zink's *Romans,* the Bibliothèque de la Pléiade issued *Chrétien de Troyes. Œuvres complètes. Edition publiée sous la direction de Daniel Poirion* (Paris, 1994). The volume contains an introduction by Daniel Poirion and editions of the following texts: *Érec et Énide* (Peter F. Dembowski, ed.); *Cligès* (Philippe Walter, ed.); *Yvain ou le Chevalier au Lion* (Karl D. Uitti, ed., and Philippe Walter, trans.); *Lancelot ou le Chevalier de la Charrette* (Daniel Poirion, ed.); *Perceval ou le Conte du Graal* (Daniel Poirion, ed.); *Philomena, Guillaume d'Angleterre, Chansons courtoises* (Anne Berthelot, ed.). Each editor was responsible for the edition and the translation (in prose, at the bottom of the page) but with the understanding that the Guiot manuscript would serve as base.[33] Each item is introduced by the editor-translator, accompanied by a short bibliography and notes and variants. The volume concludes with an Index of Medieval Terms and of Proper Names prepared by Sylvie Lefèvre and a general bibliography by Daniel Poirion. *Grosso modo,* the Pléiade texts are much improved CFMA editions, that is to say, corrections and modifications of the Guiot manuscript were introduced more frequently. In its general organization and in the presentation of variants, this edition was governed by the editorial policies of the Pléiade series.

In 1976, Douglas Kelly observed that '[t]here exists no truly critical edition of Chrétien's romances, although Hilka's *Perceval* comes closest' (*Bibliography,* p. 19). Twenty-eight years later, this statement is no longer true. We have two editions that can be qualified as *critical.* The first, *Cligés,* produced by Stewart Gregory and Claude Luttrell,[34] is a thorough edition based on the Guiot manuscript but fully supplemented by emendations from other manuscripts. In the words of the editors (I translate): 'Owing to the state of the manuscript tradition, Chrétien's text could not be fully reconstructed; our modest aim is to offer the reader a text closer to Chrétien's than to the copyist's Guiot' (p. xxxi). I believe that the editors achieved their aim. They took the Guiot manuscript as a base, but they corrected it systematically, offering, like Hilka, an exhaustive two-tier apparatus. Notes, Index of Names and a comprehensive Glossary conclude the volume.

The second new edition that merits the epithet *critical* is Keith Busby's *Perceval.*[35] It is a careful edition built, so to speak, on Hilka's. Busby, like Roach, has chosen as base B.N. fr. 12576. Rejected readings and a very substantial quantity of variants are presented in the two-tier fashion. Rich critical notes are followed by an Index of Names and an exhaustive Glossary. Clearly, future *complete* editions of *Erec et Enide, Lancelot* and *Yvain* should follow the models of Gregory/Luttrell and Busby.

Some 160 years of editing of Chrétien's romances can be considered as a history in miniature of critical editions of Old French literary works. These romances, and particularly *Perceval,* have clearly demonstrated that an *a priori*

---

33 The text of *Philomena,* and the 2000 Baumgartner edition, are based on MS Rouen 1044, O 4 controlled by de Boer's edition. The edition of *Chansons* uses Marie-Claire Zai's preliminary work for her edition.

34 *Cligés* (Cambridge, 1993).

35 *Le Roman de Perceval, ou Le Conte du Graal, Edition critique d'après tous les manuscrits . . .* (Tübingen, 1993).

established theory and practice of editing, be it of the Lachmann/Foerster or the Bédier/Roques sort, cannot render full justice to the available resources and needs. The recent editions by Gregory/Luttrell and by Busby follow the practices that combined the best aspects of Lachmannism and Bédierism. This approach is based on a renewed respect for both literary insight and common sense. This consensus acknowledges, above all, that each literary work has its own textual situation demanding its own editorial solution.

PART II
TEXTS

8

Philomena: *Brutal Transitions and Courtly Transformations in Chrétien's Old French Translation*

ROBERTA L. KRUEGER

In the Prologue to *Cligés*, the narrator introduces himself as author of a series of works 'an romans' ['in the French vernacular']: the 'commandments of Ovid'; 'the art of love'; the tale of the shoulder bite; the story of King Marc and Iseult la Blonde; and the 'muance' or metamorphosis of the hoopoe, the swallow and the nightingale.[1] Like the blurb for a modern book, these opening lines announce the author's credentials and his literary preoccupations. Chrétien portrays his engagement in a process of textual transmission, known in the Middle Ages as *translatio studii*, which involved the 'translation' or carrying over of ancient studies from Greece to Rome and into the European vernacular.[2] As he proposes to tell a new story about a Greek youth of Arthurian lineage, Chrétien refashions *translatio* in a distinctive mode. He claims to have translated or adapted a broad range of works about love, from Ovid's witty amorous verse (most likely the *Ars amatoria* and the *Remedia amoris*) and tragic Celtic lore (the Tristan legend) to the shocking story of Philomena's transformation into a nightingale (from Ovid's *Metamorphoses*). Before he embarks on an original romance about a heroine trapped in an unhappy marriage who will cleverly promote her own amorous desire, Chrétien proclaims his literary expertise in affairs of the heart.

The last work mentioned – and the text described at greatest length – is by far the most brutal account of desire. In Ovid's tale, Philomela (as she is called in Latin) is raped by her brother-in-law, Tereus, who cuts out her tongue so that she cannot speak of his crime. After the mute victim portrays the story of her misfortune in a woven tapestry conveyed to her sister, Procne, the two women kill Procne's son, Itys, and feed him to his unsuspecting father. As Tereus charges to kill the sisters, all three characters are changed into birds. Chrétien's mention of the final transformation or 'muance' of hoopoe, swallow and nightingale evokes a dreadful tale, reminding readers of the deadly impulses that subtend marital and family relations.

Philomela's story is also remarkable because it is the only one of Chrétien's non-Arthurian narrative works to have survived, at least in the eyes of many

---

[1] Chrétien de Troyes, *Cligés*, ed. Stewart Gregory and Claude Luttrell (Cambridge, 1993), vss 1–7.

[2] On *translatio* and the *Cligés* Prologue, see the discussion, below, by Joan Tasker Grimbert.

scholars. (Another work not mentioned in *Cligés*, the *Guillaume d'Angleterre*, is far less commonly attributed to Chrétien de Troyes.)[3] A French translation of Ovid's tale was 'discovered' in 1884 by the eminent medievalist Gaston Paris, who reported that he had had the pleasure of finding it in the midst of the *Ovide moralisé*, a vast fourteenth-century French translation of and commentary upon tales from the *Metamorphoses*.[4] Several features led Paris and subsequent critics to ascribe authorship to Chrétien de Troyes.[5] The *Ovide moralisé* narrator affirms four times that he tells the story as 'Crestiens' told it: once at the beginning, twice at the end, and again at the tale's precise mid-point, where he cites the author not as Chrétien 'de Troyes' but – to the great consternation of critics – as 'Crestiiens *li Gois*' (emphasis added).[6] Philomena's story in the *Ovide moralisé* ends with the marvellous transformation of the characters into the same three birds in the order that Chrétien names them in *Cligés*. Furthermore, for many critics, important aspects of *Philomena*'s language, style and moral commentary resemble features of Chrétien's Arthurian romances.

But if Paris argued that *Philomena* was originally composed by Chrétien de Troyes, he also noted the difficulty, if not impossibility, of reconstituting Chrétien's original poem from extant manuscripts. The text we know bears the mark of its fourteenth-century redactors, the author of the *Ovide moralisé* (whom Paris identified erroneously as Chrétien Legouais de Sainte-More) and the scribes who copied his original manuscript. Some critics have cast doubt on Chrétien's authorship, arguing that the grammar and lexicon are inconsistent with Chrétien[7] or doubting that *Philomena*'s lurid subject matter and its vision of love – adulterous, incestuous and cruel – could have appealed to an author whose treatment of love and marriage elsewhere is far more genteel.[8] Others concede that the work may well be Chrétien's, but that it is a work of juvenilia, penned by a brilliant pupil who applies rhetorical principles at times too diligently.[9]

---

3   The text's most recent editor names the author simply 'Chrétien'. See Chrétien, *Guillaume d'Angleterre*, ed. A.J. Holden (Geneva, 1988), p. 31.

4   Gaston Paris, 'Un poème retrouvé de Chrétien de Troyes', *Romania*, 13 (1884), 399–400. For more extensive discussion, see Gaston Paris, 'Chrétien Legouais et autres traducteurs ou imitateurs d'Ovide', *Histoire littéraire de la France*, vol. 29 (Paris, 1900), pp. 455–525.

5   See the arguments of the poem's first editor in Chrétien de Troyes, *Philomena: conte raconté d'après Ovide*, ed. C. de Boer (Paris, 1909), pp. LXXXI–CII; see also Ernst Hoepffner, 'La *Philomena* de Chrétien de Troyes', *Romania*, 57 (1931), 19–74. More recent arguments in favour of Chrétien's authorship are offered by Marie-Claire Gérard-Zai, 'L'Auteur de *Philomena*', *Revista de istorie si Teorie Literara*, 25 (1976), 361–68, and Elisabeth Schulze-Busacker, '*Philomena*: une révision de l'attribution de l'œuvre', *Romania*, 107 (1986), 459–85.

6   The first mention of 'Crestiens' occurs in vss 2211–16 of the sixth book of de Boer's edition of the *Ovide moralisé*. See C. de Boer, ed., *Ovide moralisé: poème du commencement du quatorzième siècle*, 2 vols (Amsterdam, 1920), II, p. 336. Further mentions occur at 2950, 3686 and 3842. Various hypotheses have been offered for the meaning of 'li Gois'; none of these definitively resolve the question of authorship.

7   For a summary and refutation of critics' philological arguments against Chrétien's authorship, see Hoepffner, '*Philomena*'.

8   This argument is advanced by Hans-Erich Keller, 'De l'Amour dans *Philomena*', in Giovanna Angeli and Luciano Formisano, eds, *L'Imaginaire courtois et son double: actes du VIe congrès triennal de la Société Internationale de Littérature Courtoise (ICLS), Fisciano (Salerno), 24–28 juillet 1989* (Naples, 1992), pp. 361–70.

9   A view expressed by Jean Frappier, *Chrétien de Troyes: l'homme et l'œuvre* (Paris, 1957), p. 68.

Although Chrétien's authorship cannot be claimed absolutely, there is general consensus today that the stylistic features and thematic preoccupations of *Philomena* reveal the nascent talent of the Champenois master. For example, the author makes frequent use of proverbs and proverbial expressions in a way that anticipates Chrétien's more refined deployment of proverbs in his romances.[10] The Ovidian translation has been included in recent editions of Chrétien's works and is briefly considered in several critical studies.[11] However awkward or formulaic it may seem at times, *Philomena* should not be dismissed as insignificant. As he translates Latin hexameters into Old French octosyllables, Chrétien recasts Ovid's poem in striking ways, deploying his rhetorical art to underscore a problematic *sens*, or meaning. Precisely because we are able to compare it to its source in a way that we can for no other work in his corpus, the Old French *Philomena* provides an extraordinary opportunity to study the emerging authorship of Chrétien de Troyes. If *Philomena* is indeed Chrétien's, then the founding narrative by one of the first and most influential romancers is a tale not of love and honour, but of deception, rape, incest, mutilation, infanticide and cannibalism. The intertextual connections between *Philomena* and Chrétien's later *œuvre* have only begun to be explored.

Chrétien's translation of Ovid's works places him at the forefront of twelfth-century literary innovation, when translation and adaptation of classical material were very much in vogue. The Latin poet Ovid (Publius Ovidius Naso, 43 BCE – 17/18 CE) endured as one of the most influential classical poets throughout the Middle Ages, so much so that the twelfth- and thirteenth-centuries have been dubbed the *aetas ovidiana* ['the age of Ovid']. Ovid's love poetry, his witty books of advice on love (the *Ars Amatoria* and the *Remedia amoris*) and the epic *Metamorphoses* were frequently cited, alluded to, copied, commented upon, translated and adapted, particularly from the Carolingian period onward and especially during the high Middle Ages and throughout the Renaissance.[12] Ovid also left an unmistakable imprint on courtly literature in love casuistry and wordplay, in amorous imagery – arrows, wounds and flames of desire – and in mythological characters, such as Narcissus and Piramus, who appear in numerous courtly texts. Ovid's self-conscious attention to the work-

---

Emmanuèle Baumgartner, in her recent edition and translation, repeats the general consensus that this is 'une œuvre de jeunesse de Chrétien de Troyes . . . même peut-être sa première œuvre', even as she reminds us that we cannot gauge the extent of *remaniement* [reworking] in the *Ovide moralisé*. Emmanuèle Baumgartner, ed., *Pyrame et Thisbé, Narcisse, Philomena: trois contes du XIIe siècle français imités d'Ovide* (Paris, 2000), p. 274.

10 Schulze-Busacker, 'Philomena'.

11 See, for example, *Philomena*, ed. Anne Berthelot in Chrétien de Troyes, *Œuvres complètes*, ed. Daniel Poirion (Paris, 1994), pp. 917–52 and 1391–410; and *Philomena*, ed. C. de Boer and trans. Olivier Collet in Chrétien de Troyes, *Romans suivis des Chansons avec, en appendice, Philomena*, gen. ed. Michel Zink (Paris, 1994), pp. 1225–67. Among recent studies that consider *Philomena* an early work, see Karl D. Uitti and Michelle Freeman, *Chrétien de Troyes Revisited* (New York, 1995), and Joseph J. Duggan, *The Romances of Chrétien de Troyes* (New Haven, 2001).

12 The scope of Ovid's medieval impact is represented in a special issue edited by Marilyn R. Desmond, 'Ovid in Medieval Culture', *Mediaevalia*, 13 (1989). A succinct discussion of Ovid's medieval legacy is offered by Peter L. Allen, *The Art of Love: Amatory Fiction from Ovid to the 'Romance of the Rose'* (Philadelphia, 1992), pp. 38–58. On the Ovidian mythographic tradition, see Paule Demats, *Fabula: trois études de mythographie antique et médiévale* (Geneva, 1973).

ings of poetry and narrative no doubt appealed to the nascent literary sensibilities of the twelfth century. An ambitious writer who wished to explore passion and poetics could do no better than to cut his teeth on Ovid, to imitate and adapt his complex art.

Yet Ovid's pagan beliefs and his frank portrayal of sexuality posed a problem for Christian writers, as did the work of other classical authors. Medieval theologians and clerics devised various interpretative strategies to justify or normalize classical writing: by deeming it useful for pedagogical purposes, by purifying it of indecencies, or, increasingly in the later Middle Ages, by reading it as an *integumentum*, a false covering that disguised the hidden truth of Christian doctrine. Many medieval commentaries and glosses of Ovid performed some kind of revisionary interpretaton.[13] The *Ovide moralisé*, the text in which Gaston Paris made his happy find, offers one of the most striking examples. In the first full-length French translation of the *Metamorphoses*, the author/translator intervenes and digresses so extensively that the work swells to more than 70,000 lines, over six times longer than Ovid. As critics have noted, the narrator's frequent commentary produces not a *single* moral message, but rather a proliferation of explanations, moralizations, and allegorical readings, some of which are contradictory.[14] *Philomena* is a case in point. The *Ovide Moralisé* author says that he conveys the tale 'just as Chrétien told it'. But he then glosses the myth as an allegory of the body (represented by Tereus) and soul (Procne) corrupted by sensual delights (Philomena). He interprets Philomena not as an unfortunate victim of rape, but rather as the cause of Tereus's crime. Philomena, not Tereus, represents deceitful love and capricious pleasure, and she is fittingly transformed into a 'flighty nightingale' (vss 3839–40).

The moral deduced by the fourteenth-century compiler seems to betray the meaning of Chrétien's text. It wilfully appropriates the story and forcefully re-interprets it. As Gaston Paris succinctly said of the allegory, 'Il est impossible d'être plus absurde' ['It is impossible to be more absurd'].[15] But, if we look carefully at *Philomena* itself, we see that the process of recasting Ovid has begun within Chrétien's translation. Chrétien alters his source, rendering the central characters more complex and considerably complicating the moral '*sens*'. Furthermore, *Philomena*'s narrator allies himself with the characters' drama and underscores the processes of translation, linguistic deception, corporeal appropriation, mutilation, rewriting – artistic and linguistic processes already dramatized in Ovid, as classical scholars have shown.[16] As Chrétien self-consciously explores the processes of translation, transformation and interpretation and

---

13 On medieval strategies for reading Ovid and other pagan authors, see Renate Blumenfeld-Kosinski, *Reading Myth: Classical Mythology and Its Interpretations in Medieval French Literature* (Stanford, 1997) and Rita Copeland, *Rhetoric, Hermeneutics, and Translation in the Middle Ages: Academic Traditions and Vernacular Texts* (Cambridge, 1991).

14 Blumenfeld-Kosinski, *Reading Myth*, pp. 90–136 and Ana Pairet, *Les Mutacions des fables: figures de la métamorphose dans la littérature française du Moyen Age* (Paris, 2002), pp. 97–134.

15 Paris, 'Chrétien Legouais', p. 518.

16 See, for example, Charles Segal, 'Ovid's Metamorphic Bodies: Art, Gender, and Violence in the *Metamorphoses*', *Arion*, 5.3 (1998), 9–41, and the fine essays in Philip Hardie, Alessandro Barchiesi and Stephen Hinds, eds, *Ovidian Transformations: Essays on the 'Metamorphoses' and its Reception* (Cambridge, 1999).

further probes Ovid's analysis of gender relations, he examines the problematic link between courtly discourse and uncourtly violence that will pervade later Arthurian romance. Before we examine Chrétien's artful transformations, let us consider more closely Ovid's 'Philomela', whose story occurs near the end of *Metamorphoses* VI (vss 412–674).[17]

The tale begins with the military victory of Tereus, King of Thrace, over the enemies of Athens, ruled by King Pandion, and with the victor's marriage to Pandion's daughter, Procne. This politically expedient union, in which the bride has no voice, seems ill-fated from the start. The positive forces of Juno, Hymen and the Graces are absent from the wedding; bad omens, the Furies and a screech owl, attend the conception of the newlyweds' son, Itys. After five years, Procne begs to be allowed to see her sister, and Tereus returns to Athens to entreat Pandion to allow his younger daughter, Philomela, to travel with him to Thrace for a visit. Pandion tearfully entrusts his cherished daughter to his son-in-law, enjoining him to protect her and return her as soon as possible. But as the trip nears its end, Tereus drags his sister-in-law off to a hut hidden in the woods and rapes her. When the horrified victim threatens to tell the world what has happened, the rapist cuts out her tongue. Leaving Philomela locked up under guard, Tereus feigns grief and tells Procne that Philomela is dead; the wife piously mourns her sister. But, a year later, Philomela artfully weaves her story in purple on white and sends the cloth to her sister, who exacts bitter revenge when she understands what has happened. Dressed as a Baccante, Procne rescues Philomela and devises a 'great deed' of terrible retribution. With Philomela's aid, she murders Itys, her own beloved child, throws his mutilated body into a boiling kettle, and serves him to her unsuspecting husband as part of a special sacred feast. Tereus learns his son's fate when Philomela appears and dramatically hurls the boy's head into his father's face. As the enraged King draws his sword, Procne and Philomela are transformed into birds of unspecified species. When Tereus charges forth to kill them, he turns into a hoopoe, 'with the look of one armed for war' (vs. 674).

Ovid's narrative recounts the power of desire to destabilize the family, the bedrock of society in both classical and feudal times. It portrays the force of feminine ingenuity and artifice and reveals the power of narrative simultaneously to cover and expose the truth, revealing, in this case, the violence against and silencing of women that underlies patriarchal relations, as Patricia Joplin has shown.[18] It also emblematizes a particularly brutal version of *translatio* or carrying forth from one geo-political location to another, in which the appropriated body is raped, the victim's tongue mutilated, and the treacherous 'translator' finally punished by a plot motivated by his betrayal, a revenge plot prompted by a new form of storytelling.

Chrétien's *Philomena* transmits a tale substantially similar to but also signifi-

---

[17] Ovid, *Metamorphoses*, trans. Frank Justus Miller, 2 vols (Cambridge, MA 1977), I, pp. 317–35.

[18] Patricia Klindienst Joplin, 'The Voice of the Shuttle is Ours', *Stanford Literature Review*, 1 (1984), 25–53. See also Amy Richlin, 'Reading Ovid's Rapes', in Amy Richlin, ed., *Pornography and Representation in Greece and Rome* (Oxford, 1992), pp. 158–79.

cantly different from its source.[19] The most obvious difference is length. Chrétien stretches 262 Latin hexameters to 1468 octosyllabic verses, arranged in rhyming couplets, principally by deploying the rhetorical technique known as *amplificatio*, or amplification; to a lesser extent – but at important moments – Chrétien also abbreviates the tale or eliminates particular details.

It would be impossible to enumerate every difference between the two versions; readers are encouraged to review Ovid's version for themselves before reading Chrétien's. Some of the most significant changes are authorial interventions that present narrative signposts, proverbs and moralizations; embellished portraits and enhanced characterizations; enhanced dialogue within dramatic scenes; and a focus on moral questions. The narrator calls our attention to the tale's structure, organized into two parts and further subdivided into narrative segments. As in Chrétien's later romances, the clearly delineated structure invites readers to perceive analogies and contrasts between characters and situations; these points of comparison are further enhanced by repetition, rhyme and wordplay. As he translates for his medieval audience a Latin story that was itself adapted from Greek myth, Chrétien does not simply refashion the classical tale in medieval garb. At several points, as we shall see, he notes the peculiarity of ancient customs. At other times, he introduces an explicit or self-conscious anachronism that works like a signature to remind us of his own creative intervention, highlighting the disparity between old and 'new' cultures and calling upon listeners and readers to compare social practices. Finally, Chrétien highlights the sexual tensions of the intrigue, deepens the emotional and moral complexity of the characters and underscores the drama of translation, deceptive discourse, mutilation and artistic creation and transformative storytelling – a drama in which his own clerkly performance is implicated.

Although *Philomena* has no formal Prologue (unlike Chrétien's romances), the medieval clerk insinuates his presence from the start. King Pandion of Athens is described as one who is 'poissans et larges et cortois' [powerful, generous and courtly][20] – courtly terms not present in Ovid – whose delight at marrying his daughter to Tereus is immediately called into question. Deploying a technique used frequently in *Philomena* and in Chrétien's later romances (inspired,

---

[19] Critical analyses of Chrétien's translation include Edith Joyce Benkov, '*Philomena*: Chrétien de Troyes's Reinterpretation of the Ovidian Myth', *Classical and Modern Literature*, 3.4 (1983), 201–9; Wagih Azzam, 'Le Printemps de la littérature: la "translation" dans "Philomena" de Crestiiens li Gois', *Littérature*, 74 (1989), 47–62 ; E. Jane Burns, *Bodytalk: When Women Speak in Old French Literature* (Philadelphia, 1993), pp. 115–50; Michelle Guéret-Laferté, 'De Philomèle à Philomène', in *Bien dire et bien aprandre: Bulletin du Centre d'études médiévales et dialectales de l'université de Lille III*, 15 (1997), 45–56; Marylène Possamaï-Perez, 'Chrétien de Troyes au début du XIVe siècle: Philomène "moralisé" ', in Claude Lachet, ed., *L'Œuvre de Chrétien de Troyes dans la littérature française: réminiscences, résurgences, et réécritures* (Lyon, 1997), pp. 160–85; Baumgartner, ed., *Pyrame et Thisbé, Narcisse, Philomena*, pp. 273–79; Colette Storms, 'Le Mal dans *Philomena*', in Myriam Watthée-Delmotte and Paul-Augustin Deproost, eds, *Imaginaires du mal*, (Paris, 2000), pp. 103–13; Nancy A. Jones, 'The Daughter's Text and the Thread of Lineage in the Old French *Philomena*', in Elizabeth Robertson and Christine M. Rose, eds, *Representing Rape in Medieval and Early Modern Literature* (New York, 2001), pp. 161–88.

[20] Vs. 2, Baumgartner, ed., *Philomena* in Baumgartner, ed. *Pyrame et Thisbé, Narcisse, Philomena*, pp. 154–255. All further citations will refer to this edition; English translations are my own.

perhaps, by the *Roman d'Eneas*),[21] the author engages in a dialogue with himself (or a fictive listener) about Tereus's character, which we may loosely translate as follows: '– Pandion is delighted to be marrying his daughter to a king. – To a king? No, he marries her rather to a tyrant'. The narrator's rhetorical cross-examination warns of the dangers that lurk beneath the appealing veneer of royal power and signals the perilous exchange of a woman between two rulers. Tereus is a brute, and Pandion is too easily persuaded to give his daughter away, as the rhyme of 'sa fille chiere' [his dear daughter] and 'sans grant priere' [without much entreaty] (vss 13–14) reminds us.

When Chrétien comments that neither Hymen, god of marriage, nor priest or clerk attended the wedding (vs. 18), he creates the first of many conscious anachronisms, which work as a kind of signature.[22] He highlights simultaneously the marriage's inauspicious beginning, the pagan setting and *clergie*, the Christian values of his audience. These multiple perspectives prompt readers to begin the process of comparative analysis that Chrétien fosters throughout his retelling of an ancient, barbaric tale. Although *Philomena* lacks a formal exordium, the opening lines function as Chrétien's later Prologues will do, establishing the narrator's clerkly presence and rhetorical mastery.

Chrétien's treatment of Philomena's rape and revenge is indeed distinctive. By signing 'Crestien li Gois' at the distinct mid-point – verse 734 out of 1468 verses – he calls attention to his careful structuring of the tale, which is bifurcated and further subdivided.[23] One critic has noted that he 'cuts' the text just when Tereus mutilates the maiden.[24] Indeed, his signature divides the text in half at precisely the moment Tereus leads his sister-in-law off to a 'meson gaste' [empty house] whose material – 'en bois' [of wood] – rhymes with the enigmatic name, 'li Gois'. The first half presents Tereus's negotiations and the promises made to Procne and Pandion. The second half, in four scenes, presents Tereus's brutal betrayal (the rape and mutilation); Procne's mourning; Philomena's tapestry; and the sisters' revenge. Chrétien's use of description, dialogue and moral commentary in each part enhances the tale's psychological drama, inviting the audience's engagement, if not sympathy, with characters whose actions are, as Emmanuèle Baumgartner has observed, almost uniformly monstrous.[25]

Chrétien extensively amplifies the events that lead Tereus and Philomena to the 'maison gaste': eighty lines of Latin become seven hundred lines of Old French. As he interpolates details about Tereus's voyage to Athens (strongly reminiscent of Wace's *Brut* and Thomas's *Tristan*, as has been pointed out[26]), he stresses the tragic irony of the crossing, claiming that it is a great shame that peaceful seas allowed Tereus to reach his destination (vss 80–85). Tereus's role as his wife's faithful emissary is carefully conveyed in contractual language that echo Procne's earlier promise to her husband to return with her sister. Tereus

---

[21] As noted by Baumgartner, ed., *Philomena*, p. 159.
[22] On the function of anachronism as signature in *Philomena*, see Azzam, 'Le Printemps', p. 50.
[23] The careful organization of the tale has been remarked by Storms, 'Le Mal', p. 106.
[24] Azzam, 'Le Printemps', p. 48.
[25] Baumgartner, ed., *Philomena*, p. 277.
[26] Hoepffner, '*Philomena*', pp. 36–8; Baumgartner, ed., *Philomena*, p. 163.

makes a solemn 'covent' [pledge] to bring Philomena back as soon as possible – and then gently chides Pandion for not having presented his daughter earlier; the term 'covent' recurs at strategic moments, vss 117, 535, 672. Pledges and promises precede the fateful moment when Tereus beholds Philomena.

As many have noted, Philomena's appearance before Tereus is a remarkable amplification, the first of Chrétien's celebrated literary portraits of beautiful women.[27] Expanding four lines of Ovid into nearly twenty times as many Old French octosyllables, the narrator highlights Philomena's beauty, her courtly qualities and her artistic talents as he displays his own rhetorical mastery. It may be that this passage recalls a school exercise and that Chrétien, 'just learning the art of portraiture', was 'following a manual of poetic composition'.[28] If this is so, Chrétien applied himself admirably. The clerk signals his *clergie* from the very beginning, when he proclaims, in an amusing anachronistic understatement, or litotes, that the maiden was not a 'veiled nun' and says that the wisdom of Plato, Homer and Cato could not help him describe her (vss 126–39). The passage enhances Philomena's status, transforming a maiden described in a natural setting in Ovid into a full-blown courtly heroine.[29] As E. Jane Burns has noted, Chrétien transforms the conventional physical description of the first part (which focuses on Philomena's sensual, passive beauty that will soon inflame Tereus) into a more dynamic second part that endows her with subjectivity and praises her active talents and skills.[30] Chrétien's explicit *clergie* is matched by that of his heroine in the latter part of the description, who is described as more 'sage' [wise] than 'bele' [beautiful] (vs. 172), and who has mastered courtly games, falconry, needlework, knowledge of classical authors, grammar, writing and singing (vss 176–204). In a brilliant detail, Chrétien tells us that Philomena could work cloth so well that she would have been able to depict Hellequin's troop (vss 192–93). The allusion to a band of souls wandering wildly in Purgatory foreshadows not only the skill with which the heroine later weaves her story but also her tragic transformation into flight.[31] Other details, too, seem ironically to presage the maiden's fate. That Philomena knows more of joy than do Apollonius and Tristan (vss 174–76), heroes of incest and adultery narratives, is surely ironic. Her skill in courtly games provides no protection against Tereus's designs. Her knowledge of birds and of singing poignantly evokes her final transformation as nightingale. Finally, we are told that she knows so well how to speak 'wisely' that she could have had her own school (vss 202–4). This attribute seems to anticipate her verbal sparring with Tereus; it renders her loss of tongue more poignant. The narrator's enumeration of artistic and linguistic

---

[27] For a detailed analysis of this portrait, see Alice M. Colby, *The Portrait in Twelfth-Century Literature: An Example of the Stylistic Originality of Chrétien de Troyes* (Geneva, 1965), pp. 122–38.

[28] Colby, *Portrait*, p. 125.

[29] Guéret-Laferté, 'De Philomèle à Philomène', pp. 55–56.

[30] Burns, *Bodytalk*, pp. 120–24.

[31] Hellequin's troop is explicated by Colby, *Portrait*, p. 136. The thematic connection to Philomena's fate is suggested by Burns, *Bodytalk*, p. 122, and Jones, 'The Daughter's Text', p. 173.

skills throughout this passage conveys his admiration for and complicity with a heroine whose 'sagesse' [wisdom] mirrors his own.

If the victim is more fully developed as a courtly subject in Chrétien's version, so, too, is the rapist. The scene in which Tereus first meets Philomena and persuades her father to entrust her to him is expanded from less than two hundred lines in Ovid to more than six hundred by Chrétien, who composes a narrative segment of theatrical proportions.[32] Ovid reports that Tereus was 'inflamed by love, quick as if one should set fire to ripe grain'; that he was 'pricked' 'by his own passionate nature'; and that 'love made him eloquent', leading him to 'add tears to his entreaties'.[33] Chrétien develops the motifs of amorous flames, eloquence and tears into a quintessentially courtly drama that self-consciously idealizes Tereus's transgressive passion as love at the same time that it exposes it as vile lust. Tereus is simultaneously condemned as a sinner and portrayed as the helpless victim of Amors, when the narrator comments, 'Pechiez le met en esperance / de mauvestié et de folie. / Amours vilainement le lie'. (vss 212–14) [Sin made him hope for wickedness and madness. Love bound him basely].

Yet Chrétien does more than simply condemn Tereus's depravity. He examines the very foundation of moral action and judgment. Following the lines just cited, the narrator qualifies his statement, explaining that Tereus's lust for his sister-in-law was not considered 'amour vilaine' [base love] in ancient Thrace, for one of their gods had decreed that everyone could do exactly as he pleased; such was 'la loi paienne' (vs. 228) [pagan law]. This explanation – a principle Amelia Van Vleck has dubbed 'Tereus's pleasure-law'[34] – is not present in Ovid. Kathryn Gravdal has argued that Chrétien 'justifies' Tereus's action in this passage as part of his programme of 'aestheticizing' rape throughout the tale.[35] Yet the narrator, Philomena and Procne consistently denounce Tereus as an evil tyrant. Indeed, Chrétien's striking intervention has been seen as a passage that 'denatures' the moral vision of Ovid's text.[36] Chrétien's historical explanation can be read as expressly problematic: it calls our attention to an underlying tension or inherent contradiction. 'La loi païenne' is not law but its very opposite, the brutal impulse that underlies the veneer of any civilization, including Chrétien's contemporary world. The narrator's 'denaturing' explanation invites the audience's comparative reflection about the transgression of taboos and calls into question the very nature of law. He also foreshadows a similar description of another law that endangers women, the 'custom' that purports to protect ladies from marauding knights in Le Chevalier de la Charrette (vss 1302–16), but that also casts women as objects of exchange and prizes in chivalric contests.[37]

---

[32] On the dramatization and theatrical qualities of this scene and others in Philomena, see Possamaï-Perez, 'Chrétien de Troyes au début du XIVe siècle', p. 175.

[33] Ovid, Metamorphoses, ed. and trans. Miller, Book VI, vss 455–60, 469–71.

[34] Van Vleck, 'Textiles as Testimony', p. 33.

[35] Kathryn Gravdal, Ravishing Maidens: Writing Rape in Medieval French Literature and Law (Philadelphia, 1991), p. 62.

[36] Guéret-Laferté, 'De Philomèle à Philomène', p. 49.

[37] See my analysis of this custom in Roberta L. Krueger, Women Readers and the Ideology of Gender in Old French Verse Romance (Cambridge, 1993), pp. 39–40.

Chrétien's attention to custom and social conflicts displays itself first in *Philomena*.[38]

It may be too much to argue, as has one critic, that Tereus, like Tristan, is not responsible for his actions and that he feels 'une douleur sincère' [genuine sorrow] when he weeps.[39] But it is true that Chrétien's presentation makes the rapist a more complex, and therefore more troubling, character.[40] Paradoxically, it is Tereus's feigned 'courtly' behaviour that renders him so reprehensible and memorable for the audience. His treachery foreshadows that of Meleagant in *Le Chevalier de la Charrette* (whose base impulses are fortunately thwarted by Lancelot) and of a long line of fictional scoundrels who abuse their linguistic and sexual powers, from Don Juan to the Marquis de Valmont. With remarkable perspicacity, Chrétien places love-talk in the mouth of a *fel* [wicked man] and asks the audience to reflect – as he will in all of his later romances – about the nature of Amors and the problematic ways it structures relations between men and women.

Ernst Hoepffner was the first to observe that the source of love casuistry in *Philomena* is not the *Roman d'Eneas* but rather Ovid's own amatory verse.[41] Chrétien claims in *Cligés* to have translated Ovid's 'commandments', which critics usually understand as all or parts of the *Ars amatoria* and the *Remedia amoris*. Yet *Philomena* also enacts a 'translation' of Ovidian love poetry, as Chrétien 'carries over' this material into Ovid's mythography. As he combines two Ovidian traditions in a new 'conjointure', Chrétien reflects critically on the nature of erotic desire. In a long passage in which the narrator explores Tereus's amorous distress, the narrator wonders, in a self-reflexive authorial dialogue, whether the base passion that Tereus feels can in fact be Love (vss 481–96). The extended dialogues between Tereus and Philomena and between Tereus and Pandion create a 'courtly' scenario in which Chrétien shows how a wicked man manipulates discourse to evil ends, but also how a clever maiden can use her own tongue to counter him.

When Tereus first entreats Philomena to ask her father for permission to visit his sister, she retorts that he should, in effect, 'go ask for yourself' and invokes a 'French custom', 'la coustume aus François' (vs. 280), which stipulates that whoever wants something should work hard to achieve it, if he has the knowledge and merit to do so (vss 276–86). The passage has given scholars pause, since no mention of such a 'custom', which seems proverbial in origin, has been found.[42] In any case, an allusion to a French custom made by a pagan woman in ancient Thrace is a jarring anachronism that underscores the dramatic tension and the trouble with Tereus, whose 'pagan law' of do-as-you-please contrasts clearly with Philomena's rule of working hard to persuade. Ironically, Tereus applies Philomena's French custom to the letter and subsequently uses feigned

---

38 On custom in Chrétien's Arthurian romances, see Erich Köhler, 'Le Rôle de la "coutume" dans les romans de Chrétien de Troyes', *Romania*, 81 (1960), 386–97.
39 Cormier, 'Térée, le pécheur fatal', p. 4.
40 On Tereus's complexity, see Storms, 'Le Mal', p. 106, Possamaï-Perez, 'Chrétien de Troyes au début du XIVe siècle', p.175, and Guéret-Laferté, 'De Philomèle à Philomène', p. 48.
41 Hoepffner, '*Philomena*', p. 58.
42 Baumgartner, ed., *Philomena*, p. 179.

courtly behaviour – persuasive speech, tears and false promises – to enact pagan law and get exactly what he wants.

The spirited dialogue between the scoundrel and the young ingénue establishes Philomena as Tereus's intellectual equal and makes her loss of tongue later all the more poignant.[43] It also sets up the terrible moment of Philomena's rape, when Tereus – following Philomena's advice to 'ask first on your own' – will attempt to persuade Philomena through courtly entreaty that she should love him before he rapes her (see vss 763–70). Calling her 'bele' [beautiful] (vs. 766) and proclaiming his love, he attempts to convince her to accede to his 'volentez' [will] (vs. 780). Such 'courtly' talk barely masks Tereus's lust, which soon degenerates into brute force when he declares 'Tout ferai quan que mes cuers pense' ['I will do everything just as my heart desires'] (vs. 794).

If Chrétien is, as Jones has suggested, 'eager to display his mastery of Ovidian lore'[44] in *Philomena*, he seems just as intent on showing how problematic that lore may be. Ovidian love rhetoric is unmasked as a deceptive cover-up for male lust.[45] Chrétien similarly reveals the double-edged nature of amorous discourse at various moments in his later romances and uses Ovidian topoi to signal sexual and political tensions. In *Yvain*, for example, when lovesick Yvain lusts after the wife of a knight he has just slain in battle, Ovidian imagery points to the underlying contradictions of this precarious moment.[46] In both these texts, Chrétien deploys Amors to embellish brute impulses or underlying tensions that he simultaneously reveals. Chrétien resolves these tensions comically in *Yvain*, when the hero marries the woman he desires; in *Philomena*, the force of male lust is unbridled. The critical perspective of the narrator throughout Chrétien's works invites our comparative analysis of the link between courtly discourse and sexual violence in such scenes. *Philomena*'s critical analysis of Ovidian love casuistry constitutes another 'signature' feature of Chrétien in this text, one that heralds the interpretative complexity of his mature romances.

Philomena's response to Tereus offers another highly charged rhetorical performance that is conspicuously added to the source. Ovid's Philomela is speechless before the rape and is compared to a frightened lamb and a wounded dove (vss 526–53). Chrétien's Philomena, by contrast, is outspoken. Her words sternly chastise Tereus, whom she condemns as a 'fel' in six successive lines and whom she rebukes for breaking his promise to return her safe and sound, dishonouring his verbal contract, perjuring his oath to the gods and crying false tears (vss 807–25). Adding yet another moral dimension that is lacking in Ovid, Philomena then urges him to repent, to act wisely by avoiding perjury and treachery (vss 830–32).

Chrétien's transformation of the rape scene is remarkable in several respects. He presents a forceful heroine who attempts to deploy her rhetorical skills to dissuade her attacker before the rape. In Ovid, she speaks only afterwards to

---

[43] Baumgartner, ed., *Philomena*, p. 179.

[44] Jones, 'The Daughter's Text', p. 164.

[45] On Chrétien's use of courtly rhetoric to critique love, see Guéret-Laferté, 'De Philomèle à Philomena', p. 49.

[46] As I have argued in Krueger, *Women Readers*, pp. 41–46.

lament her fate. Within this passage, Chrétien interjects a moralization about Tereus's character that attempts to gloss or interpret the event. When Philomena twice urges Tereus to repent, she evokes a Christine doctrine of considerable currency in Chrétien's time. As Possamaï-Perez has observed, Chrétien's Christian moralization in this passage seems in keeping with the framework of the *Ovide moralisé* whose author, she suggests, may have been inspired by Chrétien's methods for his larger enterprise.[47]

Whether or not we read *Philomena*'s moralization as one of the forces behind the *Ovide moralisé*, Chrétien's treatment of the rape is notable for its verbosity. Chrétien diminishes the corporeal violence of the rape depicted by Ovid, who devotes ten lines to describe the tongue, which continues to 'twitch convulsively' after it has been wrenched out by Tereus.[48] By contrast, Chrétien omits the graphic account of the tongue but amplifies the characters' verbal dispute and interjects moralizing commentary – from the heroine, as we have seen, and from the narrator, who explains the horrible cycle of events as evil issuing from evil, 'male norreture' (vss 842–43), foreshadowing the ultimate violent meal. As Chrétien translates the violent 'translation' of Philomena from Thrace by Tereus and signs his name at the mid-point, he calls attention to the use and abuse of language and to his own radical transformation of his source. His role as translator in the first part of the story shares an affinity not only with Philomena, for her wisdom and artistry, but also, more disturbingly, with Tereus, for his linguistic treachery.[49]

Just as Chrétien has deepened the moral and psychological complexity of the scenes leading up to the rape, so, too, does he dramatize the aftermath, deepening our insights into the characters and complicating our judgments about them. Tereus continues to be portrayed as a *fel* (vs. 904). The scene in which Tereus feigns tears to deceive Procne after Philomena's invented death (expanded from 5 lines in Ovid to 90 lines in Chrétien) replays his earlier deception of Pandion and further enhances the story's 'thématisation du mensonge' [thematization of lying], as Azzam has termed it.[50] As in the *trompeur trompé* plot of numerous medieval tales, the trickster will soon be punished and forced to eat far worse than his words.

It is easy to condemn Tereus, but how does Chrétien invite his audience to judge the sisters? Procne's and Philomena's brutal retribution was no doubt as troubling to medieval readers and listeners as it remains today, when it has sparked particular interest from feminist critics. Chrétien enhances the scene's drama and underscores its dubious moral nature. He expands the scene depicting Procne's grief when she is deceived by Tereus to believe that Philomena has died. Procne expresses her despair in a long lament to Death (vss 979–1004), which is ironic because Philomena is still alive.[51] Procne then

---

47 Possamaï-Perez, 'Chrétien de Troyes au début du XIVe siècle', p. 173.
48 Ovid, *Metamorphoses*, ed. Miller, p. 327.
49 For a different perspective on the affinities between Tereus and the narrator, see Azzam, 'Le Printemps', p. 58.
50 Azzam, 'Le Printemps', p. 51.
51 Chrétien later employs a similar ironic lament in the *Chevalier de la Charrette* (vss 4264–83), as Possamaï-Perez has noted, 'Chrétien de Troyes au début du XIVe siècle', p. 173.

performs with meticulous devotion the ritual sacrifice of a bull to Pluto, god of the underworld, a rite not described in Ovid. Transferring the animal's blood to a white pot, she foreshadows her preparation of Tereus's dreadful meal, another kind of sacrifice. When she later seeks revenge, she does not act in the frenzy of a Bacchic rite (as in Ovid's text); she moves with swiftness and resolve to her sister's side.

Philomena's weaving of the 'cortine', or bedcurtain, that recounts her plight is also more elaborately dramatized. Significantly, she acts not alone but in collaboration with other women – with an old *vilaine* [peasant], in whose protection Tereus 'foolishly' left her, and with the woman's daughter, another *fille* [daughter] (vs. 1093). Jane Burns has remarked the importance of female collaboration in the fabrication of the *cortine* and in preparation of the final meal; she argues that the tapestry emblematizes not only women's disembodied voices, but also the active work of their hands.[52] Nancy Jones observes that Philomena's weaving re-enacts the poetic resonance of her name, which in turn summarizes the plot and the hidden sub-plot: as a *fille* she has been lead away ('mener'); it is she who will weave the thread (*'fil a mené'*) telling the story that will lead to the destruction of the *fils* ('son').[53] She further notes alliance between Philomena's tapestry and the author's text, which are both 'products of courtly *savoir-faire'* with 'potentially dangerous effects', and which both convey hidden meanings about family violence in the ancient and feudal worlds.[54] By emphasizing the wordplay of *fil / filz / mener* throughout the text, Jones argues, Chrétien underscores the power of female sexuality to disrupt feudal marital and family relationships. Amelia Van Vleck claims that the author's choice of a *cortine* as the backdrop for the story, not only restores the bond between the sisters that marriage has destroyed but also 'silently acknowledges a common subjection to biology', as the bed is the locus of sleep, death, childbirth and dreams.[55] As Philomena expertly weaves her symbolically charged tapestry, she invents a new way of speaking, 'nouviax signes', vs. 1147, or a new sign language, evoked also in vss 1188 and 1193, to instruct the old woman and her daughter to deliver the *cortine* to her sister.[56] Many critics have noted that the *cortine* is woven not only with purple thread, as in Ovid, but with purple, red, yellow and green in profusion – as if to emblematize Chrétien's own amplification. The added threads of a sister's pious mourning, female collaboration, the wordplay with terms of weaving and lineage, 'nouviax signes' and a profusion of colours all enhance Chrétien's artful transformation as he reweaves Philomena's threads.

The narrator's creative transformation continues through to the bitter end. As

---

[52] Burns, *Bodytalk*, p. 131.
[53] See Jones, 'The Daughter's Text', pp. 170–81. Azzam ('Le Printemps', pp. 59–62) also notes the significance of the text's wordplay, although he offers a different interpretation of its significance.
[54] Jones, 'The Daughter's Text', p. 173.
[55] Amelia E. Van Vleck, 'Textiles as Testimony in Marie de France and Philomena', *Medievalia et Humanistica*, New Series, 22 (1995), 37.
[56] For this observation, I am grateful to my student Kristin W. Andrews, whose 2002 Hamilton College Senior Honors thesis in Classics and French was entitled 'Vox Silentium et *Noviax Signes*: la représentation de la voix chez Ovide et deux traducteurs du XIIe siècle français (les contes de Narcisse et de Philomèle)'.

he has done with previous segments of the narrative, he dramatizes the scene of Procne's and Philomena's revenge, adding and extending dialogue, underscoring parallels with earlier events, and interjecting proverbs and commentary that invite the audience's reflection on the final, disturbing acts. Enraged by the tapestry, Procne proceeds directly to the sylvan hideaway, where her appearance terrifies the old woman, who cannot speak, plays deaf and trembles with fear. Procne addresses three speeches of increasing length and intensity to her unfortunate 'suer' [sister], expressing her affection and her increasing rage. In her last utterance, she resolves to punish Tereus with the 'loier' [payment] his 'felonie' [treachery] deserves (vss 1290–91). As Itys enters the room, the narrator remarks his excessive beauty and misfortune: the rhyme of 'demesure'/ 'mesaventure' [immoderation / misfortune] foreshadows the extremely disturbing events that ensue.

In Ovid, Procne's slaying of her son is described with chilling dispatch. Like a tigress dragging a fawn, she carries Itys off to the woods and brutally stabs him, while Philomena cuts his throat. Ovid's narrator makes no moral judgment; his narrative emphasizes the primal violence of the act. Chrétien's murder scene is less graphic. Procne alone decapitates the boy in one line and hands the head to Philomena (who will later hurl it in Tereus's face). Chrétien's rhetoric emphasizes the moral conundrum from beginning to end. Procne's words to her son are described as a 'merveille' [amazing utterance] prompted by the 'diables' [devil] (vss 1297–98). Procne's use of the same term – 'vil diables' (vs. 1300) – as she blames her husband emphasizes the terrible symmetry of his violence and her retribution: both are wicked acts. At the very moment that Itys throws his arms around his mother, the narrator offers moral commentary: Procne should have stopped herself at that point, Chrétien says, as 'Drois' [Right], 'Nature' [Nature] and 'Pitiez' [Pity] would require this of every human being (vss 1313–17). He concludes with a disarmingly simple aphorism: 'Que mere ne doit son enfent / Ne ocire ne desmembrer' (vss 1318–19) [For a mother should neither kill nor dismember her child]. Just as the narrator's earlier interventions about 'loi' [law] and 'costume' [custom] signal a *problem* within cultural practices and mark the breakdown of social order, so here his attempt to evoke a universal law – mothers ought not to slay their children – calls our attention to the narrative's disruption, a violation that cannot be contained by cultural order, natural law or moral sentiments. Chrétien's wordplay emphasizes the terrible contradictions of this moment: Procne acts knowingly to pay the 'fel' his due, betraying his bloodline (his *fils*) in return for the treachery he has committed against her sister (*Phil*omena). But her actions are equally diabolical: they transgress a fundamental taboo and disrupt universal assumptions about law, natural order and maternal feelings. Just before Procne beheads Itys, the narrator again comments that this is a work of 'dyablie', prompted by the 'dyables' (vss 1330–31).

Recent interpretations of Procne's killing and cooking of her son reflect the text's ambivalence about female revenge and power. Burns emphasizes Procne's transformative resistance; she acts to 'extricate herself from an unwitting collusion in producing ravishers of women' and to 'stop the cycle of abuse'.[57]

---

[57] Burns, *Bodytalk*, p. 142.

Possamaï-Perez observes that Procne, more darkly portrayed than in Ovid, is as 'Machiavellian' as her husband. But she also remarks that Procne's verbal manipulation of Tereus (whom she invites to an intimate dinner for three) can be compared to Lunete's manipulation of her mistress in *Yvain*,[58] and notes further that the designation of the old lady as a *mestre* recalls the role of Thessala in *Cligés*.[59] The designing women of *Philomena* thus prefigure more positive roles of female accomplices and helpmates in the later romances. Jones reminds us that medieval audiences might have seen antifeminist fears of women's destructive sexual powers confirmed in the revenge plot,[60] but, in her final assessment, she stresses the transformative power of Chrétien's text to reveal what has been hidden, the 'savage, disruptive violence' that 'lies beneath the closest family ties'.[61]

The critics' ambivalence about the sisters' revenge reflects the paradoxical position of women in *Philomena*, which mirrors women's problematic status in Chrétien's Arthurian romances. Among his female characters, Procne and Philomena are those who are most brutally mistreated *and* those who act the most powerfully to protest their oppression. Their contradictory status differs in degree but not in kind with many of Chrétien's Arthurian women, who are both central and marginal; mistreated but also resourceful; dependent upon knights for protection, but also possessed of sexual powers that they know how to wield.[62] Similarly, Chrétien's female romance characters, through their troubling resistance or problematic presentation, are often the catalyst for the readers' critical analysis of deeper tensions and violent conflicts. Whether Chrétien invites his audience to protest women's mistreatment, admire their resourcefulness, or fear their dreadful powers, their disruptive presence often prompts critique. Readers seeking to understand Chrétien's analysis of gender relations and the violence that subtends chivalry in his Arthurian romances might well recall his representation of Tereus's treachery and the sisters' revenge in *Philomena*.

Chrétien's final textual transformation occurs at the moment of metamorphosis, when Tereus charges the sisters and all three fly up as birds. Chrétien names not only the hoopoe (Tereus), as does Ovid, but also the swallow and the nightingale – in just the order he names them in *Cligés*.[63] He deems this moment a 'merveille' (a word that he has earlier used to describe Procne's words to Itys). Ovid's bird retains his phallic and military power; he has a 'stiff crest' on his head and a long beak instead of a sword; 'he is the hoopoe, with the look of one armed for war' (vss 673–74). Chrétien moralizes and denigrates the hoopoe, depicted as a filthy bird, 'dirty, disgusting, little and base' (vs. 252), whose miserable condition reflects Tereus's moral depravity in inflicting 'sin' and 'shame' on the girl (vss 1450–51).

---

58 Possamaï-Perez, 'Chrétien de Troyes au début du XIVe siècle', pp. 174–75.
59 Possamaï-Perez, 'Chrétien de Troyes au début du XIVe siècle', p. 176.
60 Jones, 'The Daughter's Text', p. 169.
61 Jones, 'The Daughter's Text', p. 181.
62 See Burns, *Bodytalk*, pp. 151–202, and Krueger, *Women Readers*, pp. 33–67.
63 Chrétien's specific mention of the swallow and nightingale may indicate his knowledge of Hyginus's version of the myth, as noted by Edith Benkov, 'Hyginus's Contribution to Chrétien's *Philomène*', *Romance Philology*, 36 (1983), 403–6.

In the same vein, Chrétien moralizes the song of the nightingale, with a paradoxical twist. Singing 'as sweetly as she knows how' in the springtime, the
nightingale carries a bitter message: 'oci! oci!' ['kill! kill!']. Her song, the moralist
explains, reminds us that wicked men who betray a wise and courteous young
woman deserve to die a dishonorable death (vss 1454–68). The poem's last
words – 'oci! oci!' – thus offer an ambivalent image of female power.
Philomena's sweet and artful voice has been restored, but her message is blood-
thirsty. The song of the nightingale, an inspiration to lovers in numerous courtly
lyrics,[64] here delivers a warning to those who would betray love. The narrative
voice, which has previously strongly condemned men's and women's violence,
now echoes with the terrifying sweetness of a female voice. As the poet brings
his story into the courtly domain of lyric springtime, he establishes a link
between poetic discourse and bestial impulses, in the past and the present.

Philomena's Epilogue bears the mark of a master storyteller whose marvellous
transformation weaves together courtly moralization, lyric imagery and a
haunting poetic utterance of the violence that lurks beneath courtly discourse.
The conclusions of Chrétien's Arthurian romances will be no less richly textured
and provocative. They, too, will invite continuation beyond the frame of the tale.
If the author of the *Ovide moralisé* subsequently pens an interpretation that
differs 'absurdly' from Ovid's tale, as we have discussed at the beginning of this
essay, he has perhaps been led along the path of moralization by Chrétien's own
artful translation. To be sure, the allegorical exegesis of *Philomena* in the *Ovide
moralisé* bears no more resemblance to Chrétien's original *sens* than the allegory
of the *Queste del Saint Graal* bears to the enigma of Chrétien's *Conte del Graal*; in
both cases, the later medieval texts apply Christian explanations to earlier material that resists easy categorization. Yet, in a sense, just as it is possible to see how
the questions left unanswered by Chrétien's story of Perceval may have inspired
the Christianized versions that followed it, so we might understand how the
moral paradoxes of Chrétien's *Philomena* could have prompted further commentary. Chrétien sows the seeds for creative continuation of the Ovidian tradition
in the Middle Ages by crafting a troubling tale that highlights tensions inherent
in the social order and that portrays brutal acts as moral conflicts demanding
critical reflection. Recasting the myth of Tereus, Procne and Philomena as a
psychological drama that implicates all those who speak about love, probing the
political and sexual tensions that subtend courtly discourse and that romance
may both conceal and expose, Chrétien ushers in the age of Ovid and his own
Arthurian romances with bittersweet élan.

---

[64] As detailed by Wendy Pfeffer, *The Change of Philomel: The Nightingale in Medieval Literature*
(New York, 1985).

9

Erec et Enide: *The First Arthurian Romance*

DONALD MADDOX and SARA STURM-MADDOX

Erec et Enide enjoys pride of place among the works of Chrétien de Troyes and in the history of medieval narrative fiction as well. First among the Champenois poet's five Arthurian romances, it also marks a new departure in medieval vernacular narrative: it is the first Arthurian *romance*, in contrast with the earlier *romans d'antiquité*, the Latin pseudo-chronicle of Geoffrey of Monmouth, the *Historia regum Britanniae* (c. 1137), and its vernacular avatar, the *Brut* of the Anglo-Norman poet Wace (1155).[1] As regards versification, like Wace's *Brut* and such 'romances of antiquity' as the *Roman de Thebes*, the *Roman d'Eneas*, and the *Roman de Troie*, Chrétien's narratives are in rhyming octosyllabic couplets; yet he defied the metric constraints of the octosyllabic line to achieve a syntactic suppleness prefigurative of the kind of *prose* that emerged around 1200 in Old French fiction and chronicle.[2] Chrétien was also an innovator in terms of form. Whereas Geoffrey and Wace depict the rise, political and social fortunes and ultimate fall of Arthur's realm, Chrétien's Arthurian court assumes prominence only at the beginning and end of the story and sporadically in between. These 'Arthurian scenes' are largely ceremonial *loci* at which to initiate heroic exploits, positively sanction their completion, or else to bring the adventuring hero momentarily into contact with the court.[3] Chrétien thus sacrifices the comprehensive Arthurian *historia* elaborated by Geoffrey and Wace, choosing instead to portray his eponymous hero or couple against an attenuated background of Arthurian pseudo-history.[4] He relinquishes the 'epic' military campaigns

---

[1] On this background see the articles, above, by John Baldwin and Norris J. Lacy, and by Laurence Harf-Lancner. See also Erich Köhler, *L'Aventure chevaleresque: idéal et réalité dans le roman courtois*, trans. Eliane Kaufholz (Paris, 1974), pp. 10–11.

[2] See Jean Frappier, 'La Brisure du couplet dans *Erec et Enide*', *Romania*, 86 (1965), 1–21; and Emmanuèle Baumgartner, 'Vers, prose et fiction narrative', in *Shifts and Transpositions in Medieval Narrative: A Festschrift for Elspeth Kennedy*, ed. Karen Pratt (Cambridge, 1994), pp. 1–9.

[3] See Wilhelm Kellermann, *Aufbaustil und Weltbild Chrestiens von Troyes im Percevalroman* (Halle, 1936), on the 'Haupt-Artusszene'.

[4] On the 'divorce from history' in *Erec* and the emergence of a pseudo-historical mode in *Cligés*, see D.H. Green, *The Beginnings of Medieval Romance: Fact and Fiction, 1150–1220* (Cambridge, 2002), pp. 178–80; and Donald Maddox, 'Pseudo-Historical Discourse in Fiction: *Cligés*', in *Essays in Early French Literature Presented to Barbara M. Craig*, ed. Norris J. Lacy and Jerry Nash (Birmingham, AL, 1982), pp. 9–24. On the marginalization of kingship in Chrétien's romances, see Peter Haidu, *The Subject Medieval and Modern: Text and Governance in the Middle Ages* (Stanford, CA, 2004), pp. 94–100.

featured by Geoffrey and Wace in favour of heroic episodes linked by a developmentally meaningful design, a format well exemplified in *Erec et Enide*.[5]

At Easter, King Arthur decrees the observance of the customary hunt of the White Stag. His nephew Gauvain warns against it, because according to that custom the slayer of the stag must kiss the loveliest maiden at court, and the five hundred young knights will each be eager to assert in combat the supreme beauty of his own beloved. Yet Arthur insists, and the hunters all depart save Erec who, hastening after them, suddenly offers to accompany Queen Guenevere and her lady-in-waiting. They encounter an armed knight, his maiden, and a malicious dwarf who strikes first the Queen's attendant, then Erec. The latter, unarmed, vows to pursue the knight, procure arms and avenge the insults. Meanwhile the King himself has taken the stag, but as Gauvain foresaw, each knight insists that his own beloved receive the customary kiss. To forestall strife, Guenevere has the ritual deferred until Erec's return. Far from court, Erec participates in the enactment of another local tradition, the Custom of the Sparrowhawk, in which he defeats the knight with the dwarf by championing a beautiful maiden (Enide, as we later learn) and returning with her to court. There Arthur and his knights unanimously acclaim her supreme beauty, and the king bestows upon her the kiss that completes the White Stag custom. Here, says the narrator, 'ends the first verse'.

Arthur hosts the wedding of Erec and Enide and a tournament in which Erec wins the highest accolades. After the newly-weds repair to Carrant, in the kingdom of Erec's father, Lac, a crisis confronts them: Erec neglects his chivalric responsibilities to dally with Enide. Learning that his companions are resentful of his conduct, she utters a tearful lament that Erec overhears in part and exacts its reason. He orders their immediate departure and enjoins her to observe total silence. Both are severely tested in progressively dangerous adventures that culminate in their full reconciliation. Then in the supreme challenge, the redoubtable 'Joy of the Court', Erec rescues a knight and his lady from prolonged bondage to a nefarious custom. Having effected the couple's return to courtly society, Erec and Enide rejoin King Arthur who, after the death of King Lac, mounts a sumptuous coronation for them both.

In the prologue (vss 1–26) we learn that this story derives from 'D'Erec, le fil Lac' [Of Erec, Son of Lac],[6] a tale often told before 'kings and counts' by itinerant entertainers who 'mutilated and corrupted' it (vss 20–22).[7] 'Cresti̇ens de Troies' (vs. 9) is eager to enhance the fortunes of the story by setting it into writing, thus placing it into memory ('en memoire', vs. 24) unto the end of time, 'Tant con durra cresti̇entez', vs. 25 [as long as Christianity endures].[8] Despite the playful

5   Frappier noted that Chrétien prefers 'characters that progressively construct themselves, that develop by finding adventures and tests for themselves'. Jean Frappier, *Chrétien de Troyes, l'homme et l'œuvre* (Paris, 1968, 2nd edn), p. 65.

6   Chrétien de Troyes, *Erec et Enide*, ed. and trans. Jean-Marie Fritz, in *Romans suivis des Chansons, avec, en appendice, Philomena*, gen. ed. Michel Zink (Paris, 1994), vs. 19. Citations are from this edition unless indicated otherwise.

7   All English translations from the Old French are our own.

8   The appellative 'de Troies' here is a hapax legomenon in Chrétien's works. See Glyn S. Burgess, *Chrétien de Troyes: Erec et Enide* (London, 1984), pp. 12–13.

sonority of 'crestïentez – Crestïens', this is no idle boast. Unlike the courtly entertainers who trafficked this adventure tale – a 'conte d'aventure' (vs. 13) – through oral tradition, Chrétien has transformed it into a 'mout bele conjunture', vs. 14 [a very beautiful composition], notable for the superior assembly – conjoining – of its narrative components.[9] Moreover, he has made it the vehicle of profound ethical significance, by heeding the maxim of writers trained in ecclesiastical and monastic schools: 'Doit chascuns penser et entendre / A bien dire et a bien aprendre', vss 11–12 [one should determine and strive to speak eloquently and to edify well].[10] Hence an instructive design, to 'Atorne[r] a sens' (vs. 5), that is, to imbue the story with meaning.

The scope and subtlety of this ambitious poetic and moral agenda are antici-pated remarkably well in the first section of the romance, 'Li premerains vers' (vss 27–1840).[11] This account of the events culminating in Arthur's bestowal of the ritual kiss upon Enide is a miniature masterpiece; opening the first of Chrétien's romances – as well as the first vernacular Arthurian romance of the Middle Ages – it sets an extremely high standard for the nascent genre.

As in most of Chrétien's later romances, *Erec et Enide* opens in a large assembly at Arthur's court.[12] The main intrigue grows from a conflict that leads Erec to his principal exploits far afield. Clashing markedly with the hunters' nondescript surcoats, fleet hunting horses and bows and arrows, Erec first appears in sumptuous attire hardly appropriate for either hunting or jousting, and though astride a charger, he is unarmed but for a sword.[13] Although he first rides headlong in the direction of the hunts, he then deliberately lingers with the Queen and her attendant. This scene, which turns his itinerary away from both the court and the chase, hints that he, unlike the ardent hunters bent on honouring their chosen favourites, has not yet encountered his beloved.

After the encounter with the arrogant knight, Erec pursues him and his party to Lalut, on the eve of the enactment of a custom in which the knight, Ydier, is to be a contender along with his lady. Unlike the Arthurian cynegetic Custom – hunting the White Stag – the Custom of the Sparrowhawk is individual, not collective: two knights vow each to uphold by force of arms his maiden's supreme beauty, so that she may claim the sparrowhawk. Although eager to confront Ydier, Erec has no lady; then he meets the daughter of a poor vavassor,

---

9 On the background of *conjointure*, a key exordial term in Chrétien's writings, see Douglas Kelly, 'The Source and Meaning of *conjointure* in Chrétien's *Erec* 14', *Viator*, 1 (1970), 179–200; and Claudia Villa, 'Per *Erec*, 14: "une molt bele conjointure" ', in *Studi di filologia medievale offerti a D'Arco Silvio Avalle* (Milan, 1996), pp. 453–72.

10 On the evidence of Chrétien's clerical formation, see Tony Hunt, 'Tradition and Originality in the Prologues of Crestien de Troyes', *Forum for Modern Language Studies*, 8 (1972), 320–44; and his 'Chrétien's Prologues Reconsidered', in *Conjunctures: Medieval Studies in Honor of Douglas Kelly*, ed. Keith Busby and Norris J. Lacy (Amsterdam, 1994), pp. 153–68.

11 Literally, 'the first verse', thus identified in vs. 1840, which closes the section: 'Ci fine [here ends] li premerains vers'. On 'vers' as 'narrative sequence', see Kelly, 'Source', p. 189. See also Reto R. Bezzola, *Le Sens de l'aventure et de l'amour: Chrétien de Troyes* (Paris, 1947), pp. 87–88.

12 On the Arthurian opening in Chrétien's romances, see Donald Maddox, *The Arthurian Romances of Chrétien de Troyes: Once and Future Fictions* (Cambridge, England, 1991), pp. 129–32.

13 For detailed analysis of this portrait, see Alice M. Colby, *The Portrait in Twelfth-Century French Literature: An Example of the Stylistic Originality of Chrétien de Troyes* (Geneva, 1965), pp. 104–12.

his host, and offers to claim the prize for her.[14] The narrator's portrait of Enide confirms the wisdom of his choice: 'De ceste tesmoingne Nature / C'onques si bele creature / Ne fu veüe en tot le monde', vss 421–22 [Concerning her, Nature bears witness that such a beautiful creature had never before been seen in all the world].[15] Incited to prowess by her presence, Erec defeats Ydier and dispatches him to report his defeat to the Queen, now appropriately avenged.

If initially the political tensions at Arthur's court seem unrelated to Erec's solitary adventure, we soon see that within the *premerains vers* they are tightly intertwined.[16] As Arthur prepares to bestow the customary 'baisier', his knights vehemently object '*Que ce n'iert ja fait sanz deresne / D'espee ou de lance de fresne. / Chascuns vuet par chevalerie / Desranier que la soe amie / Est la plus bele de la sale; / Mout est ceste parole male*', vss 293–98 ['*that this will not be settled without recourse to the sword or to an ash-tree lance. Each one wants to prove by chivalric means that his beloved is the fairest in the hall; this word bodes ill indeed*' (emphasis ours)]. Their rejection of long-standing protocol sets them utterly at odds with Arthur, though, thanks only to the Queen's insistence, they defer the matter until Erec's return.

Significantly, each of the two interlaced narratives is organized around a *costume*, or custom. These 'legalistic' mechanisms, frequent in Chrétien's romances and elsewhere in Old French romance, are seldom reminiscent of the customary laws in contemporaneous feudal society. They are literary devices, depicted as social protocols observed in specific locales; some involve marvels or enchantments, while the 'evil' customs are often abolished by the hero.[17] The customs of White Stag and Sparrowhawk each feature, as 'prize', an exceptional creature of the natural world; the *white* stag is further suggestive of the *super*natural world of Celtic folk tradition, in which a white animal often serves as a call to adventure.[18] Moreover, the formal properties of both customs are remarkably similar, and because in both masculine prowess designates superlative feminine beauty, they could well be seen as variants of a courtly 'game' that we might appropriately call 'La plus belle'.

The *contrasts* between the two, however, are especially revealing: whereas the collective hunt prevents each participant from upholding *by force of arms* ('desranier', vs. 55) the supreme beauty of his own favourite, in the struggle for

---

[14] A vavassor (< Lat. *vassus vassorum*) is a minor vassal. Enide's father is married to the sister of the local count, his feudal lord. On Enide's kinship relations, see Donald Maddox, *Structure and Sacring: The Systematic Kingdom in Chrétien's 'Erec'* (Lexington, KY, 1978), pp. 150–55.

[15] On this description of Enide's ideal beauty, see Colby, *Portrait*, pp. 138–44.

[16] The interlacing of narrative episodes, a technique of great complexity in the thirteenth-century prose romances, is infrequent and less intricate in Chrétien's romances. See Eugene Vinaver, *The Rise of Romance* (Oxford, 1971), ch. 5, 'The Poetry of Interlace', pp. 68–98. On interlace and *conjointure* in Chrétien, see Kelly, 'Source and Meaning', pp. 197–99.

[17] On the customs in Chrétien's romances, see Maddox, *Arthurian Romances*; and his 'La Représentation du droit coutumier dans les romans de Chrétien de Troyes', in *Le Droit et sa perception dans la littérature et les mentalités médiévales*, ed. D. Buschinger (Göppingen, 1993), pp. 133–44; and Erich Köhler, 'Le Rôle de la coutume dans les romans de Chrétien de Troyes', *Romania*, 81 (1960), 386–97.

[18] See Bezzola, *Sens*, pp. 94–95; Roger Sherman Loomis, *Arthurian Tradition and Chrétien de Troyes* (New York, 1949), pp. 68–70; R. Harris, 'The White Stag in Chrétien's *Erec et Enide*', *French Studies*, 10 (1956), 55–61; and Marcelle Thiébaux, *The Stag of Love* (Ithaca, NY, 1967).

the avian prize the female contestant claims the sparrowhawk while her armed defender stands ready to uphold her claim ('desranier', vs. 575) precisely *by force of arms*. The King's Custom thus owes its peaceful completion to the couple's joint victory in the aristocratic and chivalric Custom, which legitimates determination of 'La plus bele' according to a protocol that, unlike the older Arthurian custom, exalts chivalry and the courtly couple. Hence a symbolic – and salutary – accommodation of the ambitions of the noble youths at Arthur's court, at which Enide, having at Erec's request exchanged her threadbare shift for regal attire provided by Guenevere, emerges as the radiant *mediatrix* of the feudal king *primus inter pares* – first among peers – and his restless barons.[19] Questioned by Arthur, who proposes Enide as recipient of the kiss, they proclaim in unison: 'Baisier la poez par droit, / Car c'est la plus bele qui soit', vss 1819–20 ['You may rightfully kiss her, for she is the most beautiful of all'].

Annual designation of 'La plus bele' might seem but a frivolous courtly pastime, yet the stakes are extremely high. The youthful knights – the *jeunes* – at Arthur's court are evocative of the contemporary rise in northern France of a self-conscious chivalric class with its own values and priorities.[20] These are nonetheless eclipsed in Arthur's solemn address on the state of the realm (vss 1789–1810), which evinces instead his intractable resolve to fulfill his political, social and moral obligations as feudal monarch:[21] he must ensure right and justice for all alike, but also maintain the customs and protocol of his regal heritage. His emphasis explains much about both his rigorously 'traditionalist' stance in this segment and his desire to renew the old cynegetic custom 'come what may'.[22]

In sum, the *premerains vers* subordinates the nascent amatory intrigue to the elaboration of an operative fiction of mediation between a staunchly conservative feudal monarch and a volatile chivalric class eager to assert its power and independence. Subsequently, the couple's wedding culminates in a tournament sponsored by Arthur, hence on his part a further symbolic accommodation of chivalry, while Erec, who betters all contenders, is now its somewhat idealized exemplar. Chrétien then deftly modulates from the public to the private sphere by reconfiguring the dominant emblem in each of the two customs as a figure of erotic fulfilment for both knight and lady:

> Cers chaciez qui de soif alainne
> Ne desirre tant la fontainne,
> N'esprevier[s] ne vient au reclain

---

[19] On female mediators in *Erec*, see Maddox, *Structure and Sacring*, pp. 94–101; 143–55. See also Moshé Lazar, 'Lancelot et la *mulier mediatrix*', *L'Esprit Créateur*, 9 (1969), 243–56.

[20] Georges Duby, 'Les "Jeunes" dans la société aristocratique dans la France du Nord-Ouest au XIIe siècle', in *Hommes et structures du Moyen Age* (Paris, 1973), pp. 213–25; and Hervé Martin, *Mentalités médiévales: XIe-XVe siècle* (Paris, 1996), pp. 322–24.

[21] For a detailed analysis of this passage, see Maddox, *Arthurian Romances*, pp. 25–32.

[22] Arthur's position is evocative of the coronation charter of Henry II (1154), who vows to uphold all of the 'concessions, donations, liberties and free customs' upheld by his grandfather, Henry I (1100–35), and to abolish all 'mauvaises coutumes' ('bad customs') that Henry I had abolished during his reign. That decree is excerpted by Charles Petit-Dutaillis, *La Monarchie féodale en France et en Angleterre* (Paris, 1971), p. 109.

> Si volentiers con il a fain,
> Que plus volentiers n'i venissent,
> Ainçois que il s'entretenissent. (vss 2077–82)

[The hunted stag athirst craves less the spring, the famished sparrowhawk heeds less eagerly the summons, than they hastened there then to that embrace.]

Likewise, the kiss is transposed from symbolic court ritual to the amatory register: 'De baisier fu li premiers jeus', vs. 2097 [The opening play was to kiss]. Returning to King Lac's realm, the heir-apparent and his bride are welcomed enthusiastically by the subjects of Erec's father. In some respects, Erec begins to comport himself as an exemplary monarch by cultivating chivalric solidarity through *largesse* and dispatching his handsomely equipped knights to tournaments.[23] The story of this beautiful young couple, now happily married and on the threshold of sovereignty, could logically end at this juncture.

The horizon soon darkens, however, because Erec, previously the charismatic agent of knightly enterprises, now forsakes his chivalric duties, even shunning tournaments in order to consecrate himself entirely to nuptial bliss. The couple's seclusion occasions murmuring among the nobles: 'Ce disoit trestoz li bernages / Que granz duelx est et granz domages, / Quant armes porter ne voloit / Tex bers con il estre soloit', vss 2455–58 [The barons were all saying that it was terribly sad and unfortunate that a man as valorous as he used to be no longer cared to take up arms]. Hearing of this talk, Enide is deeply distraught, and one morning as Erec slumbers beside her she tearfully bemoans her own role in the eclipse of his chivalric renown: 'Bien me devroit sorbir la terre, / Quant toz li mieudres chevaliers, / . . . / A de tout en tout relinquie / Por moi tote chevalerie. / Donques l'ai je honi por voir', vss 2494–95; 2499–2501 ['Would that the earth engulf me, that the greatest among knights . . . has utterly forsaken all chivalry for me. Thus it is I who have shamed him']. Registering only her last, enigmatic words – 'Con mar i fus', vs. 2503 ['Woe that you were there!'],[24] Erec exacts this reluctant explanation of the truth as she perceives it: 'Recreant vos apelent tuit . . . il m'en metent le blasme sus. . . . Et dïent tuit raison por qoi, / Que si vos ai lacié et pris / Que tot en perdez vostre pris, / Ne ne querez a el entendre', vss 2551; 2556; 2558–61 ['Everyone calls you a recreant. . . . They blame me for it . . . and say it's because I've captured you so completely that you care for nothing else and are losing your reputation'].

Although something has gone terribly awry here, the nature of the underlying problem is as yet obscure. Nor does Chrétien hasten to clarify matters, having us instead perceive the crisis from the point of view of Enide, until now the almost wordless member of the couple. When she timorously proposes that he alter his conduct so as to silence the charges and recover his former prestige, misunderstandings proliferate in rapid succession. Erec immediately concurs

---

23 On feudal *largesse* and its functions, see Aaron J. Gourevitch, *Les Catégories de la culture médiévale* (Paris, 1983), 'Servir et distribuer', pp. 250–63.

24 Cf. ms. BNF fr. 794: 'con mar fus' ['how dreadful for you']. *Les Romans de Chrétien de Troyes: Erec et Enide*, ed. M. Roques (Paris, 1952), vs. 2503.

with her disclosure, but then, abruptly and without explanation, he orders her to don her best attire and prepare for immediate departure. Terrified, she assumes he is sending her away, but instead he decrees that they will ride out alone together. Adamantly refusing the accompaniment of a protective retinue, he has himself ceremoniously armed in full panoply and thus, like her, will bear the outward trappings of his courtly status.[25]

As in Chrétien's later romances, this principal crisis occurs near the centre of the intrigue and necessitates a subsequent reworking of the story along corrective lines.[26] Its enigmatic outset invites, without endorsing, a gamut of speculations as to motive and misunderstanding.[27] Two elements are repeated throughout: Enide's regret for her fateful utterance – her *parole* that had awakened Erec [28] – and his command that she now maintain silence under all circumstances. The relation between the two of these, however, as well as their relevance to the fundamental issue that had occasioned her words – the stigma of *recreantise* connected with the couple's amatory self-absorption – are initially far from clear.

As the couple venture forth, Enide's beauty and conspicuous elegance create optimal conditions for the testing of Erec's prowess. Obediently preceding him on her best palfrey, she first draws the unwelcome attention of three rapacious knights, then of five others. In both situations, despite anguished hesitation and misgivings expressed in lengthy monologues,[29] she breaks her silence to warn him of impending danger. He responds with accusations of her lack of confidence in his prowess – 'Or me prisiez vos trop petit', vs. 2846 ['You held me in low esteem just now'] – and further harsh injunctions to remain silent, then acquits himself admirably. A third encounter presents a wholly different challenge: when the couple accept an invitation to lodge overnight, their apparently gracious host, Count Galoain, makes covert offers of love and marriage to Enide and plots to dispose of Erec through treachery. To gain time, Enide feigns acquiescence, then warns her husband. When her loyalty and quick wit enable the couple to escape, Galoain pursues them, and Erec, while again emerging victorious from the fray, is seriously wounded.

All of these episodes illustrate the destructive potential of chivalric aggressivity. Erec's first two sets of opponents are not low-born robbers but

---

25 Successive descriptions of arms and attire serve to nuance meaning. See Sara Sturm-Maddox and Donald Maddox, 'Description in Medieval Narrative: Vestimentary Coherence in Chrétien's *Erec et Enide*', *Medioevo Romanzo*, 9 (1984), 51–64.

26 On the comprehensive, crisis-centred organization of Chrétien's narratives, see Donald Maddox, 'Trois sur deux: Théories de bipartition et de tripartition des œuvres de Chrétien de Troyes', *Œuvres et Critiques*, 5 (1981), 91–102; and his 'Medieval Textualities and Intergeneric Form', *L'Esprit Créateur*, 33 (1993), 40–50. See also Green, *Beginnings*, pp. 123–33: 'Double Cycle'.

27 On this question, see the studies cited in Douglas Kelly, *Chrétien de Troyes: An Analytical Bibliography* (London, 1976): Hc9; Hc15; Hc17; Sb3; Ua2; Ua9; Ua10; Ua12; and in Kelly et al., *Chrétien de Troyes: An Analytical Bibliography, Supplement 1* (London, 2002): Ga66; Hc31; Hc32; Hc34; Hc37; Hc42; Hc46; Hc50; Hc51; Hc52; Hc55; Hc56; Hc59; Hc67; Hc68; Hc69; Ke11.

28 On the thematization of 'parole', see Burgess, *Erec et Enide*, pp. 51–54.

29 Beginning with Enide, Chrétien makes extensive use of interior monologue in his romances. See Peter F. Dembowski, 'Monologue, Author's Monologue, and Related Problems in the Romances of Chrétien de Troyes', *Yale French Studies*, 51 (1974), 102–14.

marauding knights, eager for easy gain. Count Galoain's attentions to Enide suggest again, as in the *premerains vers*, that competition occasioned by feminine beauty can have devastating effects on chivalric solidarity. The narrator evokes the senseless wrath of the count's hundred armed men who follow him in pursuit of Erec: 'De mautalant sunt aïrey / Vers celi qui onques nes vit, / Ne mal ne lor a fait ne dit', vss 3536–38 [They are impelled by outrage toward one who had never seen them and had never insulted them or done them harm]. Once defeated, Galoain contritely acknowledges his error, and even sermonizes his companions on his *vilenie* (base conduct), his infringement of the proper relation between beauty and prowess.

The protagonists of these chivalric and courtly lessons have not escaped them without suffering. Erec's singular prowess, however, has been spectacularly reaffirmed. And the resolution of the conjugal crisis too has been achieved, albeit more slowly and indirectly: when Enide, after anxious hesitation between protective speech and obedient silence, at last determines that she must warn her husband of yet another aggressor, the narrator confirms that Erec has learned what he needed to know about his wife:

> Ele li dit; cil la menace,
> Mais n'a talant que mal li face,
> Qu'il aperçoit et conoist bien
> Qu'ele l'aimme sor tote rien,
> Et il li tant que plus ne puet. (vss 3761–65)

> [She warns him; he threatens her, but has no desire to harm her, for he
> sees and understands well that she loves him above all else, and he
> loves her so much that more would be impossible.]

The new arrival, Guivret the Small, proves to be a knight-king who seeks to acquire neither booty nor Enide, but rather to measure himself against a worthy opponent; his armed encounter with Erec, carried out in proper chivalric form, concludes in mutual respect and pledges of aid and friendship.[30] Nonetheless, although exhausted and wounded, Erec decrees that he and Enide resume their journey. They encounter first Kay, then Gauvain, and are obliged to accept the joyful hospitality of Arthur and his travelling court, encamped in a hunting party in the forest.[31] Yet despite the king's insistence that the couple remain, Erec again vows to leave, as adamantly as on their departure from his father's court. Thus the following day they set off together, again unaccompanied, leaving the court to 'demener un duel si fort / Con s'il le veïssent ja mort', vss 4285–86 [grieve as deeply as if they saw them already dead].

At this point there is no further question of *recreantise*, and there is no further prohibition of Enide's speech. Why then this second departure? Again Erec offers no explanation, but the series of adventures that follow contrasts with the

---

[30] On the emergence of this 'knight-king', see Maddox, *Structure and Sacring*, pp. 148; 166–68; 171.

[31] Comparable Arthurian 'interludes' punctuate the protagonist's trajectory in *Le Chevalier au lion* and *Le Conte du graal* and, as here, reaffirm the hero's superior status but also that the principal objective of his itinerary has not yet been attained.

previous encounters in suggestive ways.[32] In the first, neither Enide nor Erec is directly threatened: he responds to the desperate cries of a damsel whose lover is being brutally abducted by two giants. Displaying extraordinary courage and prowess, Erec restores the beleaguered knight to his lady and hastens back to Enide, fearful for her safety. But the wounds from his many battles overcome him, and he falls into a swoon. Believing him to be dead, Enide unleashes a torrent of self-accusation for the fateful *parole* by which she had occasioned their crisis:

> 'He, qu'ai je dit? Trop ai mespris,
> Que la parole ai esmeüe
> Dont mes sire a mort receüe,
> La mortel parole entochie
> Qui me doit estre reprochie.
> Et je reconois et outroi
> Que nuns n'i a corpes fors moi;
> Je seule en doi estre blasmee'.   (vss 4638–45)

> ['Alas! What have I said? I erred grievously when what I uttered caused the death of my lord. My lethal poisonous speech must be held against me, and I realize and concede that no one is guilty but me: I alone must bear the blame for it'.]

Only God in his mercy, explains the narrator, stays her from impaling herself with Erec's sword.[33]

Like the lament of the damsel whose knight Erec had just rescued, Enide's desperate shrieking attracts a knight, the Count of Limors, who hastens to the scene with his retinue. They, like Enide, believe Erec to be dead, and the over-zealous count at once claims the lady as his wife. In an encounter reminiscent of the earlier one with Galoain, he attempts to win her over through flattery and promises; when she defiantly refuses, he determines to force the marriage. During the wedding banquet, as the presumably lifeless Erec lies nearby, the count threatens Enide and then, when she resists him, resorts to violence. Her screams rouse Erec from his swoon: he deals the count a mortal blow, as his sudden 'resurrection' sets the count's terrified entourage to flight. As the couple escape through the moonlit night on a single mount, Erec assures his wife that their period of estrangement has ended. 'Bien vos ai dou tot essaïe', vs. 4915 ['I have tested you well in everything'], he tells her, and pardons her for her unfortunate *parole*: 'Et se vos m'avez rien mesdite, / Je le vos pardoing et claim quite / Et le forfait et la parole', vss 4923–25 ['And if you have misspoken to me, I pardon you and acquit you of both the misdeed and what you said'].

This renewed bond is immediately put to the test. Intent upon claiming Erec's

---

[32] Bezzola (*Sens*, pp. 153–90) identifies them as struggles *accepted* on behalf of an 'other' ('la lutte pour le "toi" '), in contrast with the earlier series of 'aventures subies' that *befall* the couple and entail a 'struggle for selfhood' ('la lutte pour le moi').

[33] On the numerous instances of 'suicide inachevé' in Chrétien's romances, see Marie-Noëlle Lefay-Toury, *La Tentation du suicide dans le roman français du XIIe siècle* (Paris, 1979), pp. 92–140. The motif of false assumption of the hero's demise occurs frequently in Chrétien's romances to generate suspense.

body from the count of Limors and assisting Enide, Guivret the Small arrives on the scene. Neither party recognizes the other. Instructing Enide to remain hidden, Erec advances but is so weakened by his wounds that Guivret easily unhorses him. Enide emerges propitiously from her refuge and, seizing the bridle of Guivret's horse, upbraids him for ignobly attacking a grievously wounded man. Formerly silent and submissive, she now becomes an eloquent advocate for chivalric values, and Guivret complies. Learning their identities, he will preside over Erec's prolonged convalescence.

In both its affective and its societal dimensions, Erec and Enide's reconciliation has deepened and consolidated their marital bond. At this point, the tale's conjugal and chivalric threads are at last conjoined in a secure, indeed triumphant, conclusion.[34] As if to mark this juncture symbolically, Chrétien pauses to describe at length the palfrey given to Enide upon the couple's departure for Arthur's court. A vertical green line running down its forehead divides black colouration on one side from white on the other, suggesting chromatically the couple's passage from tribulation to happiness.[35] The mount's opulent trappings feature delicately carved saddle-bows depicting episodes from the life of Aeneas – of how Dido 'received him in her bed' (vs. 5333) and 'Coment Eneas puis conquist / Laurente et tote Lombardie / Et Lavine, qui fu s'amie', vss 5336–38 [How Eneas then conquered Laurentia and all of Lombardy, and Lavinia, his beloved]. Echoing the classical legacy represented by the *Roman d'Eneas* and its Virgilian model, Chrétien implies in suggestive ways a parallel between the heroic growth of Eneas and that of Erec.[36]

Read as an exemplary ascent to monarchy, the story thus far lacks only the couple's coronation, but that conclusion is significantly deferred. Journeying back to court accompanied by Guivret, they arrive at an imposing fortress, Brandigan, said to be impregnable and richly provisioned within. Erec is eager to lodge there, but Guivret warns him that within the ramparts awaits a difficult and dangerous 'corridor of evil' ['mal trespas', vs. 5414] in which, for some seven years, many a fine knight has met shame and death; none has ever returned. This, explains Guivret, is *La Joie de la cort* (vs. 5457), whose paradoxical promise of 'courtly joy' has long held King Evrain and his subjects at the point of despair.

Following upon the couple's successful quest and reconciliation, this episode might at first glance seem a belated anticlimax. There is no apparent need for further demonstration of Erec's chivalric superiority. Yet he adamantly proclaims his intention to seek the perilous *joie*: 'Car ja de rien que j'aie emprise, / Ne ferai tel recreandise / Que je tot mon pooir n'en face / Ainçois que g'isse

---

34   The couple's previous adventures fall into two consecutive series that acquire meaning cumulatively. See Peter Haidu, 'The Episode as Semiotic Module', *Poetics Today*, 4 (1983), 655–81, esp. pp. 666–73; and Maddox, *Structure and Sacring*, pp. 126–31.

35   Cf. Bezzola, *Sens*, pp. 83–84; and Burgess, *Erec et Enide*, pp. 76–80.

36   On this passage in relation to Virgil's *Aeneid*, see Joseph S. Wittig, 'The Aeneas-Dido Allusion in Chrétien's *Erec et Enide*', *Comparative Literature*, 22 (1970), 237–53; and Lee Paterson, *Negotiating the Past: The Historical Understanding of Medieval Literature* (Madison, WI, 1987), ch. 5, 'Virgil and the Historical Consciousness of the Twelfth Century: The *Roman d'Eneas* and *Erec et Enide*', pp. 157–95.

de la place', vss 5645–48 ['For never in whatever I have undertaken / shall I be so recreant as not to do everything in my power before quitting the lists']. Instead, it is as if the adventure's name itself attracts him, as a harbinger of his own destiny: '– Dex! en joie n'a se bien non, / Fait Erec; ce vois je querant', vss 5458–59 ['God! In joy there is nothing but goodness', says Erec, 'that is what I am seeking'].[37]

The enigma of this allegedly ominous 'joy' is intensified by the news that its principal venue, an orchard beyond the ramparts, is sealed by a virtually impenetrable wall of air. Passing through the sole point of entry, Erec beholds a grisly spectacle: a row of stakes, all but one bearing a helmet and a human head; on the last hangs a blast horn. As he approaches a beautiful damsel reclining beneath a sycamore, he is accosted by a knight of immense stature. Only when he finally betters this formidable challenger is the enigma resolved: the knight, Mabonagrain, once a subject of King Lac, had years ago granted a rash boon to the damsel, his beloved since childhood.[38] Not until King Evrain, his uncle, had knighted him did he learn the nature of his promise: to remain with her in the enchanted orchard and slay every knight who entered therein until a contender could defeat him. His formidable strength ensured the gruesome consequences.

The marvel of the perennially verdant orchard of delights, walled away from the world by air alone; the blast horn; the maiden governing the fate of her lover – these details possibly reminiscent of Celtic antecedents – have led some to argue that the romance stems from a Celtic tale.[39] Some have perceived a discordant amalgam of mythic and courtly/chivalric elements,[40] others a skilful adaptation of traits of the Celtic *merveilleux* to further Chrétien's own meaningful design.[41] Critical consensus nonetheless holds that it is by no means a superfluous prolongation of the fiction, and that its meaning lies in comparison of the secluded couple's mode of existence with the earlier experience of Erec and Enide.[42]

Love and prowess are already identified in Geoffrey of Monmouth's *Historia regum Britanniae* as fundamental attributes of the courtly ideal.[43] In the opening

---

[37] Hence, according to Bezzola, the adventure actively 'sought for', as a 'struggle for the community'. *Sens*, pp. 190–226.

[38] Chrétien often features a rash boon, which entails a pledge to honour a request in ignorance of its nature. See Jean Frappier, 'Le Motif du don contraignant dans la littérature du Moyen Age', *Travaux de Linguistique et de Littérature*, 7 (1969), 7–49; and Philippe Ménard, 'Le Don en blanc qui lie le donateur, réflexions sur un motif de conte', in *An Arthurian Tapestry, Essays in Memory of Lewis Thorpe* (Glasgow, 1981), pp. 37–53.

[39] See, in Kelly, *Chrétien Analytical Bibliography*, Na.d3; Na.d11;Na.d16; Na.d20; Na.e2; Na.e4; Na.e5; Na.e6; Na.e7; Na.e10; Na.e11; Na.e14; Na.e15; Na.e16; and in Kelly et al., *Chrétien Analytical Bibliography: Supplement 1*, Na.d53; Na.d58; Na.d60; Na.e21; Na.e26; Na.e46.

[40] See Gaston Paris, review of Wendelin Foerster, ed., *Kristian von Troyes, Erec und Enide* (Halle, 1909), in *Romania*, 20 (1891), 148–66; and, among other studies, Roger Sherman Loomis, *Arthurian Tradition and Chrétien de Troyes* (New York, 1941), pp. 168–84; Albert Pauphilet, *Le Legs du Moyen Age* (Melun, 1950), pp. 145–47.

[41] See, for example, Jean Fourquet, 'Le Rapport entre l'œuvre et la source chez Chrétien de Troyes et le problème des sources bretonnes', *Romance Philology*, 9 (1955–56), 298–312; and Barbara Nelson Sargent, 'Petite histoire de Mabonagrain', *Romania*, 93 (1972), 87–96.

[42] See Sara Sturm-Maddox, ' "Hortus non conclusus": Critics and the *Joie de la Cort* ', *Œuvres et Critiques*, 5 (1981), 61–73.

[43] See William A. Nitze, 'Erec and the Joy of the Court', *Speculum*, 29 (1954), 691–701; and Barbara

section of *Erec et Enide*, as we saw, their combination became the catalyst of a crisis of chivalric individualism.[44] In Lalut, Erec's newfound love for Enide rekindles his prowess as her champion: 'Tot maintenant qu'il l'a veüe, / Li est mout grant force creüe', vss 913–14 [As soon as he saw her, great strength welled up within him]. In Carrant, this solidarity of love and prowess yields to an eclipse of prowess for the sake of love, then during the couple's quest, love is seemingly overshadowed as Erec makes demonstration of his prowess contingent upon Enide's silence. By the end of their perilous adventures, however, the complementarity between love and prowess has been restored through mutual understanding, and as Erec takes leave of Enide to seek the Joy of the Court, he 'who knew her heart very well' (vs. 5825) assures her that her love makes him capable of surmounting all obstacles: 'S'en moi n'avoit de hardement / Que tant con vostre amors me baille, / Ne doteroie je sanz faille / Cors a cors nule rien vivant', vss 5848–51 ['If I had no courage other than that which your love gives me, I would surely not fear to do combat with any mortal creature'].

Have we merely come full circle, then, back to love as catalyst of prowess? Indeed not, for these two properties, initially functional within the couple's earliest private life, are now fully operative within the public sphere. In contrast, the exile of Mabonagrain and his lady from their social functions recalls, in a grotesquely exaggerated way, the reclusive newlyweds in Carrant.[45] In fact Mabonagrain is overjoyed to be released from a kind of indenture to his lady's will. The lady herself, having willed their isolation, is distraught by its termination, but Enide, now with full mastery of persuasive speech, convinces her of the happiness awaiting them upon their return to life at court. Thus both Erec *and* Enide assume key roles in putting an end to this socially disastrous *délire à deux*. Their collaborative success signifies their own transcendence of the narrowly self-serving propensities to which the *jeune* and his lady are characteristically vulnerable, as well as their hard-won qualification to assume exemplary sovereign roles within courtly society. Hence the symbolically apposite gesture that signals the joyful outcome of the episode: Erec sounds the horn to summon the kingdom to partake in the collective 'joy'. We are reminded of the festivities at Arthur's court celebrating the conclusion of the Custom of the White Stag, which we may term in retrospect an initial 'joy of the court'.[46] Thus, in the episode of the *Joie de la Cort*, Chrétien effectively rewrites the outcome of *Li premerains vers* in a new, collectively more auspicious key.

With the successive conflicts at last resolved, Chrétien returns the couple to the Arthurian court, where their arrival dissipates the King's melancholy. Upon the demise of his father King Lac, Erec requests – wisely, according to the

---

Nelson Sargent-Baur, '*Dux bellorum / res militum / roi fainéant*: La Transformation d'Arthur au XIIe siècle', *Le Moyen Age*, 90 (1984), 357–73.

[44] See Maddox, *Structure and Sacring*, chs 4 and 5.

[45] See Norris J. Lacy, 'Thematic Analogues in *Erec*', *L'Esprit Créateur*, 9 (1969), 267–74; and John F. Plummer, ' "Bien dire et bien aprandre" in Chrétien de Troyes' *Erec et Enide*', *Romania*, 95 (1974), 391.

[46] For the frequency and significant variations of the word 'joie' in the text, see Frappier, *Chrétien de Troyes*, p. 105; see also Sara Sturm-Maddox, 'The 'Joie de la Cort': Thematic Unity in Chrétien's *Erec et Enide*', *Romania*, 103 (1982), 514; 421–22; 527–28.

narrator – that King Arthur arrange the formalities of his succession and corona-tion. While thus consolidating the feudal bond between Erec's patrimonial realm and that of his suzerain, the closing segment unfolds as a glorifying sanc-tion of the couple's ascent to sovereignty. It is symbolic on multiple levels, both religious and secular: coordinated with the liturgical calendar, the sacring takes place at Christmas; the Arthurian plenary court, convened at Nantes, in Brittany, includes both insular and continental kings, counts and dukes, in unprece-dented numbers.[47] Arthur's lavish hospitality begins with the parents of Enide, who are ceremoniously received and identified by name. His *largesse* greatly exceeds even that of Alexander the Great and Caesar: he knights and generously equips four hundred sons of kings and counts, and lays open to the throngs thirty bushels brimming with pieces of silver.

Yet these are merely some of the preliminaries to the coronation itself, whose opulence defies the narrator's ability to depict it adequately (vss 6694–704), as well as his acknowledgement of Macrobius, from whose works he claims to have learned the art of description (vss 6730–35).[48] There follows a series of densely symbolic descriptions of exquisite gifts commissioned by Arthur. On Christmas morning, Erec and his suzerain sit side by side in sculpted ivory chairs identical in all respects. Erec's coronation robe is a marvel of descriptive detail. Lined with the fur of exotic, multicoloured creatures from India,[49] its exterior configures the quadrivium: Geometry limns the dimensionality of the universe; Arithmetic measures its discrete quantities and Music the harmonies that unify it; Astronomy, finally, takes counsel from the celestial bodies concerning past and future (vss 6728–82). The orb of the effulgent sceptre that Arthur places in Erec's right hand is a single emerald the size of a fist, engraved with images of every variety of man, beast, fish and fowl (vss 6862–78).[50] The figurally ornate coronation robe and sceptre 'transform the King's body into a pictorial representation of the Cosmos, . . . a living *axis mundi* – depicting iconically the sacred nature of kingship in courtly society'.[51] At the same time, the cascade of emblematic detail affirms the harmony uniting the elder Arthu-

---

[47] The constituents of this convocation are all evocative of the political sphere of King Henry II. On Christmas Day 1169, in fact, Henry II convened his court in Nantes; his son Geoffrey and his fiancée, Constance, the daughter of Conain IV of Brittany, were also present. See Beate Schmolke-Hasselmann, 'Henry II Plantagenêt, roi d'Angleterre et la genèse d'*Erec et Enide*', *Cahiers de civilisation médiévale*, 24 (1981), 241–46 ; and Helen C.R. Laurie, 'The Arthurian World of Chrétien de Troyes', *Bibliographical Bulletin of the International Arthurian Society*, 21 (1969), 111–19.

[48] The meaning of this much-discussed allusion has been plausibly clarified by Douglas Kelly, *The Conspiracy of Allusion: Description, Rewriting, and Authorship from Macrobius to Medieval Romance* (Leiden, 1999), pp. xiii; 36–37; 47–49.

[49] On these animals, see Glyn S. Burgess and John L. Curry, ' "Si ont berbïoletes non" (*Erec et Enide*, l. 6739)', *French Studies*, 43 (1989), 129–39, and '*Berbïolete* and *dindialos*: Animal Magic in Some Twelfth-Century Garments', *Medium Aevum*, 60 (1991), 84–92.

[50] Some commentators have perceived in this description overtones of late twelfth-century Chartrean neo-Platonism. According to Winthrop Wetherbee, they create the image of a philosopher-king whose significance 'comprehends and transcends the natural order itself'. See *Platonism and Poetry in the Twelfth Century: The Literary Influence of the School of Chartres* (Princeton, 1972), pp. 239–40.

[51] Maddox, *Structure and Sacring*, p. 170.

rian order with the nascent, mediatory order modelled on the exemplary experience of Erec and Enide.

After a solemn Coronation Mass and the largest banquet ever hosted by the King, Arthur bids his guests farewell, thus marking the end of the couple's story: 'E[x]plicit d'Erec et d'Enide'. Thus does Chrétien end his poetically and ethically superior version of the story 'Of Erec, Son of Lac' by transforming the new monarch into the measure of the universe.[52] As we have seen, however, his overriding concern in *Erec et Enide* has been with intimately relating, in increasingly nuanced and profound ways, the story of the eponymous *couple* and the socio-political issues adumbrated in the initial segment. Indeed, this is the only romance by Chrétien to feature the names of two protagonists in its title, and the psychological and poetic delicacy with which he portrays the nascent and deepening love between them, their eagerness and reticence, their fearful doubts and hard-won certainties, contributes in large part to the charm of the story and its telling. The couple, moreover, are joined in marriage, and the intimate dimension of conjugal life is frequently in the foreground in their lengthy period of tribulation. Chrétien's stance as an 'apologiste du mariage d'amour' in his first romance has been recognized as innovative with regard both to the notions of aristocratic courtly poetry and to contemporary reality.[53] Hence too the memorable dimension of his portrayal of Enide: the audacity, in a period that strongly tended to dissociate love and marriage, 'to make of Enide a woman completely fulfilled in and by marriage'.[54]

Moreover, it is evident in retrospect that the depiction of Enide holds a key to the significance of the work as a whole. In the early portrait of the heroine, Nature herself thrice marvels at the superlative beauty of her own creation (vss 411–41). Hence an instance of the 'Nature topos', [55] a descriptive convention that typically casts Nature as the handmaiden of God and as creator of the protagonist, as for example in the twelfth-century Latin philosophical epics of Bernard Silvester and Alain de Lille.[56] Like those authors, Chrétien associates Nature's creation of a perfect exemplar with an ethical development that progressively evolves over the course of the entire work.[57] While the kiss in the White Stag Custom was indeed a beauty prize, to be awarded to 'la plus bele', the sparrowhawk is destined for a lady who is 'Bele et sage sanz vilenie', vs. 572 [beautiful and wise without ignoble traits], and the criterion of merit is underscored by Erec's immediate decision to champion the maiden whose name is as yet unknown to him: 'se il avec soi l'en mainne, / Raison avra droite et certainne / Dou desrainier et dou mostrer / Qu'ele [en] doit l'esprevier porter', vss 644–46 [if he takes her with him, he will have just and certain cause to maintain and

---

52 See Donald Maddox, 'Nature and Narrative in Chrétien's *Erec et Enide*', *Medievalia*, 3 (1977), 59–82.

53 See Frappier, *Chrétien de Troyes*, p. 102.

54 Emmanuèle Baumgartner, *Romans de la Table Ronde de Chrétien de Troyes* (Paris, 2003), p. 48.

55 On the Nature topos in *Erec* and other twelfth-century Latin and French works, see Claude Luttrell, *The Creation of the First Arthurian Romance: A Quest* (Evanston, 1974), pp. 1–13.

56 See Brian Stock, *Myth and Science in the Twelfth Century: A Study of Bernard Silvester* (Princeton, 1972); and Wetherbee, *Platonism and Poetry in the Twelfth Century*. On Chrétien and the *De planctu Naturae* and *Anticlaudianus* of Alain de Lille, see Luttrell, *Creation*, pp. 8–13.

57 See also Maddox, 'Nature and Narrative', pp. 61–79.

demonstrate that she should carry away the sparrowhawk]. That Enide's supreme qualification for the prize is not diminished by her quiet modesty and shabby dress is underscored by Erec's insistence after their triumph in the Custom that she accompany him to Arthur's court in that same humble attire.[58] During their solitary journey, the narrator emphasizes the couple's perfect equality in beauty and moral qualities, thus bringing Erec into the sphere of exemplarity initially attributed to Enide:

> Si estoient igal et per
> De cortoisie et de beauté
> Et de grant debonaireté,
> Si estoient d'une matiere,
> D'unes mors et d'une meniere,
> Que nuns, qui le voir en vuet dire,
> N'en porroit le meillor eslire,
> Ne le plus bel, ne le plus sage.
> Mout estoient d'igal corage
> Et mout avenoient ensamble.
> Li uns a l'autre son cuer emble;
> Onques deus si beles ymages
> N'asambla lois ne mariäges.   (vss 1500–12)

> [So equally paired were they in courtesy, beauty and noble bearing, so well matched in substance, conduct and manner, that none could in truth name the better of the two, nor the more beautiful or the wiser. Very much of one mind, they belonged together, and thus stole each other's heart. Law nor marriage never joined two such beautiful figures.]

From the outset, their quasi-Platonic reciprocal attraction engages the couple in a kind of specular 'rapture'. For Erec, Enide seems to embody a powerfully reflexive quality; she was 'faite por esgarder, / Qu'en li se peüst on mirer / Ausi con en un mireour', vss 439–41 [made to be contemplated, for in her one could see oneself, as in a mirror]. Indeed, 'En li regarder se refait', vs. 1486 [seeing her uplifted him] and inspired him to greater prowess. Enide is no less enraptured by the sight of Erec: 'Mais ne regardoit mie mains / La damoisele le vassal / De bon huil et de cuer leal / Qu'il fesoit li par contençon', vss 1494–97 [But the maiden gazed no less intently nor with less devotion at the young man than he did at her in return]. In short, they are as if mesmerized by their own coequally ideal beauty. This visual euphoria recurs as a prelude to the consummation of their marriage:

> Li huil d'esgarder se refont,
> Cil qui d'amors la voie font
> Et lor message au cuer envoient,
> Car mout lor plait quanque il voient.
> Aprés le message des iauz

---

58 See Sturm-Maddox, 'The "Joie de la Cort" ', 519–21.

Vint la douceurs, qui mout vaut miauz,
Des baisiers qui amors atraient. (vss 2087–93)

[The eyes take delight in gazing, open the way to love and dispatch their message to the heart, for all they see pleases them. After the eyes' message came the more exquisite sweetness of kisses that summon love.][59]

Soon, however, this idyll *à deux* declines into idle self-absorption. The ensuing public censure, along with the *parole* that transforms Erec's reassuringly reflexive mirror into a window opening onto a disturbing reality, create at mid-course of the story an acute sense that the personal qualities of Nature's ideal creations do not alone suffice in the absence of an ethic of action, and it is this ethic that the couple now progressively construct. The scope of Erec's prowess expands outward from self-rehabilitation to service to others and ultimately to society as a whole, while Enide relinquishes the passive role of catalyst – whether of love and prowess, or of masculine aggression – to develop a deliberative voice with which to signify her love and support for Erec, and then to express her discernment and wisdom for the benefit of others as well. Over the course of the romance, they become much more than the ideally matched couple, more than the conventional hero and heroine of idyllic romance. Their liberation of the couple in the deceptively 'edenic' garden, in effecting a reconciliation of Nature and courtly society, reflects their progressive awakening to their responsibilities within the social order. The 'Joy of the Court' is a product of the active ethic they illustrate *together*, enabling them to achieve harmony between the order of human affairs and Nature's creation, the visible universe. The identical crowns designed especially for them symbolically confirm their *conjoined* qualification to reign in their own right, universalizing the cumulative significance – the *sens* – of their exemplary synthesis of love, prowess, marriage and monarchy.

Erec et Enide thus emerges as a milestone in the history of narrative fiction. Here we initially discover Chrétien as a clerical writer with an already mature mastery of the medium of romance narrative and thus capable of addressing fundamental socio-historical tensions. His affinity with the spirit of the contemporaneous philosophical epics goes well beyond a theologico-philosophical treatment of matrimony,[60] to engage many other acute problems confronting feudal society in the age of accelerated transition that saw the emergence of courtly verse romance. It is in the mode of idealism, common to contemporary Chartrean, neo-Platonic writers, that Chrétien initiates the long reflection on his age that marks his entire narrative production, elaborating in *Erec* a heuristic

---

[59] On the role of the eyes in amatory transformations, see Gerard J. Brault, 'Chrétien de Troyes' *Lancelot*: the Eye and the Heart', *Bibliographical Bulletin of the International Arthurian Society*, 24 (1972), 142–53. See also Ruth H. Cline, 'Heart and Eyes', *Romance Philology*, 25 (1971–72), 263–97; and Lance K. Donaldson-Evans, *Love's Fatal Glance: A Study of Eye Imagery in the Poets of the 'Ecole Lyonnaise'* (University, MS, 1980), ch. 1, 'The Eyes' Role in Love Literature Since Antiquity', pp. 9–49.

[60] Luttrell arrives at an unduly restrictive characterization of the overall meaning of the work as a 'mirror of marriage' (*Creation*, p. 77).

fiction that embodies a model of social adequation. While in his later romances he continued to explore some of the darkest conflicts within feudal society, he never returned to the mode of forthright idealization he so masterfully developed in *Erec et Enide*. As his ensuing romances appear in rapid succession, however, we can recognize many vibrant echoes of the work with which he originated his progressively nuanced dialectic of courtly narratives.

10

Cligés *and the Chansons: A Slave to Love*

JOAN TASKER GRIMBERT

Chrétien's versatility was such that each of his romances could be said to stand apart from the others. Yet *Cligés* probably deserves that characterization more than any other, considering its many distinctive features: the prologue vaunting the author's achievements and the pre-eminence of France's culture; the distinctive treatment of Arthur (a warrior) and his court (famous, but peripheral at best); the dominance of Byzantium both as background and source material; the existence of two heroes and two heroines; the unusually large proportion of passages devoted to warfare; the near disjunction between prowess and love; the preponderance of supremely rhetorical monologues and dialogues devoted to love; and a narrator whose ironical stance is so highly developed that it is difficult to ascertain how the author feels about the cast of characters he has created for this bizarre reworking of the legend of Tristan and Ysolt.

For the student and the casual reader, *Cligés* is undoubtedly the least appreciated of the romances; yet, in many ways, it is the key to understanding Chrétien's artistry. Not only is it 'an exercise in virtuosity and literary prowess',[1] it is also a work of intricate intertexuality where the concept of craft is foregrounded, bringing together all the threads of the romance tradition.[2] Moreover, it is the romance that reveals most clearly Chrétien's debt to the troubadours and the link with his beginnings in lyric poetry. For this reason, in my discussion of *Cligés* is embedded an analysis of Chrétien's two chansons courtoises (love lyrics).[3] Of necessity, I have allowed the martial exploits of the two heroes to be eclipsed here by the marital issues.[4] A brief summary of the romance will help situate the various aspects of the work discussed below.

Chrétien presumably modelled this bipartite romance after Thomas's *Roman de Tristan*: the story of Cligés is preceded by that of his father, Alixandre, elder

---

[1]   Jean Frappier, *Chrétien de Troyes: l'homme et l'œuvre* (Paris, rev. edn 1968), p. 121.

[2]   Friedrich Wolfzettel, '*Cligès*, roman "épiphanique" ', in *Miscellanea mediaevalia: mélanges offerts à Philippe Ménard* (Paris, 1998), p. 1490.

[3]   References are to *Cligés*, ed. Stewart Gregory and Claude Luttrell (Cambridge, 1993), and, for the Chansons, to Marie-Claire Zai's edition in *Chrétien de Troyes, Romans, suivis des Chansons, avec, en appendice, Philomena*, genl ed. Michel Zink (Paris, 1994). Translations are my own, though occasionally inspired by Ruth Harwood Cline's ingenious verse translation, *Cligès* (Athens, GA, 2000).

[4]   Lucie Polak estimates that warfare and jousting occupy 38% of Alixandre's story and nearly 30% of Cligés's. See her *Chrétien de Troyes: Cligés* (London, 1982), pp. 22–35.

son of the emperor of Greece and Constantinople. Alixandre, desirous of proving his worth, asks for leave to visit the most renowned court of the time, King Arthur's, where he is warmly received. Arthur soon sails for Brittany, leaving his kingdom in Count Angrés's hands. During the crossing, Alixandre falls in love with Gauvain's sister, Soredamors, who, normally disdainful of love, soon realizes that she is enamoured with him. Both wish to reveal their feelings but dare not. (From here until the end of this first section, the progress of the lovers' rapprochement is interlaced with episodes of war, thanks in part to Guenevere's gift to Alixandre of a silk shirt that Soredamors has stitched with gold thread and a strand of her hair.) When news of Angrés's treachery reaches Arthur, he returns to Britain and triumphs over him with the help of the Greeks, especially Alixandre, whose ruses are as effective as his prowess. Arthur offers his protégé anything he wants, save the crown and the queen. Guenevere then urges Alixandre and Soredamors to confess their love and be united honourably in marriage. Cligés is the fruit of this happy union.

Upon the emperor's death, his younger son, Alis, is crowned, when informed erroneously that Alixandre has perished at sea. Alixandre lets him keep the title of emperor if he agrees never to marry, so as not to disinherit Cligés. Alixandre exhorts Cligés to test his valour incognito at Arthur's court and then dies, as does his grief-stricken wife. Alis promptly yields to the urging of his barons to marry, choosing Fenice, the daughter of the German emperor, though she is already betrothed to the duke of Saxony. Cligés and Fenice fall passionately in love at first sight, but Fenice must marry Alis. Repulsed by the thought of giving her body to a man who does not have her heart (as did Ysolt) and of causing Cligés to be disinherited, she secures from her nurse, Thessala, a magic potion designed to convince the sleeping Alis that he is enjoying her body. Meanwhile, Cligés, combining prowess and ruse, triumphs over the Saxons and defeats the duke in single combat. Having thus secured his uncle's marriage, Cligés sails for Britain, after taking leave of Fenice, and arrives in Wallingford where he participates incognito in a tournament organized by Arthur, defeating in quick succession Sagremors, Lancelot and Perceval; he might have defeated Gauvain if Arthur had not intervened.

On Cligés's return to Constantinople, Alis confers on him all honours except the crown. (Unlike Arthur, he did not think to forbid him the queen!) Once reunited, Cligés and Fenice confess their mutual passion, which Fenice insists they may indulge only if they can avoid its becoming public knowledge. Opting for the ruse of the *fausse mort* ('feigned death'), Fenice obtains another magic potion from Thessala, her death is published far and wide, and she becomes the object of great mourning. The stratagem is nearly undone by three physicians from Salerno who recall the ruse of Solomon's wife and inflict real torture on Fenice's inert body, pouring molten lead into her palms. Eventually, Fenice is 'buried' in a magnificent tomb and then transferred to a beautiful tower, both built by Cligés's trusted serf, Jean. The lovers live happily in seclusion until the spring when Fenice longs to enjoy the garden. A youth discovers them by chance and denounces them. They flee to Britain where Cligés complains of Alis's treachery. Arthur raises a huge army and is about to cross the sea when they learn that Alis has died of grief at his inability to find Cligés. The lovers return to Greece where they are crowned and live happily ever after, though future empresses were closely guarded because of Fenice's negative example.

Chrétien prefaces this double romance with a prologue that demonstrates a highly developed literary self-consciousness and sets the tone for the work that follows. The author identifies himself as the one who composed *Erec et Enide*, wrote about King Marc and Ysolt the Blonde, and produced vernacular versions of works by Ovid (his *Ars amatoria* and *Remedia amoris* and two tales – Pelops and Philomela – from Book VI of *Metamorphoses*). Chrétien then announces his new subject, a Greek youth of Arthur's line, and identifies his source, a book supposedly found in the library of St Peter's Cathedral in Beauvais. Having thus established his credentials, he vaunts French culture, using the *translatio* topos to affirm that the prize for chivalry and learning, once held by Greece and then Rome, has come now to France where he prays it will remain.[5]

Not surprisingly, this celebrated passage, which reveals precious clues about Chrétien's literary activity and his attitude toward his art, has been the object of much critical scrutiny. For Michelle A. Freeman, the term *translatio* – which means not simply transfer, but also translation and transposition – is the key to understanding the poet's artistry or literary *craft* in a work where so much attention is lavished on the arts of Thessala and Jean. The brewing of the magic potion is elaborately depicted and occurs, significantly, at the mid-point of the romance. The construction of Jean's tower and tomb is also described at length.[6] Without the ingenuity and skill of these confidants, Fenice and Cligés would be utterly unable to forge a destiny different from that of Tristan and Ysolt.

Other critics read the *translatio* topos in terms less of cultural supremacy (*translatio studii*) than of political supremacy (*translatio imperii*) and claim that it refers to the political situation either in Chrétien's time[7] or in Arthur's fictional universe. Sharon Kinoshita believes that *Cligés* mirrors the troubled relationship between Greek and Latin Christendom in the period after the First Crusade. At a time when the Franks were simultaneously dazzled by the splendour of the East and disgusted by Byzantine treachery, 'in Chrétien's literary-revisionist version cultural capital indisputably migrates from East to West, with the chivalric pilgrimages of Alexander and Cligés demonstrating by example the ideologies of *translatio* explicitly articulated in the romance's prologue'.[8] Donald Maddox,

---

5   For a summary and update of Tony Hunt's various analyses of Chrétien's prologues, see his 'Chrétien's Prologues Reconsidered', in *Conjunctures: Medieval Studies in Honor of Douglas Kelly*, ed. Keith Busby and Norris J. Lacy (Amsterdam, 1994), pp. 153–68. On the *translatio studii* topos, see Douglas Kelly, '*Translatio studii*: Translation, Adaptation, and Allegory in Medieval French Literature', *Philological Quarterly*, 57 (1978), 287–310; and Faith Lyons, 'Interpretations critiques au XXe siècle de *Cligès*: la *translatio studii* selon les historiens, les philosophes et les philologues', *Œuvres et critiques*, 5 (1980–81), 39–44.

6   Michelle A. Freeman, *The Poetics of 'Translatio studii' and 'Conjointure': Chrétien de Troyes's Cligés* (Lexington, KY, 1979) and her 'Cligés', in *The Romances of Chrétien de Troyes: A Symposium*, ed. Douglas Kelly (Lexington, KY), 1985, pp. 89–131.

7   Fenice's betrothal successively to the duke of Saxony and the emperor of Constantinople may well echo events that occurred in 1170–76. See Fourrier, *Le Courant réaliste*, pp. 160–78; and Joseph J. Duggan, *The Romances of Chrétien de Troyes* (New Haven, CT, 2001), pp. 13–15.

8   Sharon Kinoshita, 'The Poetics of *Translatio*: French-Byzantine Relations in Chrétien de Troyes's *Cligés*', *Exemplaria*, 8 (1996), 315–54 (here, 319). Chrétien's romances were all composed between the Second and Third Crusade, and both his patrons were 'intimately involved in the affairs of the eastern Mediterranean' (317).

for his part, situates the *translatio* within Arthurian 'history'. Pointing out the unusually complicated nexus of kinship alliances found in this romance, he observes that Cligés does not bear the same relation to Alis as Tristan does to his uncle, Marc: Alis is the paternal – not maternal – uncle of Cligés, the superior role of maternal uncle being reserved for Gauvain (brother of Soredamors), who is the maternal nephew of Arthur. Cligés is thus the maternal grand-nephew of King Arthur, and when he becomes emperor of Greece and Constantinople, the Arthurian sphere of influence expands eastward considerably.[9]

The prologue also underscores dramatically the intertextual dimension of this romance, a veritable tapestry into which Chrétien has woven the threads of many different sources. For the elaborate love monologues, he clearly drew on both Ovid and the *Enéas*.[10] He modelled the episode of Angrés's treachery primarily on that of Mordred's treason in Wace's *Roman de Brut*.[11] As for the crucial episode of the *fausse mort*, he apparently used a version of the *Solomon et Marcolfus* tale. [12] The book that Chrétien alleges as his source – if indeed this allusion is more than a simple authority topos – may have contained a variant of tale eleven of the thirteenth-century collection, *Marques de Rome*, in which the hero, also named Cligés, loves the wife of his uncle, the emperor of Constantinople. The wife feigns death, undergoes the ordeal of the molten lead, and the lovers eventually escape to a refuge outside the city.[13] Since this comic tale, which has no ending, is recounted as an example of feminine deception, and Fenice indeed becomes a negative exemplum, it is likely a popularized summary of *Cligés* – and thus an analogue rather than a source. Lucie Polak speculates that Chrétien's source could have contained a Byzantinized version of the Persian tale of *Vis and Ramin*, which features a 'chastity' potion and a happy ending.[14]

The most important of Chrétien's sources for *Cligés* was clearly the legend of Tristan and Ysolt.[15] It is on this tale of Celtic inspiration (and of which *Vis and Ramin* is thought by some to be an analogue) that Chrétien constructed this most Byzantine – in both the literal and figurative senses – of his romances. He was very much influenced by Thomas's *Roman de Tristan* and drew as well on Béroul's version; yet, despite the painstaking work of identifying all the implicit and explicit allusions to the legend[16] and of demonstrating the clever ways in

[9] Donald Maddox, 'Kinship Alliances in the *Cligès* of Chrétien de Troyes', *L'Esprit créateur*, 12 (1972), 12; and his *The Arthurian Romances of Chrétien de Troyes: Once and Future Fictions* (Cambridge, 1991), esp. ch. 1.

[10] Foster E. Guyer, 'The Influence of Ovid on Crestien de Troyes', *Romanic Review*, 12 (1921), 97–134, 216–47; Alexandre Micha, 'Enéas et Cligés', in *Mélanges de philologie romane et de littérature médiévale offerts à E. Hoepffner* (Paris, 1949), pp. 237–43.

[11] Margaret Pelan, *L'Influence du Brut de Wace sur les romanciers français de son temps* (Paris, 1931).

[12] For a summary of this tale, see Urban T. Holmes, Jr., *Chrétien de Troyes* (New York, 1970), pp. 80–84. On the many variations of this popular motif, see Henri Hauvette, *La 'Morte vivante'* (Paris, 1933).

[13] See Gaston Paris, '*Cligès*', in *Mélanges de littérature française du moyen âge*, ed. Mario Roques (Paris, 1910), pp. 308–26.

[14] Polak, *Cligés*, p. 88, and Lucie Polak, '*Tristan* and *Vis and Ramin*', *Romania*, 95 (1974), 216–34.

[15] For a summary and history of the legend from the Middle Ages to the present, see my introduction to *Tristan and Isolde: A Casebook*, ed. Joan Tasker Grimbert (New York, 1995; repr. 2001).

[16] Anthime Fourrier, *Le Courant réaliste*, pp. 124–54; and Polak, *Cligés*, pp. 50–69.

which Chrétien transposed them,[17] there is no real consensus on the overall meaning of this intricate intertextual web. Most discussion has focused on Chrétien's supposed hostility to the legend, as 'evidenced' by Fenice's criticism of Ysolt's conduct. But questions abound. Did Chrétien himself take that harsh critique to heart? Was he hostile to the kind of unbridled passion unleashed by the love potion that the Cornish lovers unwittingly consumed, preferring instead the more reasoned and cautious approach adopted by Fenice? Did he see in her refusal to give her body to a man who did not have her heart a sign of her greater integrity? Many critics have thought so, especially those who see Chrétien as a moralist,[18] and many continue to subscribe to this traditional interpretation, which makes of Fenice the mouthpiece for Chrétien's purported hostility to the Tristan legend.

Fortunately, Peter Haidu's seminal study on aesthetic distance, which demonstrated the dominance of the reality/illusion dichotomy in *Cligés*, encouraged readers to examine the implications that Chrétien's pervasive irony had for interpreting this romance.[19] For example, how is the reader to construe Fenice's overriding concern for her reputation? How can her conduct be seen as morally superior to Ysolt's if she has access to a magic potion that allows her to keep from fulfilling her conjugal duty in order to give her body solely to the man who has her heart? Could Chrétien have possibly approved of the lovers' decision to choose freely to renounce their familial and feudal ties (their betrayal of Alis, Cligés's lord and uncle and Fenice's husband) and to abandon their proper roles in society in order to live together in seclusion? Their sojourn in the tower alludes indirectly to the Joie de la Cort episode in *Erec and Enide*, which presents in an unfavourable light the decision of Mabonagrain and his lady to live apart from society. Tristan and Ysolt betrayed Marc only because they could not do otherwise, dominated as they were by the love potion; they made every attempt to fulfill their roles in society because they had no desire to live on the margins. It seems clear that Chrétien could not have been presenting in Cligés and Fenice a morally superior set of lovers. Their multifaceted betrayal is underscored by the way in which the narrator slyly subverts the 'happy ending' by noting the effect of Fenice's negative example on the lives of future empresses.

Many critics who agree that the classical interpretation of *Cligés* should be nuanced in light of the author's ironic presentation of the lovers continue to believe, nonetheless, that Chrétien was hostile to the Tristan legend, and notably to the idea of a potion-induced passion. Jean Frappier contended, in a highly influential article, that Chrétien adapted the troubadours' concept of *fin'amors* (refined or loyal love) to the more marriage-oriented approach featured in his romances.[20] Frappier believed that the troubadours, who cited the Tristan

---

[17] Michelle A. Freeman, 'Transpositions structurelles et intertextualité: le *Cligès* de Chrétien', *Littérature*, 41 (1981), 50–61.

[18] Wendelin Foerster, ed., *Cligés* (Halle, 1910), p. xl; Gaston Paris, '*Cligès*', pp. 289–90; Frappier, *Chrétien*, pp. 105–6, 112–14.

[19] Peter Haidu, *Aesthetic Distance in Chrétien de Troyes: Irony and Comedy in 'Cligés' and 'Perceval'* (Geneva, 1968); and his 'Au début du roman, l'ironie', *Poétique*, 36 (1978), 443–66; Norris J. Lacy, *The Craft of Chrétien de Troyes: An Essay on Narrative Art* (Leiden, 1980), esp. pp. 23–27.

[20] Jean Frappier, 'Vues sur les Conceptions courtoises dans les littératures d'oc et d'oïl au XIIe

legend frequently, had seen no conflict between Tristan-love and *fin'amors*, whereas Chrétien had made a distinction between the fated and fatal passion of the Cornish lovers and the essence of *fin'amors* founded on the choice of a beloved involving reason and free will. In support of his theory, Frappier cited not only the love portrayed in *Cligés*, where both sets of protagonists fall in love 'naturally', but also the famous 'Tristan allusion' that Chrétien's poet-lover makes in one of his chansons, *D'Amors, qui m'a tolu a moi*.

Before examining the process of enamourment actually described in *Cligés*, let us first consider the celebrated stanza IV of *D'Amors*:

> Onques du buvrage ne bui
> Dont Tristan fu enpoisonnez;
> Mes plus me fet amer que lui
> Fins cuers et bone volentez.
> Bien en doit estre miens li grez,
> Qu'ainz de riens efforciez n'en fui,
> Fors que tant que mes eux en crui,
> Par cui sui en la voie entrez
> Donc ja n'istrai n'ainc n'en recrui. (vss 28–36)

> [Never did I drink of the brew by which Tristan was poisoned; rather, my true heart and good will make me love more than he. I should be very grateful that I was not forced in any way except in that I believed my eyes, by which I have entered the path, which I shall never leave nor renounce.]

According to Frappier, Chrétien was setting up an opposition here between a passion imposed from without, by a love potion, and a love dictated from within, by one's own heart and will. Yet, as Peter Haidu has demonstrated in a detailed semiotic analysis of this lyric, the 'bone volentez' to which the poet alludes in vs. 31 is only his will or willingness to submit to Love's commands after being seduced by the evidence presented to his eyes – his lady's beauty. In this subtle twist so typical of Chrétien's playful style, the poet-lover offers, in essence, a hyperbolic compliment to his lady by stating that her beauty represents no less a constraint than does the imbibing of the famous love philtre.[21] Indeed, the compliment draws its force from the poet-lover's (specious) claim that his ardour is greater than Tristan's.

The idea that Chrétien was celebrating the choice of a lover involving reason and free will simply does not square with the 'love doctrine' set out in the only

---

siècle', *Cahiers de civilisation médiévale*, 2 (1959), 135–56. See also Moshé Lazar, *Amour courtois et 'Fin'amors' dans la littérature du XIIe siècle* (Paris, 1964). According to Andreas Capellanus, *fin'amors* was incompatible with marriage. See his celebrated treatise, *De amore libri tres*, ed. E[mil] Trojel (Copenhagen, 1892; repr. Munich, 1972), or *The Art of Courtly Love*, trans. John J. Parry (New York, 1969). Although this treatise is actually a codification of the love depicted in Occitan lyric poetry, many critics believe in this incompatibility, a view that has been convincingly challenged by William D. Paden, et al., 'The Troubadour's Lady: Her Marital Status and Social Rank', *Studies in Philology*, 72 (1975), 28–50.

21 Peter Haidu, 'Text and History: The Semiosis of Twelfth-Century Lyric as Sociohistorical Phenomenon (Chrétien de Troyes: "D'amors qui m'a tolu")', *Semiotica*, 33 (1981), 1–62, esp. 22–25.

two courtly lyrics attributed with some certainty to him, *Amors tençon et bataille*
and *D'Amors, qui m'a tolu a moi*.[22] Both chansons are variations on the motif of
love service, on the concept that the poet-lover,[23] totally subjugated by 'Amors'
(Love), is willing to serve her without expectation of the slightest reward.[24] In
the first lyric, he complains that Amors acts unjustly, offering him no compensa-
tion for his devoted service, whereas she often rewards false lovers; yet he
would never seek to be free of her dominion. He introduces a significant theme
in vss 23–24, stating that in order to be worthy of Love, 'Raison li covient
despandre / Et mettre mesure en gages' ['One must forfeit reason and pawn
moderation']. It is the 'toll' that he himself paid to enter Love's domain (vss
35–36), and quite willingly did he forfeit *raison* and *mesure,* for he announces that
he is quitting their company for good and intends to remain always under
Love's sovereignty, even if he never obtains mercy. As is well known, the relation of the *fin amant* (loyal lover) to his lady is patterned on that of the vassal to
his lord, but the feudal relation involves reciprocal duties, and although the
poet-lover complains that his suzerain does not reward his service as she should,
he feels bound to remain in her 'domain' – a virtual slave to love.

   The poet-lover's attitude is remarkably similar in *D'Amors, qui m'a tolu a moi*,
where he claims that Love has 'taken him out of himself', depriving him of all
personal initiative and action independent of Love's will.[25] Indeed, he asserts
the very futility even of redoubling his efforts to serve her: he cannot send her
his heart, since it is already hers,[26] and indeed wonders if he is really *serving* her,
as he is only giving her what he owes her! In light of the helplessness expressed
by the poet-lover throughout this lyric and the willing forfeiture of *raison* and
mesure underscored in the other lyric, it is clear that Chrétien's poet-lover is *not*
setting up a distinction between Tristan (*compelled* to love Ysolt) and himself
(*choosing* to love of his own free will).[27]

   The situation is the same for the two sets of lovers in *Cligés*, where the birth of
love is described in a set of monologues and dialogues far more elaborate than

---

22 See Anne Berthelot's commentary on these two lyrics in the Pléiade edition/translation of
    Chrétien's works under the direction of Daniel Poirion, Chrétien de Troyes, *Œuvres complètes*
    (Paris, 1994), pp. 1041–49.
23 I distinguish between Chrétien the trouvère (lyric poet) and his poet-lover narrator.
24 Since 'amors' was feminine in Old French, it is sometimes difficult to decide whether the femi-
    nine pronoun is referring to Amors or to the lover's lady, but the fusion is significant, for there
    is no real need to distinguish between these two imperious 'mistresses'. I refer to Amors as
    feminine in my discussion of the Chansons, but when discussing *Cligés*, where the reference
    to Love's arrow is reminiscent of Cupid, I bow to tradition and refer to it as masculine. Amors
    makes more than forty appearances in *Cligés*, slightly over half of all its appearances in
    Chrétien's romances (Duggan, *Romances*, p. 156).
25 On this chanson as part of an intertextual dialogue with Bernart de Ventadorn's *Can vei la
    lauseta mover* and Raimbaut d'Aurenga's *Non chant per auzi ni per flor*, see Luciano Rossi,
    'Chrétien de Troyes e i trovatori: Tristan, Linhaura, Carestia', *Vox Romanica*, 46 (1987), 26–62,
    esp. 58–59; and Don Monson, 'Bernart de Ventadorn et Tristan', in *Mélanges de langue et de
    littérature occitanes en hommage à Pierre Bec* (Poitiers, 1991), pp. 385–400.
26 On the motif of the displaced heart, see below.
27 For a more detailed analysis, see my 'Chrétien, the Troubadours, and the Tristan Legend: The
    Rhetoric of Passionate Love in *D'Amors qui m'a tolu a moi*', in *Philologies Old and New: Essays in
    Honor of Peter Florian Dembowski*, ed. Joan Tasker Grimbert and Carol J. Chase (Princeton,
    2001), pp. 237–50.

any found in the other romances. Chrétien combined the artistry learned in his activity as a trouvère (lyric poet) with his knowledge of classical and contemporary works – Ovid, troubadour lyric, Thomas's *Tristan* and the *Enéas*. He may owe some motifs, such as the eye conceived as the gateway to the soul and represented as a mirror, to Plato's *Phædrus* and to Arabic erotic literature (*The Dove's Neck Ring* and *The Arabian Nights*).[28]

In *Cligés*, as in *D'Amors*, the catalyst for love is the wondrous beauty of the beloved, a sight that dazzles the beholder, entering the eye like an arrow and lodging in the heart. The force unleashed is as sudden and irreversible as any love philtre.[29] It is the result neither of free will nor of reason, and although the lovers reflect at length on the effects of love and wonder at their inability to resist, when they finally express their desire to love, as do Soredamors and Alixandre, it is only after having been surprised by the abrupt onset of love (described as an assault) and forced to align their own will on that of the imperious god Amors. This surrender is particularly well illustrated by Soredamors's enamourment, which she herself develops in two long monologues. The maiden, described initially as 'disdainful' of love (vs. 446), goes through several stages, first accusing her eyes of treason for wanting to gaze at Alixandre, then stating that, since one cannot love with one's eyes, she must not be in love. In any case, she reasons, she cannot blame her eyes since she controls them, but then she admits that her gaze would not be fixed on someone who did not please her heart. If, by the end of the first monologue, she realizes that her heart is somehow engaged, she still thinks she controls her feelings, a conviction the narrator undermines by framing her lament with comments showing that Amors has taken its revenge on this proud beauty. At the beginning, he notes: 'Bien a Amors droit assené, / Qu'el cuer l'a de son dart ferue. / Sovant palist, sovant tressue, / Et maugré suen amer l'estuet', vss 460–63 [Love has aimed its arrow straight and true, and through the heart she was impaled and often sweats and often pales and despite herself is compelled to love]. And he concludes: 'Vers Amors se cuide desfandre, / Mes ne li a mestier desfanse', vss 528–29 [Against love she thinks she can prevail, but her defence is of no avail].

Only in the middle of her second monologue does Soredamors recognize that Love has assailed her and that she must do its will: 'Par force a mon orguel donté, / Si m'estuet a son pleisir estre. / Or vuel amer, or sui a mestre / Que m'aprandra Amors? Et quoi! / Confeiteman servir le doi', vss 944–48 ['By force he has subdued my pride, now I must be at his pleasure. Now I wish to love. Now I have a master. What will Love teach me? – What indeed! How I must serve him']. She adduces further proof that she was destined to do Love's will when she analyzes her name and realizes that it means 'gilded with love': *sor* (refined gold) + *amors* (love).[30]

Alixandre likewise falls in love at first sight. As he gazes at Soredamors, her

---

[28] Ruth H. Cline, 'Heart and Eyes', *Romance Philology*, 25 (1971), 263–66, 289.

[29] Chrétien's lovers all experience that imperious constraint, and when Love chooses to lodge in the heart of a villain like Tereus (*Philomena*), it can lead to unspeakable brutality, if that love is not reciprocated; see Roberta L. Krueger's essay in this volume.

[30] See Douglas Kelly's analysis of this example of paranomasia (wordplay) in his essay in this volume.

luminous beauty passes like an arrow through his eyes and lodges in his heart. Unlike his proud beloved, he knows he is in love, and his anguish stems from his reluctance to express it. Although he blames Love for hurting its disciples, he refuses to disdain this lesson from his master. Accusing both his eyes and his heart of treason, he characterizes his helpless state by describing the arrow that has subdued him, a description that becomes interwoven with a portrait of Soredamors, for that arrow is none other than her surpassing beauty: 'Li penon sont les treces sores / Que je vi l'autre jor en mer. / C'est li darz qui me fet amer', vss 790–93 ['The feathers are the golden tresses I saw the other day at sea. This is the arrow that makes me love'].

Thus begins the portrait that Alixandre makes of Soredamors, lovingly detailing every trait starting at the top and proceeding downward until his gaze reaches her throat and can descend no farther because the arrow is in its quiver![31] Once he recognizes the links between his sickness, the arrow (and Soredamors) and love, he commits himself solemnly to do Love's will, whatever the cost: 'Or face de moi tot son buen / Si com il doit feire del suen, / Car je le vuel et si me plest; / Ja ne quier que cist max me lest', vss 865–68 ['Now let (Love) do with me all his will, as he should do with one who is his, for I wish it, and it pleases me; never do I want this sickness to leave me'.]

Both Alixandre and Soredamors, then, reach, at the end of their long monologues, a conclusion concerning their relationship with Amors that mirrors perfectly the attitude in Chrétien's lyrics of the poet-lover, who pronounces himself happily constrained to do Love's will. Alixandre's reference to 'the golden tresses' that he 'beheld at sea' reminds us that for Alixandre and Soredamors, as for Tristan and Ysolt, Love's 'assault' occurred while they were at sea. Indeed, as Guenevere sees the couple grow pale, sigh, and tremble, she wonders if they are not seasick. The narrator explains in a passage clearly inspired by Thomas's play on the sonorities of *la mer* (the sea) and *l'amer* (love):[32]

> Espoir bien s'an aparcëust
> Se la mers ne la deceüst.
> Mes la mers l'angingne et deçoit
> Si qu'an la mer l'amor ne voit,
> Qu'an la mer sont, et d'amer vient,
> Et s'est amers li max ques tient.   (vss 547–52)

> [Perhaps she would have realized if the sea had not deceived her. But the sea abuses and deceives her, such that on the sea she does not see love, for they are on the sea and it comes from love, and love is the sickness that holds them.]

These first allusions to the famous legend underscore the similarity of the two situations. Love's arrow, like the love potion, is a symbol for the onset of love in

---

31 See Alice M. Colby, *The Portrait in Twelfth-Century French Literature: An Example of the Stylistic Originality of Chrétien de Troyes* (Geneva, 1965); of the thirty-seven portraits analyzed, ten are from Chrétien's romances and demonstrate his innovative artistry.

32 The corresponding passage in Thomas, where the wordplay includes the adjective *amer* (bitter), appears in the Carlisle fragment edited by Michael Benskin, Tony Hunt and Ian Short, 'Un Nouveau Fragment du *Tristan* de Thomas', *Romania*, 113 (1992–95), 289–319.

two exemplary individuals who are destined to love each other and powerless to resist. The single way in which the enamourment described in *Cligés* differs from that seen in Chrétien's lyric *D'Amors* is that the love is reciprocal (as it is for Tristan and Ysolt). Although the love that binds Alixandre and Soredamors is mutual, they do experience the anguish described in the typical chanson courtoise while waiting to discover if their feelings are indeed reciprocated.

The manner in which this love differs the most from Tristan-love is in the absence of an obstacle – an obstacle that is, however, present in the case of Cligés and Fenice, where allusions to Tristan, and especially to Ysolt, abound. Not only does Fenice rail against Ysolt's conduct, which she considers profoundly immoral, but also she transforms significantly two key elements of the legend, enlisting Thessala's aid to turn the love potion into a brew designed to make Alis a husband in name only, and later to reconfigure the Cornish lovers' real death as a false death that allows Cligés and Fenice to live together in private and leads eventually to the 'happy ending'. Emmanuèle Baumgartner notes that just as Fenice's namesake, the phoenix, rises from the dead, she comes back to life and to love – another inversion of the meaning of the love potion, which in the legend leads to death.[33] Frappier lamented that Chrétien had misunderstood the human and tragic truth of the Tristan legend,[34] but the poet's playful presentation of Fenice's ingenious solutions and her disregard for certain moral issues demonstrate that his intention was hardly to offer a 'new and improved' version.[35]

Nor did he likely wish to parody it. Medieval authors sought to *instruire* (instruct) and *plaire* (please), and Chrétien's romances, besides being highly entertaining, are provocative, designed to engage his listeners/readers in a process of reflection that often parallels that of the hero.[36] None of the four protagonists in *Cligés* appears to evolve, but given the shifting perspectives and the popularity of the Tristan legend, Chrétien's audience could only have been intrigued by the problems posed in this romance. Lucie Polak suggests that the question of whether Fenice was a purer Ysolt or an adulteress could have been a topical debate at the time for courtly listeners who may well have been acquainted with the issues in marriage and annulment proceedings. The second half of the twelfth century was crucial in the formation and development of matrimonial legislative practices in Western Christendom when the Church was both claiming jurisdiction regarding the marriage ritual and grappling with the very definition of marriage.[37] In his *Decretum* (1145), which was rapidly trans-

---

[33] Emmanuèle Baumgartner, *Romans de Chrétien de Troyes* (Paris, 2003), pp. 63–64.

[34] Frappier, *Chrétien*, p. 121.

[35] See my 'On Fenice's Vain Attempts to Revise a Romantic Archetype and on Chrétien de Troyes's Fabled Hostility to the Tristan Legend', in *Reassessing the Heroine in Medieval French Literature*, ed. Kathy M. Krause (Gainesville, FL, 2001), pp. 87–106.

[36] See my *'Yvain' dans le miroir: une poétique de la réflexion dans le 'Chevalier au lion' de Chrétien de Troyes* (Amsterdam, 1988).

[37] David J. Shirt, 'Cligés – A Twelfth-Century Matrimonial Case-Book?' *Forum for Modern Language Studies*, 18 (1982), 75–89. See also Georges Duby, *Medieval Marriage: Two Models from Twelfth-Century France*, trans. Elborg Forster (Baltimore, 1978); A[dhémar] Esmein, *Le Mariage en droit canonique*, 2nd edn, rev. by R[obert] Génestal and Jean Dauvillier, 2 vols (Paris, 1929–35), and James A. Brundage, *Medieval Canon Law* (New York, 1995).

lated into Anglo-Norman, Gratian had argued that a marriage contract was not valid without both *disponsatio* (betrothal or an exchange of vows) and *commixtio* (sexual union).[38] For Peter Lombard, *consensus* was the central ingredient, and once that stage was reached, the union was as difficult to dissolve as a consummated one. At the time, canonists were also discussing grounds for annulment. Among them, they recognized *impossibilitus (coeundi) accidentalis* – impotence caused by physical accident or drug. Given the effects of Thessala's brew, one might question the validity of Fenice's marriage to Alis and, consequently, her adultery with Cligés.[39]

On the other hand, the text never leaves in doubt that she and Alis are married,[40] (nor does Fenice dispute it), as Sally L. Burch points out; she cautions against assuming that the lovers are excused. The lovers' eventual marriage is tainted by adultery and incest (since Fenice is Cligés's aunt by marriage), which is not the case in *Amadas et Ydoine*, written some twenty-five years later, where the author clearly condemns the marriage of adulterers. Although those lovers are in a situation similar to Cligés and Fenice,Ydoine, married unwillingly to the count of Nevers, refuses to consummate her love with Amadis until her marriage has been dissolved, fearing that it would destroy their hopes of a valid marriage. Although, at the time, marriage between adulterers was allowed, public opinion reflected earlier condemnation. The Council of Meaux (845) had specified certain conditions under which an adulteress could marry: the couple had to make public penance, could not be linked by consanguinity or affinity and had to be innocent of the husband's death. Gratian himself, while quoting canons showing that adulterers could marry, cited more than six times the principle of 'Nullus ducat in matrimonium quam prius polluit adulterio' ('No one shall take in matrimony the woman he has previously polluted in adultery'). Burch, noting that the Eastern Church had a stricter code than in the West and that adultery and incest were rampant among the aristocratic laity, suggests that Chrétien's playful treatment of Cligés and Fenice's marriage may have been meant to underscore the decadence of Byzantine society. In any case, it seems clear that *Cligés* was not meant as an epithalamium or hymn to marriage, as earlier critics claimed.[41]

Whereas the romance may have provoked reflection on these issues among Chrétien's listeners, Fenice's own internal debate does not, of course, raise any such issues, although her focus on avoiding the split between her body and her heart certainly relates to the question of consent in marriage. Moreover, it is surely significant that in a bipartite work, which naturally encourages comparison between the two sets of protagonists, two starkly different marriage models are presented.[42] Alixandre and Soredamors are betrothed only after they have

---

[38] See *Gratiani Decretum: la traduction en ancien français du Décret de Gratien*, ed. Leena Löfstedt (Helsinki, 1992), cited by Sally L. Burch, '*Amadas et Ydoine* and *Cligès*, and the Impediment of Crime', *Forum for Modern Language Studies*, 36 (2000), 185–95 (here, n. 27).

[39] Polak, *Cligés*, pp. 89–90.

[40] Burch, '*Amadas et Ydoine* and *Cligès*', p. 191.

[41] Burch, '*Amadas et Ydoine* and *Cligès*', p. 192. These 'earlier critics' include Paris, *Cligés*, I, pp. 229–327, and A.G. Van Hamel, 'Cligés and Tristan', *Romania*, 33 (1904), 465–89.

[42] Duggan, *Romances*, p. 68, calls *Cligés* 'the romance of Chrétien that most directly celebrates the new matrimonial practices imposed by the church'.

ascertained that their love is reciprocal. In fact, Alixandre, when told by Arthur that he can have anything he desires, dares not ask for Soredamors until he is certain she loves him. Fenice, on the contrary, is not consulted regarding her betrothal to either the duke of Saxony or Alis, whom she dutifully marries, though she is in love with his nephew. Indeed, as Kathryn Gravdal points out, this situation makes of Fenice the repeated victim of *raptus*: Cligés wrests her away from the Duke, who responds with a counter abduction, leading Cligés to 'rescue' her, only to hand her over to a man she does not love. Once the pair have confessed their love and are seeking a way to consummate it without incurring public shame, Cligés proposes to abduct her and take her off to Britain. Fenice prefers the solution of the *fausse mort*, which results in her being 'kidnapped' from her tomb, and, when the lovers are discovered, carried off to Britain to escape Alis's revenge.[43] Thus, although Fenice firmly believes she is mistress of her own destiny, time and again she is proven wrong.

Elements of this uncomfortable situation in which the lovers find themselves remind us again of Chrétien's vocation as a lyric poet. Cligés is cast in the role of the courtly lover, whereas Alis is relegated to that of the jealous husband, with Fenice incarnating both the lady of the courtly lyric and the heroine of the chanson de malmariée [lament of the unhappily married wife]. In the chanson courtoise, the focus is on the poet-lover and his beloved; the husband, if he exists, remains in the background. But in the chanson de malmariée, as in many a fabliau [short comic tale], the husband is foregrounded: he is a ridiculous figure, a potential – if not actual – cuckold. Moreover, description of the lovers' passion takes a backseat to ruse, the ingenuity required to bring the lovers together in secret. The story of Cligés and Fenice begins in the register of the chanson courtoise, but as soon as they declare their love, it resorts precipitously to the comic style typical of the chanson de malmariée. It is this stunning contrast, not only between the two sets of lovers but also between the pre- and post-declaration stages in Cligés and Fenice's story that gives the romance its strange allure.

The early stage is dominated by extended discussion of the heart, especially as it relates to the body: it is the *cuer/cors* [heart/body] dichotomy, which Chrétien undoubtedly borrowed from Thomas's *Tristan*. When Cligés and Fenice first lay eyes on each other, each is literally dazzled by the other's radiant beauty, and since they cannot avert their gaze, there is an exchange of eyes: 'Par boene amor, non par losange, / Ses ialz li baille et prant les suens' ['With sincere true love, not flattery / She offers him her eyes and takes his' (vss 2788–89)]. Because of his great beauty, Fenice 'Ses ialz et son cuer i a mis, / Et cil li ra son cuer promis', vss 2797–98 [Her eyes and heart she did impart, and he in turn promised his heart]. But Cligés did not simply *promise* his heart, rather he gave it to her outright, notes the narrator, who, suddenly taking the figure of speech literally, goes on to reject the idea that two hearts can inhabit a single body. He explains that whereas two people can have the same desire, a heart cannot be in two places (vs. 2820), and a body cannot have two hearts (vs. 2827). Those who share the same desire are like people singing in harmony; the voices may seem

43 Kathryn Gravdal, *Ravishing Maidens: Writing Rape in Medieval French Literature and Law* (Philadelphia, 1991), pp. 53–55.

like one, but they are not, and a body can have but one heart (vs. 2834). Polak
analyzes in detail the narrator's long digression here as an exceptional example
of *expolitio* [reiteration using various figures] and concludes that the poetic metaphor is apparently 'rejected in a series of axiomatic, common sense *sententiae*
[sententious formulae] into which is inserted an explanation of the true meaning
beneath the "lying" figure of speech'.[44]

Chrétien's poet-lover uses the same metaphor in *D'Amors, qui m'a tolu a moi*:
'mon cuer, qui suens est, li anvoi', vs. 16 ['my heart, which is hers, I send to her']
and 'Cuers, se ma dame ne t'a chier / Ja mar por cou t'an partiras', vss 37–38
['Heart, if my lady does not hold you dear, never for that will you leave her'].
Moreover, despite the narrator's insistent rejection of this image at this point in
the romance, both Cligés and Fenice will go on to make ample use of it. With
both hearts engaged, the two are firmly committed but – as is usual with *fins
amants* – reluctant to express their feelings, all the more so because their love is
forbidden. Fenice requests Thessala's help to avoid giving her body to a man
who does not have her heart. When Cligés is about to depart for Britain, he tells
Fenice tearfully of his intention, adding: 'Mes droiz est qu'a vos congié praigne
/ Com a celi cui ge sui toz', vss 4306–7 ['But it is proper that I ask leave from you
as the one to whom I belong totally']. Cligés's parting words leave Fenice
pensive:

> Car quant ce vint au dessevrer
> Dist Cligés qu'il estoit toz suens.
> Cist moz li est si dolz et buens
> Que de la leingue au cuer li toche,
> Sel met el cuer et an la boche
> Por ce que mialz en soit seüre.   (vss 4364–69)

> [For when it came time to leave, Cligés said that he was totally hers.
> This phrase is so sweet and good that from her tongue it reaches to
> her heart, for she puts it in her heart and her mouth in order better to
> safeguard it.]

As she savours the phrase, which alone sustains and nourishes her, she
wonders *at length* (vss 4319–554!) how to interpret it[45] – does he mean that Love
has him 'en ses lïens', vs. 4408 ['in its bonds'], or is he simply using a cliché or
flattering her? If he is not sincere, he has slain her, for he has stolen her heart.
The motif of the displaced heart is the object of a long, anxious development in
which at one point Fenice casts Cligés in the role of the *losengier* (flatterer or false
lover), a familiar figure in courtly lyric:[46]

---

[44] See Polak, *Cligés*, pp. 79–82, and the entire chapter devoted to Chrétien's 'craft' (pp. 70–86).
For a complete list of rhetorical devices, see Valerie Bertolucci, 'Commento retorico all'*Erec* ed
al *Cligés*', *Studi mediolatini e volgari*, 8 (1960), 9–51.

[45] Her long meditation echoes the passage where Soredamors is carefully considering the pros
and cons of calling Alixandre 'amis' when Guenevere arrives and unhesitatingly addresses
him as such (vss 1381–420). Indeed, the context is crucial: although 'amis' often means
'friend', it means 'beloved' in the songs of the women troubadours and trouvères.

[46] It reappears in *Yvain*, when Laudine's messenger denounces Yvain as a flatterer and liar for
having stolen his lady's heart. See below.

'Morte sui, quant celui ne voi
Qui de mon cuer m'a desrobee,
Tant m'a losengiee et lobee.
Par sa lobe et par sa losenge
Mes cuers de son ostel s'estrenge
Ne ne vialt o moi remenoir,
Tant het mon estre et mon menoir.
Par foi, donc m'a cil maubaillie
Qui mon cuer a en sa baillie.
Qui me desrobe et tost le mien
Ne m'ainme pas, je le sai bien'.   (vss 4436–47)[47]

['I am slain when I do not see the man who stole away my heart, so
much did he flatter and deceive me. By his deceit and flattery my
heart forsakes its lodging and does not wish to remain with me, so
much does it hate me and my home. By faith, then, he has mistreated
me, he who has my heart in his possession. I know well that he who
steals and takes mine surely does not love me'.]

Since the heart's 'ostel' or 'menoir' is really Fenice's body, Chrétien is allowing
his heroine to use the very metaphor condemned earlier by the narrator. Fenice
decides eventually that their two hearts may well be different, for 'Li suens est
sire et li miens sers / Et li sers maleoit gré suen', vss 4478–79 ['His is the lord and
mine is the serf'], a formulation that recalls the equanimity with which the
poet-lover in both of Chrétien's lyrics accepts his state of bondage. Fenice
concludes her monologue by noting that since Cligés is so beautiful, noble and
loyal, she wills her heart to serve him. She can hardly do otherwise, for as she
has just demonstrated, he took her heart with him!

The metaphor of the displaced heart also proves useful as the clever means
by which the lovers confess their love. When Fenice asks Cligés, upon his return,
if he loved a lady while in Britain, he admits that he did – but no one who was
there: 'Ausi com escorce sanz fust / Fu mes cors sanz cuer an Bretaingne',
vss 5160–61 ['Like bark without its wooden core was my body without my heart
while in Britain']. Revealing progressively more of his passion in answer to
Fenice's carefully graduated set of inquiries, he finally tells her that his heart
remained with *her*, and when she claims that her heart was with him too, they
conclude their avowals: 'Dame, don sont ci avoec nos / Endui li cuer, si con vos
dites, / Car li miens est vostres toz quites. / – Amis, et vos ravez le mien: / Si
nos antr'avenomes bien', vss 5210–14 ['My lady, then they are here with us, both
hearts just as you say, for mine is totally yours. – My friend, and you have mine:
so we are in accord'].

Cligés's admission that his heart is hers 'toz quites' brings the pair around
full circle to the enigmatic phrase he pronounced upon leaving. The meaning is
now abundantly clear, and Fenice's reference to their 'accord' alludes to the
narrator's preferred metaphor for the displaced heart. In fact, most manuscripts

---

[47] This passage is an excellent example of *annominatio* (play with form or meaning of words)
described by Douglas Kelly in this volume. The rich rhyme of most of the couplets is particularly striking.

substitute for 'antr'avenomes' the expression 'entr'acordomes', which refers more explicitly to singing in unison. Fenice continues to use the *cuers/cors* dichotomy as she goes on to explain how she managed to avoid this loathsome split that characterized Ysolt's behaviour: 'Car quant mes cuers an vos se mist, / Le cors vos dona et promist / Si qu'autres ja part n'i avra', vss 5233–35 ['For when my heart was placed in you, you were given and promised the body such that no other man would ever have a share'].

As Fenice segues into the conditions under which Cligés might actually enjoy her body, the romance is transmuted from the chanson courtoise back to the chanson de malmariée glimpsed during the episode recounting the ruse of Thessala's magic potion, where the narrator maliciously underscores that when Alis, emperor in name only, lay down with his wife, he became husband in name only as well. In the space of thirteen lines, he repeats 'neant' (nothing) ten times, hammering home the point that Alis reaps nothing, believing all the while that he has 'taken the fortress' (vss 3336–48). This 'colossal deception' or 'delusively specular dream of carnal love', notes Donald Maddox, occurs at the mid-point of the romance, and the second half 'exploits the narrative potential of this fraudulent fiction'.[48] The quickened pace of the last third of the romance and the low-comic style of the *fausse mort* episode,[49] especially the surprising brutality employed by the three doctors from Salerno suggests the fabliau, in which lively action predominates over psychological analysis.

It is ironic – and amusing – that Fenice, in order to enjoy her lover, is closed up in a tower, like the unhappy wife of the jealous husband in the chanson de malmariée – and like the empresses who were to follow her on the throne! The courtly lyric re-emerges briefly in the scene where Fenice, attracted by the signs of springtime, is drawn out of her tower confinement into the garden. The description recalls the traditional springtime exordium (beginning) found in most troubadour chansons:

> Au renouvelemant d'esté,
> Quant flors et fuelles d'arbres issent
> Et cil oiselet s'esjoïssent
> Qu'il font lor joie an lor latin,
> Avint que Fenice un matin
> Oï chanter le rossignol.   (vss 6328–33)

> [With summer's renewal, when flowers and leaves burst forth on trees, and those little birds rejoice and voice their joy in their language, it happened that Fenice one morning heard the nightingale sing.]

One almost expects another lyrical expansion typical of the pre-avowal stage, but this idyll is short-lived. As the lovers lie naked under a pear tree, reality

---

48 Donald Maddox, *Fictions of Identity in Medieval France* (Cambridge, 2000), p. 85.
49 In Tibaut's *Roman de la poire* (c. 1250), which gives voice to four sets of lovers, each describing a famous episode from their respective stories, Cligés and Fenice are, significantly, represented by the *fausse mort* torture, thanks to which they narrowly avoid the tragic death that characterizes the other couples (Tristan and Yseut, Pyramus and Thisbe, Paris and Helen).

intrudes abruptly when the knight Bertrand scales the wall in search of his sparrowhawk, causing a pear to fall on Fenice's ear. This bizarre scene is one of Chrétien's many ironic transpositions, here combining elements of two famous episodes in Béroul's *Tristan* (the lovers' tryst under the pine tree and their discovery by Marc in the forest of Morrois), but since the pear and the pear tree are symbols of sensuality, there may well be a further allusion to the fabliau of the enchanted pear tree.[50]

The end of the romance, which finds Cligés and Fenice happily married, may constitute the ultimate deformation of the Tristan legend. As Denis de Rougemont (who believed marriage to be incompatible with *fin'amors*) remarked famously, can one imagine Ysolt as 'Madame Tristan'? Would not marriage spell the end of their passion?[51] Chrétien, conscious of the paradox he presents, makes sure we understand that, even married, Cligés and Fenice still behave like *fins amants*:

> De s'amie a feite sa fame,
> Mes il l'apele amie et dame,
> Et por ce ne pert ele mie
> Que il ne l'aint come s'amie,
> Et ele lui tot autresi
> Con l'en doit feire son ami.
> Et chascun jor lor amors crut.
> Ne querela de nule chose . . .   (vss 6731–38)

> [Of his beloved he has made his wife, but he calls her beloved and lady, so she loses not his loving her like his beloved. And she loves him in the same way as one should love one's beloved. And every day their love grew, and they never quarrelled about anything . . .].

By assuring us that as husband and wife their love grew daily and they never quarrelled, Chrétien turns his romance into a fairy tale – or *fable*, which in Old French means both a fiction and a lie. The Tristan legend is a great love story, but it is a fiction that Chrétien has used to construct a work whose fictional quality is squarely in the forefront.

At the beginning of *Yvain*, the narrator laments that loyal lovers of the kind found in Arthur's time no longer exist and that love has been turned to *fable* because people claim they are in love, whereas they are not (vss 24–28).[52] It is the familiar problem of the *faux amants* or *losengiers* evoked by the troubadours and by Chrétien in the works discussed here. We have seen that Fenice, before she is sure that Cligés loves her, frets about his sincerity. In *Amors Tençon et bataille*, the poet-lover complains that Amors treats faithless lovers better than her faithful devotees, and he ends *D'Amors, qui m'a tolu a moi* by describing himself as 'cil qui ne set a gas / Amors servir ne losengier', vss 53–54 ['he who does not know

50 This fabliau may have originated in the East. See Polak, *Cligés*, pp. 68–69, and her 'Cligés, Fenice et l'arbre d'amour', *Romania*, 93 (1972), 303–16.

51 Denis de Rougemont, *L'Amour et l'Occident* (1939; definitive edn, Paris, 1972), *Love in the Western World*, trans. Montgomery Belgion (1940; rev. 1983).

52 References are to David Hult's edition of *Yvain* in Zink's *Chrétien de Troyes, Romans*, cited in n. 1 above.

how to serve Love by joking or using flattery']. In *Yvain*, the narrator, by situating his story in Arthur's time, would have us believe that we will hear the
story of a loyal lover. Although Yvain gives every *appearance* of one when he
confesses his love to Laudine, he proves to be faithless and is roundly
denounced as an insincere lover, trickster, liar and seducer (vss 2719–24). It is
only through Lunete's guile that he is reunited with Laudine, so the narrator's
assurance that everlasting peace has been made 'De mon signor Yvain le fin / Et
de s'amie chiere et fine', vss 6802–3 ['Between my lord Yvain the true / And his
dear and true beloved'] is hardly convincing.[53] As Tony Hunt asks, what is the
significance of Chrétien's treatment of the love intrigue in that romance,
including the conclusion? Why are we constantly reminded of the lament in the
prologue about false lovers?[54]

In Chrétien's romances and in *Philomena*, the protagonists who are under the
sway of love range from the most devoted to the most brutal. All adopt some of
the trappings of *fin'amors*, but at times their behaviour belies their words: their
conduct is rarely that of the perfect lover depicted in Chrétien's two chansons.
The courtly lyric is short enough to strike a note of intense yearning and to
sustain it right up until the end, for in a short piece a satisfying closure is easily
reached and is thoroughly believable. However, when that desire is transposed
into a narrative work of several thousand lines, 'reality' necessarily intervenes,
just as when lovers transform their idyll into marriage. Chrétien concludes his
romance by stating that future empresses were not allowed the company of
males, except eunuchs: 'De ce n'est crienme ne dotance / Qu'Amors les lit an
son lïen. / Ci fenist l'uevre Crestïen', vss 6760–62 ['So that they had no fear nor
doubt lest Love join them in its bonds. Here Chrétien finishes his work']. In the
last two lines, where 'fenist' evokes the name of Alis's notorious consort, the
name of 'Crestïen' rhymes with 'lïen', leaving us with the troubling image of
Fenice as a slave to love.

The irony that pervades the 'happy ending' in *Cligés* is virtually inevitable,
especially since the illusion/reality dichotomy permeates the romance. In the
long prose romances of the later Middle Ages, Chrétien's narrative poetry will
be 'flattened out' – his playful irony stifled – by the earnestness of authors like
the one who penned the fifteenth-century Burgundian prose reworking of
Cligés.[55] Only at that point are the romance characters that Love joins in its
bonds portrayed as true lovers who never fail at their vocation.

[53] See Tony Hunt's essay in this volume, and Grimbert,'*Yvain' dans le miroir*, pp. 171–81.
[54] See his essay, below.
[55] See Norris J. Lacy, 'Adaptation and Reception: The Burgundian *Cligès*', *Fifteenth-Century
Studies*, 24 (1998), 198–207.

11

Le Chevalier de la Charrette:
That Obscure Object of Desire, Lancelot

MATILDA TOMARYN BRUCKNER

Lancelot is a name that still reverberates for the modern public with the intensity discernable in his medieval reception from the moment Chrétien's romance launched him into Arthurian history in the provocative guise of the Knight of the Cart. Efforts to understand what makes him such a compelling figure lead inevitably to the question of desire, Lancelot's for Guenevere, of course, but also our desire for him, the desires of so many inside and outside the romance world, which Chrétien has crystallized around the hero himself. In *Le Chevalier de la Charrette*, Lancelot generates a magnetic field of erotic potential at once positive and negative, productive and disruptive, as singular and extraordinary as his heart and as paradoxical as the romancer's art. Indeed, story and romance mirror each other in a kind of infinite regress that traps readers in an open-ended quest for meaning, the *san* that Chrétien claims to receive from his patroness, that we can only seek to uncover in the arrangement of fiction produced by 'sa painne et s'antancïon' [his effort and creative intention].[1] Since Chrétien has crafted a romance as enigmatic as Lancelot's love story, we will have to follow the writer's ploys as much as the hero's exploits. A quick summary will set the stage.

Commanded by the Countess of Champagne, Chrétien has undertaken to write a romance entitled the *Knight of the Cart*. It begins on Ascension Day as an unknown knight erupts into court and challenges Arthur to send the Queen into the forest with a champion who will fight, double or nothing, for the release of the King's subjects held captive in the stranger's land. By the manipulations of a Rash Boon, Keu claims the role of defender and leads off the Queen. Gauvain and others belatedly follow: Keu's riderless horse reveals the unfortunate results. Gauvain next encounters a hard-riding knight who pursues the Queen with even greater haste. Catching up a second time, Gauvain sees the knight step, after a moment's hesitation, into a cart driven by a dwarf, who promises information on the Queen's whereabouts. The narrator explains the shame associated with carts, used in those days for felons and murderers. Gauvain follows

---

[1] Chrétien de Troyes, *Le Chevalier de la Charrette ou Le Roman de Lancelot*, ed. and trans. Charles Méla, in *Romans suivis des Chansons avec, en appendice, Philomena*, genl ed. Michel Zink (Paris, 1994), vs. 29. All translations are my own.

them to a castle, where they spend the night. Although his hostess scorns him, the Knight of the Cart insists on sleeping in the Perilous Bed and survives the adventure of the flaming lance. Both knights set out the next morning and meet a damsel who names Meleagant as the queen's abductor. The rescuer's entrance into Gorre must pass over one of two bridges. Given first choice, Gauvain sets off for the Bridge Under Water; we follow the Cart Knight's progress to the more daunting Sword Bridge.

His adventures include combat with a knight guarding a ford and a series of encounters engineered by a damsel offering hospitality in exchange for an agreement that he share her bed. The extraordinary prowess of the knight becomes more and more evident, as does his absorption in love for the queen. In a cemetery containing the future graves of Arthur's knights, the knight discovers a tomb reserved for the one who will rescue the queen and liberate the prisoners in Gorre – he easily lifts its heavy stone cover and thus confirms his future success without revealing his identity. Resuming his journey, he makes contact with prisoners ready to join in their liberation. Rumours circulating about the Knight of the Cart and the liberator collide, when a haughty knight challenges him. The unknown coolly defeats the Orgueilleux and a damsel arrives requesting his head. Torn between Pity and Largess, the victor satisfies both by giving the Orgueilleux a second chance in battle and then awarding his head to the maiden (later identified as Meleagant's sister). She promises future help.

Wounding his unprotected hands, feet and knees, the Cart Knight crosses the Sword Bridge and claims his combat, which takes place next morning despite the king of Gorre's efforts to make his son relinquish the queen. Lancelot of the Lake is finally identified when Guenevere reveals his name to a damsel who calls out that the queen is watching from a tower; initially interrupted by ecstatic contemplation, Lancelot's prowess soon triumphs, only to be interrupted again when Bademagu's request that his son be spared is seconded by the queen. After an agreement is arranged for a second combat to take place at Arthur's court, Lancelot is taken to the queen who surprisingly refuses to speak with him. When Lancelot leaves to find Gauvain, he is taken prisoner and rumours of death and suicide fly. The queen's monologues reveal her love for Lancelot, and when he returns to court, they arrange a night-time rendezvous during which their love is consummated.

The next morning Meleagant finds the queen's sheets bloodied, deduces treason against the king and accuses Keu, who sleeps in the same room. Lancelot fights Meleagant in a judicial combat, which is again suspended by Bademagu's intervention. Through treachery, Meleagant imprisons Lancelot while the queen, Gauvain and the prisoners return to Logres. Knowing the queen will be present at a tournament, Lancelot manages to participate as an unknown knight in red arms. Suspecting his real identity, the queen twice requires the unknown to fight as a coward before commanding his best performance. After triumphing, Lancelot returns to his imprisonment. More than a year later, Meleagant's sister finds Lancelot's tower and releases him; he arrives at Arthur's court just in time to replace Gauvain in a final combat against Meleagant, whose death occasions great joy. An epilogue reveals that Godefroi de Leigni has completed the romance according to Chrétien's direction.

As in previous romances, Chrétien uses the prologue to establish his relationship with the public and introduce the story that follows, thereby giving us his credentials as an author well schooled in the rhetoric of composition and supplying us with clues on how to read what he has composed. In this particular case, the romancer foregrounds a new element: the role of his patroness, Marie de Champagne, whose name appears in the very first line and whose praises overflow the majority of the prologue's verses. Marie has supplied 'matiere et san', vs. 26 [storymatter and sense], Chrétien, the creative arrangement. Since prologues traditionally multiply the guarantors of a work's value – sources, patrons, titles, author's name – we should not be surprised to see the romancer spotlight the Countess of Champagne's authorization.[2] Nor should we fail to notice, even as Chrétien's words assert willing submission to his lady's command, that other elements nuance, even if they do not completely efface, his humility and foreground his art as much as the lady's worth: in those opening lines, she occupies the subordinate clause, the author/narrator's first person commands the main clause. The puzzle fashioned by Chrétien's praise for Marie appropriately introduces the puzzle of a romance whose title oxymoronically links a knight to a cart. How can the poet servant praise without the risk of flattery, use the hyperboles the countess deserves without the appearance of exaggeration, without sounding like the conventional flatterer he models in order to discredit and then paradoxically endorse?

> Qui i volsist losenge metre,
> Si deïst, et jel tesmoignasse,
> Que ce est la dame qui passe
> Totes celes qui sont vivanz,
> Si con les funs passe li vanz
> Qui vante en mai ou en avril.
> Par foi, je ne sui mie cil
> Qui vuelle losangier sa dame;
> Dirai je: tant come une jame
> Vaut de pelles et de sardines,
> Vaut la contesse de reïnes?
> Naie, je n'en dirai [ja] rien,
> S'est il voirs maleoit gré mien.   (vss 8–20)

> [One who would want to flatter would say, and I stand witness for it, that she is the lady who surpasses all those who are living, just as the wind that blows in May or April surpasses other breezes. By my faith, I am not one who wants to flatter his lady. Will I say: as much as one gem may be worth of pearls and sards, the countess is worth queens? No, I will not say it and yet it is true in spite of me.][3]

---

2 Anne Berthelot, *Figures et fonction de l'écrivain au XIIIe siècle* (Montreal, 1991), especially pp. 66–96.
3 Chrétien's prologue has received abundant critical attention: see, for example, Jean Rychner, 'Le Prologue du *Chevalier de la Charrette*', *Vox Romanica*, 26 (1967), 1–23, and Jean Frappier's response in 'Le Prologue du *Chevalier de la Charrette* et son interprétation', *Romania*, 93 (1972), 337–77. These verses are especially problematic because of the vocabulary: the hapax 'li funs' resists translation and 'jame' in the singular sits ill with the two plurals that follow. See Karl D. Uitti, 'Autant en emporte *li funs*: remarques sur le prologue du *Chevalier de la Charrette* de

There is clearly an excess in Chrétien's rhetoric here that calls attention to itself through the doubling of sample praises, the repetition of key terms, the inverted comparisons where less is more, and the repeated interventions of the narratorial 'I' framing his examples with comment, question and answer. Chrétien plays an ironic game of not saying and saying at the same time; he seeks to establish a difference while using the common tools of praise, a truth that rings false and then true in spite of the pitfalls of language and the poet's volition.[4]

This problem of excess anticipates Lancelot's characterization in the romance proper, and there, too, issues connected with the status of hyberbole will problematize our efforts to evaluate the hero's actions as well as the nature of his love. Consider the excess of either too little or too much attached to the title event itself, which the narrator left with no comment in the prologue – his silence the more mysterious by contrast. When Lancelot actually arrives at the cart, a lengthy narratorial intervention explains how carts served as a kind of pillory in those days, causing unending shame for anyone who rode in them, hence the common saying to make the sign of the cross when a cart passes by (vss 321–44). We may thus appreciate the unreasonableness of Lancelot's love, elaborated in his interior monologue (vss 365–77), before it thrusts him into the cart. Although the narrator appears to more than satisfy our need for explanation with this accumulation of commentaries – his excess the perfect correlate of Lancelot's – we will discover that his unusual prolixity covers over as much as it reveals. What about the cart's mix of crimes, its mythic overtones linked to death? Why will Lancelot regret his two-step hesitation? And later, how does the queen learn about it? Why does the shame of the cart-ride disappear from the romance once Lancelot is named? Our questions accumulate, as we remember the implicit warnings of the prologue not to take at face value what words say. They may or may not be true and will certainly require interpretation to verify.

Indeed, interpretations of Chrétien's praise for the countess have introduced another level of excess in the romance's puzzles. After the dazzling performance of not flattering by flattering with flattery that is not flattery but the truth, Chrétien declares that Marie's commandment plays a greater role in the romance than his own contributions (vss 21–23). Is he now serious, flattering – or both? The countess's exact contribution to Chrétien's work has occasioned endless speculation, and many critics since Gaston Paris see the romancer engaged in an effort to disengage his responsibility.[5] This line of argument depends on some tenuous threads that have nevertheless kept a remarkable hold on modern readers. They are anchored on the assumption that Marie's *san*

Chrétien de Troyes', *Romania*, 105 (1964), 270–91; and Jan Janssens, 'Le prologue du "Chevalier de la Charrete": une clef pour l'interprétation du roman?' *Bien dire et bien aprandre*, 4 (1986), 29–57.

4   On Chrétien's irony, see Peter Haidu, *Aesthetic Distance in Chrétien de Troyes: Irony and Comedy in 'Cligès' and 'Perceval'* (Geneva, 1968); 'Au début du roman, l'ironie', *Poétique*, 36 (1978), 443–66. For a recent discussion, see Ana Sofia Laranjinha, 'L'ironie comme principe structurant chez Chrétien de Troyes', *Cahiers de civilisation médiévale*, 41 (1998), 175–82.

5   See the article by Gaston Paris that launched the term 'courtly love': 'Etudes sur les romans de la Table Ronde. Lancelot du Lac, II. *Le Conte de la Charrette*', *Romania*, 12 (1883), 459–534.

can be defined as an apology for adulterous love, based on her decision, as reported in Andreas Capellanus's *De Amore*, that love and marriage are incompatible.[6] Since Chrétien is viewed as the poet of love in marriage, based on the plots of his previous romances, he must have been unhappy with the task imposed on him by his patroness, hence his 'abandonment' of the project to Godefroi de Leigni. But once we recognize that the Latin author's treatise is not a historical document but a fictional game played with irony and wit (and based in part on his reading of Chrétien's romances), we have no outside witness, no unimpeachable authority to specify what Marie's meaning may have been, only the romance as written by Chrétien.

If we have properly read the prologue (and the romance as a whole), we can have few illusions about the romancer's ability to write whatever he wants, but the persistence of a presumed antagonism between Chrétien and Marie in some readers' minds bears further investigation.[7] It is, I believe, a fiction only partially authorized by what we read in the romance, shaped in part by Chrétien's manipulations, in part by cultural and psychological factors in his society, as in ours. It begins in the prologue when Chrétien describes his obedient service to the countess with the same language he later uses for Lancelot's submission to the queen. 'Come cil qui est suens antiers', vs. 4 [as the one who is completely hers] finds repeated echoes, exact or approximate (vss 1264, 4187, 5656), which culminate at the tournament in the queen's recognition that Lancelot is as completely hers as she is his (vss 5874–75). Given the overlap between couples inside and outside the romance, readers have understandably been tempted to elaborate a story about Chrétien and Marie that imitates Lancelot's with the queen. But when the duplication of couples inexplicably continues and a second author declares (after the fact) his obedient submission to the first author's will, Chrétien moves to the position of queen and patroness. Is this a logical contradiction of his opening claim? Some efforts to grapple with the substitution have led to speculation that Chrétien invented Godefroi as a fiction to problematize the ending of his romance.[8]

In any case, the shifts between prologue and epilogue frame repeated disruptions between cause and effect, words and deeds, words and their meanings, which will characterize the characters' actions as well as the romance's construction. If historical reasons for the change in authors elude us as much as the actual contents of Marie's gifts, Chrétien's combination of silence and excess still fuels our desire to interpret: we invent, using what we find in the romance or supply from cultural contexts. Is Chrétien a victim or a manipulator, both or neither? As

---

6   Andreas Capellanus, *De amore libri tres*, ed. E. Trojel (Copenhagen, 1892), or *The Art of Courtly Love*, trans. John J. Parry (New York, 1969), pp. 106–7.
7   Although he still assumed a conflict with Chrétien's personal morality, Jean Frappier began the process of questioning this view of the author's relation to his patroness. See Frappier's *Chrétien de Troyes* (Paris, 1968), pp. 122–44, for a nuanced appreciation of Lancelot's and Guenevere's characterizations, as well as Chrétien's art. For a feminist reading of inscribed female readers and patrons in *Yvain* and the *Charrette*, see Roberta L. Krueger, *Women Readers and the Ideology of Gender in Old French Verse Romance* (Cambridge, 1993), pp. 33–67.
8   For example, David F. Hult, 'Author/Narrator/Speaker: The Voice of Authority in Chrétien's *Charrete*', in *Discourses of Authority in Medieval and Renaissance Literature*, ed. Kevin Brownlee and Walter Stephens (Hanover, NH, 1989), pp. 76–96.

the author/narrator alternately pulls us into romance passions and invites us to stand back and reflect, we may wonder if these categories make sense for him or his characters Lancelot and Guenevere. The story of a romancer in conflict with his patroness may be a fiction that reflects more faithfully the difficulties men experience with women placed in positions of power (in contemporary society, as in twelfth- century France) than the realities or even the actual representation of Chrétien's position vis-à-vis Marie de Champagne.[9] Perhaps Lancelot, who appears to have no trouble accepting whatever the queen commands, operates as the exception here, as he does in so many other categories, so it is to him and his relations with women (and men), to his problematic identity constructed between the overlapping demands of love and chivalry, that we should now turn, before coming back to the problem of endings.

Lancelot's anonymity, carefully maintained by both the narrator and the Cart Knight until the middle of the romance, compounds our desire to know who this hero is. Throughout the romance, the process of discovery is thematized over and over again, as if to warn us that the question itself remains in place even when we think it has been resolved at one stage or another. Delay and deferral appear not only as techniques that dramatize the gradual revelation of Lancelot's identity; they are the constants of his character, paradoxically essential components of the uncommon force that makes him the extraordinary hero designated to rescue the queen and liberate the prisoners. In the romance world, women have the greatest access to the many facets of Lancelot's identity as knight and lover, as it operates elusively across the constraints of public and private domains. The anonymous damsels at crossroad and ford, his hostesses unwilling and too willing, the damsel on the mule who reappears as Meleagant's sister, the seneschal's wife, the queen's serving maidens and all the eligible damsels hoping to find husbands at the tournament – an exceptional number of female characters proliferate along Lancelot's journey and participate in the hero's adventures for his or their own benefit, as his absorption in love for the queen generates a magnetic force field pulling the desire of others toward him even as his overflows into service for all. When the spectators observe that Meleagant has begun to triumph against Lancelot, weakened by the wounds inflicted during his punishing crawl across the Sword Bridge, 'une pucele molt sage', vs. 3635 [a very wise maiden] thinks that the knight would not have undertaken such a battle for her sake nor that of the other prisoners, but only for the queen (vss 3636–42). Indeed, Lancelot's love for Guenevere appears to be an open secret for a number of female characters; this one understands how to use it to revive Lancelot's prowess and thereby secures for us the cart rider's name, pronounced by the very object of his love. The maiden's first reaction assures us that Lancelot is a figure already known and respected in the Arthurian world, yet the intended effect of her intervention seems to backfire when his ecstatic contemplation of the queen results in an even worse performance, as Lancelot defends himself ineffectually from behind. This is not the first time we have seen a pensive Lancelot comically out of touch with what a proper knight is supposed

---

[9] Georges Duby, 'Women and Power', in *Cultures of Power: Lordship, Status and Process in Twelfth-Century Europe*, ed. Thomas N. Bisson (Philadelphia, 1995), pp. 69–85.

to be doing: lured by the receding figure of the kidnapped queen, he nearly commits suicide at the window of his first hostess; failing to heed the ford knight's warnings, he suddenly finds himself unhorsed, splashily awakened as he hits the water.

The comedy recalls Chrétien's other pensive hero, the simpleton Perceval, who has generated among romance readers and writers as much passion as Lancelot himself. The two have much in common – their role as liberators, their anonymity and ex-centric relationship to Arthur's court, their pairings with Gauvain and even their appearance in red arms. Most importantly, both of their stories are stories of desire so intense that the very notion of closure becomes problematized, although the specifics of that dynamic differ radically. Perceval's comic energy and the faux pas it entails are presented as the products of an incomplete and ongoing education; the objects of his passion remain split between Blancheflor and the grail quest, their resolution left uncharted. The contrast with Lancelot's single-mindedness could not be more striking: everything he is and does intersects his love for the queen. The comic moments coincide with his most intense expressions of passionate devotion, and it is the same devotion that moves him to his greatest achievements: the sublime and the comic are inextricably intertwined in this paradoxical hero.

Lancelot's love explodes into romance without any beginning revealed or end foretold, fully formed and symbolized by the extraordinary fullness of his heart. As the narrator describes it during their union, Love has slighted all other hearts, having so perfectly invested itself in Lancelot's alone (vss 4664–68), an imbalance that gives him the capacity to love the queen a hundred thousand times more than she loves him. The dynamic movement of the romance comes not from any change in his love, such as we can see in the queen's, but rather from the gradual discovery of its power and impact. The narrator highlights the process of revelation by closely following the perceptions, reactions and interactions of his characters. Thus as soon as Lancelot's paralysis before the queen becomes an object of the maiden's ridicule, he quickly follows her directions to put Meleagant between him and the tower so that he can simultaneously fight and gaze at the motivating force of his prowess. Love and mortal hatred now quickly combine to vanquish the queen's abductor, until obedience to Guenevere's word leads Lancelot to stop fighting again, even as Meleagant's blows continue to rain down on him. Extreme passivity and extreme activity alternate and combine in Lancelot's heroic performance, which has frequently polarized the debate about his love and its relationship to the values of chivalry. Has love humiliated or elevated the knight? Is Lancelot ennobled or emasculated by his submission to the queen? The polemic is anticipated in the romance by the diversity of evaluations attached to a figure who refuses to limit his trajectory by any reputation or name already established. We can get some sense of this mobility in Lancelot's identity, as well as the range and import of other characters' judgments, by briefly examining the adventures initiated by the Immodest Damsel.[10]

[10] For detailed analysis, see Matilda Tomaryn Bruckner, 'An Interpreter's Dilemma: Why Are There So Many Interpretations of Chrétien's *Chevalier de la Charrette?' Romance Philology*, 40 (1986), 159–80.

After the scornful criticism of his first hostess sets the tone for a pattern of insults that follow the cart rider, the second hostess is the first to give voice to the laudatory and superlative evaluations that form in counterpoint, first in the privacy of her bedchamber, then in the significant exchanges that take place in the meadow and at the cemetery, as Lancelot escorts her. The bargain she imposes on Lancelot in exchange for her hospitality allows her to test first Lancelot's prowess – when he has to prove his mettle in defending her from a simulated rape – then his fidelity to the queen, when he must share her bed and resist the powerful attraction of her charms, which are, as she observes, powerless to entice him even to touch her, as he remains silent and unmoving in her bed, his heart and thoughts fixed elsewhere under the rule of Love's justice (vss 1228–40). Before leaving him, she affirms that Lancelot has completely fulfilled his promise 'to go to bed with her' (the ambiguities of the verb *couchier* are cleverly deployed throughout this scene) and thus anticipates crucial moments when Lancelot will do the impossible – like Chrétien – by bringing together contradictions and impossibilities. Even without access to his private thoughts, this damsel correctly surmises Lancelot's exceptional character and mission (vss 1270–78).

With her knowledge of Lancelot as both lover and knight, the Immodest Damsel functions as an analogue of the queen and offers an implicit commentary on the bond linking him to Guenevere.[11] Lancelot himself makes the connection, while he hesitates, outnumbered and outarmed, before deciding to rescue his hostess. Severely reproaching himself with the charge of *Malvestiez*, vs. 1102 [cowardice] – a key word that will reappear in the discussions of his performance at the tournament, where he will once again allow his conduct to be directed by the manipulations of a woman – Lancelot experiences an acute sense of shame which pushes him to new heights to be worthy of his quest for 'la reine Guenievre' (vs. 1099), appropriately named here for the first time by the man who loves her. Conflicts of honour and shame introduced by the cart episode continue to thread through Lancelot's adventures, as he chooses to act unreasonably in accord with his understanding of what love for the queen requires, regardless of risk or reputation.

But Lancelot is just as capable of choosing moderation as immoderation, depending on the circumstances. When he accompanies his hostess according to the custom of Logres – which, the narrator explains (vss 1302–16), allows any knight to possess her without incurring shame, as long as he can defeat her escort – Lancelot's conduct with her unwanted suitor remains unruffled despite the young knight's presumption and boasting. When they arrive in the meadow, since the narrow passage of their meeting prevented immediate combat, the Proud Son is restrained by his father who immediately recognizes Lancelot's worth and delays their combat until his son is persuaded to abandon his claim, finally convinced by Lancelot's feat in the cemetery. Analogues multiply through the romance and connect its episodes: this father-son couple clearly

---

11 On Chrétien's use of analogues, see Norris J. Lacy, *The Craft of Chrétien de Troyes: An Essay on Narrative Art* (Leiden, 1980), pp. 68–71; 'Thematic Structure in the *Charrette*', *L'Esprit créateur*, 12 (1972), 13–18.

anticipates Bademagu and Meleagant, offering a model of proper restraint exercised over unruly pretensions, which contrasts with the king of Gorre's failure to prevent his own son's treachery. For his part, Lancelot has no need to broadcast his superior prowess; he is willing to avoid unnecessary combat, or accept it when unavoidable, as he will demonstrate again with the Orgueilleux, the last public voice of shame accusing the cart rider before Lancelot and the queen redefine the problem within the exclusively private concerns of love.

Through the custom of Logres, Lancelot enters into a triangular relationship with the Immodest Damsel and her unwanted suitor that mirrors the triangle set up in the opening scene by Meleagant when he challenges the queen and her escort. With Keu's defeat, the same triangle is then repeatedly replayed with Lancelot in the position of challenger. To this series of triangles we might add that of the simulated rape when Lancelot defends the damsel against three knights and four sergeants. We can then appreciate how the outrageous conduct of his hostess (who dismisses the men attacking her once Lancelot has sufficiently demonstrated his prowess) usefully brings out the triangulation of desire left unstated in Meleagant's initial challenge. Bademagu's protection prevented his son from taking possession of his prize and fuels his rage when he discovers bloody sheets announcing erroneously that the loser has replaced him in the queen's bed. The sequence and parallels suggest that Lancelot might rightly claim Guenevere as his reward for defeating her abductor, but that claim runs into two obstacles: on the one hand, the problem of adultery phrased as a case of treason against Arthur and deflected by misinterpretation, on the other, the actions of the queen herself who by her unexpectedly cold reception has disrupted the connection between Lancelot's triumph in combat and their night of love. In that scene, Guenevere first shows the kind of initiative and game-playing we associate with the Immodest Damsel, a change which brings out by contrast her earlier passivity, when she was manipulated and endangered by Keu and King Arthur's failure to protect her. The transformation signals not only the way we gradually discover her character in the course of the narrative but the way her love changes and develops, especially through the complex series of actions set into motion by her initial rejection of Lancelot.

The queen's behaviour in this scene and at the tournament has often been viewed through the model of the troubadour's lady, the *domna* who commands and frequently rejects her lover's service. Chrétien composed at least two, possibly four, poems in the mode of the troubadours[12] and certainly finds models for his lovers in the variety of poses and the characteristics of *fin'amor* explored in troubadour song: loss of self, humbling service to the lady that paradoxically raises the lover to her superior level, the split of heart and body, dying for love, antitheses of wisdom and folly, measure and *desmezura*, pain and joy, etc. Guenevere's and Lancelot's monologues reflect troubadour ideas as well as style in their argumentation about the rights and wrongs of refined loving. In that light, we might interpret the queen's cold reception as a way to preserve her love as a gift, like *fin'amor* freely chosen and bestowed, not commandeered by

---

[12] Marie-Claire Zai, ed., *Les Chansons courtoises de Chrétien de Troyes: édition critique avec introduction, notes et commentaire* (Bern, 1974).

the automatism of a custom. She says to herself that the rejection was meant as a joke ('cuidai ge feire a gas', vs. 4205 ['I thought to do it in jest']), but Lancelot failed to perceive it with the spirit of play she shares with so many troubadour poets. Now that the queen believes herself responsible for Lancelot's death, she pronounces judgment on her cruelty and regrets not holding her lover at least once in her naked arms, a desire often expressed in both troubadour song and chansons de femme. Such is the preparation that leads to the night of fully shared love, once Lancelot returns to Bath alive and well despite the rumours of death and suicide.

In the process of constructing his lovers, Chrétien exploits not only lyric models – which play games as they pass into narrative – but other representations of love recognizable by a twelfth-century public. Ovidian material appears in his comic variations on double suicide borrowed from Pyramus and Thisbe and, of course, Tristan and Iseut remain here as elsewhere in Chrétien's corpus powerful figures for reinvention. Their mutual and physical passion finds echoes in Lancelot and Guenevere's consummation of love, to which Lancelot's adoration of the queen adds the embellishment of religious language, in order to express the excess of his reverence. As he enters and leaves her bedchamber, 'Si l'aore et se li ancline, / Car an nul cors saint ne croit tant', vss 4652–53 [He adores and bows to her, for he believes in no saint's relic as much as in her]. Lancelot's immoderation in love intertwined religious tropes and the Tristan story earlier during his journey with the Immodest Damsel, when their path led to a fountain and the queen's comb, still threaded with golden hair. 'Iseut la blonde', already evoked in the golden hair Soredamors worked into the shirt given to Alexandre in Cligés, reappears metonymically here to channel Lancelot's devotion to the queen, once he verifies that the queen in question is indeed 'the wife of king Arthur' (vs. 1423). First nearly fainting with pain, Lancelot catches himself in time before the damsel can catch him falling from his horse, then touches his eyes, mouth, forehead and face with the hairs a hundred thousand times before placing them next to his heart, judging them better protection than medications or saints (vss 1462–78). As in the prologue, hyperboles pile up, in Lancelot's mind and in the language of the text, as the narrator anticipates that we will take him for a crazy liar when he describes how golden those hairs really were (vss 1481–95).

With words and their meaning foregrounded, the religious echoes that furnish a kind of aura around Lancelot not surprisingly raise questions about how to read them: literally, figuratively, parodically, allegorically?[13] Chrétien surely expects his readers to recognize the Christological overtones given to the suffering martyr of love and redeemer of the captives. The passage into Gorre echoes Christ's Harrowing of Hell; His wounds on the cross anticipate Lancelot's, nicked on the side by the flaming lance, cut by the Sword Bridge on hands, feet and less holy knees. Gorre's mythic possibilities include not only Christian

---

[13] Jacques Ribard reads the romance as allegory: e.g., Chrétien de Troyes, Le Chevalier de la Charrette: essai d'interprétation symbolique (Paris, 1972). Robertsonian interpretations generally treat Lancelot as parody and look for allegorical meanings: e.g., D. C. Fowler, 'Love in Chrétien's Lancelot', Romanic Review, 63 (1974), 5–14.

but Celtic resonances – the Other World in an abduction story that Chrétien may have adapted from Marie's 'matiere' – as well as Classical antecedents in the story of Orpheus and Eurydice.[14] Chrétien's art, as expressed in the prologue to *Erec et Enide*, plays constantly on his ability to put together 'une mout bele conjunture', vs. 14 [a most beautiful conjoining]. Reading through this multiplicity of allusions, I suggest that the sacred echoes in Lancelot's story are neither blasphemous nor parodic: the knight lover is not a figure of Christ; rather, messianic reverberations effectively translate the extraordinary quality of Lancelot's secular heroism for a medieval public.

What about references to the adulterous triangle of Tristan, Iseut and King Mark, cued into the narrative by bloody sheets and Lancelot's variation on Iseut's ambiguous oath? With Lancelot and Guenevere, Chrétien has profoundly reimagined the lovers' tragic story, transforming the asocial character of their subversive and disordered passion by inextricably linking Lancelot's love for the Queen to his service on behalf of Arthurian society.[15] Alluding to the end of Arthur's kingdom in the cemetery episode, relocating and cropping the story of the Queen's abduction, adding a new hero and a new villain to eliminate incestuous overtones in the role of the King's nephew (common to Wace's *Roman de Brut* as well as the Tristan story), Chrétien's art of conjoining opens the possibility for rewriting the end of Arthur's reign in a less tragic mode, in consonance with his more comic impulses.[16] These choices reframe but do not entirely remove the dangers conjured up by disordering passion, hence the secrecy and isolation of the lovers' one night of love, which takes place in Gorre far from Arthur's kingdom of Logres; hence the difficulties of coordinating public and private values, love and chivalry, social roles and personal ties. However indirectly, the tensions and contradictions tied to an adulterous love are unavoidably expressed in the romance, especially in the parallels and contrasts which align the characterizations of Lancelot and Guenevere.

Their differences emerge with particular clarity in the tournament episode, the last scene written by Chrétien, according to Godefroi's epilogue.[17] While the lovers have much in common, they are located on opposite trajectories in terms of one characteristic feature already mentioned: their use of delay. Put most succinctly, the tournament allows the Queen to demonstrate how she has learned to hesitate where necessary, to accept the limitation of her public role and use it as a cover for private feelings, while Lancelot's performance, hesitating and not hesitating, confirms his ability to break through any limit, inasmuch as his public actions are always propelled by the direct expression of his love, whether or not it can be deciphered as such. How does this appear in the specifics of the episode, which highlight the tournament as spectacle observed and commented? The Queen's presence is the magnet that draws great crowds of knights, including Lancelot, who arrives from his imprisonment incognito

---

[14] Frappier, *Chrétien*, pp. 134–36.
[15] Jean-Charles Payen, 'Lancelot contre Tristan, ou la conjuration d'un mythe subversif', in *Mélanges Pierre Le Gentil* (Paris, 1973), pp. 617–32.
[16] Cf. *Cligés*'s variations on the same themes.
[17] For more extensive analysis, see Matilda Tomaryn Bruckner, *Shaping Romance: Interpretation, Truth and Closure in Twelfth-Century Fictions* (Philadelphia, 1993), pp. 60–108.

and prevents a herald, who discovers him by chance, from revealing his identity. The herald's enigmatic cry, 'Or est venuz qui l'aunera!' ['Now is come the one who will give the measure!', vss 5563, 5564, 5571, 5963], raises a whirl of excitement and mystery around the knight in red arms, which initially accords with his outstanding prowess and rivets all eyes on him. Everyone wants to know who he is, and the queen, who has perhaps remarked Lancelot's signature delay (entering the action only after the opening clash of arms, just as he was absent in the opening scene of the romance), sends her maiden to him with a message in the form of a pun. He should fight 'au noauz' (vs. 5654), which can be understood as an invitation to fight on the side of the lady of Noauz, one of the organizers of the tournament, or as a secret command, decipherable only by her lover, that he should appear as the worst. Lancelot immediately signals his willingness and transforms his prowess into a comic performance of cowardice, thereby confounding the crowd's expectations and the herald's cry. The queen now knows that this is Lancelot, but she repeats the same process the second day, until the report of Lancelot's response quickly prompts her to send a third message that he do his best.

We, like the crowd and the queen, must decipher obvious (and less obvious) disruptions and reconnections in the chain of cause and effect produced by Lancelot's contradictory performances. Following the play of intratextual echoes, readers readily interpret the choreography of actions as a response to two earlier scenes: Lancelot's two-step hesitation before the cart, used by the queen to explain her cold reception in Gorre, has now been corrected; his cowardly hesitations on the field of combat are the very proof of his unhesitating acceptance of any and every command love or the queen may send him. Critics who see the second day's repetition as gratuitous are inclined to blame the queen as a haughty *domna* who punishes her lover's earlier disobedience and humiliates him, as well as the values of chivalry. It seems to me more convincing to ask further questions about the apparent gratuity of the repetition: why might the queen hesitate to trust the first day's proof and how might the first and second proofs give different results? Let us recall first that words and signs frequently do not mean unambiguously what they say in this romance: indeed, the last time Guenevere received news about Lancelot, whose whereabouts had long remained a mystery for the court, it was in the form of a letter possessing 'entresaignes tes / Qu'il durent croire', vss 5270–71 [signs such that they had to believe them], despite the falsity of its claim that he had already returned to Arthur's court. Under these circumstances a second trial does not appear unwarranted, but there is also the further advantage of using it to reveal (and conceal) the perfect love and perfect knowledge of each other that the lovers share.

The queen certainly intervenes to manipulate Lancelot's performance, but her instructions show with what subtlety she understands the knight lover we have discovered in the course of the romance. The role she gives Lancelot 'au noauz' reprises his own voluntary and involuntary play with delay, disguise, even travesty, as his anonymous progress in the quest led repeatedly through momentary eclipses that set the stage for extraordinary feats. No one can do what Lancelot does, and all that he does is guided first by his trust in love, which may occasionally seem to suspend chivalry but ultimately raises it to unimagined heights. The misplaced scorn of those who witness the red knight's transformation at the tournament includes the accusation of *Malvestiez* (vss 5741, 5866) that Lancelot himself used to propel himself into battle against all odds and triumph. Here, too, the queen's goal is not to undermine Lancelot's prowess – witness the celerity of her third message – but to allow the maximum display of his love, as it explodes in a dazzling chivalric performance that galvanizes the attention of all who watch, including Gauvain (the Arthurian standard-bearer), who no more recognizes his friend here than he did earlier in the romance.

In fact, Lancelot remains the focus of desire throughout the tournament, whether he does his worst or his best. None of the young ladies will deign to marry anyone else in the year ahead, although the tournament was purposely arranged as a kind of reverse beauty pageant to let them choose husbands among the participants. The simultaneous disappearance of Lancelot and marriage at the end of the day hints again at the potentially disruptive force of his love for the queen. Although in the first part of the romance Lancelot identified himself several times as a knight of Logres, though his service for the queen overflows to the benefit of the king and his subjects, and is, in fact, essential and irreplaceable in light of Arthur's, Keu's and even Gauvain's failures, the Knight of the Cart remains a figure from elsewhere, a man raised by a fairy whose ring allows him to discern where there is or is not enchantment, a knight lover who crosses boundaries no one else can.

The tournament, a gratuitous escape inserted between two moments of imprisonment, offered the lovers their first opportunity to come together in Arthur's kingdom. Their indirect, displaced reunion in that public arena reconfigures the more perfect and private union in Gorre, as it anticipates the difficulties of future rendezvous. Indeed, in the final scene at Arthur's court, the narrator will give us access to the queen's joy when Lancelot reappears, while at the same time emphasizing her circumspection: body and heart separate; reason hides her crazy thoughts (vss 6820–53). The queen has learned to avoid the kind of problematic exposure that occurred with her cold reception; she has accepted the necessity to wait for the appropriate moment to show her private feelings (cf. Lancelot's regret after the night of love that no future meeting has been arranged, vss 4704–5). No closure will be found in the romance for the love story initiated between Lancelot and the queen, only expectations for something more, expectations the public no doubt shares with the lovers, though we all remain uncertain about what form their future may take. Desire that seeks and defers fulfillment, characteristic of lyric *fin'amor*, has survived the passage into romance despite narrative's need to translate feeling into action.[18] In recognizing the open-endedness written into the lovers' story, we thus return to the problem of how Chrétien managed to end *Le Chevalier de la Charrette*, how

---

[18] Desire that cannot obtain satisfaction is also a staple of psychoanalytic theory, which perhaps explains the attraction courtly love continues to exert over Jacques Lacan, Julia Kristeva et alia. See, for example, Kristeva's *Histoires d'amour* (Paris, 1983), pp. 263–76; Toril Moi, 'Desire in Language: Andreas Capellanus and the Controversy of Courtly Love', in *What is a Woman? and Other Essays* (Oxford, 1999), pp. 400–21; E. Jane Burns, 'Courtly Love: Who Needs It? Recent Feminist Work in the Medieval French Tradition', *Signs*, 27 (2001), 23–57.

indeed he managed to put it all together, the principal task he claims for himself in the prologue. What can we learn from the shape and architecture of his romance to help us determine what *san* it might convey?

All of Chrétien's romances use a series of episodes as the basic building block of narrative, but their organization into meaningful sequence differs considerably across a corpus which illustrates how the romancer's art of conjoining constantly experiments in putting together stories. The typical pattern of bipartition that operates generally in medieval narrative thus appears in a variety of guises in Chrétien's romances: scholars dispute whether they are two- or three-part in their basic organization, but all agree that multiple divisions established in the combination of episodes shape the perceptions and understanding of the public.[19] Since *Le Chevalier au lion* makes three references to *Le Chevalier de la Charrette*, and therefore ties together the actions of both romances through the echo of their titles as well as the movements of Gauvain, the contrast between them is particularly instructive, as long as we remember that comparisons among Chrétien's works are revealing without necessarily implying a judgment with respect to a norm. The overall structure that underlies both *Erec* and *Yvain* builds two parts around a crisis that requires correction; 'before and after' install a recognizable hierarchy, the final resolution of conflict superior to preliminary satisfactions achieved in the first part. In the *Charrette*, we cannot read the second part as a correction of the first: unlike the sequence of separate quests that organize the adventures of Erec and Yvain, Lancelot's single-minded quest to rescue the Queen operates from beginning to end; the conflict introduced in the opening scene by Meleagant's challenge is not finally resolved until the very last. Indeed, all closure in the romance is securely tied to the defeat of Meleagant in combat, a defeat that seems imminent in the middle of the romance, when Lancelot meets him on the field of arms not once but twice. Imminence turns out to be a false lure, however, when victory and resolution are repeatedly interrupted by the interventions of Bademagu and the Queen, delayed until the initial setting of Arthur's court can set the stage for the final destruction when Meleagant returns for the third time and unexpectedly meets the champion he had arranged to avoid. The tactics of delay and deferral clearly characterize the author/narrator as much as the lovers (cf. his positioning with first one then the other in the prologue and epilogue). Indeed, each of the characters in turn serves Chrétien's need to keep the story going, propelled to and from the problematic middle: Meleagant's disloyalty aids the romancer as much as Lancelot's loyalty, perhaps even more considering how much the art of deception characterizes the narrator's linguistic sleights of hand and the author's organizational strategy.

What differs considerably on the two sides of the middle is the episodic structure that connects the adventures. The confusing circularity of the midsection

---

[19] Donald Maddox, 'Trois sur deux: théories de bipartition et tripartition des œuvres de Chrétien de Troyes', *Œuvres et critiques*, 5 (1980/81), 91–102; Peter Haidu, 'Narrative Structure in *Floire et Blancheflor*: A Comparison with Two Romances of Chrétien de Troyes', *Romance Notes*, 14 (1972), 383–86; Douglas Kelly, *'Sens' and 'conjointure' in the 'Chevalier de la Charrette'* (The Hague, 1966), p. 68.

itself – where the narrator's and the plot's repeated departures and returns to Bath seem to lose all forward momentum – operates as a significant change in gears. In the first part, the linearity that propels Lancelot's quest is signalled by the detailed chronology, each day and night in the series indicated: seven days until Lancelot can first confront Meleagant, then two days more to their second combat, at which point the chronology shifts into the long periods of unspecified time designated in the second part, whose rhythms are marked by a refrain, the year's delay between the second and third combats, accorded at Bath and then moved forward after Meleagant's second visit to Arthur's court. A different kind of contrast appears in the patterns of causality linking the episodes of the two parts. Despite the linear clarity of the time frame, the juxtaposition of events in the first part appears illogical: a series of real or apparent non-sequiturs, loose ends, puzzles or mysteries often left unsolved and unsolvable, characterize Lancelot's adventures on the way to the Sword Bridge. Adventure in romance is by definition what unpredictably lies ahead, as the narrator keeps his focus aligned with the characters' so that we as much as they will be caught up in the play of anticipation and surprise. Adventures lie along the journey waiting for the designated hero; chance and necessity combine to reveal his identity, the special nature of his heroism. The marvellous, used discretely in the *Charrette*, carries with it an air of the supernatural that enhances Lancelot's value and gives lustre to his sangfroid, as he puts out the flames in the Perilous Bed or prepares to get a good grip on the sharp sword edge of the bridge by disarming his hands and feet (an act which the narrator characterizes as 'molt estrange mervoille', vs. 3096 [a very strange marvel]).

Of course, what appears illogical from a point of view based in the reality of the world outside romance may reveal a different kind of logic operating in the non-mimetic patterns of romance, as the series of analogues and intratextual echoes discussed above have already suggested. What seems unmotivated or gratuitous at the surface level yields possible meanings when we superimpose the matching elements and note the variations, reflect on their implicit commentary and make interpretations, that is, look for the romance's *san*. On the other hand, Chrétien does not hesitate to use the resources of realism when it suits his purpose, and this too has an impact on the quest for meaning. Episodes beginning in Bath and extending through the second part of the *Charrette* appear more logically linked according to the normal constraints of cause and effect, which has suggested a comparison with *Cligés* for Jean Frappier and disappointment for any number of critics who wonder if the romancer has lost his inspiration without the mythic overtones of the first part.[20] Their dissatisfaction with the change often translates into the familiar story about Chrétien, dissatisfied with his lady's command, happy to leave Lancelot suspended in Meleagant's tower and let Godefroi de Leigni finish the job. The possible let-down in the move from fantasy to realistic constraints – figured by the interplay between Logres and Gorre – may, however, have other roles to play in the world of romance, especially in a romance that does not hesitate to expose its own fictions in order

[20] Frappier, *Chrétien*, p. 132. Among the disappointed, Paule Le Rider, 'Le Dépassement de la chevalerie dans *Le Chevalier de la Charrette*', *Romania*, 112 (1991), 83–99.

to use fictionality as a tool necessary for working in the arena of human complexities that resist resolution.

The appearance of logic in the second part's sequence of events does not prevent certain confusions that help cover over what is happening at other levels of cause and effect. Recall the impression that the circular movements of the middle section in Bath paralyze the action and stall further development. While that may be true in relation to a plot line anchored on Meleagant, rumours that turn out to be false, repetitions that seem only to go back and forth, in fact move the love story forward and make possible the startling progress from cold rejection to the indescribable joys the lovers experience during their night of love. Once consummated, however, Lancelot and Guenevere's love becomes more problematic for Arthurian society, as we saw in the tournament episode, itself a kind of gratuitous interlude since the plot makes a circle around it. Its removal would make no difference in Lancelot's status as prisoner, yet its presence acquires necessity on other levels, as it encapsulates the paradoxes of Lancelot's role and the puzzle of his author Chrétien, who stops writing, we are told, at its completion, thereby making what follows a continuation of romance. Did we get the end desired? Do we really desire the end? The destabilizing effect of Godefroi's epilogue, which throws open the problem of ending just when the romance seemed so definitively ended by Meleagant's death, inevitably goes back to the destabilizing logic of the romance's middle, where circularity and linearity combine, as the contradictions of Lancelot's identity as knight and lover deepen and demand a search for meaning through interpretation.

In twelfth-century usage the term *san(s)* covers a gamut of semantic possibilities: meaning, but also direction, wisdom and good sense. The overlap appears in the prologue when the same word characterizes not only Marie's gift but the talents Chrétien brings to the project (vs. 23); the associations extend into the romance as well, further linking inside and outside worlds. If Lancelot has doggedly refused to turn in any other direction ('Je ne tornerai autre san', vs. 1381), off the 'droit chemin' [the right road],[21] the narrator has likewise promised repeatedly (and often deceptively) to avoid detours and delay by sticking to the straight road of his tale: 'je ne la [ma matire] vuel boceier, / . . . / Mes mener boen chemin et droit', vss 6249, 6251 [I don't want to put bumps in my story . . . but lead it along the good and right road].[22] The verbal thread that leads from *san* to the *droit chemin* also leads to the sense of right and wrong, the care and even anxiety the characters have for doing the right thing (or not), as well as the public's efforts to make sense of those decisions. The concatenation also leads back to the heated question of whether courtly love constitutes Marie's *san*, along with the debate about Chrétien's position for or against it. If one of the aims of this essay is to debunk the assumptions that underlie that polemic, the analysis presented here nevertheless confirms love as a major concern of the *Charrette*, which examines its multiple facets as well as its effects on courtly and chivalric behaviour. Far from showing love fixed into doctrine, as defined either

---

21 See vss 1345, 1359–60 and passim.
22 These verses are in Godefroi's part (see also vss 7098–10, 7111–12), but they echo Chrétien's narrator, e.g. vss 2989–90 and 3181–84.

by Andreas Capellanus or Gaston Paris, the 'Knight of the Cart' captures how difficult it is to reduce the complexities of 'right' loving. But if love undeniably operates as an important theme in the romance, it still needs to be located in a broader nexus of problems, if we are to properly discern the kind of meaning(s) put into play by Chrétien's total orchestration of the tale.

Just as the cart emblematically locates Lancelot at a difficult moment along his path, Chrétien's romance offers obstacles to guide us along the right road and outlines a direction to take in the search for significance, without marking a final destination. Framed by the shifting points of view introduced by the narrator's constant filtering of his story, Lancelot serves as a touchstone to reveal not only problems connected to love but larger issues of identifying and evaluating appropriate behaviour for a society where multiple systems of value make claims on individuals' choices and actions. Chrétien's romance constructs the fiction of Arthurian society as an ideal even as it examines the ideal's limitations and potential. Customs and private agreements, family and feudal hierarchy, marvellous adventures, love, chivalry and courtesy, all enter into competition and each requires a code of behaviour that may not be compatible with the others. If Lancelot's love for the queen is the most obvious and extended example – supreme joy and treasonous adultery, service to Guenevere and service to all, especially all ladies – it is by no means the only source of conflict and contradiction. Arthur fails to exercise the protection he owes his wife and queen when, despite the court's dismay, he determines to honour the Rash Boon promised Keu. Bademagu's pity for his son allows Meleagant's treachery to operate almost unchecked, despite the king of Gorre's own sense of loyalty and courtesy. These two kingdoms have much in common, whatever mythic resonances separate them, and together suggest that kingship in relation to chivalry, not just love, remains a crucial question in Chrétien's romances.[23]

Even within a single code of conduct, competing values may arise, as when Lancelot must answer requests from the Orgueilleux and Meleagant's sister for the knight's head: mercy and generosity make equally valid claims on him as a chivalrous knight and Lancelot says yes to both in his inner monologue before defining a set of actions that satisfies each of the claimants. Where conflicts and paradoxes multiply, solutions must be negotiated and Lancelot's process of reasoning, however unreasonable it may occasionally appear, establishes guidelines for making decisions. He does not eliminate competing values but sets up a hierarchy that subordinates all to love, whenever it comes into play. Lancelot is presented as 'the one who will give the measure', and the measure he gives is both exemplary and exceptional. On the one hand, the extreme shifts in his conduct 'for the best' and 'for the worst' furnish a model of the way appropriate action may change according to circumstance and perception. When Lancelot first appears in the romance he grabs the closest horse offered by Gauvain without regard for which one is better or worse, as he immoderately pursues the queen's abductor. Later, he demonstrates a keen sense of a horse's value and his

---

[23] Cf. Maddox, *Structure and Sacring* (Lexington, KY, 1978). On the conflict between kingship and chivalry as crucial to the history of the period, see Geoffrey Koziol, 'England, France, and the Problem of Sacrality in Twelfth-Century Ritual', in *Cultures of Power*, pp. 124–48.

own modesty, when he insists that the horse offered to replace the one killed by the Orgueilleux – the best his host owns (vs. 2978) – go rather to the new knight, the son of an earlier host who has accompanied the unknown liberator on his journey and whose own horse Lancelot now mounts.[24] Calling attention to his hero's gift for moderation and humility ('Mes une chose vos cont gié / Por ce que rien ne vos trespas / . . . ce vos voel conter', vss 2988–89, 2993 [But one thing I will tell you so that I pass over nothing for you . . . this I want to tell you]), Chrétien calls attention to his own gift for the 'petit fait vrai' that brings his story and characters alive before us.

On the other hand, Lancelot's conduct, always lively, is not always so easily deciphered, and it may not always be transferable either inside or outside the romance. Starting in the prologue, the author/narrator has insistently demonstrated how much interpretation is required to deal with the pitfalls of language, the multiplicity of points of view limited by what a given viewer knows or ignores, the mistakes that may proliferate in the misreading of signs. When Meleagant unintentionally deflects the charge of adultery away from Lancelot by incorrectly connecting the bloody sheets in two beds, we are at the heart of the contradictions that characterize both Lancelot and the romance that first introduces him as the queen's lover. Lancelot and Guenevere's love is and is not adultery – that is to say, viewed from a certain angle, of course, it is an act of treason against Arthur as husband and king. Viewed from another angle, the question of adultery – a word never used in the romance – disappears and then reappears along another route, which turns it into a conundrum that requires reflection and resists resolution. How to make sense of an apparent impossibility, the paradox in which Lancelot is Arthur's best knight and Guenevere's lover, not one or the other but both, not Arthur's best knight in spite of, but because of his love for the queen?

The impossibility topos appears directly in the language of the text, introduced repeatedly by characters grappling with Lancelot's performance. According to the vavassor's sons (vss 3050–65), even if he managed to cross the Sword Bridge, he could no more survive the two lions that await him on the other side than one can forbid the winds to blow (remember the prologue's praise) or the birds to sing, no more than a man can re-enter his mother and be reborn or the sea emptied – and yet the lions disappear when Lancelot arrives on the far side in the land from which no stranger has ever returned. In Gorre and in Logres, he will continue to do the impossible, successfully combining contradictions, resolving paradox as no one else can. No one else? But the romancer, too, plays with the possible and the impossible, uses fiction to ask questions about real human complexities, stretches the possible by imagining the impossible. The problems represented – from the social to the hermeneutic – suggest that Chrétien's *Charrette* is not arranged to offer unambiguous meaning. It does not codify a single value, recommending or disapproving courtly love, rather it

---

[24] The *cheval* [horse] is, of course, the sign par excellence of the *chevalier* [knight]. On Lancelot's connection with horses, see Rosanna Brusegan, 'L'Autre Monde et le Chevalier de la Charrette', in *Lancelot, Lanzelet: hier et aujourd'hui*, ed. Danielle Buschinger and Michel Zink (Greifswald, 1995), pp. 77–85.

aims at a wider ethical problem, the contradictions of human experience explored within a secular and courtly ideal. Chrétien invites movement toward that ideal, as much as he signals the conflicts that prevent its attainment. In *Le Chevalier de la Charrette,* he offers not answers but questions, direction embedded in the complex texture of romance. His art requires debate, interpretation and judgment, without removing the burden of decision from his public nor the power of emotion to capture our desires. Chrétien's success can be measured by the passionate enthusiasm of the medieval response, expressed in the immense prose romances of the thirteenth century, the positive and negative views of Lancelot elaborated in successive branches of the Vulgate Cycle. It continues today, filling scholarly shelves and popular movie theatres, as the Knight of the Cart continues to generate multiple interpretations and new approaches to satisfy and increase our desire for more.[25]

---

[25] See, for example, the Charrette Project on the Web, which makes available all the manuscripts, as well as a critical edition by Karl D. Uitti and Alfred Foulet and a modern French translation (http://www.princeton.edu/~lancelot and http://www.baylor.edu/lancelot); the collection of articles on the *Charrette* and critical theory published in a special issue of *Arthuriana,* 6 (1996), plus Lacanian interpretations offered by Robert S. Sturges, 'La(ca)ncelot', *Arthurian Interpretations,* 4 (1990), 12–23, and Jeffrey Jerome Cohen, 'Masoch/Lancelotism', *New Literary History,* 28 (1997), 231–60; as well as popular films from *Monty Python and the Holy Grail* to *First Knight.*

12

Le Chevalier au Lion: *Yvain Lionheart*

TONY HUNT

As King Arthur celebrates Pentecost, one of his knights, Yvain, overhears a cousin, Calogrenant, narrating an adventure in which he had lost face. Yvain at once vows to avenge him and precipitately leaves court for the scene of the adventure, a magic fountain in the forest of Brocéliande. He defeats the defender of the fountain, Esclados le Ros, and pursues the mortally wounded knight to his castle, where he promptly falls in love with the knight's widow, Laudine, whom he persuades to marry him through the ingenious help of her quick-witted hand-maiden Lunete. No sooner has the wedding taken place than Yvain is lured away to the tournaments by his best friend Gauvain and, heedless of the period of leave which his new wife has generously granted him, fails to return to her on time and is repudiated by her. A short period of madness follows, with the hero retreating to the forest as a sort of wild man. Rescued by the Lady of Noroison and three maidens, he embarks on a series of adventures, six in all, before being reunited with his lady through a stratagem devised by Lunete in the manner of the ruse she had employed to arrange the marriage in the first place. It is in the course of his adventures that Yvain rescues a lion from combat with a dragon and unexpectedly becomes the beneficiary thereafter of its devoted service, so that when he has an incognito meeting with Laudine he identifies himself to her as The Knight of the Lion, a pseudonym which is instrumental in the stratagem which reunites them.

Most critical introductions to *Yvain* begin by praising the clarity of its structure and the harmoniousness of its general design.[1] This is a first impression, but certainly strong enough to have led to its long being considered the perfect para-digm of medieval romance, a view reinforced by the number of close medieval translations or adaptations which were made of it, attesting to its popularity in Germany, Scandinavia, England and Wales, no less than in France, where the Lyonnais Pierre Sala rewrote it as late as 1522.[2] These are painstaking formal

1   As one example amongst many see Francis Dubost, '*Le Chevalier au lion:* une *"conjointure"* signifiante', *Le Moyen Âge*, 90 (1984), 195–222.
2   These are indicated in Tony Hunt, 'The Medieval Adaptations of Chrétien's *Yvain*: A Biblio-graphical Essay', in *An Arthurian Tapestry. Essays in Memory of Lewis Thorpe*, ed. Kenneth Varty (Glasgow, 1981), pp. 203–13, to which should now be added the contributions in *Die Romane von dem Ritter mit dem Löwen*, ed. Xenja von Ertzdorff (Amsterdam, 1994). On the Norse *Saga* see Régis Boyer, '*Ivens saga*: présentation de l'œuvre', *PRIS-MA*, 3 (1987), 15–22, and Jonna Kjaer, 'Franco-Scandinavian Literary Transmission in the Middle Ages: Two Old Norse Trans-lations of Chrétien de Troyes – *Ivens saga* and *Erex saga*', *Arthurian Yearbook*, 2 (1992), 113–34;

imitations with many of the problematic features removed, or at least simplified, a fact which proves instructive in identifying such features and assessing their contribution to the success of Chrétien's composition, both in the Middle Ages and today.[3]

By the mid-1980s a certain consensus seemed to have been established concerning the main interpretative problems in *Yvain*,[4] especially its pervasive irony and apparent critical detachment.[5] This may account for the fact that in the ensuing years it has received proportionally less critical discussion than Chrétien's other romances.[6] Nevertheless, there has been no interruption to the flow of studies on the manuscripts,[7] on the medieval French reception of the work,[8] or on its influence in art,[9] and it continues to be translated into modern European languages.[10] Against this background of critical perseverance the

and, on the Welsh, Ceridwen Lloyd-Morgan, 'Tradition et individualité dans le conte gallois d'*Owein*', *PRIS-MA*, 3 (1987), 129–35. On Pierre Sala see François Suard, 'Le Réécriture du *Chevalier au lion* par Pierre Sala', in Danielle Quéruel, *Amour et chevalerie dans les romans de Chrétien de Troyes* (Paris, 1995), pp. 329–41, Pierre Servet, ed., *Pierre Sala. Le Chevalier au lion* (Paris, 1996) and Claude Lachet, '*Le Chevalier au lion* au XVIe siècle', *Le Moyen Age*, 104 (1998), 545–49; and for echoes of *Yvain* in seven other works, see his study 'A la griffe on reconnaît le lion: quelques échos du *Chevalier au lion* dans les romans en vers des XIIIe et XIVe siècles', in Lachet, ed., *L'Œuvre de Chrétien de Troyes dans la littérature française: réminiscences, résurgences et réécritures* (Lyon, 1997), pp. 73–86.

3   See Tony Hunt, 'Beginnings, Middles and Ends: Some Interpretative Problems in Chrétien's *Yvain* and its Medieval Adaptations', in *The Craft of Fiction: Essays in Medieval Poetics*, ed. Leigh A. Arrathoon (Rochester, MI, 1964), pp. 83–117.

4   See, for example, Tony Hunt, 'Chrétien de Troyes' Arthurian Romance, *Yvain*', in *The New Pelican Guide to English Literature*, vol. 1:2, *Medieval Literature: The European Inheritance*, ed. Boris Ford (Harmondsworth, 1983), pp. 126–41, Tony Hunt, *Chrétien de Troyes, Yvain* (London, 1986), Joan Tasker Grimbert, '*Yvain* dans le miroir: une poétique de la réflexion dans le 'Chevalier au Lion' de Chrétien de Troyes* (Amsterdam, 1988), and Emmanuèle Baumgartner, *Chrétien de Troyes: Yvain, Lancelot, la charrette et le lion* (Paris, 1992).

5   A dissenting voice was Renée L. Curtis, 'The Reception of the Chivalric Ideal in Chrétien de Troyes's *Yvain*', *Arthurian Interpretations*, 3 (1989), 1–22.

6   See the entries in Douglas Kelly, *Chrétien de Troyes: An Analytic Bibliography, Supplement 1* (London, 2002). The paucity of monographs is partly compensated for by chapters devoted to *Yvain* in the studies by Per Nykrog, *Chrétien de Troyes: romancier discutable* (Genève, 1996), pp. 151–78, and Donald Maddox, *The Arthurian Romances of Chrétien de Troyes* (Cambridge, 1991), pp. 54–81.

7   See *Les Manuscrits de Chrétien de Troyes / The Manuscripts of Chrétien de Troyes*, ed. Keith Busby, Terry Nixon, Alison Stones and Lori Walters, 2 vols (Amsterdam, 1993) and the transcription by Kajsa Meyer, *La Copie de Guiot. fol.79v–105r du manuscrit f.fr.794 de la Bibliothèque Nationale, 'li chevaliers au lyeon' de Crestien de Troyes* (Amsterdam, 1995).

8   *The Legacy of Chrétien de Troyes*, ed. Norris J. Lacy, Douglas Kelly and Keith Busby, 2 vols (Amsterdam, 1987–88); Beate Schmolke-Hasselmann, *Der arthurische Versroman von Chrestien bis Froissart: zur Geschichte einer Gattung* (Tübingen, 1980), English trans. *The Evolution of Arthurian Romance: The Verse Tradition from Chrétien to Froissart* (Cambridge, 1998) by Margaret and Roger Middleton (Cambridge, 1998); Emmanuèle Baumgartner, *Chrétien de Troyes*, pp. 107–15. On the striking uptake of lines and motifs from *Yvain* in Guillaume le Clerc's *Fergus*, see Tony Hunt, 'The *Roman de Fergus*: Parody or Pastiche?' in *The Scots and Medieval Arthurian Legend*, ed. Rhiannon Purdie and Nicola Royan (Cambridge, 2005).

9   James A. Rushing, *Images of Adventure: Ywain in the Visual Arts* (Philadelphia, 1995); and Stephanie Cain Van D'Elden, 'Specific and Generic Scenes: A Model for Analyzing Medieval Illustrated Texts Based on the Example of *Yvain / Iwein*', *Bibliographical Bulletin of the International Arthurian Society*, 44 (1992), 255–69.

10 E.g., for the first time into Danish (*Loveridderen*) by Kajsa Meyer (Kopenhagen, 1991), into Dutch (*Ywein, de ridder met de leeuw*) by C.M.L. Kisling (Amsterdam, 1994), into Hungarian (*Az oroszlános lovag*) by A. and L. Vajda (Budapest, 1998), into Japanese by Yoshiko Kikuchi

present essay seeks to revise and update the position that had been reached in the 1980s.

It should be said at once that no such essay would come near to doing justice to *Yvain* if it were to offer firm, ostensibly authoritative conclusions about the work's 'meaning' and function, for Chrétien's ludic, theatrical, interrogatory tone makes it clear that almost everything in *Yvain* is debatable, deliberately so, and that it is a deeply paradoxical work, which tests its readers' intelligence and alertness at every turn. Some of the paradoxes run deep and merit illustration from the outset.

For example, the theme of visibility / invisibility, most prominently and comically presented in the scene of Yvain's imprisonment in Laudine's castle, is naturally enough correlated with the notion of identity / anonymity (incognito)[11] and focusses our attention on the problematic moral identity of the hero in the manner of Calogrenant's words to the forest herdsman enquiring if he is 'boine chose ou non', vs. 327 ['friend or foe'], in other words, whether he is what he seems and whether he has a stable identity at all.[12] This is an important issue in *Yvain*: how much of the hero do we really see, and are appearances reliable? When the inhabitants of Laudine's castle search for their master's assailant they know that he is present – the bleeding of the corpse (*cruentatio cadaveris*) proves that[13] – but they cannot see him at all. All they know of Yvain is what he has done, but chivalric feats in this romance turn out to be ambiguous. The grieving widow Laudine considers the invisible Yvain to be a coward (vss 1222–28) to whom her husband could never have fallen victim 'if he had seen him' (vs. 1236). The situation in which Laudine concludes that the hidden Yvain is 'a phantom or a devil' (vs. 1220) ironically recalls Calogrenant's initial suspicion that the herdsman was an evil shape-shifter. Yvain has something of the impostor about him, requesting a glimpse of his enemy's burial, when he really has eyes only for the distressed widow (vss 1271–81) – a voyeuristic trait which casts further doubt on the probity of Yvain's private agenda in the first part of the romance.

Paradoxically, the love plot unites an *ami* with his *anemie*[14] (vss 1364–65, 1454–65) in what is depicted as an act of revenge by Amors (vss 1366–70) on a

---

(Tokyo, 1994), into Spanish by Isabel de Riquer (Madrid, 1988) and Marie-José Lemarchand (Madrid, 1999).

11 See Antoinette Saly, '*Le Chevalier au lion*: un jeu de cache-cache ?' in her *Image, structure et sens: études arthuriennes* (Aix-en-Provence, 1994), pp. 23–32.

12 Unless otherwise indicated, references to *Yvain* are to the edition by David Hult in *Chrétien de Troyes, Romans, suivis des Chansons, avec, en appendice, Philomena*, gen. ed. Michel Zink (Paris, 1994). Translations are my own.

13 See Henri Platelle, 'La voix du sang: le cadavre qui saigne en présence de son meurtrier', in *La Pitié populaire au Moyen Age, Actes du 99e Congrès National des Sociétés Savantes, Besançon 1974*, Section de Philologie et d'Histoire jusqu'à 1610, 2 tomes (Paris, 1977), 1, pp. 161–79, and Marina Cometta, 'La "Bahrprobe" e la sua rappresentazione nel Nibelungenlied e in altri poemi epici medievali', *Acme: Annali della Facoltà di Filosofia et Lettere dell'Università di Milano*, 26 (1973), 331–57.

14 For 'the metaphor of battle [as] the principal vehicle for the story of their relationship until the very end of the poem', see Peter Nicholson, 'The Adventures at Laudine's Castle in Chrétien de Troyes's *Yvain*', *Allegorica*, 9 (1988), 195–219, who sees the romance as the narrative realization of the figurative imagery of courtly lyrics.

man who himself is an avenger (vss 58,746) and who is finally accepted by the people of the castle who at first seek to avenge (vs. 1058) their dead lord, the fountain knight. At the nadir of his fortunes, in the period of his madness, Yvain is depicted as a man who hates himself, has 'killed' himself, and who would rather lose his mind than fail to avenge himself (vss 2793–95). His solitariness (vss 2785, 2799) 'comme hom forsenés et sauvage', vs. 2828 [like a deranged wild man] exceeds that of the prospecting Calogrenant who set out 'seus comme païsans', vs. 176 [solitary as a peasant]. In an astounding characterisation of Love as all too often indiscriminate and apt to consort with low life (vss 1399–406), which fits ill with the picture presented in the prologue, as we shall see, Yvain, against all expectation, is said by the narrator to be an undeniably fitting and noble host (vss 1407–9). This is not how Yvain sees himself, for he considers himself crazy to want the one woman he surely cannot have, but cynically derives hope from the misogynistic adage that 'la donna è mobile' which does not rule out a change of heart on the part of Laudine.

The claim that Love may lodge in a 'vil lieu', vs. 1401 [base setting] recalls the opposition *cortois-vilain* [courtly / churlish] which certainly has an important role to play in the romance (see below) and constitutes yet another paradox. At first, it might seem that the herdsman in Brocéliande[15] and the lion in the forest clearing embody such a polarity, but this view is too simple. The herdsman is much more than a specimen of acromegaly; he remains civil throughout his encounter with the slightly overbearing Calogrenant and reveals without fuss, but with a legitimate pride, 'Ainsi sui de mes bestes sire', vs. 353 ['In this way I am master of my animals']. Far from being an evil shape-shifter, as the knight fears, he is both benign and efficient in fulfilling his role in the social order, and bows to the knight's desire for adventure by directing him to the fountain despite knowing that the raising of the storm will ravage the forest and the wild life within it. The lion, by contrast, is having less success in fulfilling its traditional role as the 'king of beasts', and reacts with such humble gratitude that there occurs one of the rare indications of Yvain's personal response to what is happening to him: 'Si li plaist mout cheste aventure', vs. 3407 [This event pleases him greatly], for he perceives in the lion 'la grant amor qu'en li ot', vs. 3453 [the great affection that resided in him]. Instead of the gratuitous destruction of the forest's wildlife, we now have the lion's discriminate hunting – 'Che veut nature', vs. 3423 [the prompting of nature] – of wild beasts to sustain life, that of his master and himself. *Vilain* and *cortois* turn out to be less transparent labels than we might have imagined.

As for the lion, it too embodies a paradox, a combination of opposites, for it was thought, throughout the Middle Ages, to unite two attributes, those of being humble to the meek and fierce to the proud.[16] An author like Chrétien must have realised in how many different ways it could be interpreted and

---

[15] See Alice Planche, 'Les Taureaux et leur maître: sur un épisode discuté de l'*Yvain* de Chrétien de Troyes', *PRIS-MA*, 4 (1988), 9–19.

[16] See Tony Hunt, 'The Lion and Yvain' in *The Legend of Arthur in the Middle Ages: Studies Presented to A.H. Diverres by Colleagues, Pupils and Friends*, ed. P.B. Grout et al. (Cambridge, 1983), pp. 86–98.

deemed its polyvalence appropriate to this constantly questioning and provoca-tive romance.[17] The notion of reciprocity with which the lion is associated finds obvious application to Yvain. The lion is introduced at the mid-point of the romance and remains inextricably connected with the hero's rehabilitation, however that rehabilitation is understood.

Another paradox is represented by the forest and the storm at the fountain,[18] which in this romance constitutes the gateway to adventure. For all its destruc-tive properties, vividly depicted by Chrétien, the storm also affords a glimpse of an ideal harmony, in the singing of the birds. The birds are at first expatriated (vs. 398) by the storm along with every other living creature of the forest, but when God quells it (vss 449, 452, 805) the birds return and sing in a joyful polyphony (vss 454–56, 468, 471; 809, 811) – a motif drawn from the Brendan legend – which hints at the possibility of a happier outcome than the combat with Esclados, just as the imprisoned Yvain at Laudine's castle is told by Lunete 'Grans biens vous en porra venir', vs. 1316 ['Good fortune may yet be yours']. Subsequently, Yvain returns to the forest where he is sustained, during the period of his madness, by the deer which furnish his meat (an obvious imitation of the forest of Morrois in the Tristan story). His 'folie', of course, is incalculably more serious than the 'folly' acknowledged by Calogrenant (vss 576–77) whom he set out to avenge.[19] It is Yvain's return to the fountain which instigates the machinations of Lunete which win him back his lady.

Yvain is a difficult work for feminists. Though intimately connected, Lunete and Laudine offer two very different faces when confronting men.[20] Lunete may

17 For an almost exhaustive review of interpretations of the lion, see Dietmar Rieger, '"Il est a moi et je a lui". Yvains Löwe – ein Zeichen und seine Deutung', in *Die Romane von dem Ritter mit dem Löwen*, pp. 245–85, and ' "Il est a moi et je a lui" ': Le Lion d'Yvain – un symbole et son champ sémantique', in *Ensi firent li ancessor: mélanges de philologie médiévale offerts à Marc-René Jung*, ed. Luciano Rossi, 2 vols (Alessandria, 1996), 1, pp. 349–69. On the ubiquity of the lion in medieval iconography, see Jean Dufournet, 'Le Lion d'Yvain' in Jean Dufournet, ed., *Le Cheva-lier au lion: approches d'un chef-d'œuvre* (Paris, 1988), pp. 77–104, and Robert Favreau, 'Le Thème iconographique du lion dans les inscriptions médiévales', *Comptes rendus de l'Académie des Inscriptions, juillet–octobre 1991*, pp. 613–36. The leonine literary evidence is assembled by Paule le Rider, 'Lions et dragons dans la littérature, de Pierre Damien à Chrétien de Troyes', *Moyen Age*, 104 (1998), 9–52, who thinks Chrétien was inspired by certain crusade stories and quite specifically the Old French epic *Les Chétifs*; and Michel Stanesco, 'Le lion du chevalier: de la stratégie romanesque à l'emblème poétique', *Littérature*, 19 (1988), 13–31, and *Littérature*, 20 (1989), 7–13. See also Helen C.R. Laurie, 'Beasts and Saints: a Key to the Lion in Chrétien's *Yvain*', *Bibliographical Bulletin of the International Arthurian Society*, 39 (1987), 297–306.
18 Cf. Marie-Luce Chênerie, 'Le Motif de la fontaine dans les romans arthuriens en vers des XIIe et XIIIe siècles', in *Mélanges de langue et littérature françaises du moyen âge et de la Renaissance offerts à Monsieur Charles Foulon*, 2 vols (Rennes, 1980), 1, pp. 99–104.
19 See Jean-Marie Fritz, *Le Discours du fou au Moyen Age* (Paris, 1992), Muriel Laharie, *La Folie au Moyen Age (XIe–XIIIe siècles)* (Paris, 1991), esp. pp. 146f, 227–30, Monique Santucci, 'La Folie dans *Le Chevalier au lion*', in Dufournet, *Le Chevalier au lion*, pp. 151–72.
20 See James R. McGuire, 'L'Onguent et l'initiative féminine dans *Yvain*', *Romania*, 112 (1991), 65–82 (with bibliography); Ellen Germain, 'Lunete, Women, and Power in Chrétien's *Yvain*', *Romance Quarterly*, 38 (1991), 15–25; Judith Rice Rothschild, 'Empowered Women and Manip-ulative Behaviors in Chrétien's *Le Chevalier au lion* and *Le Chevalier de la charrette*', *Medieval Perspectives*, 7 (1992), 171–86; R. Allen, 'The Roles of Women and their homosocial context in the *Chevalier au Lion*', *Romance Quarterly*, 46 (1999), 141–54; J.M. Sullivan, 'The Lady Lunete: Literary Conventions of Counsel and the Criticism of Counsel in Chrétien's *Yvain* and Hartmann's *Iwein*', *Neophilologus*, 85 (2001), 335–54.

be thought to represent women's empowerment, for she is much more than a *suivante* [attendant], whereas the haughty, though certainly wronged, Laudine might suggest women's vulnerability.[21] Is there such a thing as a 'heroine' in this romance? Laudine remains isolated, whilst Lunete participates in the significant theme of friendship, rather than amatory relations, enjoying a remarkable independence from both the courtly world (she was lacking in 'courtoisie', which is why nobody at court would speak to her, vss 1004–9) and from Laudine's dominion and control.[22] A strong contrast, in her loyal, determined and unwavering assistance, to the touchy Laudine, she stands out for her masculine independence and initiative, appropriating a set of male roles without difficulty as well as possessing a lucid capacity for manipulating and influencing events. Her success in backing the misbehaving hero and in arranging Laudine's final, forced surrender leaves a number of question marks at the end of the work.

Such are some of the paradoxes which permeate the romance of the Knight of the Lion. Yvain's adventures are somewhat kaleidoscopic, forming different patterns for different critics, who are left without any guidance from the protagonist himself.[23] It may at least be said that the adventures are all concerned with helping women. For some readers they may be seen as reflecting victory over the hero's own flaws or vices; they can be said to begin with the moral obligation of gratitude to the Lady of Noroison, who has cured Yvain; and some degree of responsibility for Lunete's predicament likewise explains the hero's involvement with, and defeat of, her accusers, but only after he has exhibited a newly acquired sense of punctuality in championing the nieces and nephews of Gauvain against the giant Harpin de la Montaigne. For most critics the central symbolic episode remains the rescue of the lion. But arguably the most important adventures, which are interlaced, are the last two, the liberation of the silkworkers at Pesme Aventure,[24] and the settling of the inheritance dispute between two sisters, daughters of the Lord of Noire Espine, two adventures in which the lion plays no role. These culminating adventures both contain striking elements of social realism and also remain unknown to Laudine and are thus 'gratuitous', playing no part in the formation of her opinion of the 'Knight of the Lion' before he is revealed as her husband. These and many other views are under regular critical discussion. More generally, the adventures may be thought to be the product of chance (*aventure*) or of Christian Providence.[25] How

---

[21] See Marc Glasser, 'Marriage and the Use of Force in *Yvain*', *Romania*, 108 (1987), 484–502.

[22] See Herta Zutt, 'Die unhöfische Lunete', in *Chevaliers errants, demoiselles et l'Autre: höfische und nachhöfische Literatur im europäischen Mittelalter: Festschrift für Xenja von Ertzdorff zum 65. Geburtstag*, ed. Trude Ehlert (Göppingen, 1998), pp. 103–20.

[23] My view that Yvain's 'inner life is hidden from us', referring to Chrétien's conspicuous avoidance of revealing Yvain's own possible insights into his actions and their motivation, is opposed by Saul N. Brody, 'Reflections on Yvain's Inner Life', *Romance Philology*, 54 (2000–01), 277–98. He discusses elements of Yvain's adventures as symbolic representations of struggles within him, notably the moral flaws which he must overcome, thus relegating them to his old self (Yvain) as opposed to the new man called the Knight of the Lion. Whatever the persuasiveness of Brody's analysis, it has nothing to do with Yvain's self-consciousness and awareness of what is happening to him.

[24] See Jean Subrenat, 'Pourquoi Yvain et son lion ont-ils affronté les fils de netun?' in Dufournet, ed. *Le Chevalier au lion*, pp. 173–93.

[25] Cf. Tony Hunt, 'The Christianization of Fortuna', *Nottingham French Studies*, 38 (1999), 95–113.

far they should be considered to constitute a 'quest' is a moot point. The *Erec* incorporates a double quest: one in which the hero tests and confirms his wife's loyalty in a series of chivalric encounters in which he is the defender; and one in which he exemplifies the ethical imperative of chivalry by succouring those in need of his aid. Similarly it might be said that *Yvain* presents two sequences of adventures: the first, in which the hero acts out of gratitude or obligation (Dame de Noroison, Lunete) and the second in which he gratuitously comes to the aid of distressed young women who need help. But this still leaves the question of the lengthy 'adventure' involving the avenging of Calogrenant which brings Yvain to the fountain for the first time and, paradoxically through the killing of Esclados, lays the foundation of his marriage.

Yvain's declared innocence of any misdemeanour concerning Esclados's death – 'la mort dont je n'ai rienz meffait', vs. 1995 ['the death which involved no wrongdoing on my part'] – when he first comes before Laudine requires some consideration. On his reunion with her he refers to his 'mal / non / fol savoir', vs. 6772 ['foolish state of mind'], and the line which follows, 'Folie me fist demourer', vs. 6774 ['Stupidity prolonged my absence'], seems to indicate quite clearly that he is referring to his enthusiasm for the tourneys at which he is detained by Gauvain. His protestation of innocence at his first meeting with Laudine finds surprisingly easy acceptance from her, as she bids him tell her if he committed any misdemeanour, and, when asked in turn whether a man who defends himself victoriously against an aggressor does wrong, she replies 'Nenil, qui bien i garde a droit', vs. 2007 ['Not from a strictly legal point of view'] and promptly acquits him of 'touz torz et touz meffaiz', vs. 2014 ['all wrongs and misdeeds']. Are we persuaded that she is right? What about the moral point of view? Certainly Yvain embarks on the fountain adventure impetuously and pre-emptively, neglectful of the standard court proprieties: he departs clandestinely, without the leave of his monarch (his isolation is emphasized in vss 677, 689–92, 723). At the fountain he behaves impatiently (vs. 800). Throughout, his principal desire is to arrogate to himself a mission of vengeance which he fears may otherwise be accorded to Kay or Gauvain (vss 680–88), a rivalry which receives neither explanation nor justification. The combat with Esclados is fierce, though initially respectful of chivalric etiquette (neither combatant seeks to harm his opponent's horse), and all the more satisfying for the knights' wish to continue fighting on horseback and not to dismount. But when the decisive moment comes, the infliction of a mortal wound on Esclados, it is clearly marked by the narrator with the comment 'S'i foï puis, n'ot mie tort, / Car il se sent navrés a mort, / Que riens ne li valut deffence', vss 871–73 [He then fled and had good reason to, for he could tell he was mortally wounded, that further resistance was futile], whilst close by preparations are made to receive the defeated knight in his castle. In the meantime he is subjected to the unbridled ferocity of the pursuing victor, who follows so closely that he can hear his victim's agonized moaning. Yvain's own safety is not at risk, so why does he pursue the fountain knight so relentlessly? The answer is that Yvain is still smarting from Kay's earlier taunts and is bent on gaining at all costs some visible token of his victory in order to allay future criticism or mockery (vss 890–97). As an example of courtly romance *Yvain* is strikingly unusual in that the moral probity of the hero appears to be impugned even before the crisis of a disintegrated marriage.

And how can we describe the hero's aberration from the chivalric quest of revenge to one of love, which involves his memorable transition from a literal prison (between the portcullises of Laudine's castle) to a metaphorical one (vss 1924–44), with its lesson 'sanz prison n'est nus amis', vs. 1942 ['There is no lover who is not a prisoner'], 'bien est en prison qui aime', vs. 1944 ['Every lover is a prisoner']? We may well feel that when first seeking 'pes et acorde', vs. 1970 (cf. 6761, 6769) ['peace and conciliation'] with the widow Laudine, Yvain strikes a humbler and less confident pose than in the final reconciliation scene: 'Mesire Yvains maintenant joint / Les mainz, si s'est a genoulz mis, / Et li dist comme vraiz amis', vss 1974–76 [My lord Yvain at once clasps his hands, falls to his knees, and speaks like a true lover], an eager and absolute submission which even astonishes the lady herself (vss 1984–87) and finds expression in lines like: 'Dame, ja voir ne crïeray / Merci, ainz vos mercïeray / De quanque vous me vouroiz fere, / Que riens ne me porroit desplere', vss 1977–80 ['Lady, I shall not ask for mercy, but will be grateful for whatever you are disposed to do with me, for nothing could displease me']. Yvain here pledges subservience with a well tried formula, 'pour vous, a delivre, / veil, c'il vous plaist, mourir ou vivre', vss 2033–34 ['For you, unreservedly I will, if it is your wish, happily live or die'], a humility whose success is reflected in the narrator's assurance 'Et mesire Yvains est plus sire / Quë il n'osast penser ne dire', vss 2053–54 [My lord Yvain now exercises such lordship as he could ever have dared imagine]. This is very different from Yvain's coercive strategy (see vss 6507–16) at the end, which causes such destruction in and around Laudine's town that the inhabitants curse their very choice of settlement (vss 6537–45), for it is then they who become prisoners (vss 6551–54)! The wooing of Laudine is often comically theatrical as Yvain seeks, morally speaking, to marginalize his act of homicide, on which he must perforce depend for his claim that he will be an effective defender of Laudine's fountain, which has become a pressing priority. It is thus difficult to see the hero's amatory quest as any less precarious than his chivalric one.

The ambiguities and paradoxes of the romance's main scenes need now to be viewed in the more general frame in which Chrétien has placed them. The *ex abrupto* opening of the work deviates from the standard romance prologue[26] and upsets the expected equilibrium of the authorial introduction. For many readers it establishes subversiveness as a characteristic feature of the entire work. Technically, the first forty-one lines may be considered an indirect approach (*insinuatio*) to the work's substance which initially draws us into the genre of Arthurian romance by praising Arthur as an exemplar of prowess and courtliness, by referring to his rich Pentecostal celebrations, and by an appreciation of the ready audience his court provided for stories of love and the experiences of members of love's 'community' or 'order' (*covant*). But halfway through this

---

26 See Tony Hunt, 'Chrétien's Prologues Reconsidered', in *Conjunctures: Medieval Studies in Honor of Douglas Kelly*, ed. Keith Busby and Norris J. Lacy (Amsterdam, 1994), pp. 153–68 and, more generally, *Seuils de l'œuvre dans le texte médiéval: études recueillies par Emmanuèle Baumgartner et Laurence Harf-Lancner*, 2 vols (Paris, 2002).

introduction there is a striking change of direction beginning with a temporal contrast: 'then' (*lors*) the order of love was rich and good, 'but now' (*mes ore*) it has few adherents. The adversative conjunction *mes* articulates a series of contrasts between historical past (Arthurian society) and authorial present,[27] the former highly valued, it seems, and the latter firmly depreciated. The touchstone of judgment is love and this triggers a series of paradoxes. Writing in an age dubbed the 'Age of Ovid' (*aetas ovidiana*), an age saturated in writings – spiritual, fictional, didactic – on love, the author rejects the age's commitment and good faith and reverts to the past: 'Let us leave alone those now alive and speak of those from the past' (vss 29–30). In arguing that contemporaries make a mockery of love, the narrator employs the words *fable* and *menchonge*, both of which are also used to describe literary fictions: Calogrenant, in his own, recognizably 'literary' prologue to the account of his misadventure (vss 149–74)[28] protests that he has no intention of speaking of 'songe, / Ne de fable ne de menchonge, / Dont maint autre vous ont servi', vss 171–73 ['some fantasy, fiction or lie of the sort plenty of others have dished out to you']. We wonder, therefore, whether both these prologues voice a critique of contemporary literature (if so, of the troubadours or of the romancers?) as well as, or instead of, amatory mores. The end of Chrétien's prologue reinstates the Arthurian Golden Age, but not without having glossed the temporal distinction with a moralising formula: 'Qu'encor vaut mix, che m'est a vis, / Un courtois mors c'uns vilains vis', vss 31–32 [For it seems to me that a courtly person, even when dead, is preferable to a churl who is alive]. The application of this apophthegm occurs strikingly at the moment of Yvain's precarious marriage to the widow of the fountain knight, the courtly Esclados: the narrator tells us, somewhat insensitively, that the dead knight is now forgotten, his killer is married to his wife and sleeping with her, and her people praise 'le vif', vs. 2171 [the living man] more than they ever did 'le mort', vs. 2171 [the dead man]. This is also a literary allusion to Oedipus's marriage to Jocasta in the *Roman de Thèbes* (vss 482–86), but the connexion with Chrétien's prologue is too obvious to be overlooked. Is Yvain presented, by implication, as a 'vilains vis', vs. 32 [living churl]?

The Arthurian company depicted in the romance is revealed to be very much less ideal than is suggested in the prologue and the elements of contemporary feudal reality incorporated in the protagonist's adventures are also less than reassuring. Arthur's court finds room for an ineffectual knight, Calogrenant, with little comprehension of his function; a bilious seneschal, Kay, whose rudeness to the Queen justifies his final ignominy at the fountain; and a chivalric butterfly, Gauvain, whose inopportune absences from court are the result of an overzealous and somewhat indiscriminate sense of chivalric duty to ladies. All three are nevertheless instrumental in the directing of Yvain's chivalric career. Arthur himself is scarcely a rock of stability: he creates a stir by retiring with the Queen to the royal bedroom at the height of the Pentecostal festivities, thus

---

[27] See the analysis by Grimbert, *'Yvain' dans le miroir*, pp. 13–34.

[28] The conflation of knight and romancer, both errant, with its unmistakable echo of Wace, *Roman de Rou*, vss 6395–98, suggests the equivalence of 'trover aventures' to both 'find' and 'compose'.

missing Calogrenant's carefully crafted narrative of his adventure ('les noveles Calogrenant') which has been displaced from the conventional preprandial slot reserved for the arrival of 'noveles' [news] at Arthur's court; he fails to admonish the elder sister in the inheritance dispute although he knows she is in the wrong (vss 5905–7, confirmed by the king vss 6380–81);[29] and he obstinately declines to separate Yvain and Gauvain in their inconclusive duel (vss 6176–86), despite the entreaties of the younger sister of Noire Espine and all her supporters, who include kings and knights, ladies and townspeople, and the Queen herself, named here for the first time (vs. 6172). When Gauvain pronounces himself defeated, Arthur's 'leave it to me' rejoinder (vss 6362–68) is somewhat pompous, and in the end he is obliged to intimidate the elder sister (vss 6410–18) to gain any concession at all. Arthur's last act is to procure medical treatment for the two combatants in the duel, and thereafter he disappears.

The Arthurian court does not, therefore, seem to exemplify the chivalric excellence which Chrétien at the beginning had claimed for it nor to define the values that courtly romance is expected to incorporate. Nor does it embody an amatory ideal. Gauvain and Yvain display varying degrees of ineptitude concerning love, the hapless Laudine is from outside the court (from Landuc[30]), and Lunete is not from Arthur's court either, having been snubbed by all save Yvain when she once visited it. The hero's successful relationships are in fact those of friendship – with a fellow knight (Gauvain), a female well-wisher (Lunete) and a grateful beast (the lion). In view of all these discrepancies and surprises we may say that the major interpretative challenge posed by *Yvain* is to bring the prologue into a coherent relationship with the narrative to which it is so provocatively prefixed. That *Yvain* actually subverts both courtly love and the courtly romance is a possibility that surprises, yet cannot simply be dismissed.

At the other end of the structural spectrum, the romance's conclusion embodying the final reunion of the hero and his lady is, though less complicated, just as problematic. Compared with the hero's marriage the situation is here inverted, the question being not whether, when Laudine is said to love Yvain (vss 2111–14, 2139–42), she really does so, but, rather, whether, when she claims *not* to love him (vss 6752–53, 6756–61) she truly does not? In the conclusion the word love (*amor / amer*) is studiously avoided, its implementation and acknowledgement being desired by God (vss 6740–41) and by Lunete (vs. 6753), but never conceded by Laudine herself. Instead, the key word is *pes*, 'reconciliation', which sits nicely on the surface of things and occurs no fewer than ten times in the finale. On its last occurrences it appears alone, whereas earlier it is used in binary constructions 'pais ne acorde' (vss 6761, 6769), 'boine pais et boine amour' (vs. 6741), 'pais . . . pardon' (vs. 6725). However much the audience may desire an expression of love from Laudine, it remains lacking and has to be supplied by the narrator, who resolutely presents only Yvain's point of

---

29 See Maddox, *Once and Future Fictions*, pp. 69–81.
30 See Alfred Foulet and Karl D. Uitti, 'Chrétien's "Laudine": *Yvain*, vv. 2148–55', *Romance Philology*, 37 (1984), 293–302, and Brian Woledge, *Commentaire sur Yvain (Le Chevalier au lion) de Chrétien de Troyes*, 2 vols (Geneva, 1986), 1, pp. 135–38 (seven out of nine manuscripts simply call her 'la dame de Landuc').

view, that of Laudine herself being completely ignored: 'Mout en est [sc. Yvain] a boin chief venus, / Qu'il est amés et chiers tenus / De sa dame, et ele de luy', vss 6793–95 [He has come to a happy end, for he is loved and cherished by his lady, and she by him]. The enjambement leading to the words 'sa dame' as a 'rejet' makes the omission of Laudine's feelings all the more conspicuous and reminds us of the moment when the terrified Yvain first comes face to face with her 'la ou il iert mout chier tenuz', vs. 1947 [where he will be greatly appreciated]. How much of the narrator's commentary is subject to the possibly ironic qualification found in Foerster's text 'Si poez croire', ed. Reid vs. 6801 [You may well believe] is uncertain, particularly as the phrase is absent from some manuscripts.[31] Nevertheless the conclusion remains shaky, not least because the basis of the allegedly permanent union remains entirely nugatory, whilst the coercive fear of perjury is prominent, substantial and unequivocal.[32] It is true that after his incognito meeting with her earlier Yvain tells Laudine that he could only accept her invitation to return (vs. 4617, a nice irony!) when he felt sure 'Que le boin gré ma dame eüsse', vs. 4620 ['That I had gained my lady's favour'] an expression no doubt carefully chosen so as not to alarm Laudine, whilst his *sotto voce* aside uses the amatory metaphor of the casket, lock and key which contain his 'joie', which would certainly have alerted her to his identity. So much for the 'reconciliation' of Yvain and Laudine, a scene as serious as the original courtship was comic in its earlier mixture of virtuoso talk and humour.[33]

But, we may ask, how is the apparent reconciliation of the Knight with the Lion and his wife related more precisely to their earlier incognito meeting (vss 4574–4628)? Is not the latter the most significant turning point in Yvain's chivalric odyssey?[34] The inevitable question arises as to why Yvain does not at that meeting appear to seek reconciliation. It seems in some ways a propitious moment, for Laudine has herself, through Yvain's intervention, just been reconciled with Lunete. Cannot Yvain hope for the same fate? Both the audience and the hero, perhaps, hear warning bells: the narrator, echoing Ovid,[35] remarks on the condign punishment meted out to the seneschal who had instigated the charge of treason against Lunete: 'Que chë est raison de justiche / Que chil qui autrui juge a tort, / Doit de chelui meïsme mort / Morir quë il li a jugie', vss 4566–69 [For it is a principle of justice that whoever wrongly sentences another should die the same death as he intended for him] – the enjambement foregrounds *mort* as a 'rejet' and opens up disturbing possibilities for the hero's future. Moreover, Laudine, in criticising Yvain's 'lady' (vss 4588–89), lets slip a qualification which may inhibit any attempt on his part at reconciliation at this

---

31   As it is from Hult's text. For Foerster's text, see Chrestien de Troyes, *Yvain (Le Chevalier au lion): The Critical Text of Wendelin Foerster with Introduction, Notes and Glossary* by T.B.W. Reid (Manchester, 1942).

32   For a totally opposite view, see Micheline Dessaint, *La Femme médiatrice dans de grandes œuvres romanesques du XIIe siècle* (Paris, 2001), esp. p. 152.

33   See Philippe Ménard, 'Rires et sourires dans *Le Chevalier au lion*', in Dufournet, *Le Chevalier au lion*, pp.7–29, esp. p. 13.

34   See Maurice Accarie, 'La Structure du *Chevalier au lion* de Chrétien de Troyes', *Moyen Age*, 84 (1978), 13–34.

35   Ovid, *Ars amatoria*, I, 653ff.

point: that lady, opines Laudine, should not bar her door to a knight of such distinction 'Se trop n'eüst vers li mespris', vs. 4592 ['unless he had greatly wronged her']. Yvain ironically declares that he prefers not to reveal his wrong-doing save to those who already know it, i.e., to Lunete! Laudine asks, 'Does anyone else know about it apart from you two?' (vs. 4599) but curiously does not persist with the question when Yvain retorts, 'Yes, indeed' (vs. 4600). Instead she asks him his name and he reveals only his pseudonym, 'the Knight with the Lion' (vs. 4607), which Laudine does not recognize, prompting Yvain's humble explanation 'ne sui guaires renommés', vs. 4614 ['I am not very well known']. Both Laudine and Yvain display elements of hesitation, yet it is after this encounter that the knight perceives the way forward:

> Mesire Yvains, qui sans retour
> Avoit son cuer mis en amour,
> Vit bien que durer ne porroit,
> Mais pour amors enfin morroit
> Se sa dame n'avoit merchi
> De li; qu'il se moroit pour li.   (vss 6501–6)

> [My lord Yvain, whose heart was irrevocably set on love, realized only too well that he would not be able to go on, but would in the end die of love, unless his lady forgave him, for he was pining away for love of her.]

His future strategy is overtly one of coercion, but his concealed departure for the fountain now recalls his solitary, clandestine disappearance (vss 691–92, 717–19) at the beginning of the romance after hearing Calogrenant's tale:

> Et pense qu'il s'en partiroit
> Toz sols de court et si iroit
> A se fontaine guerroier,
> Et s'i feroit tant fourdroier
> Et tant venter et tant plouvoir
> Que par force et par estouvoir
> Li couvendroit faire a li pais,
> Ou il ne fineroit jamais
> De la fontaine tourmenter,
> Si feroit plouvoir et venter.   (vss 6507–16)

> [He makes the decision to leave the court, alone, and to create havoc at her fountain, producing such lightning, wind and rain, that she would be compelled to make her peace with him, else he would continue for ever more to cause disruption by storm, rain and wind.]

The beginning, the deferred reunion of the lovers, and the romance's conclusion thus provide plenty of puzzles.

How far does 'The Romance of the Knight with the Lion' reflect within it the problems of romance composition and thus function as a self-reflexive experiment? Before the post-crisis sequence of the protagonist's chivalric adventures we have already witnessed a significant combination of narrative (*conte*) and adventure (*aventure*)[36] in the fountain expedition, of which we are given no fewer than three versions.[37] Calogrenant's quest with its literary prologue represents in embryo (*mise en abyme*) the courtly tale or *conte*, whilst his self-definition as 'uns chevaliers, / Qui quier che que trouver ne puis', vss 356–57 ['a knight in search of what he cannot find'], namely 'Aventures, pour esprouver / Ma proeche et mon hardement', vss 360–61 ['adventures to test my prowess and mettle'], is also a *mise en abyme* of the knight errant. Calogrenant had already been introduced to this idea by his host, who had revealed how long it was since he had lodged 'chevalier errant / Qui aventure alast querant', vss 259–60 ['a knight riding in search of adventure'] and who begged Calogrenant to return and relate his experience. The host's company, a microcosm of the chivalric court, receive him no less courteously on his return (Calogrenant scrupulously keeps his promise), when the pain of disgrace and defeat is somewhat mitigated by the revelation that he is the first knight to escape from the fountain with his life, perhaps in recognition of his innocence. At any rate Calogrenant did not, unlike Yvain, attempt to pursue his attacker, 'Que folie faire doutaisse', vs. 549 ['from fear of acting foolishly']. Calogrenant's adventure, in short, combines many paradoxical features with a unified sense of composition as if it were a self-contained *lai* or *conte*,[38] or miniature romance. As for romance, the context is ironically inauspicious, for does not Chrétien – we here reach the height of irony – depict the reading of a romance, 'ne sai de cui', vs. 5362 [I do not know about whom] as the privileged act of an adored daughter whose father owes his wealth to the shameless exploitation of other young women in a sweatshop.[39] The reciter of the romance is so beautiful that the god of love would willingly have become a man and been smitten by her, but, says the narrator, though he himself could expatiate at length on the wound of love, he would have few listeners, 'Que le gent n'est mais amoureuse, / Ne n'aiment mais si com il seulent, / Que nis oïr parler n'en veulent', vss 5390–92 [for people no longer fall in love nor do they love any longer as they used to; they don't even want to hear about such things]. What is the significance of this reminder of the prologue for Chrétien's conduct of the love plot and the way it is concluded? Love conquers all things except, apparently, irony.

---

[36] See Bernard Marache, 'Le Mot et la notion d'aventure dans la "conjointure" et le "sen" du *Chevalier au Lion*', in Dufournet, *Le Chevalier au lion*, pp. 119–38.

[37] See Christine Ferlampin-Acher, *Merveilles et topique merveilleuse dans les romans médiévaux* (Paris, 2003), pp. 421–22.

[38] See Leigh A. Arrathoon, 'Jacques de Vitry, the Tale of Calogrenant, *La Chastelaine de Vergi*, and the Genres of Medieval Narrative Fiction' in Leigh A. Arrathoon, ed., *The Craft of Fiction*, pp. 281–68, 307–15, and Jacques Ribard, 'L'Enigme Calogrenant', in *'Por le soie amisté': Essays in Honor of Norris J. Lacy*, ed. Keith Busby and Catherine M. Jones (Amsterdam, 2000), pp. 425–34. For some later references to it, see Keith Busby, 'The Reception of Chrétien's Calogrenant Episode', in *Tussentijds: Bundel Studies aangeboden aan W.P. Gerritsen ter gelegenheid van zijn vijftigste verjaardaged*, ed. A.M.J. van Buuren, et al. (Utrecht, 1985), pp. 25–40.

[39] See André Maraud, 'La Lectrice dans le roman (*Yvain*, vss 5354–5395)', in *Le Lecteur et la lecture dans l'œuvre*, Fac. des Lettres et Sc. hum. de l'Univ. de Clermont-Ferrand II, n.s. 15 (Clermont-Ferrand, 1982), pp. 155–62.

13

Le Conte du Graal: *Chrétien's Unfinished Last Romance*

RUPERT T. PICKENS

Chrétien's commentary in the prologues and epilogues of his last three romances reveals a shifting perspective with respect to his primary protagonists. In earlier works they are referred to in ways that eventually give rise to eponymous titles: 'Cil qui fist *D'Erec et d'Enide'* [The one who wrote about Erec and Enide],[1] and, in reference to *Cligés*, 'Un novel conte recomance / D'un vaslet qui an Grece fu / Del linage le roi Artu', vss 8–10 [begins a new story about a youth descended from King Arthur who lived in Greece], where the metonymic circumlocution reflects the narrator's plan not to name his main protagonist until it is time for his story. Later, in the intertwined 'twin romances',[2] Chrétien modifies the strategy exemplified in *Cligés*: 'Del *Chevalier de la charrete* / Comance Crestïens son livre'[3] [Chrétien begins his book about the Knight of the Cart], where the hero is not named until the mid-point, and 'Del chevalier al lion fine / Crestïens son romant issi' [Thus Chrétien ends his romance about the Knight of the Lion],[4] where Yvain is not seen until after Calogrenant tells his story. In these references Chrétien retains generic terms (*conte, livre, romans*) and continues using verbs defining the narrative act (*rancomance, comance, fine*), but he now claims possession of his work ('*son* livre', '*son* romant') and, more significantly, metonymy shifts from circumlocution to the use of surnames in anticipation of the principle, expressed by Perceval's mother, that a man's surname is the key to knowing who he is.[5] The cart and the lion are an object and a creature

---

1   Chrétien de Troyes, *Cligés*, ed. Claude Luttrell and Stewart Gregory (Cambridge, 1993), vs. 1, where it is listed first among Chrétien's previous works. No such reference appears in *Erec et Enide* itself, but Chrétien mentions his source: 'D'Erec, le fil Lac, est li contes' [The story is about Erec, son of Lac] (Chrétien de Troyes, *Erec et Enide*, ed. and trans. Jean-Marie Fritz, in *Romans suivis des Chansons, avec, en appendice, Philomena*, genl ed. Michel Zink [Paris, 1994], vs. 19). In the *Cligés* catalogue (vss 1–7), *faire* takes the preposition *de* followed by protagonists' names in reference to works in the *matière de Bretagne*, but the Ovidian translations have stand-alone titles.
2   Karl D. Uitti, with Michelle A. Freeman, *Chrétien de Troyes Revisited* (New York, 1995), pp. 59–89.
3   Chrétien de Troyes, *Le Chevalier de la Charrette ou Le Roman de Lancelot*, ed. and trans. Charles Méla, in *Romans suivis des Chansons*, genl ed. Michel Zink (Paris, 1994), vss 24–25.
4   Chrétien de Troyes, *Le Chevalier au lion, ou Le Roman d'Yvain*, ed. and trans. David F. Hult, in *Romans suivis des Chansons*, gen. ed. Michel Zink (Paris, 1994), vss 6804–5.
5   'Par le sornon [variant: non] connoist on l'ome' [by the (sur)name one knows the man]. Chrétien de Troyes, *Le Roman de Perceval ou Le Conte du Graal*, ed. Keith Busby (Tübingen, 1993), vs. 562. Translations of the *Conte du Graal* are from Chrétien de Troyes, *The Story of the*

encountered while *en aventure* [pursuing adventure] that become so intimately associated with the protagonists that the latter are transformed.[6]

One of many distinctive features of Chrétien's last romance is that he endows it with a title, whereas 'Cil qui fist d'Erec et d'Enide' and 'Del chevalier al lion fine / Crestïens son romant issi' are not titles at all, but contain germs from which titles eventually emerge in tradition. 'Ce est li Contes del Graal', vs. 66 [It is the story of the Grail] presents a stand-alone title that can be extracted from Chrétien's verse without alteration where genre and subject matter are not distanced but conjoined. As in the 'twin romances', where eponymy in the emergent titles involves surnames, the title *Li Contes del Graal* highlights an object encountered by a knight *en aventure* that grows in importance as the text advances, for it serves as the object of successive secondary narratives and commentaries within the story – 'contes du Graal' that continually reinterpret it and eventually spawn the *Conte du Graal* – up to a certain point when it is fragmented and submerged in an ever-expanding account of a second protagonist's adventures. Unlike the cart and the lion, however, the Grail remains distant and does not attach itself to a knight's identity – there is no *chevalier au Graal* – for indeed the protagonist who encounters it is surnamed 'li Galois', vs. 3575 [the Welshman].

The *Graal*, which for all intents and purposes Chrétien invented, is privileged as the primary object of discourse, but in our own world, where the term Grail is so highly charged with incongruent meanings, where it is related in so many ways with the holy, the unholy and the non-holy, it is difficult for heirs of Chrétien's successors to imagine the reception of a 'story about the grail' or 'a story about the Grail' (though capitalization is irrelevant to the medieval text) by Chrétien's first readers, for whom 'un graal' [a grail] was nothing of transcendent value. Chrétien's title initially might have prompted questions of the sort Perceval thinks about when he sees a grail in an unexpected context but fails to ask. At the outset, however, Chrétien's presentation of the title begins a process wherein an ordinary serving piece used at banquets, even if only the rich could afford to own it, is transformed into something exceptional. In this process, the texture of his *Conte du Graal* is enriched, given weight and density, by an uncommon amount of intradiegetic referencing, very often in the royal courts, where it is proper that *Li Contes del Graal*, as 'le meillor conte / Qui soit contez a cort roial', vss 64–65 [the best story that has been told in royal court] and 'contes du Graal' and 'contes de Perceval' are told: events are repeatedly recounted and interpreted as characters become performers like Chrétien himself. No other work by Chrétien demonstrates to such a degree how narrative, imperative, ironic, sarcastic, expository and didactic discourse, its production and its reception, shapes and directs human lives and human events. No other work by Chrétien is driven to such a degree by intradiegetic matter.

The *Conte du Graal* is unique in many other respects. Even though it is unfin-

---

Grail (Li Contes del Graal), ed. Rupert T. Pickens, trans. William W. Kibler (New York, 1990); deviations from Kibler's translations appear in parentheses within the brackets.

6   See Norris J. Lacy, *The Craft of Chrétien de Troyes* (Leiden, 1980), pp. 15–27.

ished, it is by far the longest of Chrétien's romances.[7] No other work by Chrétien is so infused with religious sentiment and doctrine. None, not even *Yvain*, where Calogrenant tells Arthur's court a misadventure that generates the romance about his cousin,[8] is so thoroughly informed by prediegetic matter – organized accounts of sacred history, British history, events in communities in exile from Arthur's kingdom, genealogy, customs[9] – and by extradiegetic matter concerning the Grail kingdom, a mysterious world that remains largely hidden to those outside it. None, with the possible exception of *Erec et Enide*,[10] is to such a degree complemented by and interacts with a work outside itself, namely Wace's *Brut*.[11] Finally, none, not even *Cligés*, offers a second protagonist in a parallel 'romance' who threatens to overshadow the one presumed to dominate.[12]

Analysis of the narrative organization of the *Conte du Graal* brings to light essential textual features that further distinguish Chrétien's last romance from its predecessors. Bipartition is an important principle, but a system of more refined episodic division has arisen in the tradition of scholarship that recognizes seventeen textual segments following the Prologue.[13] Prior to the Hermitage (segment 14), episodes correspond either to a main protagonist's departure from one specified place and his stay at another place, usually a castle, where hospitality is offered or demanded, or else to an extended encounter along the way with one or more other characters who do not reappear, if at all, until much later. Some episodes include codas in which events in the division are passed in review, as when the Tent Maiden and her lover discuss Perceval's visit (segment 3) and knights sent to Arthur's court give accounts of his prowess (segments 4, 6, 9).

1. Prologue (vss 1–68).[14] Chrétien quotes the Parable of the Sower and related Biblical texts as he likens his writing to sowing seed (the seminal word) and introduces in exegesis the theme of Christian charity; his romance embodies

---

[7] The *Conte du Graal* surpasses the longest of the others, the *Charrette* at over 7100 verses, by more than 2000.

[8] See Marie-Louise Ollier, 'Le Discours en "abyme" ou la narration équivoque', *Medioevo Romanzo*, 1 (1974), 351–64.

[9] On 'anterior order' in the *Conte du Graal*, see Donald Maddox, *The Arthurian Romances of Chrétien de Troyes* (Cambridge, 1991), ch. 4.

[10] Uitti and Freeman, *Chrétien de Troyes Revisited*, ch. 3.

[11] The *Brut*, a *translatio* of Geoffrey of Monmouth's *Historia regum Britanniae* dated 1155, undergirds many arguments in Maddox, *Arthurian Romances*. See also Sara Sturm-Maddox, ' "Tenir sa terre en paix": Social Order in the *Brut* and in the *Conte del Graal*', *Studies in Philology*, 81 (1984), 28–41.

[12] This essay is consonant with work in my *The Welsh Knight: Paradoxicality in Chrétien's Conte du Graal* (Lexington, KY, 1977); in 'Le Conte du Graal (Perceval)', in *The Romances of Chrétien de Troyes: A Symposium*, ed. Douglas Kelly (Lexington, KY, 1985), pp. 232–86; and in Chrétien de Troyes, *The Story*.

[13] Keith Busby, *Chrétien de Troyes: Perceval (Le Conte du Graal)* (London, 1993), organizes his discussion of the romance with respect to these divisions, except for Orquenie; his edition sets off all eighteen.

[14] For a well-organized review of the extensive scholarship on the Prologue alongside an insightful reading, see Barbara N. Sargent-Baur, *La Destre et la senestre: étude sur le 'Conte du Graal' de Chrétien de Troyes* (Amsterdam, 2000), pp. 1–23.

translatio studii and *translatio imperii*, transfers of knowledge and political power from Antiquity to modern times that imply discovery of things hidden.

Perceval Adventures

2. The Waste Forest (vss 69–634).[15] An adolescent boy sees knights for the first time in his life, barrages them with questions about their nature, and feels compelled to become one of them. Before he sets out for Arthur's court, his mother, who has isolated him from the world, tells him his family history and gives him advice that he will attempt to follow. He sees her fall in a faint as he leaves.

3. The Tent Maiden I (vss 635–833). He sees a tent in a forest and thinks it is a church. Remembering his mother's advice about courtship, he attempts to embrace the lady he finds inside, steals her ring and takes bread and wine from her table. After he leaves, her lover returns and, believing that she has entertained a knight, imposes a punishment on her.

4. Carduel (vss 834–1304). The boy finds Arthur at Carduel and asks him to make him a knight. Kay sarcastically grants him the arms of the Vermilion Knight, who has just threatened to seize Arthur's kingdom and waits outside to fight Arthur's champion. As he leaves in pursuit of the knight, a maiden smiles[16] and calls him a great knight. He sees Kay slap her and kick the court Fool, who predicted that she would not smile until she saw the best of knights. He kills the Vermilion Knight, takes his horse and armour, and rides away. Yvonet informs the court, and the Fool predicts that the boy will avenge him and the maiden by breaking Kay's arm.

5. Gornemant de Gorhaut (vss 1305–698). The boy rides until he reaches a castle whose lord, Gornemant, instructs him in military and courtly arts. When he insists on returning home because he is worried about his mother, Gornemant inducts him into the order of knights.

6. Biaurepaire (vss 1699–2975). The 'new knight' reaches Biaurepaire, which is besieged by Engygeron, seneschal of Clamadeus des Illes, who seeks to marry the lady of the castle (Blanchefleur). She begs him to defend her. He vanquishes Engygeron and sends him to Arthur's court for imprisonment. When Clamadeus arrives, the boy defeats him and orders him to follow Engygeron. They find Arthur at Disnadaron, where they praise the prowess of the knight who vanquished them. Meanwhile, at Biaurepaire, the boy takes leave of Blanchefleur, with whom he has fallen in love, to resume his quest for his mother.

7. The Grail Castle (vss 2976–3421). He meets two men fishing in a boat. One offers him hospitality. During their lavish meal, a banquet procession featuring a

---

[15] As Maddox, *Arthurian Romances*, pp. 83–90, observes, the *Conte du Graal* lacks Chrétien's conventional court 'opening', which in this instance Chrétien delays until Carduel.

[16] '. . . li rist' (vs. 1037) is usually read as 'laughed at him', and 'en riant' (vs. 1038) as 'laughingly', but Barbara N. Sargent, 'Medieval *ris, risus*: A Laughing Matter?' *Medium Ævum*, 43 (1974), 116–32, demonstrates that the Old French terms are ambiguous.

bleeding lance and a grail repeatedly passes through the hall. The boy wishes to ask about the procession, but remembers Gornemant's advice against talking too much and decides to wait. The next morning, the castle is deserted.

8. The Weeping Maiden (vss 3422–690). He rides until he meets a young woman mourning over her beheaded lover, killed by another knight (the Orgueilleux de la Lande). She asks him questions about the previous evening, tells him about his host, the Fisher King, and berates him for failing to ask questions. Prompted by her, he correctly guesses that his name is Perceval the Welshman. She tells him that his mother is dead and that his sin in leaving her prevented him from speaking. As his mother is dead, Perceval rides away to wander aimlessly.

9. The Tent Maiden II (vss 3691–4143). He again encounters the Tent Maiden, who has suffered long and hard from her punishment. Her lover, the Orgueilleux de la Lande, attacks Perceval and is defeated. Having avenged the maiden and expiated the wrong he committed, Perceval orders the Orgueilleux to care for her and then take her to Arthur's court. They find Arthur at Carlion, and the Orgueilleux's account of Perceval's prowess spur the king to search for him.

10. Blood Drops on the Snow (vss 4144–602). Perceval rides onto a snow-covered heath. He is transfixed by three drops of blood from a goose that have fallen on the snow: the red on white reminds him of Blanchefleur's face. The court, camped nearby, are curious about him. Sagremor greets him impolitely and is unhorsed. Kay, more ill-mannered, has his arm broken as Perceval brings him down, avenging the Smiling Maiden and the Fool. When Gauvain speaks courteously, Perceval goes with him to see Arthur.

11. Carlion (vss 4603–815). In joyful reunion the court returns to Carlion for the night. Celebration is disrupted by the arrival of a hideous maiden who denounces Perceval for his failure at the Grail Castle. She invites all knights to undertake a variety of quests, but Perceval swears to find out why the lance bleeds and whom the Grail serves. Guigambresil, seneschal of the king of Escavalon, comes to accuse Gauvain of murdering the king's father and challenges him to go to Escavalon for judgment.

Gauvain Adventures

12. Tintagel (vss 4816–5655). On the way Gauvain attends a tournament at Tintagel, vowing not to participate. Ladies watching the tournament observe him setting up camp. The lord's elder daughter sneers that he must be a merchant; she slaps her little sister who declares that he is a better knight than her sister's lover, Meliagant. Offered hospitality in the city, Gauvain agrees to champion the little girl, who is avenged when he defeats Meliagant.

13. Escavalon (vss 5656–6216). Led to Escavalon by a white doe, Gauvain meets the king leaving for a hunt. The king invites him to wait for him at his castle. There he meets the king's sister and begins to seduce her. He is recognized and the alarm is raised. A mob attacks the castle while Gauvain and the lady defend themselves by hurling chess pieces and using the chessboard as a

shield. After they are rescued by Guigambresil and the king, a wise vavassor advises postponement of the judgment for a year because Gauvain is protected by the king's hospitality; meanwhile, Gauvain must quest for the Bleeding Lance, which will one day destroy the kingdom of Logres.

Perceval Adventures

14. The Hermitage (vss 6217–518). In five years Perceval has fought sixty knights and sent them to Arthur. On Good Friday he meets penitent knights and ladies who ask him why he is armed on such a day. Having forgotten God, he questions them in detail about the day's significance, then seeks the Hermit who has shriven them. He confesses to him that he has visited the Fisher King's castle and failed to ask the appropriate questions. When the Hermit learns Perceval's name, he explains how he and his mother are related to him, to the Fisher King, and to the king who is served by the Grail. The sin he committed against his mother 'cut his tongue'. He gives absolution to Perceval, who stays with him through Easter Eucharist.

Gauvain Adventures

15. Galloway I (vss 6519–7370).

a. Gauvain leaves Escavalon the day of the chessboard battle. He enters Galloway and comes upon a wounded knight (Greoreas), who sends him to a nearby castle to face the adventure in which he was injured (vss 6519–650).

b. Instead of combat, Gauvain finds a maiden (the Orgueilleuse de Logres)[17] who becomes his companion and subjects him to never-ending scorn (vss 6651–903).

c. Gauvain heals Greoreas, who recognizes him as the one who punished him for raping a maiden.[18] He takes Gauvain's horse, Le Gringalet, and rides away with his lover. Much to the Orgueilleuse's delight, Gauvain must ride a female nag, an insult to his manhood (vss 6904–7231).

d. They ride until they see a great castle across a large body of water (vss 7232–330).

e. Meanwhile, Greoreas's nephew appears on Le Gringalet. Observed by maidens at the castle's windows, Gauvain wins him back in single combat astride his nag. The Orgueilleuse disappears (vss 7331–70).

16. Galloway II (vss 7371–8371).

a. Gauvain crosses the waterway in a ferry. The Ferryman, who lays claim to

---

[17] Variant: No(r)gres (vs. 8639).

[18] The Custom of Logres guarantees the safety of unaccompanied maidens (Maddox, *Arthurian Romances*, pp. 104–8). Perceval's attempt to seduce the Tent Maiden by force (#3) is a violation of the custom (p. 96), which Perceval expiates when he defeats the Orgueilleux de la Lande (#9) (pp. 98–99), as is Le Guiromelant's treatment of the Orgueilleuse de Logres (#17c) (pp. 106–8).

the knight Gauvain has defeated, offers him lodging in his house beneath the castle (vss 7371–637).

b. The next day the Ferryman takes him up to the castle, where a queen rules with her daughter, another queen, and granddaughter. Gauvain submits to an impossible, spectacular test, the Bed of Marvels, and succeeds (vss 7638–8032).

c. The Old Queen declares that he is the expected liberator, the lord and defender of the castle, which he must never leave (vss 8033–371).

17. Galloway III (vss 8372–9188).

a. Gauvain sees a knight in the company of the Orgueilleuse. The queen allows him to meet him in combat, and he defeats him. The Orgueilleuse tells him that the knight is her lover, and she challenges him to jump his horse across the Perilous Ford (vss 8372–497).

b. After a partial failure, Gauvain meets the ford's owner (Le Guiromelant), who tells him the scornful maiden's name and informs him that the castle is called the Roche de Canguin. When he learns Gauvain's identity, he challenges him to combat in the presence of King Arthur because Gauvain's father Lot killed his father and Gauvain murdered his cousin. Gauvain must send for Arthur, who holds Pentecost court at Orquenie. Gauvain clears the ford before returning to the Orgueilleuse (vss 8498–913).

c. She confesses that the knight Gauvain defeated is a substitute for her true love; he was killed by Le Guiromelant, who then raped her. Consequently, she hated all men and was so unhappy that by being scornful she tried to provoke Gauvain to kill her. Repentant, she rides to the castle with Gauvain to join the ladies there (vss 8914–78).

d. After a celebratory banquet, Gauvain knights the castle's 500 squires and dispatches a squire to Orquenie to summon Arthur (vss 8979–9188).

18. Orquenie (vss 9189–234) (incomplete). The squire arrives and finds the town and court mourning for the loss of Gauvain.

Immediately apparent in the foregoing is the double plot structure recalling that of *Cligés*. Unlike *Cligés*, however, where the son's story is twice as long as the father's, and unlike the other romances, where Gauvain is clearly subordinated to the eponymous protagonists, in the *Conte du Graal* he nearly matches Perceval in importance. The discrete Perceval section plus the Hermitage accounts for about 55% of the text and the extant Gauvain adventures for nearly 45%. If Blood Drops is discounted from Perceval's adventures on the grounds that Gauvain's prominence rivals his, however, and if Gauvain is credited with the portion of Carlion in which attention shifts exclusively to him (vss 4747–815), then Perceval's portion shrinks to 49% and Gauvain's increases to 46%, while they share 5% and Gauvain's adventures have yet to conclude.

Meanwhile, the episodic conceptualization of the two sections is radically different. On the one hand, the Perceval episodes are significantly shorter than the Gauvain episodes. The 5049 lines in the discrete Perceval section are organized into thirteen divisions averaging 459 lines each. The Gauvain section consists of five divisions in 4071 lines, excluding Orquenie, for an average of 814 lines, almost twice that of the Perceval section. Every division in the Gauvain section is longer than every Perceval episode except Biaurepaire. On the other hand, the three Galloway divisions are incongruent with all Perceval episodes as well as with the analogous Tintagel and Escavalon episodes in the Gauvain section for at least three reasons: (1) After Escavalon, Gauvain does not find lodging until he accepts the Ferryman's hospitality in the town below the Roche de Canguin (segment 16a); (2) after he leaves the Ferryman's house the next morning, his host remains his companion; and (3) the Great Hall becomes a base from which he rides out to other adventures, for displacement of linearity by centrifugality is a consequence of Gauvain's new identity as imprisoned lord of the castle. In short, in the Gauvain section discrete episodic structuring gives way to other patterns, and by previous standards the Galloway divisions all together (vss 6419–9188) constitute one long 'mega-episode'.

What are the implications in the textual ballooning manifest in the inordinate length of Tintagel and Escavalon and in the remarkable elasticity of Galloway? Chrétien explodes romance as he pushes the form he has developed previously beyond all expectations. He does this by amplifying the role of Perceval's double so that he approaches parity with him and by informing the largely secular Arthurian world with a new religious or quasi-religious vision and offering an overt critique of its values: Perceval's acquisition of chivalric manners leads to his failures at the Grail Castle and during the five years following Carlion, while the boy who questions knights in the Waste Forest (vss 171–342) and the newly reawakened man who interrogates other knights at the Hermitage (vss 6261–308) would have succeeded immediately, although they might not have understood the answers. Emblematic of Chrétien's achievement in his transformation of the romance form are the ways in which the Perceval and the Gauvain sections are conjoined via *translatio*, for Perceval's accomplishments and his failures are mirrored in Gauvain. The *Conte du Graal* presents Perceval's biography in an episodic ordering of unfolding events. In rewriting Perceval's life in the Gauvain section, Chrétien fragments its constitutive elements and scatters them across the new, expanding constellation.

It is interesting to observe that the *Conte du Graal* as we have it ends, at the Roche de Canguin, where it begins, in the Waste Forest.[19] The Galloway episode is reflective of multiple aspects of the Perceval section, some of the most important of which occur in the Waste Forest – the 'gaste forest soutaine', vs. 75 [deserted, uncultivated forest], 'gaste forest', vs. 392, 'forest gaste', vs. 451 – which Chrétien recalls literally in describing the landscape of Galloway as Gauvain and the Orgueilleuse ride through 'forés gastes et soutaines', vs. 7225 [deserted, uncultivated forests] before reaching the plain by the river across which rises the Roche de Canguin. In addition, the community of the Waste Forest manor and the Roche de Canguin share a common history, for both were founded shortly after the death of Uther Pendragon (vss 442–54, 8739–47). In *Erec et Enide*, Arthur's nostalgia for an emblem of his father's reign, when he seeks to restore the Custom of the White Stag, attests to a sense of decline and a desire to retrieve a vestige of past glories, however divisive that beauty contest

---

[19] On analogical relationships, see Lacy, *Craft*, esp. pp. 67–72, 100–12.

may prove to be.[20] In fact Enide's triumph in Arthur's day surpasses anything known before. In the *Conte du Graal*, evocations of Uther's time are more complex and perhaps also more sinister.

In the Gauvain section, it is Le Guiromelant who evokes the transition from Uther's reign to Arthur's. He tells Gauvain, whose identity he does not yet know, that the Old Queen is King Arthur's mother (vss 8732–33), Ygerne (vs. 8742) or Ygraine, who, after Uther Pendragon's death, came there with her treasury to build her castle, the Roche de Canguin (vs. 8817), and the Great Hall (vss 8740–48). The Young Queen, her daughter, wife of King Lot and mother of Gauvain, came later, when she was pregnant with her daughter (vss 8757–63), elsewhere named Clarissant (Clarissans, vs. 8269), the love of Le Guiromelant's life (vss 8760–61). The Young Queen, whom Chrétien never names, is called Enna (or Anna) in Wace and Morcadés (or Morchadés, etc.) elsewhere.[21] Gauvain expresses surprise at this news: Arthur's mother must be dead, for he is more than sixty years of age (vss 8735–38), while his own mother has been dead for at least twenty years (vss 8753–56). Finally, Le Guiromelant's hatred of Gauvain because of a dispute between their fathers and their own contemporaries, also exemplifies the shift from 'Utherian' to Arthurian time.

Although Gauvain and Le Guiromelant have sworn to tell the truth (vss 8605–15), the latter is caught in at least one lie that maligns Clarissant's love for her brother (vss 9027–42, cf. vss 8790–99). According to the Orgueilleuse de Logres, who is also not known for her truthfulness, he is a murderer and a rapist (vss 8931–46). However, Le Guiromelant's revelations chime with and give renewed depth to the playful, exquisitely courtly conversation Gauvain has with Ygraine the evening before when they exchange information about Arthur, his Queen and his court, including most especially the sons of King Lot (vss 8114–98) – a conversation that Gauvain avows has rid him of depression brought on by the knowledge that his success at the Bed of Marvels has led to his imprisonment (vss 8199–205). Moreover, Chrétien's narrator explicitly affirms the familial relationship between Gauvain and the three ladies when he observes that the Young Queen does not recognize that Gauvain and her daughter are brother and sister (vss 9065–73).

Le Guiromelant's account is also consonant with information about the Roche de Canguin that the Ferryman, a rich, privileged dependant of the castle, imparts to Gauvain (vss 7520–604) information concerning the castle's history and the absence of a lord he cannot name. He describes the castle's mechanical defences and other wonders, which Gauvain will encounter in the Great Hall as he endures the Bed of Marvels test, designed by '.I. clers sages d'astrenomie', vs. 7548 [a learned astronomer].[22] Finally, the castle hopes for a knight-liberator who will restore property to exiles, find husbands for orphaned maidens and

---

[20] See Maddox, *Arthurian Romances*, pp. 14–34.

[21] G.D. West, *An Index of Proper Names in French Arthurian Verse Romances 1150–1300* (Toronto, 1969), p. 55.

[22] 'Astronomy' is astrology and implies the occult arts. This 'clerk' recalls Thessala and Jehan in *Cligés*.

knight five hundred squires. Those awaiting deliverance also include old widows wrongfully deprived of their inheritances after their husbands' deaths.

As Le Guiromelant's story recalls Gauvain's salutary conversation with his grandmother as well as the Ferryman's accounts, so it also resonates with what Perceval's mother tells her son about the founding of the Waste Forest community in the wake of a disaster that, following Uther Pendragon's death, brought misfortune to all who were truly noble (vss 432–58). Perceval, raised in ignorance of the outside world, encounters knights – knights from Arthur's court for whom Gauvain would be an exemplary model – and, driven by his nature, he desires to be made a knight himself. His mother informs him that he is in fact descended from knights on both sides. His father, apparently fighting in a conflict related to the disaster, was wounded 'parmi les jambes', vs. 436 [right through or between his legs][23] and was crippled. Unlike Ygraine, whose treasury was intact when she migrated, Perceval's father lost his wealth along with his landholdings at a time when even the noblest men were impoverished and brought to ruin and those who could took flight as he did. When Perceval was barely two years of age, he was brought on a litter to his manor 'en ceste forest gaste', vs. 451 [in this wild forest]. Meanwhile, Perceval's two elder brothers were trained in foreign courts, the one by the King of Escavalon and the other by King Ban of Gomorret. Both were knighted the same day and both were killed in combat the same day as they came home to visit, and Perceval's father died of grief.

The two parallel communities, where the mothers of the two primary protagonists rule,[24] were founded outside Arthur's kingdom of Logres by émigrés from Logres, the one in a remote area of Wales and the other in Galloway. The Orgueilleuse de Logres is also an exile from Arthur's kingdom, according to Le Guiromelant, as she was brought from there to Galloway when she was a child (vss 8635–40). A cataclysmic event, the death of Uther Pendragon, preceded or caused the foundation of both communities. Both communities lack male leadership and both are prosperous, yet both hold peculiar dangers at the hands of their *suzeraines* for the males who would take possession of them: the accomplished Gauvain must not leave the castle except by permission from Ygraine, while the immature Perceval is hampered, because of his mother's fears, by ignorance of the outside world and by his lack of training for what he was born to do.

In important ways the stories of these communities also find resonance in the world of the Grail, which remains hidden from the world outside it except when Perceval visits the Grail Castle. The Grail Castle episode is the one instance when Chrétien directly portrays mysterious events taking place in the world of the Grail and describes a locale where they occur, but silence reigns there. Chrétien's narrator resolutely refrains from mediating the mysteries, except to

---

[23] Chrétien de Troyes, *Story*, ed. Pickens, trans. Kibler, p. 453n. The wound is the same as that suffered by the Fisher King.

[24] Debora B. Schwartz, '"A la guise de Gales l'atorna": Maternal Influence in Chrétien's *Conte du Graal*', *Essays in Medieval Studies*, 12 (1996), 95–118. Perceval is also, like Gauvain, of royal descent through the maternal line.

describe what is plainly, yet superficially, visible to observers on the scene, while the one there who knows about them, the Fisher King, avoids commenting and the one who is apparently destined to learn about them, Perceval, purposely refuses to ask questions about them. But subsequently Perceval's experience is repeated and narrated anew by himself and others who have knowledge of it.

When Perceval encounters the Weeping Maiden, she realizes that he has just left the Grail Castle and asks him what he saw there. First he met two men in a boat, one rowing and the other fishing; the fisherman offered him lodging and gave him directions to his castle (vss 3499–506). She responds that this is a king who was so maimed in battle that he is helpless. He was struck by a javelin 'Parmi les hanches ambesdeus', vs. 3513 [through both thighs]; the wound is still so painful that he cannot ride a horse, so for distraction, while others hunt in his forests, he has himself put in a boat to go fishing, which is why he is called 'li Rois Peschierre', vs. 3520 [the Fisher King] (3507–33). When Perceval went into the castle, he found the king already seated. The king apologized for not rising to greet him and invited him to sit down beside him (vss 3534–44). The lady observes that this was a very great honour (vss 3545–46) and then, in rapid-fire interrogation, she asks what else he saw point by point, for she is obviously familiar with the Grail procession. Did he see a lance bleeding from its tip? Yes. Did he see the Grail? Yes. Who was holding it? A maiden. Where did she come from? A room. Where was she going? Into another room. Was anyone going before the Grail? Two serving boys carrying candelabra full of candles. After the Grail? A boy carrying a little silver carving platter. Did he ask why the lance bled? No. He behaved badly. Did he ask where the Grail was going? No. Even worse (vss 3548–71). If he had asked questions, the Fisher King would have been healed and he could have ruled his lands in peace. Much good would have come from that, but now great misfortune will befall him and others (vss 3586–92). She also tells him that his mother, whom he saw fall in a faint when he left her (cf. vss 620–26), died of grief for him; the sin he committed against her has brought these disasters about.[25] She knows these things because she is Perceval's cousin and was in fact raised with him at the Waste Forest manor (vss 3596–601).

Among the reasons why Perceval's interrogation is important is the fact that Perceval, who at this point knows nothing about what *the* Grail is, recognizes what *a* grail is: when she asks if he saw 'le graal?', vs. 3556 ['the grail?'], he responds, 'I certainly did' (vs. 3557), not 'What is a grail?' Mentioning the Grail for the first time, Chrétien takes it for granted that his readers likewise know what '.I. graal', vs. 3220 [a grail] is. Thus a country lad of limited experience in the world outside Wales knows that it is an appropriate object to see in a procession of dishes at a lavish banquet.[26] It is also noteworthy that Perceval has total recall of his experience, but no concept of the significance of the things he has seen. The Weeping Maiden is the first to begin ascribing meaning to them.

Later, at Carlion, as all are celebrating Perceval's accomplishments and his

---

[25] On Perceval's sin, see Sargent-Baur, *La Destre*, ch. 7.

[26] See Richard O'Gorman, 'Grail', in *The New Arthurian Encyclopedia*, ed. Norris J. Lacy (New York, 1991, rev. 1996), pp. 212–13, and 'Ecclesiastical Tradition and the Holy Grail', *Australian Journal of French Studies*, 6 (1969), 3–8.

return to Arthur's court, a remarkable monstrous storyteller, the Hideous
Damsel, addresses a much wider audience, which includes Perceval, in the
venue of storytelling *par excellence*, the royal court. She opens her discourse by
repeating and amplifying the Weeping Maiden's explanations, but her account
also resembles that of Chrétien himself. Perceval went to the Fisher King's castle,
but he did not open his mouth to ask why the lance was bleeding or what rich,
powerful man they were serving from the Grail ('Quel riche home l'en en
servoit', vs. 4661). Instead he put off asking about it until a more appropriate
time, which never came. If he had asked questions that were already formulated
in his mind, the King would have been cured of his agonizing wound and he
would have ruled his land in peace. Because Perceval kept quiet, much harm
will come because the King cannot rule and will not be healed: ladies will lose
their husbands, lands will be laid waste, maidens will be orphaned, knights will
die, all because of him (vss 4646–83). The Hideous Damsel uses the future here
in imitation of the Weeping Maiden (vss 3591–92), but her meaning is most
certainly that there will be a prolongation of what is going on in the present, for
the Fisher King's condition, which has endured for some time, will remain
unchanged. She goes on (vss 4685–714) to propose various adventures to knights
seeking ways to 'faire chevalerie', vs. 4699 [perform deeds of chivalry] and
Gauvain is the first among several to volunteer, but Perceval swears to undertake an entirely different quest: to find out whom the Grail serves and why the
lance bleeds. As the knights prepare to leave, Guigambresil comes to accuse
Gauvain of murdering the former king of Escavalon.

The Hideous Damsel excoriates Perceval in language that suggests that she
might have read Chrétien's account of the Grail processions – her version of the
Grail question is the same as his and, more significantly, she shares his narrator's
insights into Perceval's motivation in maintaining silence, which contradicts the
Weeping Maiden's notion of sin (cf. vss 3292–309). The originality of her speech,
aside from her powerfully vivid metaphors, lies in her amplification of the
Weeping Maiden's reference to future calamities in the Fisher King's lands. In
addition, her proposal of disparate adventures gives Perceval an opportunity to
define his unique quest ('tout el', vs. 4727 [a different oath]) in terms of conventional chivalric adventure.

In the Hermitage episode (segment 14), which Chrétien strikingly sets apart
from the Gauvain adventures it interrupts, narration of Perceval's Grail adventure advances to another level. Perceval's renewed quest proves to be a failure
after five years of 'practising knighthood'. His sense of guilt for keeping silent at
the Grail Castle, apparently stirred by the Hideous Damsel's words, has driven
him to a form of insanity. On Good Friday, penitents direct him to a hermit who
can console him. On Good Friday, he confesses that he did not ask the appropriate questions at the Fisher King's castle, that his failure has depressed him
('S'en ai puis eü si grant doel / Que mors eüsse esté mon wel', vss 6381–82
['since that day I've suffered such affliction that I would rather have died']) and
that he has forgotten God.

When the Hermit learns Perceval's name, he understands the reason for his
predicament. As the Weeping Maiden has said, but Perceval has forgotten ('.I.
pechiez dont tu ne sez mot', vs. 6393 ['a sin of which you are unaware']), it is his

sin in causing his mother's death that made him keep silent about the Bleeding Lance and the Grail, and it is only the efficacy of her prayer in commending him to God that has spared him death and imprisonment (vss 6392–414) – whereas Chrétien's narrator has ascribed Perceval's reticence to his memory of Gornemant de Gorhaut's advice about a knight's courteous behaviour (cf. vss 1648–56). Scholars have had difficulty reconciling these conflicting explanations,[27] and some simply opt for one or the other, but rather than mutually exclusive, they are complementary and account for the same events in different perspectives. At the Grail Castle Perceval adheres too strictly to his mentor's precepts (vss 3243–51). In fact, when Gornemant knights Perceval, his 'parole', vs. 3247 [advice (word, credo)] replaces that of Perceval's mother: Perceval must not quote her and her advice all the time or he will be taken for a fool (vss 1674–84), but instead he should heed the counsel of his (new) mentor, 'Li vavasors . . . / Qui vostre esperon vos caucha', vss 1686–87 ['the vavassor who attached your spur']. Abandoning his mother's *parole* and his rude garrulousness, Perceval puts away childish things and begins to accept manhood in chivalry. At the same time, he loses the last material vestiges of the Welsh clothing made for him by his mother as Gornemant dresses him in aristocratic linen and silk (vss 1597–621). Substitution of Gornemant de Gorhaut for his mother, of knighthood for the Waste Forest, is foreshadowed when he looks back and sees that she has fallen in a dead faint at the head of her bridge but keeps riding (vss 620–25). Fears of the consequences of her faint prompt Perceval to quest for her and in fact precipitate his induction to knighthood (vss 1579–94) in the course of which he figuratively kills her as he abandons her, her gifts and her word. When his quest leads him beyond Biaurepaire, he learns on the day his horse jumps from the Grail Castle's drawbridge (vss 3403–09) that he has literally killed her and that his 'sin' rendered him impotent when confronted by the Grail mysteries.

While the Hermit seems uninterested in the Bleeding Lance, he *partially* answers the Grail question Perceval failed to ask when he describes the king served by the Grail without naming him: 'Cil qui l'en en sert est mes frere, / Ma suer et soe fu ta mere', vss 6415–16 ['He who is served from it is my brother. My sister and his was your mother'], and for twelve years he has been confined to the room into which Perceval saw the Grail being carried (vss 6429–31). The Fisher King is the Grail King's son (vss 6417–19). Finally, he reveals the nature of the Grail, that which turns a grail into the Grail: it does not contain a pike, a lamprey, or a salmon, as Perceval might expect, for he saw his host fishing, but a single consecrated host, which is all 'li sains hom', vs. 6422 [that holy man] needs to sustain his life.[28] Perceval does penance for his sin and, in stark contrast

---

27 Lacy, *Craft*, p. 108, reconciles them as examples of analogy by contrast in Perceval's misconception of the nature of chivalry: in his haste to be made a knight he leaves his mother in a faint, while, thinking that knights should keep their silence, he delays asking questions.

28 Thus the Grail in Chrétien has the function of a ciborium, while the cutting platter resembles a paten. The context the Hermit creates is highly charged spiritually, but the Grail is not an object of devotion. Chrétien's Grail is 'Tant sainte chose', vs. 6425 [such a holy thing] because it conveys life-sustaining holy food, not because of its essence. Robert de Boron's 'translation'

to the Grail banquet, takes simple meals with his uncle and receives Communion on Easter Sunday.

Some of the links between the hidden world of the Grail kingdom and the Waste Forest community lie in family relationships which the Hermit outlines. Perceval would have learned these things if he had asked the right questions, and he could have related them to the genealogy his mother sketches out for him. When she teaches him about the high nobility he can boast of on her side of the family (vss 420–31), she has in mind her brothers and her nephew, Perceval's uncles and cousin, as well as their common forebears. She also affirms that her family has suffered a downfall and implies that it happened simultaneously with the ruin of her husband. Meanwhile, Perceval's other cousin, the Weeping Maiden who has knowledge of the Grail mysteries, was also raised in the Waste Forest manor. Family ties also strengthen associations between the Waste Forest and the Hermitage that are implicit thematically. The Waste Forest manor is in a remote *terre gaste* where Perceval's family are in exile from Logres, while the Hermitage is within a copse (vs. 6324) in a 'desert', vs. 6239 [desert (wilderness)] where the Hermit is in exile from the world. In addition, Perceval encounters knights and ladies in the *desert* to whom he addresses simplistic questions on the subject of religion, about which he is ignorant because he has forgotten God (vss 6254–314), and they inspire him to seek redemption; while in the Waste Forest he meets knights to whom he addresses absurd questions on the subject of knighthood, about which he knows nothing because his mother has kept him isolated, and they spur him on to pursue his destiny in the world outside. Finally, Perceval's father was injured 'parmi les jambes [variants: *hanche(s)*]' (vs. 436) fighting during a catastrophe in which he lost position, wealth and property, while the Fisher King suffered a similar wound 'parmi les hanches [variant: *jambes*] ambesdeus' (vs. 3513) also in a battle that cost him the ability to rule his kingdom. Perceval's father is implicitly identified with the Fisher King, which opens the possibility of incest,[29] but in the present discussion it is the simultaneity of the two disasters that is more pertinent.

Elements of the Grail kingdom are also transformed and dispersed in Galloway, which is also a reflection of the Waste Forest. The Grail Castle and the knight who the Grail mediators hope – or have hoped – will restore their kingdom are reflected in the Roche de Canguin and along its approaches in the knight who is its long-expected liberator. Moreover, not unlike the Waste Forest and the Hermitage, where Perceval learns about knighthood and is reminded of the Christian religion in flurries of questions, the Grail Castle and the Roche de Canguin are both places where questions lead to answers that gradually reveal their mysteries: Perceval fails to articulate the questions that form in his mind, but Gauvain begins penetrating the secrets of his grandmother's castle by interrogating both the Ferryman and Le Guiromelant.[30] As already suggested,

---

of the *Conte du Graal* makes the Grail the historical chalice of the Last Supper, while in more 'baroque' transformations it is also the source for all food at banquets.

29 See Jeff Rider, 'The Perpetual Enigma of Chrétien's Grail Episode', *Arthuriana*, 8 (1998), 6–21.
30 Maddox, *Arthurian Romances*, p. 114.

however, linkage is most often achieved not by replication, but in processes of transformation and refraction. Both Perceval and Gauvain are informed by accounts of their family histories and both visit wondrous castles where awe-inspiring experiences await them. Perceval's experience occurs in an aura of other-worldly mystery – in a disappearing castle, where reside two kings, father and son, Perceval's uncle and cousin, and where Christian spirituality, Celtic myth and courtliness converge. Gauvain's comes under the sign of clerkly ingenuity – in an intricately and expertly designed, heavily defended fortress, where 'Les enchantemens del palais', vs. 7604 [(the Great Hall's) magic spells] which constitute Gauvain's irresistible adventure result from a conjoining of the mechanical and military arts with the occult that produces decidedly man-made marvels to test his heart and his skills. Perceval fails where Gauvain succeeds, of course, but Gauvain's is an ironic and bitter victory, for it leads to his confinement in the place of his triumph.

Along the way, moreover, Gauvain, who epitomizes Arthurian courtesy, and Perceval, who acquires it, are both subject to the indignities of *ramprosnes*, the kind of discourteous, harmful, uncharitable speech that Chrétien's patron, Philip of Flanders, cannot bear to hear (vss 21–24). Both suffer from forms of depression. Both meet boatmen who offer them hospitality and both fall or nearly fall into water, Perceval when the Grail Castle's drawbridge is raised by invisible hands (vss 3402–13), Gauvain when he first unsuccessfully attempts the test of the Perilous Ford (vss 8511–20).[31] Both are treated to copious banquets: at the Grail Castle Perceval is served a sumptuous feast, of which Gauvain's two, at the Ferryman's house before his Bed of Marvels triumph and in the Great Hall afterwards to celebrate it, are modest imitations. Finally, whereas the Fisher King directs Perceval to the Grail Castle, Gauvain, guided by the Ferryman, sees at the entrance to the Great Hall, where the Bed of Marvels awaits him, a peg-legged man who reflects the Fisher King,[32] as well as Perceval's father,[33] and the Grail that sustains the hidden king (vss 7648–59). He is the guardian of the Great Hall, but he says not a word as they pass, nor do they address him. Gauvain asks his companion about him, as Perceval might not. He is a rich and powerful man, perhaps a castle dependant with special honours and privileges like the Ferryman himself; if the Ferryman were not Gauvain's escort, the guardian would challenge him (vss 7669–75). Oddly, not to say perversely, his prosthesis bears a refracted image of the Grail. The Grail is made of refined gold, studded with many kinds of the most costly precious stones surpassing all others (vss 3232–39); the guardian's artificial leg, although it is silver and worked with black enamel, has regularly-spaced bands of gold and is likewise encrusted with precious stones (vss 7652–55).

The history of the Roche de Canguin further abounds in direct and indirect references to the Grail world. The founding of Ygraine's castle, which parallels

---

[31] Rider, 'Perpetual Enigma', 17.
[32] Peter Haidu, *Aesthetic Distance in Chrétien de Troyes: Irony and Comedy in 'Cligès' and 'Perceval'* (Geneva, 1968), ch. 2.
[33] Rider, 'Perpetual Enigma', 17.

that of the Waste Forest community, is also consonant with that of the Grail Castle, which the Fisher King had built after he was maimed (vss 3528–33). By inference, the peg-legged man was wounded at the same time. That the origins of the Roche de Canguin are linked to a cataclysm is indicated by the state of many women there who have awaited a liberator: orphans and old ladies whose husbands are dead – implicitly, slain in battle – and who have been unjustly dispossessed of their lands. No knights are there at all – implicitly, they have been killed – but an over-abundance of squires of all ages are waiting to be knighted. These present conditions and the prior events that have implicitly caused them recall the Hideous Damsel's list of the disasters awaiting the Grail kingdom because of Perceval's failure, for the Fisher King will continue to be incapable of ruling: a domain without a lord, ladies without husbands, lands laid waste, orphaned maidens, dead knights. It comes to light in these comparisons that the disasters that have happened in Logres and affected the Waste Forest community as well as the inhabitants of the Roche de Canguin have also occurred and continue to occur in the Grail kingdom. Perceval missed his opportunity to bring them to an end and to restore peace there.

Chrétien never directly portrays the miseries suffered in the Grail kingdom, except as they are embodied in the Fisher King; rather they are related by mediators who have knowledge of the Grail mysteries and who mirror the narrators of past disasters. In the last lines he was ever to write, however, in the fragmentary Orquenie episode (segment 18), Chrétien shows that Arthur and his subjects have become afflicted in ways that reflect, in fact concretize, the pains endured in the hidden kingdom.

In this remarkable 46-line passage are condensed many of the *Conte du Graal*'s prime concerns. While in the Gauvain section the Arthurian court all but disappears as a centre of gravity, Orquenie represents a renewal of Chrétien's practice, so prominent in the Perceval section, of interspersing analogous court scenes among adventures away from court (five Arthurian courts account for almost 30% of the text). Moreover, an important narrative principle involving play on perspective and perception is brilliantly featured as citizens watch Gauvain's messenger ride into the city and comment on his mission (vss 9193–203), only to be rebuked by their fellows for not minding their own affairs (vss 9204–11). After Chrétien's narrator comments on the rebuke, he adopts the point of view of the squire (vss 9215–19) and then shifts to that of King Arthur (vss 9220–22). Meanwhile, from a gallery above Arthur's hall, Lady Lore watches the scene the narrator goes on to describe (vss 9227–29). Moreover, the townspeople who observe the squire predict that, like the tellers of 'contes de Perceval' and 'contes du Graal', he brings 'de loing / Estranges noveles', vss 9196–97 [from far away (. . .) wondrous news] to tell the court. Conversely, this 'vallés', vs. 9189 [squire] riding to court also recalls the 'vallés', vs. 834 [boy] coming to Arthur's court at Carduel who is the subject of those 'contes', and just as the young Perceval meets a charcoal burner who tells him that he will find the king both 'dolant', vs. 845 [sad] and happy, so the onlookers know that Gauvain's messenger will find Arthur 'plains de doel et d'ire', vs. 9200 [upset and sad]. Indeed Arthur has no reason to be happy at Orquenie – or in fact at Carduel. When Perceval arrives at

Carduel, he finds the king 'pensis . . . et mus', vs. 911 [disheartened and silent] just as, in Orquenie, he is 'mu et sort', vs. 9198 [deaf and dumb].[34]

The observers are physically afflicted: 'contraint et . . . ardant', vs. 9193 [crippled and mangy (or gangrenous)], perhaps from wounds suffered in battle. More to the point, they are poor people who have been reduced to abjection because they have lost Gauvain, 'Qui por Dieu toz nos revestoit / Et dont toz li biens nos venoit / Par almosne et par charité', vss 9209–11 ['who gave us all clothing in God's name, and from whom we received everything (worthwhile) in charity and alms']. At the other end of the spectrum, Arthur in his court is attended by kings, counts palatine and dukes, but grief and depression reign: 'Li rois fu mornes et pensis / Quant il vit sa grant baronnie / Et de son neveu n'i vit mie', vss 9220–22 [(the king) was sad and downcast to see all his many barons and no sign of his nephew], and, like Perceval's mother, he falls in a faint. Lady Lore observes 'Le doel qu'en fist parmi la sale', vs. 9229 [the lamentations (people made) throughout the hall] and becomes 'Ausi comme tote esperdue', vs. 9232 [(completely distraught)]. Donald Maddox ascribes this misery to the destruction of Logres by the Bleeding Lance predicted in Escavalon (segment 13), and he remarks that, as Galloway has done and as the Grail kingdom still does, Arthur's kingdom now 'awaits its champion'.[35]

Amid such distress and suffering the word *charité* gleams like the gems that encrust the Grail – and the peg leg's prosthesis. Perhaps it is used in its debased sense as interchangeable with alms, for the parallel expressions in 'Par almosne et par charité', vs. 9211 ['in alms . . . in charity'] imply synonymy. Or perhaps *almosne* is ennobled by its juxtaposition with *charité* because Gauvain clothed the poor 'por Dieu', vs. 9209 [in God's name]. In any case, the particular association of charity with Gauvain links it with *largesse*, the supreme virtue of generous giving exemplified in Arthurian chivalry, but it is *largesse* turned to social good and not only courtly enhancement. The charity evoked in Chrétien's last lines arcs back across the entire romance to connect Gauvain's acts to the substance of the Prologue, where, even as Chrétien solicits the patronage of Philip of Flanders, he develops an extraordinary discourse on *charité* as the supreme theological virtue in which the word occurs no fewer than six times:[36]

> Et la destre que senefie?[37]
> Carité, qui de sa bone oevre
> Pas ne se vante, ançois se coevre,
> Si que ne le set se cil non
> Qui Diex et caritez a non.
> Diex est caritez, et qui vit
> En carité selonc l'escrit,
> – Sainz Pols[38] le dist et je le lui –
> Il maint en Dieu et Diex en lui.   (vss 42–50)

---

34 Busby, *Perceval*, p. 85.
35 Maddox, *Arthurian Romances*, p. 113.
36 On exegesis in the Prologue, see Sargent-Baur, *La Destre*, pp. 9–21.
37 In Matthew 6:3, '. . . let not thy left hand know what thy right hand doeth'.
38 The quote in vss 47–50 is from I John 4:16. The error may be a slip-up on the part of Chrétien, who has just referred to St Paul's I Corinthians 13:4 in vss 43–44 and who quotes II Corinthians

[And what does the right hand stand for? Charity, which does not
boast of its good deed, but hides it, so that only He whose name is
God and Charity knows of it. God is Charity, and he who abides in
charity, according to Holy Writ – St Paul says it and I read it there –
abides in God and God in him.]

Chrétien goes on to posit charity as the force at work in the operations of
translatio. He has identified *translatio* with the seminal word topos by representing Philip of Flanders as the 'good ground' in which he sows his romance,
the modern prince whose *largesse* surpasses that of the ancient pagan emperor
Alexander, conventionally a paragon of generosity (vss 7–15).[39] Now it is
precisely charity as the greatest Christian virtue that sets Philip and his *largesse*
apart from the ancient exemplar (vss 51–59). Finally, in this context Chrétien
names himself as translator of the book Count Philip has given him (vs. 62), and
thus identifies himself personally and his literary project with the Christian
values he extols.[40]

It is tempting to apply the polarity of Chrétien's *translatio* model (Alex-
ander-Philip, pagan generosity-Christian *largesse*, pagan knighthood-Christian
chivalry, etc.) to the binary relationship of Perceval and Gauvain. After all it is
Perceval whom Gornemant de Gorhaut explicitly makes a Christian knight
when he gives him his spurs and advises him to go willingly to church to 'Proier
celui qui tot a fait, / Que de vostre ame merchi ait / Et qu'en cest siecle terrïen /
Vos gart comme son crestïen', vss 1667–70 ['pray Him who made all to have
mercy on your soul and keep you a true Christian in this earthly life']. Moreover,
the Hermit recasts the chivalric advice of Perceval's mother as well as
Gornemant de Gorhaut in more explicit Christian terms and sums up: 'Dieu croi,
Dieu aime, Dieu aeure', vs. 6459 ['Believe in God, love God, worship God'].

However, Chrétien's romance is more subtle, for Gauvain's charity is also
centred in God, although his flaw may be that, contrary to the Prologue's
precepts, he has not kept it hidden. In any case, he and Perceval have parallel
missions. Gauvain seems destined to reconcile the Roche de Canguin with
Arthur's kingdom, which appears to have been struck by the Bleeding Lance,
while Perceval is concerned with mediating between the Arthurian world and
the Grail kingdom. That Christian charity operates in the enterprise of the more
worldly Gauvain is evident in the fact that his absence and the absence of his
charity from Arthur's kingdom deprive it of joy and prosperity, which the poor
regard as a function of his *largesse*. Gauvain is inextricably bound up in the
history of the transfer of power from Uther Pendragon to Arthur and its aftermath as recounted in Wace's *Brut*. Although Chrétien fails to keep his narrator's
promise to resume Perceval's adventures (vss 6514–18), the opening into the
operations of his romance provided by the Orquenie fragment offers a shadowy

---

9:6 in the Prologue's opening line: 'Ki petit semme petit quelt', vs. 1 [He who sows little, reaps
    little].
[39] See Tony Hunt, 'The Prologue to *Li Contes del Graal*', *Romania*, 92 (1971), 359–79, esp. 366–73.
[40] Chrétien's name is subject to wordplay in its associations with both Christianity and Chris-
    tendom, as in the prologue of *Erec et Enide*. It has a more explicitly Christian connotation when
    Gornemant de Gorhaut knights Perceval and in the Hermitage episode when a penitent lady
    remarks that it is a Christian's duty to confess (vss 6312–14).

glimpse into the future of Gauvain's double. As a Christian knight absolved of his debilitating sin and redirected by his Easter Communion, Perceval seems destined to re-enter the world of the Grail. If the confrontation with the Bleeding Lance implicit in Gauvain's projected reunion with Arthur reflects in any way Perceval's reconnection with the Grail mysteries, then the reconciliation of the invisible kingdom with the visible world must come about through acts of transcendent charity. Such a vision is discernable in the prolific tradition of continuations, rewrites, and other *translationes* of Chrétien's last romance that were produced over the next several decades in efforts to bring Perceval's and Gauvain's incomplete adventures to perfection.

PART III

MEDIEVAL RECEPTION AND INFLUENCE

14

The Continuations of the Conte du Graal

ANNIE COMBES

[Translated by Alexia Gino-Saliba]

Left unfinished, the *Conte du Graal* was soon provided with its first continuation. The last lines of Chrétien's romance virtually cry out for a sequel, since the narrative breaks off in mid-episode: a squire, entrusted by Gauvain with a message for Arthur, has just arrived at court in Orcanie. It is easy enough to imagine what is to follow: the happiness of the royal couple when they hear that Gauvain is well and the departure of the court for the Roche de Champguin where Arthur's nephew is to face Le Guiromelant. However, beyond this imminent turn of events, the *Conte* leaves us wondering about Perceval's fate, the Bleeding Lance and the Grail. Chrétien's incomplete romance presents the problem of how to end it: how to resolve the enigmas linked to the Grail, the Lance and the Fisher King, and what roles to attribute, respectively, to Perceval and Gauvain.

Any continuation project necessarily requires that further developments be harmonized with the original text. The *Conte du Graal* imposed the following constraints in particular:

– preserving a precise temporal and spatial context: the kingdom of Logres in Arthur's time, sharing frontiers with the lands of Galloway and those of the Fisher King, at the very gates of the Other World;

– organizing the narrative around the characters of Perceval and Gauvain, just as Chrétien had presented them;

– achieving the goals the Ugly Damsel had set for Arthur's knights using the Chastel Orguellos (vs. 4689), where one can test one's valour, and Montesclaire (vs. 4706), where a besieged maiden awaits her deliverance;

– fulfilling the prophecies announced by several characters: Perceval will some day become the best knight in the world (vss 1039–44), but his failure on the Fisher King's land will cause the death of many men and leave the land desolate (vss 4678–82); furthermore, the kingdom of Logres will be destroyed by the Bleeding Lance (vss 6188–71). More generally, we expect to rediscover the strange atmosphere of the *Conte* with its obsessive set of themes involving past, present and future disasters.

One could say that to continue Chrétien's romance implied realizing all those narrative promises, but in that case it would also mean neglecting another major aspect of the *Conte* itself: its very proclivity toward non-fulfilment. In the course of the narrative, this tendency is manifest several times. For instance, Perceval had promised his friend Blanchefleur that he would meet her at Beaurepaire; however, soon after their parting, he dreams only of adventures and knighthood, 'd'aventure et de chevalerie' (vs. 4167). Wishing to return to the Fisher King's castle, he forgets his quest, loses his memory and is preoccupied only with knightly combat. It is well known that romance has no rules and is forever tempted to reflect its codes within the fictions it develops. One of the codes of the *Conte du Graal* is without any doubt suspension and postponement. What is supposed to take place does not. Perceval forgets Blanchefleur and the Grail; Gauvain forgets the quest of the Bleeding Lance even though he swore he would pursue it assiduously. Thus, on the one hand, the *Conte du Graal* traces the path of a precise narrative continuation while, on the other hand, faithful to its internal contradiction, it continuously postpones the time of fulfilment.

Caught in a dialectical movement of convergence and divergence with respect to Chrétien's work, four 'continuations' modulated the distance they would take with respect to the original work, and almost all preferred the option of suspension.[1] In the manuscripts they follow one another in a continuous sequence, but not all of them are present in all the manuscripts. Of the fifteen manuscripts of the *Conte du Graal*, eleven contain the First Continuation (C1), ten the Second (C2), seven the Third (C3) and two the Fourth, Gerbert's (GC).[2] Only four manuscripts contain Chrétien's romance alone, whereas all the others present at least one continuation, often even two: 'it is clear that in all the manuscripts that have preserved both the First and the Second Continuations, the redactors and the copyists thought of the corpus as a single, continuous story'.[3] At the end of the twelfth and beginning of the thirteenth century, reading the *Conte du Graal* meant reading Chrétien's romance, C1 and C2; GC and C3 were written later on, after the *Lancelot-Graal*. Only C3 closes the cycle. These protracted verse narratives (each longer than Chrétien's romance) do form a whole with the *Conte*, even though each one seems to have a different author; the mysterious Bliobliheri is mentioned in C1, Wauchier de Denain in C2, Manessier in C3 and Gerbert (commonly identified as Gerbert de Montreuil) in GC.[4] Therefore, there seems to be one narrative flow but four

---

[1] William Roach edited the first three continuations in five volumes: *The Continuations of the Old French 'Perceval' of Chrétien de Troyes* (Philadelphia, 1949–83). *The First Continuation*, vol. I, II, III, 1949, 1950, 1952; *The Second Continuation*, vol. IV, 1971; *The Third Continuation*, vol. V, 1983. Written by Gerbert de Montreuil, the Fourth Continuation was edited by Mary Williams and Marguerite Oswald under the title *La Continuation de 'Perceval'*, 3 vols (Paris, 1922–75). My comments will be based on these editions. Instead of referring to the Fourth Continuation, I will call this last work Gerbert's Continuation (GC); we will see that this narrative does not extend the action of C3. The verse numbering is continuous in *Continuation 1* (long version), 2 and 3, edited by Roach; Gerbert's Continuation has its own numbering.

[2] See *Les Manuscrits de Chrétien de Troyes*, 2 vols, ed. Keith Busby, Terry Nixon, Alison Stones and Lori Walters (Amsterdam, 1993), I, pp. 9–15 (Terry Nixon, 'List of Manuscripts of Chrétien de Troyes'), II, pp. 249–62 (Appendix 1: 'Other Contents of the Manuscripts of Chrétien de Troyes', by Keith Busby, Laurence Harf-Lancner, Terry Nixon, Alison Stones and Lori Walters).

[3] Roach, *The Continuations*, IV, p. XVII.

[4] With the *Conte du Graal*, the Continuations form a true Grail cycle: see Keith Busby, 'The Other Grail Cycle', *Cyclification*, ed. Bart Besamusca, W.P. Gerritsen, C. Hogetoorn and O.S.H. Lie (Amsterdam, 1994), pp. 176–78.

distinct authors, hence four aesthetic perspectives, four different takes on the task of continuation.[5]

C1 furnishes ample proof that continuing does not mean completing. The First Continuation definitely presents the largest number of deviations from Chrétien's romance.[6] The organization of this narrative differs completely from the *Conte*'s structure: Chrétien's romance was built upon the alternation between Perceval and Gauvain, whereas the new narrative offers a structure fragmented by six sections independent of one another. The work proceeds in one direction, then goes off in another and yet another one. . . . The nearly constant presence of Gauvain and his lineage (his brother and father) endows the narrative with a very relative unity; Perceval for his part is completely absent.[7] And his absence may be linked to the disappearance of the religious theme, which was so important in the *Conte*. This infidelity to the original text is even more striking in that, at first, C1 appears intent on providing a scrupulously faithful continuation.

Indeed C1 follows directly on the final lines of the *Conte*, 'Et quant la reïne la [dame Lore] voit, / Si li demande qu'ele avoit' [And when the Queen sees Dame Lore, she asks her what is wrong], with the following words: 'Et qui si l'a espoëntee' [and who has frightened her so]. The narrative coherence is also excellent since the court accepts Gauvain's invitation and leaves for the castle of the Roche de Champguin in Galloway. These two worlds are thus reunited after a long separation: Arthur sees his mother again, and Gauvain reveals his identity to his own mother and sister. This first section does fulfil the promises of the end of the *Conte*. However, the marvellous castle of the Roche de Champguin loses its other-worldly aura and vanishes almost immediately from the narrative. After Le Guiromelant is defeated, Gauvain and Arthur leave, as if the Roche had never even existed.

The notion of integrating this atemporal site into the Arthurian kingdom seems thus to be evaded in a narrative that distances itself abruptly from the *Conte*'s networks of meaning. Absent from C1 are the communities of exiles and the desolate lands. From then on, all castles are wealthy and all confrontations end in joy. There are countless celebrations in which Arthur shows his 'largesse' by distributing lands to his newly appointed liegemen.

Moreover, the king initiates the only narrative episode that was begun in the *Conte* and actually completed in C1: when he sees that Girflet is absent from the Round Table, he sets in motion his quest to the Chastel Orguellos. In this episode, full of unexpected events, one scene in particular illustrates the extent to which C1 deviates from the *Conte*: the questing knights stop in a deserted castle where they discover one hundred silver 'graaus' [grails] set out on tables,

---

[5] On the particular narrative structures of these four continuations, see Martine Séguy, *Les Romans du Graal ou le signe imaginé* (Paris, 2001).

[6] I will only mention here the short version of C1 (vol. III of Roach's edition). The long and mixed versions, dated later, occasionally interpolate complete scenes. On these different versions, see Pierre Gallais, *L'Imaginaire d'un romancier français à la fin du XIIème siècle. Description raisonnée, comparée et commentée de la 'Continuation–Gauvain', première suite du Conte du Graal de Chrétien de Troyes*, 4 vols (Amsterdam, 1988–89).

[7] Hence the designation of this narrative as the Gauvain-Continuation.

each containing a boar's head (vss 4047–53). Neither fish nor host is present:[8] this is *something else entirely*.

The process of displacement is obvious when Gauvain arrives at the Grail Castle after an odd combination of events. This particular episode will be quite important for the following continuations. It begins when a knight passes in front of the Queen without greeting her; Keu fails to convince the unknown knight to turn around and do so. Gauvain succeeds, but the knight is mortally wounded by a lance thrown at his back; before he dies, he asks Gauvain to mount his horse and let it lead him away.[9] Gauvain is then taken on a wild ride until a storm forces him to take shelter in a chapel. There, a disembodied hand extinguishes a candle set on the altar while a loud moan can be heard: frightened, Gauvain sets off again. The following night, he reaches a castle where a funeral service is taking place: on the chest of the corpse lies a piece of a blade. The knight is then greeted by a lively king who invites him to share his table, after which Gauvain 'vit parmi un huis entrer / le rice Graal qui servoit', vss 7276–77 [saw coming in through a door the precious serving Grail]. The Graal, moving on its own, serves the wine and the dishes of the feast. Later, Gauvain sees a lance fastened within a silver vase; blood drips from its point. The king asks his guest to resolder the sword, a piece of which was lying on the corpse, but the knight fails. Nevertheless, the King reveals to him that this very lance pierced Christ's heart when He was on the Cross. But Gauvain dozes off and the king falls silent. The following morning, the knight awakens on a shore; the castle has vanished.

This episode obviously contests the *Conte du Graal*: its elements reveal a constant discrepancy with those found in Chrétien, and some are in complete contradiction with them.[10] The King is no longer infirm, there is no procession (the candlesticks and platter have disappeared) and the Grail resembles more a cauldron of plenty than a 'tant sainte chose', vs. 6425 [a very holy thing]. Furthermore, if the Lance is synonymous with disaster in the *Conte*, here, as the King explains in detail, it has become the symbol of mankind's redemption. The Lance and the Grail of Chrétien's romance thus undergo a true metamorphosis. Moreover, new motifs are added: the haunted chapel, the corpse in the coffin and the broken sword. This last object assumes all by itself the sinister past referred to in the *Conte*: according to the King, it was used to deal a fatal blow, thus provoking the ruin of many lords and their families during the awful disaster that destroyed the kingdom of Logres (vss 7474–78). The sword is a product of the era linked to the twilight of Utherpendragon's rule and the subsequent migration that led to the founding of the communities of the Roche de

---

[8] We are reminded of the hermit's words concerning the Grail in the *Conte*: it does not contain 'a pike, lamprey, or salmon', but rather a single mass wafer, vss 6420–22.

[9] About this episode and the numerous representations of the Other World in the Continuations, see Keith Busby, '"Estrangement se merveilla": l'autre dans les *Continuations* de *Perceval*', *Miscellanea Mediaevalia, Mélanges offerts à Philippe Ménard*, 2 vols (Paris, 1998), 1, pp. 279–97.

[10] The following analysis is partially based upon the one in Annie Combes and Annie Bertin, *Ecritures du Graal* (Paris, 2001), pp. 36–42.

Champguin and the Grail. This weapon, which postpones further the revelations, will be handsomely exploited by the authors of the other continuations.[11]

Whereas C1 distances itself from the *Conte* as much as possible, C2, on the contrary, seeks convergence with it. C2, a narrative 13,000 lines long, has a linear structure and is almost exclusively centred on Perceval: Roach showed it to be composed of 35 episodes, 27 of which are concerned with Perceval as the main character, and only 4 with Gauvain, whose sole noteworthy action is that he twice recounts his night at the Fisher King's castle (the one narrated in C1).[12] He would like to return to that place but this ambition will remain unfulfilled. However, Perceval will go to the Fisher King's castle, but he will do so only after wandering at length and encountering many adventures. C2 pushes the process of postponement to the extreme by intertwining a second quest with the Grail quest and by plunging its hero into a faery world.

Although Perceval wants to reach the Grail Castle as quickly as possible, his quest is constantly suspended, deflected, in fact, postponed, because other necessities must be attended to first. At the beginning of the work, Perceval is very close to success since he recognizes the river where he once saw the Fisher King in his boat (vss 20,009–16). While searching for a bridge or a ford, he notices a superb castle on the other shore. A helmsman helps him cross the river and shows him 'uns chemins pleniers / Qui le manront sans nul trestor / A la court lou Roi Pescheor', vss 20096–98 [a convenient path that will lead him straight to the Fisher King's court]. But Perceval chooses to go instead to the beautiful castle that he has glimpsed. There, he meets a lady with whom he falls violently in love: 'je vos ain plus que ma vie', vs. 20250 ['I love you more than my life'], he tells her, but she agrees to grant him her love only on condition that he hunts the white stag and brings her the head. She lends him a hunting dog to help him accomplish this task, advising him not to lose the animal. Perceval kills the stag, but soon afterwards another knight steals the dog and the stag head. Before he can return to his lady, Perceval must recover what was stolen from him. He swears never to abandon his quest as long as he has not recovered the head and the dog . . . and learned the truth about the Grail and the Lance (vss 23124–40). In this double project, the secular love quest clearly occupies the foreground.

Perceval's wandering unfolds in a territory that is obviously the kingdom of Logres, but the supernatural emerges incessantly. In the *Conte* and in C1, the signs of the Other World are tied to particular lands and castles. Here, the colour associated with the faery world invades the narrative: castles, clothing and animals are all white. Perceval himself will ride a white mule. A knight lives in a tomb, another in an invisible castle. Elsewhere, one must pass over a glass bridge that appears to crack when one starts across it. These supernatural places are most often the work of fairies. Obviously, the lady Perceval loves is a supernatural creature.

---

[11] See Alexandre Leupin, 'La Faille et l'écriture dans les *Continuations du Perceval*', *Le Moyen Age*, 88 (1982), pp. 253–69.
[12] On these accounts by Gauvain, see Combes and Bertin, *Ecritures du Graal*, pp. 45–48.

In this faery universe, space assumes oneiric qualities. The hero seems to move within a dream in which obsessive images, originating from a time preceding his amnesia, appear to be clothed in fragments of his memory; from the point of view of the reader, these memory shards are also narrative fragments from the *Conte*. For instance, one day, Perceval sees 'deus pecheors an une nef', vs. 22439 [two fishermen in a boat]; he also discovers a dwelling linked somehow to the Fisher King's castle, le 'chastiaus as pucelles', vs. 24595 [the castle of the maidens]. There, Perceval dines lavishly then asks the type of questions he should have asked at the Grail Castle, even though the objects he asks about – a hammer and a table – are more pedestrian (vss 24606–11). In the course of this work, Perceval returns to Beaurepaire. Blanchefleur is still there, awaiting her friend; as before, she joins him in his bed and, as before, the knight leaves promising to return (vss 23069–70). The reminiscences are thus fulfilled in as much as they are repeated, and all innovation that would point to the future seems eliminated. This impression is confirmed when Perceval arrives by chance in the 'Gaste Forest' [Waste Forest] of his childhood (vs. 23548). His mother is no longer there to serve as interlocutor; she is replaced by a daughter, a sister whom Perceval did not know existed. It would be futile to wonder too much about this character whose biography seems improbable and whose sole purpose is to be the voice of the past and recount, in the form of a family legend, her brother's departure and the pain and loneliness suffered by the inhabitants of the domain.

Despite this semblance of permanency, Perceval is nevertheless no longer exactly as he was in Chrétien's work; besides the fact that he is very much in love (and he does spend a night with the lady, vss 28132–39), he has obviously become the best of knights: he alone succeeds in crossing the glass bridge, he alone is capable of undergoing the ordeal of Mont Douloureux mentioned by Keendin in Chrétien's romance (vss 4724–26). The *Conte* does not describe this ordeal, but C2 gives it form: the knight must tie his horse to a pillar, but if he is not the best of knights, he will lose his mind (vss 19918–29). Thus, the Perceval who at the end of the narrative arrives at the Grail Castle is a knight who has proven his valour. It becomes clear, then, that the Grail and the faery elements, though closely intertwined in the plot, do not share the same imaginary world. The Grail, in C2, takes on a definite Christian quality.

Once more on a path leading 'tot droit' [directly] to the Fisher King (vs. 32021), Perceval goes through a storm and arrives at a chapel, none other than the C1 chapel featuring the frightening hand. Unlike Gauvain, Perceval is not afraid in the least. Later on, a lady to whom he relates his night tells him: 'Ce est senefience / Que dou Graal et de la Lance / Savroiz par tens la verité', vss 32233–35 ['It means you will soon know the truth about the Grail and the Lance']. Perceval arrives at the Fisher King's castle and attempts in vain to question his host. A procession then appears: one young lady holds the 'Saint Graal' (vs. 32400); another, the Bleeding Lance; and finally a young man, carrying the broken sword, sets it down near the King. With respect to the sword, Perceval learns that only a knight 'qui sainte eglyse anorast' [who honours the holy church] will be able to resolder it and, having done so, will be rewarded with the knowledge of anything he wants to know. However, Perceval fails: there remains 'une creveüre, / Petitete, non mie granz', vss 32558–59 [a very tiny break, really not large]. The king explains to Perceval that he does not possess all the qualities one could hope for. Nevertheless, he invites him to stay with him. 'Et Percevaux se reconforte' // [And Perceval is comforted]: with this line ends C2, contradicting the prophetic words of the lady who had announced 'Saroiz par tens la verité'.[13] It is a deceptive ending to a narrative that Gerbert de Montreuil and Manessier, respectively, will continue in different ways.

Gerbert de Montreuil's long narrative (17,000 lines) is found in only two manuscripts.[14] It follows directly on the last sentence of C2: 'Et Percevaux se reconforte // qui parole au Roi Pescheor / Mais molt se tient a pecheor ' [And Perceval, who speaks to the Fisher King, is comforted but considers himself a true sinner]. According to the king, the remaining crack in the sword indeed points to a state of sin demanding penance. The narrative, deliberately moralizing, leads Perceval into a redemptive path in order to make him worthy of reaching the truth for which he yearns. However – and this is truly a remarkable aspect of this text – its ending loops back to its beginning.[15] At the conclusion of his adventures, Perceval returns to the Grail Castle, witnesses once more the procession and manages to resolder the sword perfectly. He is so happy that 'a por un poi qu'il ne chanta', vs. 17087 [he was close to singing]. Fourteen lines follow, the same ones found in C2, ending with 'Et Percevaux se reconforte', vs. 32594. This work, perfectly circular, does not aim to close the story but rather to continue it, as if the main goal were to postpone the ending by adding thousands of lines framed by two identical – or nearly identical – moments. If Perceval finally succeeds in eliminating the crack in the blade, it is because he is no longer the same: he has redeemed some of his mistakes and instances of negligence, and he has corrected his past errors.

GC's rhythm is more flexible, structured upon the alternation between weeks of wandering that are summarized in a few lines, and adventures narrated with great precision. The narrative unfolds from the obsessive desire the hero has to know the truth about the Lance and the Grail: Perceval defines himself as a man who is seeking these objects, who saw them twice but failed to gain access to their truth (vss 4682–87). Adventures and encounters follow on one another, constantly reminding us of how well the hero has proven his valour, as seen in C2: this is why he now succeeds in occupying a dangerous seat at the Round Table whereas six knights died previously in this ordeal. But most of all, *GC* shows Perceval's redemption thanks to a process of anamnesis, bringing back into the narrative characters that may have been forgotten since the *Conte*, for instance Gornemant de Goort and the Vermilion Knight.

The meeting with Gornemant gives Perceval the opportunity to recall his wanderings and his failure at the Grail Castle. As he reflects on his sins, all of which he has confessed and atoned for, he understands that one oversight

---

[13] The double slash (//) indicates the end of the text.
[14] This is why we can call *GC* an interpolation: Louise D. Stephens, 'Gerbert and Manessier: the Case for a Connection', *Arthurian Literature*, 14 (1996), 53–68.
[15] See Matilda Tomaryn Bruckner, 'Looping the Loop Through a Tale of Beginnings, Middles and Ends: From Chrétien to Gerbert in the *Perceval* Continuations,' *'Por le soie amisté.' Essays in Honor of Norris J. Lacy*, ed. Keith Busby and Catherine M. Jones (Amsterdam, 2000), pp. 33–51.

remains to be repaired: he promised Blanchefleur he would marry her. Gornemant approves this initiative and warrants that it will allow him to resolder the sword and finally to learn the secrets of the Lance and the Grail (vss 5168–77). Nevertheless, Gerbert wants nothing to do with a hero who indulges in the pleasures of the flesh, even within the bonds of matrimony. His Perceval is able to resist all the devil's temptations, even when they take the shape of a woman who promises to give him access to the secrets of the Grail and the Lance (vss 2536–41) in exchange for sexual relations. At Beaurepaire, the wedding takes place, but, thanks to a surprising trick, it is not consummated: the wedding night provides the newly-weds with the opportunity to engage in an edifying discussion about the merits of Chastity and Virginity (vss 6827–53). In this way, Perceval fulfils his promise to Blanchefleur without sacrificing his purity (GC has clearly forgotten the night of love that Perceval spent with the fairy in C2). The hero also takes charge of his sister's fate, bringing her to the Château des Pucelles where he had gone before (in C2). Perceval thus 'fulfils' his duty as a husband and as a brother, and the shadows of the past, which tended to conceal a latent or obvious culpability, are dispersed. Gerbert also evokes the Vermilion Knight, killed by the young hero of the *Conte*. Was it a wrongful death? Facing the sons of the Vermilion Knight, Perceval gives his own interpretation of the episode, recalling his naiveté and the responsibility that the king and Keu bore regarding this action (vss 11021–55). He ends up making his peace with this mourning family, achieving thus his own redemption.

A purer knight, Perceval is also a more Christian one, as witnessed by the fact that he alone is able to grasp the shield with the vermilion cross.[16] With this shield (which contains a piece of wood from the Cross), Perceval concludes an adventure presented by the Ugly Damsel in the *Conte*, one originally meant for Gauvain: the siege of Montesclaire. Perceval succeeds in delivering the besieged maiden, who had been waiting in vain for Gauvain's help (vss 9352–55). At the end of his adventures, the hero returns to the Grail Castle, asks an odd variety of questions regarding previous and more recent events, resolders the sword and . . . 'se reconforte'.

GC ties together all the adventures left in suspense from the *Conte* and from C2 and brings them to fruition in a way that exalts the perfection of the harvester of the adventures. However, the narrative, despite its great length, neglects the field of the Grail. The mysteries of the Fisher King's castle remain intact. It will be C3's mission to elucidate them.

'Et Percevaux se reconforte // Qui de l'avanture a tel joie / Que je ne cuit mie que j'oie / Jamés de tel joie parler' [And Perceval is comforted, feeling such a great joy in this adventure that I do not believe I have ever heard anyone speak of a comparable joy]. Manessier clearly opts for the notion of success after the ordeal of the broken sword. Nevertheless, the Grail quest is not over: C3 is the romance of successive closures, which arrive in waves, with the knots of

---

[16] This cross, and also the motif of temptation and the apology of chastity, suffice to prove the influence that the *Queste del Saint Graal* exercises on this continuation.

meaning untangling successively within the unfolding narrative. Manessier gives a final ending to all that can be ended in the complex story of the Grail.

At the Fisher King's castle, Perceval sees once more the procession of the Lance, the Grail and the silver platter (vss 32617–19) and asks, 'Cui l'an an sert et don il vienent', vs. 32645 [whom they are serving and where do they come from].[17] The king's answers give an unambiguously Christian reading of the elements in the procession: the Lance is the holy lance of Longinus, and the blood dripping from it belongs to Christ (an explanation already given in C1); Joseph of Arimathea used the Grail to collect Christ's blood at the Crucifixion; the platter is used to cover the Grail.

In a way, then, the narrative begins with an epilogue; however, if the wave of explanations exhausts the need for further elucidation, it does not close off the action, since the end of the work is further postponed thanks to the broken sword: at the very moment that it is resoldered, its history gives a formidable second wind to the narrative by integrating the vengeance theme into the semantic sphere of the Grail. To do so, Manessier invents the character of Goondesert, brother of the Fisher King, treacherously slain by Partinal, lord of the Red Tower, using the fateful sword. The blow was so violent that it broke the sword; mad with grief, the Fisher King used the broken pieces of the sword to mutilate himself (vss 32913–15). Partinal's death alone will be able to cure his infirmity.

This brand new scenario obviously contradicts both the cousin's and the Ugly Damsel's revelations in the *Conte*. However, it is in perfect harmony with the tone of the adventures narrated in this continuation. Discovering, perhaps, meanings buried within the Grail motif, Manessier focuses his narrative on this theme of vengeance.[18] His imaginative world is based on the idea that wrongs need to be redeemed in a universe where violence and treachery reign. Perceval, but also Sagremor and Gauvain, must constantly intervene to prevent rapes, abductions or the burning of young maidens at the stake. A brutal death is also the origin of the second mission the king entrusts to Perceval: he will have to purify the haunted chapel, occupied by a devil ever since a matricide was committed within its walls. The black hand caused the death of four thousand knights, and this scourge will end only when a knight is able to vanquish it.

Thus, after bringing closure to the *Conte du Graal*, Manessier proposes to end an ordeal put in place by the author of C1 and maintained by the authors of the other continuations. He does so in a very efficient manner: Perceval eliminates the black hand, not by force but by the sign of the cross; he then sprinkles holy water in the chapel. This new link to religion is confirmed when, using the same method, he drives away a demon who took the appearance of Blanchefleur and tried to seduce him. All these victories confirm the fact that Perceval has indeed become the best of the knights of Christendom. As a matter of fact, in this

---

[17] On the changing form of the questions asked by the Grail questers, see Emmanuèle Baumgartner, 'Del Graal cui l'an an servoit: variations sur un pronom', 1990, repr. *De l'histoire de Troie au livre du Graal* (Orléans, 1994), pp. 445–52.
[18] J. C. Lozac'hmeur, 'Du héros civilisateur à Perceval ou les transpositions successives d'un mythe', *Bien dire et bien aprandre*, 13 (1996), 133–43.

continuation, Perceval is under the direct protection of God as we can see during his fight against Partinal; the combat is long since the two adversaries are of equal strength, but finally, 'Percevaux an ot la victoire / Par le voloir au roi de gloire', vss 41807–8 [Perceval won by the will of the King of Glory]. The knight goes back to the Grail Castle, where his arrival triggers the Fisher King's recovery. Perceval once more watches the procession, and this time the Fisher King himself asks questions and requests to know the name of his guest. The King, who turns out to be Perceval's maternal uncle, is ready to let him have his kingdom, but Perceval refuses his offer and goes back to Arthur's court.

Finding his way back to the Grail Castle and then, from there, returning to Arthur's court poses no more problems. Manessier achieves the junction between the kingdom of Logres and the Grail domain, freeing the castle of the Fisher King from its supernatural prison. When his uncle passes away, Perceval is crowned king and Arthur attends the ceremony. During the feast, the Grail, the Lance and the platter are paraded before them; Arthur asks for an explanation and Perceval tells him 'D'outre en outre la verité', vs. 42514 [the whole and complete truth]. Following this apotheosis, the narrative goes on to tell of the spiritual ascension of Perceval. After a seven-year reign, he withdraws to a hermitage, followed by the Grail, the Lance and the platter. Five years later, he becomes a priest and performs the divine service for ten years, fed by the Grail, and living through prayers, fasts and vigils. When he dies, God takes his soul to Heaven, and the Grail, Lance and platter vanish from the earth.

Perceval's astonishing success contrasts with the definitive failure of Gauvain in the order of spirituality. Indeed, one after the other, the continuations have illustrated the extent of Gauvain's moral and ethical shortcomings. Manessier uses this character mainly to elucidate the story of the knight mysteriously killed in C1. His resolution of this adventure may, however, leave the reader somewhat dissatisfied: we are told that the stranger's name is Silimac and that the lance that slew him was thrown by Keu, according to Silimac's sister, who is skilled in 'astronomie' (vs. 35880). She asks Gauvain to avenge her brother's death, and he does so when he injures the seneschal quite seriously. It would be difficult to claim that all the mysteries are resolved. What was Similac's exact mission at the Grail Castle? Why did Keu kill the knight? The episode does receive narrative closure, but an unpolished one it is.

Nevertheless, with Manessier, it is clear that the *Conte du Graal* has been brought to an end. At the same time, the whole Arthurian universe seems to have reached its limits. The principles of the medieval adventure narrative are present in this narrative, but they seem devoid of meaning and are repetitive and static: without recounting the countless interchangeable jousts, I will at least mention a sumptuous bed, reminiscent of the Marvellous Bed in the *Conte*, but which here is neither the object nor the stimulus of any adventure; a knight simply sleeps in it and awakens there (vss 33098–145). The lines 36627–28 are emblematic of this lack of events and this deconstruction of the mechanics of the narrative: 'Li rois qui ne fu pas pansis / Estoit a son disner asis' [the king, who was not pensive, was seated at the table]. This bizarre statement – why indicate that the king is *not* pensive? – seems at odds with lines 865–66 of the *Conte*: 'Et li rois Artus est assis / Au chief d'une table pansis' [and King Arthur is seated, pensive, at one end of a table] or of line 3421 of C1 when Arthur 's'entr'oblie en ce penser' [loses himself in his thoughts]. In each case, the king's thoughts are a powerful motor of the plot. In C3, the 'récit de l'épuisement' [narrative of exhaustion],[19] the usual mechanisms of the narrative disappear at the same time that the Grail loses its narrative force.

The other continuators, who chose incessantly to exploit the theme of questioning, were more faithful to the *Conte*'s logic than was Manessier. Instead of closing the narrative, they preferred to adopt a dual initiative, which consisted of lending closure to certain threads of the narrative only on condition that new threads were introduced. And no doubt, being faithful to the spirit of Chrétien's work implied less a principle of systematic coherence than some sort of sporadic correlation with the *Conte* in order to preserve and prolong its enigmatic dimension.

---

[19] Séguy, *Les Romans du Graal ou le signe imaginé*, p. 317.

15

Medieval Translations and Adaptations of Chrétien's Works

MICHELLE SZKILNIK

Chrétien's romances enjoyed a huge success almost immediately after being written. They were copied, imitated, transposed, quoted broadly and consistently throughout the thirteenth century in French-speaking domains. Two of them, the *Chevalier de la Charrette* and the *Conte du Graal*, were used extensively (with major adjustments) in the Arthurian prose cycles. The transposition of the *Charrette* into the prose *Lancelot* especially testifies to the perfect familiarity with Chrétien's romances shared by prose writers and their audiences. But this familiarity also meant that French writers did not try to adapt them *stricto sensu*.[1]

The situation was quite different outside France, where some writers – but not their public – could read French and gain direct access to Chrétien's romances. One of the clearest signs of Chrétien's spreading fame is that, very early on, his romances were deemed worth translating. German, Dutch, Norse, Swedish, English translations and/or adaptations were composed before and during the first half of the fourteenth century. Only three of Chrétien's romances, however, gained fame abroad: *Erec*, *Yvain* and *Perceval*, the most popular being *Yvain*. This is all the more striking because Erec and Yvain were precisely those of Chrétien's heroes whom his French epigones (imitators) tended to ignore.[2] Yet the reason they were favoured outside France is probably the same reason they were avoided by French-speaking writers: masterly in composition, morally satisfactory, these romances embodied the spirit of courtly life. They represented the highest achievement in the art of romance. French authors could not dream of rewriting these stories, but foreign writers could appropriate them. Yet these adapters did not feel constrained to imitate their models slavishly. Indeed, while they often closely followed the plot line, they introduced many changes to reorient interpretation. They tended to motivate situations more thoroughly and to clarify what remained ambiguous and obscure in the original work (a feature that later French adaptations exhibit as well). Fully aware of the audiences they were addressing, they reshaped the romances in order to meet the expectations of their public and to convey their own understanding of the story.

---

1   See the following chapter, Emmanuèle Baumgartner's discussion of Chrétien's influence.
2   See, again, Baumgartner's discussion, below.

The case of the *Perceval* is different: Chrétien's work was fragmentary; it raised many questions that the adapters, like their French counterparts, tackled as best they could. It is rather the romance's incompleteness and enigmatic quality that appealed to them, as those qualities also fascinated Chrétien's continuators in French. All the adapters did manage (with varying degrees of success) to bring Perceval's story to an end.

The first foreign text derived from Chrétien is Hartmann von Aue's *Erec*, dating from c. 1180, which survives in one complete manuscript and in a few fragments. Much longer than its source (about 10,200 lines compared to about 6960), it is a free adaptation of *Erec et Enide*. Hartmann follows Chrétien's plot but expands some scenes and at times introduces new ones, thus giving a new tonality to the story. One of the most significant changes is that Erec apologizes for testing Enite's love and treating her rudely, thus suggesting Enite's innocence. Indeed, Hartmann depicts Erec's departure from court as a necessary atonement for *his* sin of *verlingen*, i.e., his failure to understand his social and religious duties. The *Joie de la cour* episode shows how he succeeds in overcoming his failings with Christian virtues.[3] Thus the couple has finally found the right balance between love for each other, love for God and social duties.

Hartmann's second Arthurian romance *Iwein*, roughly 8000 lines long, follows Chrétien's *Chevalier au lion* more closely. Its high sophistication points to a later date of composition than *Erec* (around 1205). The work remained very popular from the thirteenth century to the sixteenth: as many as thirty-two manuscripts (complete or fragmentary) have survived. Like Erec, Iwein suffers from an inability to balance his love for Laudine with his love for knighthood, although, contrary to Erec, he chooses the latter, thus showing *untriuwe* (faithlessness) to Laudine. Iwein must atone for this sin by performing a series of charitable exploits. Thanks to Lunete's intervention, he is finally reconciled with Laudine. The conclusion of Hartmann's romance, however, is different from Chrétien's in that Laudine also repents for treating Iwein harshly and asks for forgiveness. In the French romance, Laudine remains an ambiguous character whose enigmatic behaviour threatens the couple's happiness. Hartmann's conclusion is more optimistic: Christian virtues, such as *caritas*, will enable Iwein and Laudine (like Erec and Enite) to achieve peace and harmony. Hartmann thus gives a deeper religious tonality to Chrétien's stories.

At about the same time (c. 1200–10), a second German writer, Wolfram von Eschenbach,[4] expanded Chrétien's *Conte du Graal* into an outstanding composition. *Parzival*, written in rhymed couplets, numbers roughly 25,000 lines (compared to about 9200 lines for the *Conte*), divided into sixteen books. This work was hugely popular throughout the Middle Ages: sixteen complete manuscripts, more than sixty fragments and an early edition (1477) are extant.

3　See Silvia Ranawake, 'Erec's "verligen" and the Sin of Sloth', *Hartmann von Aue, Changing Perspectives*, ed. Timothy McFarland and Silvia Ranawake (Göppingen, 1988).

4　See Timothy McFarland, 'The Emergence of the German Grail Romance: Wolfram von Eschenbach, *Parzival*', in *The Arthur of the Germans*, ed. W.H. Jackson and S.A. Ranawake (Cardiff, 2000), pp. 54–68.

Wolfram used the *Conte* for the central part of his romance: the story of Parzival intertwined with that of Gawan reproduces Chrétien's plot, with significant additions and modifications. But he also conceived the story of Parzival's father, Gahmuret, whose amorous and heroic adventures take place first in the East, where he marries a heathen queen and fathers a son, Feirefiz, then in the West, where he marries Herzeloyde, Parzival's mother, before returning to Baghdad where he dies in combat. Wolfram also brought Chrétien's unfinished romance to a conclusion: Parzival goes back to the Grail castle, asks the right question, thus healing the Grail King. He then becomes the new Grail King and rules with his wife Condwiramur (the counterpart of Chrétien's Blanchefleur), who has been called to the Grail castle and has given birth to twin boys, Loherangrin and Kardeiz. Before his return to the Grail castle, Parzival had met his half-brother Feirefiz in combat. Having revealed their identity to each other, the two brothers go to Arthur's court, then to the Grail castle, where Feirefiz falls in love with the Grail damsel. He converts to Christianity in order to marry her. The couple then depart for India, and their union is blessed with a son: Prester John.

This sketchy summary barely gives an idea of Wolfram's thorough and complex reworking of the *Conte du Graal*. One of the most striking modifications concerns the Grail itself, as revealed by Trevrizent, Parzival's hermit uncle. Whereas the Grail is some sort of a dish in the *Conte*, it becomes a stone, mysteriously called 'lapsit exillis'. The Grail is kept at Munsalvaesche, a hidden castle, where beautiful maidens tend it, while young knights (*templeise* or Templars), forming a military and religious order, protect it.

Conscious of departing from Chrétien, Wolfram elaborated a complex fiction: he claimed to have found this new material in another source, Kyot, a Provençal poet, who had read in some abandoned manuscript in Toledo the first version of the story of the Grail, written by a pagan named Flegetanis. Kyot had then looked through many chronicles to find out who were the present guardians of the Grail and had finally discovered that they were from Anjou. This sophisticated (and no doubt imaginary) filiation of texts can be related to the care with which Wolfram develops intricate genealogies, tightly linking all the characters.

Parzival connects three worlds: the Orient, Arthur's kingdom and the Grail kingdom. All of them present communities that are, or have been, dysfunctional at some point: Anfortas, the Grail King, forgot his duties, fought for the love of a woman and was gravely injured. He is expecting the stranger who will ask the question and release him from his terrible pain. Arthur's world, as exemplified in the Gawan part of the narrative but also in the episode involving the Red Knight, is prone to violence, particularly directed against women. The same is even truer in the pagan East. In all three of these worlds, Wolfram explores failures, followed by successes that will finally restore peace and harmony. Although Wolfram obviously used the *Conte du Graal* as his primary source, *Parzival* is much more than an adaptation of Chrétien's romance. It is an entirely new and original composition that in terms of later influence is comparable to the prose *Lancelot*.

As for the *Lanzelet* by Ulrich von Zatzikhoven, dating from the beginning of the thirteenth century, it bears little resemblance to Chrétien's *Chevalier de la*

Charrette, except for the name of its main character. A skilful rewriting of many Arthurian motifs used in Chrétien's romances (*Le Conte du Graal*, *Erec*, *Yvain*) and from German original works or adaptations, it testifies to Chrétien's fame but is not a rendition of any of his romances.[5]

Chrétien's romances were adapted in Dutch as well. *Perchevael*, part of the cycle known as the *Lancelot Compilation*, is a translation of the Gauvain part of Chrétien's *Conte du Graal* (mixed with a few other adventures). A first and seemingly faithful translation (of which only fragments are preserved) had been composed at the beginning of the thirteenth century by a Brabantine poet and was later integrated, with many adjustments, into the Compilation.[6]

Towards the middle of the thirteenth century, *Yvain* was translated into Norse prose (with some alliterative passages) for the Norwegian king Hákon IV Hákonarson.[7] As for the other Norse adaptations of Chrétien's romances, the *Erex saga* and the *Parcevals saga* followed by *Valvens þáttr* [Tale of Gawain, corresponding to the Gauvain section of Chrétien's *Perceval*), they might have been written around the same time for the same king. All four of these texts are preserved in late Icelandic manuscripts (some dating from the seventeenth century).[8] *Ivens saga* is a close rendering of Chrétien's *Chevalier au lion*, albeit with many passages either shortened or suppressed. Some of Chrétien's long descriptions, such as the lion's hunt, the women's condition at Pesme Aventure, the effects of love on Yvain and Laudine, the subtle rhetorical development on love and hate before Yvain and Gauvain's fight, have disappeared altogether.

Erex saga follows Chrétien's plot line with some substantial modifications: during their wanderings, Erex and Evida do not stay at Arthur's court. Instead, Erex rescues a knight who has been captured by a flying dragon and then kills seven men who were taking some prisoners to their castle. Erex and Evida encounter Kiaei (Kay) after the episode with Jarl Placidus (the counterpart of the Count of Limors). The reconciliation scene between the spouses takes place four days after their departure from the castle of Limors. There is no second fight against Guimar (Guivret). These changes profoundly alter Chrétien's *bele conjointure*. One more detail is interesting in that it is also found in later French adaptations of Chrétien's romances:[9] after their coronation, Erex and Evida go back to their kingdom, where they lead a happy life, blessed by the birth of two sons.

The *Conte du Graal* was adapted into two separate Norse texts: *Parcevals saga*

---

5   See Danielle Buschinger's recent update in the introduction to her French translation of the *Lanzelet* (Paris, 2003), pp. 12–26.

6   See Jozef D. Janssens, 'Le Roman arthurien en moyen néerlandais', *Arturus Rex, Acta Conventus Lovaniensis 1987*, 2 vols (Leuven, 1991), vol. II, ed. Willy Van Hoecke, Gilbert Tournoy and Werner Verbeke, pp. 330–51; and Bart Besamusca, 'Introduction' to 'The Medieval Dutch Arthurian Material', in *The Arthur of the Germans*, pp. 205–6.

7   See Knud Togeby, 'La Chronologie des versions scandinaves des anciens textes français', in *Les Relations littéraires franco-scandinaves au Moyen Age* (Liège, 1975), pp. 181–91.

8   See *Riddarasögur*, ed. E. Kölbing (Strassburg, 1872); Georges Zink, 'Les Poèmes arthuriens dans les pays scandinaves', in *Les Relations littéraires franco-scandinaves au Moyen Age*, pp. 77–95; Marianne E. Kalinke, *King Arthur, North-by-Northwest* (Copenhagen, 1981); Geraldine Barnes, 'Arthurian Chivalry in Old Norse', *Arthurian Literature*, 7 (1987), pp. 50–102.

9   See, below, my discussion of the Burgundian adaptations of Chrétien.

tells Perceval's story while still including Gawain's first two adventures; *Valvens Þáttr* recounts the end of the *Conte* as told by Chrétien and breaks off with Valven sending a message to his uncle, Arthur. Both texts however are found together in the same fifteenth-century manuscript. The beginning of *Parcevals saga* differs from the *Conte*: we are told that Parceval was the son of a peasant knight who, during a military raid, had captured and married a princess before retiring to the wilderness. He died when Parceval was twelve. The Norse adapter has considerably reduced the mystery found in his source: in the scene at the Grail castle, there is no indication of the Grail passing and repassing before the guest, and the question of 'who is served from the Grail?' is not mentioned. The ugly damsel who comes to Arthur's court to curse Parceval does not refer to the plight that will affect the Fisher King's land. The allusion to the destruction that the vengeful lance will bring to Arthur's kingdom disappears as well. Parceval's hermit uncle does not reveal Parceval's family connection with the Fisher King's father. The Grail does not contain a host. Moreover Parceval's story ends up with the hero going back to Beaurepaire after being forgiven by the hermit, marrying Blankiflur and spending the rest of his life in chivalrous deeds.[10]

One more adaptation was produced in Scandinavia: *Herr Ivan Lejonriddaren* is a Swedish verse translation of *Yvain*. This text belongs to the *Eufemiavisor* [Eufemia's Lays], poems that were commissioned by Queen Eufemia (wife of Hákon Magnusson of Norway) in 1303, probably as a present for the Duke Erik Magnusson of Sweden, who was to wed her daughter. This faithful translation bears the influence of Germanic literature, although the translator probably did not know Hartmann's *Iwein*. However, he very likely knew and used *Ivens saga* along with Chrétien's *Yvain*, as suggested by the prologue, which contains, like that of *Ivens saga*, a comparison between Arthur and Charlemagne. *Herr Ivan* was later translated into Danish.[11]

Yvain was also translated into English in the second half of the fourteenth century by a minstrel from the northern part of England. *Ywain and Gawain* survives in one manuscript dating from the fifteenth century. The anonymous text, in octosyllabic rhymed couplets, is 4032 lines long, about a third shorter than its French counterpart. Interestingly, the suppressed or shortened passages are the same ones that other *Yvain* redactors (whether French or foreign) also condensed and deleted: the rhetorical developments on love inspired by Ovid, the minute discussions on points of honour (can Laudine marry a man who just killed her former husband?) or on the conflicting demands of marriage and chivalry, the clever dialogues and monologues that show insights into the characters' psychology. At times, the adapter corrects Chrétien's casual treatment of *realia*. For example, he keeps the action in Britain (thus deleting the mention of Broceliande) and rearranges the episode of Yvain's captivity in Laudine's castle

10   Zink, 'Les Poèmes arthuriens', pp. 82–86.
11   Zink, 'Les Poèmes arthuriens', pp. 80–82; Carl Ivar Ståhle, 'Eufemiavisorna', in Johannes Brøndsted and John Danstrup, *Kulturhistorisk leksikon for nordisk middelalder fra vikingetid til reformationstid* (Copenhagen, 1958–78), IV, cols 55–57.

in order to lend credibility to the physical details.[12] Clearly he was addressing a different audience from Chrétien's, probably male, who did not care much for amorous casuistry and liked a faster pace for the narrative.

Sir Percyvell of Gales, preserved in one manuscript, is an anonymous poem composed in tail-rhyme stanzas during the fourteenth century. Neither a translation nor an adaptation strictly speaking of the *Conte du Graal*, it was nonetheless very likely influenced by Chrétien's romance. Much shorter (2288 lines), it gives more or less the same account of Percyvell's life up to the conquest of Lufamour (Blanchefleur's equivalent), whom he rescues and marries.[13] But it then omits the episode at the Fisher King's castle and the succeeding adventures related to the Grail. Instead, Percyvell goes on looking for his distraught mother who is wandering in the woods, cures her and brings her back to his kingdom. He then journeys to the Holy Land, where he is killed. At times a comic parody,[14] the romance is carefully structured around the revenge motif (Percyvell's father was killed by the Red Knight) and family ties.[15]

Whether the three Middle Welsh prose tales, *Geraint ab Erbin*, *Owain* and *Peredur*, all probably dating from the first half of the thirteenth century or even the end of the twelfth, should be included in a chapter on adaptations and translations of Chrétien, is a thorny question. Their relationship with *Erec et Enide*, *Yvain* and the *Conte*, respectively, has not yet been (and may never be) satisfactorily defined. Were they derived from Chrétien's romances? Did they use an Old French source that Chrétien had known too? If so, was this French source drawing from Welsh and Breton oral tales? *Geraint* is close to its French equivalent and clearly bears signs of a French influence. It has however been reshaped according to the Welsh formulaic system and contains many elements from Welsh tradition.[16] *Owain*, which seems to have enjoyed an enduring popularity, differs from *Yvain*, noticeably in the absence of the quarelling sisters' episode and the position of the *Pesme Aventure* episode, which, in the Welsh tale, takes place after Owain's reconciliation with his wife.[17] As for *Peredur*, it is quite strikingly different from the *Conte* even though the hero, a naïve boy raised by his mother away from chivalric society, does experience some of the same adventures as Perceval. Many episodes diverge farther. For example, Peredur successively stays at the courts of his two uncles. The first one (a cross between Gornemant and the Maimed King, since he is lame) urges him never to ask ques-

---

[12] *Ywain and Gawain*, ed. Albert B. Friedman and Norman T. Harrington (London, 1964). See introduction, pp. xvi–xxxiv, for a detailed comparison of the two texts. On the romance, also see its presentation by Maldwyn Mills in *The Arthur of the English*, ed. W.R.J. Barron (Cardiff, 1999), pp. 117–24.

[13] The Gornemant de Goort episode is, however, missing.

[14] On the treatment of the scene with the Red Knight, see Keith Busby, 'Sir Perceval of Galles, le Conte du Graal, and La Continuation-Gauvain: The Methods of an English Adaptor', *Etudes Anglaises*, 31.2 (1978), 198–202.

[15] See Maldwyn Mills's presentation of the romance in *The Arthur of the English*, pp. 136–41; David C. Fowler, 'Le Conte du Graal and Sir Perceval of Galles', *Comparative Literature Studies*, 12 (1975), 5–20.

[16] See Roger Middleton, 'Chwedl Geraint ab Erbin', in *The Arthur of the Welsh*, ed. Rachel Bromwich, A.O.H. Jarman and Brynley F. Roberts (Cardiff, 1995), pp. 147–57.

[17] See R.L. Thomson, 'Owain: Chwedl Iarlles y Ffynnon', in *The Arthur of the Welsh*, pp. 159–69.

tions about what he sees. At the court of the second, Peredur witnesses the procession of a bleeding lance and a head but refrains from asking about the meaning of the scene. He will much later learn that the head is his cousin's and that he was destined to avenge him as well as his lame uncle. Other episodes, absent from the *Conte*, involve witches (responsible for beheading Peredur's cousin and injuring his uncle) and recount Peredur's fourteen-year-long reign alongside the 'Empress of the Great Constantinople'. *Peredur*'s author was obviously combining many traditions, some also found in the *Conte*, but some unknown to Chrétien.[18]

Whereas, outside of France, Chrétien's romances gave birth to autonomous poems,[19] within France, they were rapidly absorbed by huge prose compilations. The popularity of the prose romances, in which episodes from Chrétien's texts were introduced and rewritten, and the popularity of the prose style itself progressively overshadowed Chrétien's fame. His name faded away while his characters, and the *motifs* and *loci* he had created continued a life of their own. What is quite remarkable is that we *do* have an *Erec* romance and even a fragmentary *Yvain*, but they are inserted (not to say dissolved) in prose compilations that cannot acknowledge Chrétien's authorship. The anonymous prose *Erec*, for example, composed at the end of the thirteenth century or at the beginning of the fourteenth and found in two manuscripts,[20] is included in the Grail cycle and bears little relation to Chrétien's romance, the most striking difference being the total disappearance of Enide. Only one episode is clearly taken from Chrétien's *Erec et Enide* (yet with very different consequences): Erec's meeting with an arrogant knight, his lady and an aggressive dwarf who lashes him with his whip.[21] Thus this romance is less an adaptation of Chrétien than a new biography of Erec, a tragic one at that: Chrétien's luminous knight becomes a sad character, cursed by his obsession with truthfulness, who, instead of bringing back the *joie de la cour*, kills his own sister and indirectly prompts his own death at the hands of Gauvain.

As for the fragmentary prose *Yvain*, preserved in one manuscript and dating from the fourteenth century, it was long thought to be a prose rendition of Chrétien's *Chevalier au lion*. However, only the first episode, Yvain's rescue of the lion and the animal's subsequent submission to the knight are indeed derived from Chrétien's romance. The rest consists of adventures involving numerous knights and seems derived partly from the prose *Tristan*, partly from *Guiron le Courtois*.[22]

The *dérimage* ['de-rhymed' version] of the *Chevalier de la Charrette*, a close rendering of the original verse romance, given by a few prose *Lancelot* manu-

18 See Ian Lovecy, 'Historia Peredur ab Efrawg', in *The Arthur of the Welsh*, pp. 171–82.
19 The only exception is the Dutch rendering of *Perceval* that was included in the Middle Dutch *Prosa Lancelot*.
20 See *Erec, roman arthurien en prose*, ed. Cedric E. Pickford (Geneva, 1959), pp. 37–38.
21 Besides C. Pickford, *Erec*, see Norris J. Lacy, 'The Form of the Prose *Erec*', *Neuphilologische Mitteilungen*, 85 (1984), 169–77; Friedrich Wolfzettel, 'Le Roman d'Erec en prose du XIIIe siècle: un anti-*Erec et Enide*?', in *The Legacy of Chrétien de Troyes*, ed. Keith Busby, Douglas Kelly and Norris J. Lacy, 2 vols (Amsterdam, 1987), II, pp. 215–28.
22 See Lynette R. Muir, 'A Reappraisal of the Prose *Yvain* (National Library of Wales, MS. 444–D)', *Romania*, 85 (1964), 355–65.

scripts dating from the middle of the fourteenth to the fifteenth century, may be the only French example of punctilious fidelity to Chrétien, but it too is included in a prose compilation.[23]

Only in the fifteenth century were Chrétien's romances rediscovered on their own. However, in order to be fully understood and appreciated, this faint revival must be placed into the context of the intense activity of *mises en prose* [prosifications] characteristic of the end of the Middle Ages.[24] Like many *chansons de geste* and other verse writings, Chrétien's romances were then turned into prose and transformed to suit the taste of their new readers. The language was modernized, old French becoming increasingly foreign to a fifteenth-century audience, and the name of their author was either totally ignored or considered not worth transmitting.

Around the middle of the fifteenth century, a prose *Erec* and a prose *Cligés*, both anonymous, were composed at the Burgundian court. What, in *Erec et Enide* and *Cligés*, appealed to a fifteenth-century audience is not easy to determine. In the case of the latter romance, it could have been its attention to the genealogy of its main characters. As for the former, the simplicity of the love story (at least as transposed by the prosifier) might have been part of the attraction.

Although probably written by different redactors, these two texts exhibit common features.[25] While they faithfully maintain Chrétien's plots, both adapters introduce modifications that might seem minor but are significant indicators of new expectations and new trends in later romances. They modernize not only the language but the story itself to adapt it to its new audience (a process of 'acculturation', in Taylor's words).[26] They explain what is ambiguous in the twelfth-century text and focus on some specific aspects of the original. While they relish depicting military exploits, they shorten love scenes and especially the long and subtle discussions or monologues that are so characteristic of Chrétien's first romances.

Erec is not precisely dated. One manuscript preserves the complete romance. Two fragments (one fairly long) are inserted into versions of *Guiron le Courtois*,[27] as was the case with the thirteenth-century prose *Erec*. Divided into forty-two chapters, each of them introduced by a long title, the Burgundian text reduces

---

23 On this version of the *Charrette*, see Annie Combes, *Les Voies de l'aventure: réécriture et composition romanesque dans le 'Lancelot' en prose* (Paris, 2001), pp. 240–48.
24 See Georges Doutrepont, *Les Mises en prose des épopées et des romans chevaleresques du XIVe au XVIe siècle* (Brussels, 1939).
25 *L'Histoire d'Erec en prose, roman du XVe siècle*, ed. Maria Colombo Timelli (Geneva, 2000); *Le Livre de Alixandre empereur de Constentinoble et de Cligés son filz, roman en prose du XVe siècle*, ed. Maria Colombo Timelli (Geneva, 2004). In her editions, Colombo Timelli offers very extensive and useful bibliographies on these works as well as on late prosifications. Among the works quoted, see especially Norris J. Lacy, 'Adaptation as Reception: the Burgundian *Cligés*', *Fifteenth Century Studies*, 24 (1998), 198–207; Lacy's 'Motivation and Method in the Burgundian *Erec*', in *Conjonctures: Medieval Studies in Honor of Douglas Kelly*, ed. Keith Busby and Norris J. Lacy (Amsterdam, 1994), pp. 271–80; and Jane H.M. Taylor, 'The Significance of the Insignificant: Reading Reception in the Burgundian *Erec* and *Cligès*', *Fifteenth Century Studies*, 24 (1998), 183–97.
26 Taylor, 'The Significance of the Insignificant', p. 183.
27 For the precise relation among the three texts, see the long introduction to Timelli's edition of the prose *Erec*.

Chrétien's romance by almost half. Colombo Timelli, in her thorough analysis of the techniques used by the redactor of the prose *Erec*,[28] notices that dialogues are often either suppressed or drastically abridged in such a way that psychological motivations tend to disappear. On the other hand, monologues tend to be amplified and reveal a more theatrical sensibility. What is notably new is Enide's role and position. As Lacy has clearly shown,[29] by leaving court and taking his wife along, Erec, in the Burgundian romance, merely intends to test Enide's love. The question of Erec's other motivations (wounded pride, necessity to prove his knighthood) is eluded. Focusing mainly on Enide's shortcomings but also on her patience in enduring the rigours of the love test and on her willingness to learn her lesson, the fifteenth-century redactor portrays the ideal wife: in this work, as Lacy notes, 'the proper duty of a wife is to love, honour, and obey her husband without reservation'.[30]

The end of the prose *Erec* is arresting: after his victory against Mabonagrein, Erec, Guivret and Enide go back to Arthur's court, where Erec learns of his father's death. Then on Christmas day, Arthur has Erec and Enide crowned king and queen of the Lac kingdom. However, the coronation takes place in London and not in Nantes, and the famous descriptions that conclude Chrétien's romance (of the ivory thrones, Erec's coat, gold crowns) are omitted. Instead, the redactor imagines another tournament during which Erec, as an anonymous black knight, fights remarkably well. Identified by Arthur, he is praised for his prowess, and the story goes on telling about Erec and Enide's happy, glorious and virtuous life, blessed with several beautiful children, the eldest becoming king after his father's death. This is an almost staple conclusion in late chivalric romances, whether Arthurian or not:[31] the last tournament guarantees the perennial superiority achieved by the hero (who will never lapse into *recreantise* [recreance]) and the mention of the happy life, saintly death and children succeeding their parents, inscribes the romance in a genealogical frame.

The *Livre de Alixandre empereur de Constentinoble et de Cligés son filz* offers many similarities with *Erec*. It was finished on March 26, 1454 and is preserved in one manuscript only. Here, too, the redactor is concerned with rationalization and simplification. The most striking (and noted[32]) example of his taste for explaining and justifying is the introduction of a whole new episode: in the forest near Arthur's court, Cligés meets a fair lady grieving her lover's departure. He is then reminded of his own involvement with Fenice and thus decides to leave Arthur to go back to his country.

The redactor's treatment of the love scenes (abridgment of monologues, dismissing of Chrétien's complex rhetorical meditations replete with metaphors) reflects a new conception of love, a love in which 'there is no room for chance, choice, irony, or doubt'.[33] Indeed, one of the main features of these later

---

[28] See the introduction to her edition, pp. 15–44.
[29] Lacy, 'Motivation and Method', p. 273.
[30] Lacy, 'Motivation and Method', p. 279.
[31] See for example the end of *Jehan d'Avennes* or *Cleriadus et Meliadice*, two non-Arthurian biographical romances.
[32] See Lacy, 'Adaptation as Reception', p. 199.
[33] Lacy, 'Adaptation as Reception', p. 204.

prosifications is their lack of irony, their willingness to obliterate any ambiguity in their model.[34] The conclusion of the prose *Cligés* fits that impression. Chrétien ends his romance by saying that Cligés loved Fenice and never mistrusted her, while later Greek emperors, fearing Alis's misadventure, kept their wives confined indoors. The prose version does not mention this consequence of Cligés's and Fenice's cunning, but states that the couple lived a happy life, had children, founded many churches and gave alms. They died in peace and their oldest son succeeded his father as emperor – a morally satisfying ending, very similar to that of the prose *Erec*. But this conclusion is also politically reassuring: worthy sons legitimately replace worthy fathers, so that every kingdom, every domain, will be ruled by peaceful, just and generous lords. The concern for order and justice is certainly also found in Chrétien's romances, but while Chrétien describes Arthur's rule as uncertain and possibly threatened, fifteenth-century redactors depict a much more powerful ruler whose edicts and decisions are not subject to discussions.[35]

The Burgundian prose renderings provide an interesting (albeit depressing) insight into later audiences' expectations and reception of Chrétien. They also enable us to measure the political and social gap between Chrétien's time and that of the Burgundian court.

Two more adaptations of Chrétien's romances were composed in the sixteenth century. Although they seem to fall outside the scope of this chapter, they must be included as witnesses of the interest that Arthurian literature was still exciting to some degree in the Renaissance. It should be noted however that in comparison to the success enjoyed by prose romances such as *Lancelot, Guiron le Courtois, Tristan* or *Perceforest*, and moreover to the even better fortune of *chansons de geste*,[36] Chrétien's fame remained very modest.

One of the two adaptations is a prose rendering of the *Conte du Graal*, entitled *La Tresplaisante et Recreative Hystoire du Trespreulx et vaillant Chevallier Perceval le galloys*. Printed in Paris by Jean Longis and Galliot du Pré in 1530, it was probably composed shortly before, and the redactor, who remains anonymous, used a manuscript (now lost) that contained the *Elucidation* and the *Prologue de Bliocadran*,[37] both texts prefacing, as it were, the prose *Perceval*. The prose version is a close adaptation of the *Conte*, characterized like the earlier ones by the desire to rationalize and explain. Perceval is thus named from the very beginning of the story, the plight of his family described even before he is introduced. Many events are referred to long before they actually happen.[38] According to the goal

---

[34] Sometimes, as shown by Lacy ('Motivation and Method'), they end up unwittingly creating their own ambiguities.

[35] On this aspect, particularly in the prose *Erec*, see Taylor, 'The Significance of the Insignificant', pp. 187–91.

[36] See Cedric E. Pickford, 'Les Editions imprimées de romans arthuriens en prose antérieures à 1600', *Bibliographical Bulletin of the International Arthurian Society*, 13 (1961), 99–109.

[37] See Pierre Servet, 'D'un Perceval l'autre: la mise en prose du *Conte du Graal* (1530)', in *L'Œuvre de Chrétien de Troyes dans la littérature française, réminiscences, résurgences et réécritures*, ed. Claude Lachet (Lyon, 1997), p. 199.

[38] See Servet, 'D'un Perceval à l'autre', p. 202; Jean Frappier, 'Sur le Perceval en prose de 1530', *Fin du Moyen Age et Renaissance: mélanges de philologie française offerts à Robert Guiette* (Antwerp, 1961), p. 242.

defined in the prologue, the redactor moralizes Perceval's adventures to make him the perfect knight almost from the start. Thus Perceval's *niceté* [naiveté] is played down, and both protagonists, Perceval and Gauvain, are made to embody the knightly virtues celebrated at the French court of King François I. The prose *Perceval* enjoyed but little success. Only one edition was published, whereas Jean Maugin's rendering of *Tristan*, for example, composed around the same time, was edited four times between 1554 and 1586.

At around the same time, probably in 1522, Pierre Sala (1457–1529) produced a rhymed version of the *Chevalier au Lion*.[39] For once, we know quite a lot about this author, who lived in Lyon, at times occupied minor positions at the royal court and wrote a great many works: treatises, poems, fables, historical texts. He seems to have had a taste for Arthurian literature, since he also composed a *Roman de Tristan le Leonnois et de la Belle Reine Yseulte*, which focuses on Tristan and Lancelot's friendship.[40] Sala's *Chevalier au lion* is preserved in one manuscript and was never printed before Pierre Servet's modern edition. It might seem strange that he chose verse rather than prose for his adaptation of Chrétien's romance. Yet in the light of his other works, this choice seems less curious. Sala obviously liked writing poetry and had some mastery of it, as testified by his dedicatory poem, written in decasyllabic verse.

He then used octosyllabic verse (as had Chrétien) and is at times very close to his model, whose name he seems not to have known. Sala's *Chevalier au lion* exhibits many of the same features displayed in the prose renderings: rationalization and simplification. The storyline is more clearly defined. Sala deletes many details that he probably deemed superfluous. On the other hand, he stresses logical links, anticipating future events or recalling previous scenes to underline both the logical and chronological development of the romance. The *merveilleux* [marvellous] plays a much lesser role. What disappears as well is the sophisticated reflection on love. Sala intends to write a love story in which sensual love supplants Chrétien's *fin'amor*. Servet, the editor of Sala's *Chevalier au lion*, mentions the atmosphere of *fêtes galantes* that characterizes the beginning of the sixteenth century and accurately replaces Sala's image of love in this social and historical context, very different from Chrétien's own.[41] This feature sets Sala's *Chevalier au lion* apart from previous adaptations of Chrétien's romances, as most of them focused less on love than on heroic endeavours. This is indeed another profound difference from the fifteenth-century prose versions, testifying to readers' new expectations: whereas fifteenth-century redactors enjoyed depicting battles and even introduced details showing their interest in new military techniques, Sala, while preserving most of Yvain's exploits, describes them more cursorily and in less detail than Chrétien. He seemingly did not sense the gradation from Yvain's first fight against Count Alier to Yvain and Gauvain's final judiciary combat. Indeed, he totally omits that battle as well as two other major episodes: Yvain's stay at the castle of *Pesme Aventure* and the story of the

---

[39] Pierre Sala, *Le Chevalier au lion*, ed. Pierre Servet (Paris, 1996).
[40] On Pierre Sala, his life and his works, see Servet's introduction to his edition of Sala's *Le Chevalier au lion*, pp. 9–14.
[41] Servet, Introduction, pp. 73–74.

two Noire Espine sisters. Thus his *Chevalier au lion* is only 4272 lines long compared to Chrétien's 6808 lines. It also means that the general structure is quite altered: the lion's rescue, which is central both symbolically and literally in Chrétien's romance, is displaced and loses part of its meaning.[42]

Sala's *Chevalier au lion* and the prose *Perceval* are the last attempts at adapting Chrétien's romances.[43] Why did Chrétien's name vanish for almost four centuries? Why did his own romances suffer such a long eclipse? As was suggested, their decline during the late Middle Ages may well be due to the huge success of prose romances. After that, their fate seems consistent with the general disaffection that beset Arthurian literature in France.[44]

What is remarkable in Chrétien's reception in non-French-speaking lands is that it shows the same chronological trend as in French-speaking parts: whereas Chrétien's romances were eagerly translated and adapted throughout the thirteenth century, this enthusiasm lessened in the fourteenth, and later on Chrétien seems to have been forgotten altogether, displaced in Germany by Wolfram's renown, in England by Malory's achievement.[45]

---

[42] See Servet, Introduction, p. 67.
[43] On Chrétien's return in the eighteenth century, see Keith Busby, 'Roman breton et chanson de geste au XVIIIe siècle', *Echoes of the Epic: Studies in Honor of Gerard Brault*, ed. David P. Schenck and Mary Jane Schenck (Birmingham, AL, 1998), pp. 17–48.
[44] See Jean Frappier, 'Les Romans de la Table Ronde et les lettres en France au XVIe siècle', *Romance Philology*, 19.2 (1965–66), 178–93; Pickford, 'Les Editions imprimées de romans arthuriens'.
[45] One might argue however that Chrétien's fame endured somewhat in Scandinavia, since adaptations of his romances were still being copied in the seventeenth century.

16

Chrétien's Medieval Influence: From the Grail Quest to the Joy of the Court

EMMANUÈLE BAUMGARTNER

[Translated by Véronique Zara]

From the very beginning of *Erec et Enide* – 'Un jor de Pasque, au tens novel, / A Caradigant son chastel / Ot li rois Artus cort tenue' [One day at Easter, in the new season, King Arthur held court in his castle of Caradigan][1] – Chrétien de Troyes plunged the Arthurian world, which Geoffrey of Monmouth had conceived in historical terms, into the realm of fiction. The mention of Arthur and his court, the choice of a 'cyclical' feast day, the evocation, shortly thereafter, of the unusual custom of the hunt for the white stag, the hierarchical list of the knights of the Round Table, all sketched out an immutable world for generations of readers and writers, a world that existed prior to the group of narratives that modern critics refer to as 'Arthurian romances'.[2] From one romance to the next, indeed, first those of Chrétien then those of his successors, the same characters will reappear repeatedly and within an identical framework. Within this space, a new type of hero, the knight errant in quest of adventure,[3] is created and perpetuated. These adventures, with their apparently gratuitous nature and frequent ties to the *merveilleux* [marvellous], alone determine the narrative's course of action and meaning. However, the last romance of Chrétien, the *Conte du Graal*, partially breaks with this type of narrative that seems to have immediately found and captivated its audience. By giving a literary existence to a hero, Perceval, who is as new as he is *nice* [naïve], and to such curious objects as the Grail, the bleeding lance, or the broken sword (which must be mended), Chrétien introduced into the field of fiction a character and a motif, the Grail quest, that fed extremely diverse forms of literary and artistic creation for centuries, even until our own time.

Among the authors who, from the end of the twelfth century, followed Chrétien's lead in associating the composition of verse romances with Arthurian

---

1 Chrétien de Troyes, *Erec et Enide*, ed. and trans. Jean-Marie Fritz; in *Romans suivis des Chansons, avec, en appendice, Philomena*, genl ed. Michel Zink (Paris, 1994), vss 27–29.
2 These were once more accurately categorized as 'Romances of the Round Table', as is shown by the title of the first general study devoted to verse romances: Gaston Paris, 'Romans en vers du cycle de la Table Ronde', *Histoire littéraire de la France*, 30 (1888), 1–270.
3 See Marie-Luce Chênerie, *Le Chevalier errant dans les romans arthuriens en vers des XIIe et XIIIe siècles* (Geneva, 1986).

themes,[4] several – the authors of the Continuations of the *Conte du Graal*[5] – undertook the task of concluding the Grail quest and fulfilling Perceval's destiny. Even more writers remained within the spatial/temporal framework inherited from Chrétien, seeking to exploit its resources. Multiple reasons exist for this early interest, which would last until the end of the thirteenth century.[6] One can hypothesize that by reaping the fruits of their mentor's legacy, writers were answering the public's demand for the entertaining and escapist literature represented by Arthur, his realm, and its wonders. In the twentieth century, numerous film-makers have catered to the appetite for westerns or for musicals, and many authors have taken to writing serialized novels or, more recently, detective fiction. The new and unusual nature of a spatial/temporal structure and a narrative mode based from the outset on repetition and return, the numerous possibilities for narrative variations on a given scenario, as well as the freedom allowed by the use of the faery *merveilleux* surely presented a further compelling attraction for writers. Similarly appealing were the aesthetic attraction and 'moral' allure of a world where chivalric feats and love had long been inseparable, where the knight worthy of his mission strove to destroy the manifestations of evil and to impose the Arthurian order, and where it was thus possible for one to realize, more so than in contemporary times, a utopian model of civilization, *courtoisie*, a dream long nurtured by the medieval nobility.[7]

Even if, shortly after 1350, the romances of Chrétien were no longer recopied and his works (like his name[8]) seem to have been soon forgotten in their original form,[9] his influence was deep and long-lasting, with respect both to the themes of the texts and to the new style of writing that these works forged. Was it not to this indissoluble alliance of content and form that the term *conjointure* referred in the prologue of *Erec and Enide*? Nevertheless, the nature of this alliance was to vary considerably from one verse romance to the next, as Beate Schmolke-Hasselmann demonstrated as early as 1980[10] in the seminal study that she devoted to the 'genre' of Arthurian verse romance and its evolution from Chrétien to Froissart. Moreover, the great thirteenth-century prose cycles, especially that of the *Lancelot-Graal*, which, following the *Conte du Graal*, combined

---

4   For a general bibliography, see Richard Trachsler, *Les Romans arthuriens en vers après Chrétien de Troyes* (Paris, 1997).
5   Trachsler, *Les Romans arthuriens en vers*, passim.
6   The last Arthurian verse romance, Froissart's *Méliador*, nevertheless dates from the end of the fourteenth century.
7   Numerous contributions from *The Legacy of Chrétien de Troyes*, ed. Norris J. Lacy, Douglas Kelly and Keith Busby, 2 vols (Amsterdam, 1987–88), pertain to the literary tradition stemming from Chrétien's works. See especially ch. 9, 'Intertextuality', I, pp. 224–65, by Matilda Tomaryn Bruckner. Also useful are the studies compiled in Claude Lachet, ed., *L'Œuvre de Chrétien de Troyes dans la littérature française: réminiscences, résurgences et réécritures* (Lyon, 1997). Additionally, see section P, 'Influences', in Douglas Kelly, *Chrétien de Troyes, An Analytic Bibliography, Supplement 1* (London, 2002).
8   The references to Chrétien's name outside his works have been compiled by Colette-Anne Van Coolput in 'Références, adaptations et emprunts directs', the Appendix to Lacy, Kelly and Busby, eds, *Legacy*, I, pp. 333–37.
9   On the prose rewritings of the texts, see the preceding chapter by Michelle Szkilnik.
10 See *Der arturische Versroman von Chrestien bis Froissart* (Tübingen 1980); trans. Margaret and Roger Middleton as *The Evolution of Arthurian Romance* (Cambridge, 1998); see Foreword by Keith Busby and Supplement to the Bibliography.

the Arthurian world and the Grail quest, represented another manner in which the universe of Chrétien's romances was appropriated. Undoubtedly more cryptic and difficult to interpret,[11] the prose cycles nevertheless extended his influence until the beginning of the sixteenth century at least, when printed editions of the main prose romances took over from the manuscripts. It must be remembered that the thirteenth-century Arthurian prose romances were recopied, expanded and modified throughout the Middle Ages, thus perpetuating the fictional world invented by Chrétien. Still, the prose rewriting of *Cligés* in the fifteenth century and of *Erec and Enide* at the beginning of the sixteenth, the recasting in verse of *Yvain* by Pierre Sala, the printed prose version of *Perceval* or even a late romance such as the fifteenth-century *Chevalier au Papegau* [The Knight with the Parrot] all testify that the original form of these works was known until the end of the Middle Ages.

In the prologue of the short anonymous narrative traditionally titled *Le Chevalier à l'épée* [The Knight with the Sword], the narrator, after having announced his purpose, 'conter de monseigneur Gauvain' [to tell of Sir Gauvain], whose feats and refined manners are too great for words, added:

> L'en [en] doit Crestïen de Troies,
> Ce m'est vis, par raison blasmer,
> Qui sot dou roi Artu conter,
> De sa cort et de sa mesniee
> Qui tant fu loee et prisiee
> Et qui les fez des autres conte
> Et onques de lui ne tint conte.
> Trop ert prodon a oblïer.[12]

> [I believe that blame is due Chrétien de Troyes, who knew how to tell of King Arthur, of his court and his entourage, which was so greatly praised and valued, and who recounts the exploits of others and takes no account of him (Gauvain); he is too great a man to ignore.]

This statement is particularly revealing of the attitude that writers of verse had toward Chrétien's works. Indeed, the anonymous author of the *Chevalier à l'épée* unapologetically made free use of the setting of Arthur's court, held one summer in Cardueil, and of the triggering event, Gauvain's leaving to seek adventures (or, implicitly, pleasure and entertainment). Like the 'once upon a time' formula used in fairy tales, these elements introduced the fictional Arthurian world and framed the listener/reader's expectations.[13] Most important, however, as the author himself notes, the emphasis on Gauvain, Arthur's

---

[11] In the later romances, especially those in prose, it is sometimes difficult to distinguish clearly between direct borrowing from Chrétien and the reuse of motifs, places and characters stemming from the post-Chrétien tradition.

[12] See *Two Old French Gauvain Romances* [*Le Chevalier à l'épée* and *La Mule sans frein*], ed. R.C. Johnston and D.D.R. Owen (Edinburgh, 1972), vss 18–25. The reading 'l'en en doit', replacing the 'l'en ne doit' of the critical edition, is my own.

[13] Similar openings can be found, among numerous examples, in Renaud de Beaujeu, *Le Bel Inconnu*, ed. Michèle Perret and Isabelle Weill (Paris, 2003), or in *L'Atre Périlleux*, ed. Brian Woledge (Paris, 1936).

beloved nephew, whom Chrétien never chose as the protagonist of a romance, signalled the wish to exploit the 'gaps' in Chrétien's universe and to push back the outer limits of the Arthurian world. This phenomenon mirrored the change in the seating of the Round Table, where the number of seats seemed to grow perpetually from one text to the next, accommodating ever more potential heroes whose stories had been written or were waiting to be told.[14]

Until the *Conte du Graal*, Chrétien's romances were organized, as is evidenced by their titles, around one character and his destiny. This reveals the importance of the character (or individual?) in romance creation according to Chrétien. However, significantly, none of the verse romance authors risked reusing one of his heroes as the central figure. In the case of Erec and Yvain, the reasons for their disappearance seem clear enough. As heroes who had achieved their heroic and amorous destiny, Erec and Yvain no longer had a place in the world of knight errantry where heroes were in the process of realizing their destiny. Instead, their presence continued to be felt through the motifs and places with which they were associated. Although Erec more or less drops from sight, the original motif of the 'Joie de la Cour' [Joy of the Court] recurs throughout Arthurian texts. The 'fountain by the pine', where Yvain's heroic and amorous destiny unfolded, becomes one of the places most visited by Arthurian romance heroes, especially in the prose versions, whether to encounter chivalric adventures or, as is the case for Tristan in the Prose *Tristan* and its sequels, to seek poetic inspiration. Moreover, the influence of the fountain was not limited to the Arthurian world. In Guillaume de Lorris's *Roman de la Rose*, Narcissus's fountain, the departure point for the hero's quest for love, was also sheltered under a magnificent pine, evoking the shadow of the Arthurian romance's influence. Furthermore, the episode of Yvain's love-induced madness would for centuries represent the test that a worthy lover must pass, with literary echoes reverberating at least until *Don Quixote*.

Thus, apart from Perceval, predictably the central figure of the Continuations of the *Conte du Graal*, and Lancelot, who can claim the *Lancelot-Graal* cycle, it was Gauvain, never the central figure in any of Chrétien's works, who became the favourite of thirteenth-century verse romances, cast both as the central figure (*Atre périlleux, Chevalier à l'épée, Mule sans frein, Vengeance Raguidel*) and as co-star (*Chevalier aux deux épées, Hunbaut, Gliglois*). Gauvain's more prominent status can be easily explained. Unlike Perceval, the chosen Grail knight in Chrétien, who incarnated *par excellence* the quest for closure of adventure and narrative, Gauvain, as he appeared in Chrétien before the *Conte du Graal*, was a subject of new beginnings, departing on adventures that never led to a conquest that attached him to a place outside the Arthurian world, unlike in the case of Erec and Yvain. Also, until the *Conte du Graal*, Gauvain was less a hero than a role model for new knights, for whom he incarnated knightly and courtly values. However, from 'parangon de chevalerie' [paragon of knighthood], in the felici-

---

[14] Examples of this expansion exist in the prose romances, from *Merlin* to the Prose *Tristan* and also in the Round Table iconography in later manuscripts such as ms BNF 112, for instance, or ms BNF 116 of the Prose *Lancelot*.

tous words of Jean Frappier,[15] Gauvain became, in verse romances after Chrétien, a character in his own right, possessing distinct attributes and involved in the plot.

It is beyond the scope of this study to analyze in detail the verse narratives in which Gauvain subsequently appeared. We must simply note the skill with which the authors developed and emphasized, sometimes to the point of caricature and burlesque (in *Hunbaut*, for instance) the possibilities that his character suggested in Chrétien. Without a pre-programmed heroic and amorous destiny, Gauvain is the always-available hero of narratives based on new beginnings. However, as has long been noted,[16] the narratives of which he became the protagonist call into question the excellence of this knight – Arthur's nephew, who was first on the list of Round Table knights in *Erec and Enide* – and thus questions the tradition established by Chrétien. At the beginning of *L'Atre Périlleux*, Gauvain hesitates a little too long to avenge the humiliation suffered by Arthur. Confronted with his own death – and his cadaver – he who never conceals his name must recover his identity again and 'remake' a name and a reputation for himself. In the *Chevalier à l'épée*, his knightly prowess remains intact, but his sexual abilities (and what is one without the other?) are found wanting. In *La Mule sans frein*, a short narrative in which the author, by antiphrasis, calls himself Païen de Maisières, Gauvain is portrayed as a liberating hero. However, the narrative, ending with a kind of 'summary' of his adventures, curiously resembles a school exercise in pastiche. *Hunbaut*, an unfinished romance in which the author claims at the beginning that he does not seek to plunder 'les bons dis Crestïen de Troies'[17] [the good words of Chrétien de Troyes] depicts Gauvain instead as a brutal and vulgar knight, quite unworthy of the maiden who still believes that he resembles the statue that she had had made in his likeness and that she venerates in secret. Gauvain's discordant hero status and his new companions, such as Hunbaut or Mériadeuc (hero of the *Chevalier aux deux épées*[18]), provide the authors of romances with ways to explore the Arthurian world anew and playfully – or sometimes jarringly – take a fresh and often critical look at its unusual customs and rituals.

On the other hand, Lancelot is significantly absent from verse romances, and his love for Guenevere seems sometimes unknown to the authors or, rather, is concealed; he is even ridiculed in a late romance such as *Les Merveilles de Rigomer*.[19] This depiction is less a sign of the difficulties presented by the adulterous passion than of the impossibility in the world of romance of bringing closure to his and the Queen's relationship. Or perhaps this should be read as an act of defiance toward a hero too prone to submitting to feminine values, and whom the *Merveilles de Rigomer* depicts as a kitchen servant, the victim of a spell

---

[15] See Jean Frappier, *Etude sur 'Yvain' ou le 'Chevalier au Lion'* (Paris, 1969), p. 141.

[16] One can refer, among others, to Keith Busby, *Gauvain in Old French Literature* (Amsterdam, 1980); Schmolke-Hasselmann, *The Evolution of Arthurian Romance*, pp. 104–41; and more recently to Stoyan Atanassov, *L'Idole inconnue: le personnage de Gauvain dans quelques romans du XIIIe siècle* (Orléans, 2000).

[17] *Hunbaut*, ed. Margaret Winters (Leiden, 1984), vs. 187.

[18] *Le Chevalier aux deux épées*, ed. W. Foerster (Halle, 1877).

[19] *Les Merveilles de Rigomer*, ed. W. Foerster and H. Breuer, 2 vols (Dresden, 1908–15).

that made him forget his past. The fate awaiting Perceval, the other figure markedly absent from Arthurian verse romance, is less disconcerting but represents a definite impoverishment. Of the character's potential, authors merely reused the motif – so vulnerable to caricature and to the facile effects of the *naïf* – of the uncivilized youth who has to learn everything, even if he quickly progresses in his knightly and courtly 'education'. Thus, in *Fergus*,[20] the hero, despite his initial naiveté, even coarseness, successfully navigates adventures that parody the Grail quest and, unlike Perceval, completes his nuptial quest with a certain brio.

The place awarded to Gauvain, whose traditional figure was open to reinterpretation, as well as the choice of new or skilfully altered heroes, testifies as much to the influence exerted by Chrétien as to the natural desire of his successors to artfully revisit his model and differentiate themselves from it. The same tension can be observed in the concerted reuse and repackaging of romance structures and motifs. In both *Erec et Enide* and *Le Chevalier au lion*, Chrétien made the completed nuptial quest the preliminary event to the crisis where the couple lose each other before finding each other again. This two-part structure (too complex, too clearly divided?) was reused at the beginning of the thirteenth century only by Raoul de Houdenc, the skilful author of *Méraugis de Portlesguez*.[21] The other romance authors did not choose this narrow path. Lacking any great originality, the 'endings' of *Fergus* (dated around 1230–50), *Yder* (early thirteenth century)[22] or *Jaufré* (around 1220–30)[23] superimposed the completion of the adventures, however numerous and perilous they might be, on the wedding festivities and the new couple's happiness. *Durmart Le Galois* (early thirteenth century)[24] is virtually the only romance that challenged these limits. The hero, whose destiny had already begun to unfold outside of the Arthurian world, did indeed become a knight of the Round Table (successfully passing the test of the 'Perilous Seat') before freeing and marrying his love. Nevertheless, his heroic mission is completed in Rome, which he saves from a terrible invasion by pagans threatening all of Christendom. Moreover, it was under the direct influence of the prose romances that the author of the *Merveilles de Rigomer* (1250–68) sets fifty-eight knights – most of the cast of the Arthurian world – on a quest to deliver Lancelot and the other prisoners of Rigomer, only to make then a drastic choice regarding the ending of the romance, as did the author of the *Quête du Graal*. After the author recounts the quest of seven of the knights, the focus of the action falls on Gauvain, who frees the prisoners but refuses the hand of the mistress of the castle, thus short-circuiting the expected dénouement.

Le Bel Inconnu, written by Renaud de Beaujeu, is in many respects a revealing and original illustration of the oblique manner in which the best of Chrétien's

---

[20] Guillaume le Clerc, *The Romance of Fergus*, ed. Wilson Frescoln (Philadelphia, 1983).
[21] Raoul de Houdenc, *Méraugis de Portlesguez*, ed. M. Friedwagner (Halle, 1897); ed. and trans. Michelle Szkilnik (Paris, 2004).
[22] *Yder*, ed. Alison Adams (Cambridge, 1983).
[23] *Jaufré*, ed. René Lavaud and René Nelli, in *Les Troubadours. Jaufré, Flamenca, Barlaam et Josaphat*, 2 vols (Paris, 1960), I, pp. 17–618.
[24] *Durmart Le Galois*, ed. Joseph Gildea (Villanova, PA, 1965).

imitators confronted their mentor and of the tension between the respect that later writers sometimes displayed for their model[25] and the re-creation of the text. In this romance, the *Bel Inconnu* – the bastard son of Gauvain (and of fiction, according to Chrétien) – had to discover his name (Guinglain) and impose his reputation.[26] Critics have long noted, sometimes a bit excessively, the passages in which Renaud de Beaujeu used precise quotes and elements reminiscent of Chrétien's romances, particularly *Erec et Enide*. This 'borrowing' ranged from the reuse of lines to the recasting of motifs, leading some to speak of plagiarism.[27] However, viewed in context, quotations and reuse of material appear as a means of revealing, doubtless ironically, the process of composing an Arthurian romance while appropriating the resources of fanciful motifs not exploited by Chrétien ('Le Fier Baiser', for instance) or of motifs and situations borrowed from the courtly lyric genre. This phenomenon is illustrated by the canonical motif of the nuptial quest. The romance author does eventually insert his hero into the Arthurian world thanks to a marriage, imposed by Arthur with the approval of the Queen (whom the young man liberated from a horrible enchantment). However, the resulting equilibrium is immediately threatened by the suggestion that the hero might return to the fairy (a return subject to the will of the lady, who is loved by the narrator). The open and disconcerting ending (contrary to that of *Erec and Enide*) was a way to resist the tried and tested formulas of the Arthurian romance.

For authors of Arthurian verse romances, the use, observable early on, of a distanced treatment of the motifs, even to the point of parody or burlesque, was in the end the best way to handle the anxiety of influence and to bring about a renewal that acquired its full meaning only in light of the tradition in which Chrétien operated. The Occitan romance devoted to Jaufré son of Do (in French, Girflet son of Doon), who became in *La Mort le roi Artu* the last of the companions of the King, opens with the inherited motif of the King who refuses to eat during a day of great feasting before the realization of the event that will trigger the new narrative and designate its hero. Since nothing happens, the King decides to go with his knights to the forest of Brocéliande where the official court enchanter volunteers to play one of his tricks on the King, a procedure that he will repeat at the end of the narrative. Here the author cleverly underscores for his public the artificial and nearly compulsory nature of this false start of the narrative, despite his subsequent use of the no less traditional motif of the arrival in court of an unknown young man who vows to avenge the insult to Arthur by the horrible Taulas de Rougemont (thus representing the opposite of Perceval's attitude toward the 'chevalier vermeil' [red knight]) and who sets off

---

[25] Huon de Méry, for instance, declares at the beginning of *Tournoiement Antéchrist* his admiration for Chrétien and Raoul (de Houdenc): 'c'onques bouche de crestïen / ne dist si bien com il disoient' [never did any Christian mouth speak as well as they did].

[26] Regarding this romance, see in particular Jean Dufournet, ed., *Le Chevalier et la merveille dans Le Bel Inconnu ou le Beau Jeu de Renaut* (Paris, 1996).

[27] Along these lines, see Madeleine Tyssens, 'Les Sources de Renaut de Beaujeu', in *Mélanges offerts à Jean Frappier* (Geneva, 1970), pp. 1043–55. On the other hand, the very strange late thirteenth-century romance *Floriant et Florete*, ed. Annie Combes and Richard Trachsler (Paris, 2003), which combines Arthurian content with elements of diverse origin, borrows roughly eighty lines mainly from *Erec et Enide* and the *Conte du Graal*.

on a quest leading to glory, love (the hand of the beautiful Brunissent) and the wondrous presents of the fée du Gibel (Morgain). The anonymous author of *Jaufré* does not abandon, any more than did the author of the *Bel Inconnu*, the tradition of the adventure that sets the Arthurian narrative into motion and designates its hero, in the same way that the detective novel opens with the crime committed and the assassin who must be discovered. However, the enchanter's 'trick' or, in the *Bel Inconnu*, the (mock) contemptuous attitude of the message-bearing maiden apparently seeking, by all available means, to rid herself of a knight who seems to her to be too inexperienced, serves to reveal this discrepancy and the indirect way of appropriating a heritage by distancing oneself from it.

Moreover, the results are sometimes surprising. Chrétien, as we know, often delighted in providing a rational (reassuring?) veneer to the motifs, redolent of the *merveilleux*, that he drew from the Celtic tradition. In *Erec and Enide*, although many elements designated the orchard of the Joy of the Court as a space of the Other World, the reader suddenly discovers that it is the locus of the happiness of a great knight and of a very beautiful young woman, avatars of the couple formed by the giant and the fairy, but in this instance one of Erec's companions and a cousin of Enide, pure products of the Arthurian world to which they will return. However, the orchard of the fairy of the Ile d'Or, in the *Bel Inconnu*, revives the mythical figure of the fairy who mercilessly exposes her successive lovers (whose heads are nailed onto stakes surrounding the orchard) to the risks of knightly encounters. The resurgence of a mythic scenario is most interesting. However, the fact that Renaud de Beaujeu abandons Chrétien's prudent treatment of this type of motif also dramatizes one of Chrétien's essential contributions to the art of romance writing. After Chrétien, fiction no longer needed to hide beneath a veneer of pseudo-realism. It could freely assert itself as such and play unhampered with the *merveilleux* and the suspension of the natural and moral laws governing the 'real' world – until other authors would at the same time be bolder still and turn realism itself into fiction, as exemplified by the work of Jean Renart.[28] Nevertheless, the rivalry between Chrétien and the writers of the thirteenth century, Arthurian or not, is indicated by such signs (even if they are topoi) as Renart's need to emphasize, in *Guillaume de Dole*, the extent to which his heroine, Liénor, surpasses in beauty the young women who used to bring joy to the court of the good King Arthur, or how, in the *Lai de l'Ombre*, the young and, as he notes, anonymous hero's qualities equalled those of Gauvain.

Chrétien's influence on later literature was not limited, however, to providing characters, some of whom, too closely identified with their destiny, were 'forgotten' by verse romance authors. Nor was this influence confined to proposing motifs largely borrowed from Celtic myths and traditions, which Chrétien had already reworked and no doubt adapted to suit his early readers. Chrétien's tremendous influence lay as well in his ability to invent a new literary language that departed from the cumbersome devices of the romances of antiquity. Along

---

[28] Another means is of course allegorical fiction, produced at the same time by Guillaume de Lorris in the first *Roman de la Rose*.

with the characters, the structures and the motifs, it was this language that became a sort of 'standard' for Arthurian verse romances. How can one draw a portrait, risk a long description or linger on the superfluous, when Chrétien has already decreed that one must be brief, aim for what is essential and never interfere with the progression of the narrative, even though he himself also, when appropriate, inserts numerous monologues and dialogues, sketches out (with the means available in his time) a psychological analysis and ultimately, and excessively, surrenders to the pleasure of description? How can one not be inspired by a discourse that dissects *ad infinitum* the sorrows and the joys of love and by long metaphors – for the fascinating beauty of the gaze of the beloved, for the arrow of desire, or for the heart, alternately given, imprisoned, taken back or shared – that reach the pinnacle of refinement (of baroque excess?) in *Cligés*, but also in the *Le Chevalier de la Charrette* or *Le Chevalier au Lion*? In addition, romance authors almost literally reused the formulas that ensured a narrative control that was as efficient as it was offhand ('Que vous dirais-je de plus? Pourquoi vous ennuyer? A quoi bon m'attarder . . .?' [What more can I tell you? Why try your patience? Why pause . . .?]) or intervened in the transparent guise of a self-assured and mischievous narrator. These authors made the expressions, which became real 'romance clichés', their own. They also appropriated the rhyming games[29] that became crystallized, as early as *Erec et Enide*, around key words such as 'aventure', 'merveilleux', 'périlleux' or that became attached to important locations such as the Round Table (Table Ronde comme le monde [round like the 'world']), the castle (the 'castel', almost always 'bel' and 'bien assis' [beautiful and well situated]), the forest ('aventureuse', 'périlleuse' [full of adventure and danger]), the tree and the fountain, the carefully enclosed orchard, the crossing, the ford or the bridge. As is evidenced by the visible discomfort of some authors, trapped by the formulas and commonplaces that they tried to renew, or possibly to disarticulate, one instantly senses the weight of the influence exerted by Chrétien and the desire, often unrealized, to rediscover the secrets of a compact, lean and efficient style of writing. The author of *Yder* confirmed this trend by making fun of these *troveors* who exert themselves in their description of orchards, tents and other objects, and by unconditionally condemning the recourse to hyperbole, the source of error.[30]

It seems – but perhaps this is a retrospective illusion – as if Chrétien's successors neatly divided up their inheritance. Too 'byzantine', Alexandre and Cligés appear to have been soon forgotten. However, it may be that *Cligés* started another trend, that of the heroic love-quest oriented toward the East and toward an exoticism of a different kind, as is exemplified by the quest undertaken by the young Partonopeu de Blois,[31] the lover (soon to be rewarded) of a fairy, the mistress of Byzantium.[32] We have noted the disappearance of Yvain and Erec and, by contrast, the new importance given to Gauvain in the verse romances.

---

[29] See Emmanuèle Baumgartner, 'Jeux de rimes et roman arthurien', *Romania*, 105 (1984), 1–15, repr. in E. Baumgartner, *De l'histoire de Troie au livre du Graal: le temps, le récit (XIIe–XIIIe siècles)* (Orléans, 1994), pp. 49–59.
[30] See *Yder*, ed. Adams, vss 4444–58.
[31] See *Partonopeu de Blois*, ed. Joseph Gildéa (Villanova, PA, 1967).
[32] On the intertextual relationship between Chrétien and the author of *Partonopeu*, see Bruckner,

On the other hand, it was around the figures of Lancelot and, to a lesser extent, of Perceval[33] that the enormous textual corpus of the prose Arthurian romances crystallized, especially the central cycle of the *Lancelot-Graal*. In this cycle, Chrétien's influence is seemingly more diffuse and less exclusive. Throughout the different parts of the *Lancelot-Graal*, his influence competes with other sources, other 'matières', and other styles of writing. Merlin the prophet, absent from Chrétien's universe, reappears. The cycle again borrows from Geoffrey of Monmouth and Wace the 'historical' dimension of Arthur's reign, unfurling in time. Lancelot and Guenevere's love is inspired by scenes from the 'matière' of *Tristan*.[34] Chrétien's influence, however, appeared much more openly in certain parts of *Lancelot*, the most visible example being the episode of Guenevere's abduction, a recasting of the *Conte de la Charrette*.[35] More generally, Chrétien's oeuvre provides the basis for the *Lancelot-Graal* (and of the romances that it in turn influenced, particularly the Prose *Tristan*), which fuse aspects of the *Chevalier de la Charrette* with those of the *Conte du Graal*. The *Lancelot-Graal* relies on the tension at the heart of the Arthurian world between the motif of the Grail and its quest, on the one hand, and, on the other, the adventures that unfolded in a knightly universe dominated by the figure of Lancelot, and in which love would long remain what would ensure the strength, the cohesion and the duration of Arthur's kingdom.[36]

If the primary goal of the *Lancelot-Graal* cycle was indeed to give an accurate representation of Arthurian/fictional time based on the Christian model of History (the only model available at the time), Lancelot and Perceval, as well as the motifs associated with them, seem *a priori* to be the most suited to this purpose. With their origins and destiny left uncertain by Chrétien, Lancelot and Perceval incarnate, in a complementary manner, the two temporal modes upon which the romance fiction plays. Perceval is the embodiment of the linear time of the quest, which, since the *Conte du Graal*, means the end of adventures, and thus of Arthurian times. The lover of a woman whom he can never make his queen, Lancelot, rather than the too available and overused Gauvain of the verse romances, is *par excellence* the hero whose wandering is prolonged indefinitely by the same desire. Perceval would, however, soon be eclipsed in the cycle by Galaad, the newcomer. Yet, that Galaad is the son of Lancelot means by the same token the procreation of these times, the moment when the circular time of the adventures would yield to the unwavering trajectory of the Grail quest, of which

---

'Intertextuality', pp. 227–31. For an opposing perspective, see Penny Eley and Penny Simons, '*Partonopeus de Blois* and Chrétien de Troyes: A Re-assessment', in *Romania*, 117, (1999), 316–41.

[33] Perceval is the chosen Grail hero in the prose trilogy of the pseudo-Robert de Boron (*Joseph, Merlin, Perceval*) and in the *Perlesvaus*, a prose romance no doubt contemporary with the *Lancelot*.

[34] However, one must remember that the Tristan legend and Thomas's romance cast a long shadow over the work of Chrétien.

[35] A formula by which the prose writer no doubt refers to his source. See *Lancelot du Lac*, ed. and trans. François Mosès, 5 vols (Paris, 1991–99); I (ed. and trans. Yvan G. Lepage and Marie-Louise Ollier), p. 66.

[36] See Emmanuèle Baumgartner, 'Arthur et les chevaliers *envoisiez*', *Romania*, 105 (1984), 312–25, repr. in Baumgartner, *De l'histoire de Troie au livre du Graal*, pp. 263–76.

the cycle would soon announce the absolute origin, in the latest romance of the cycle, *L'Estoire del saint Graal*. One can only speculate as to a possible end of the *Conte du Graal* and the meaning of the complementarity that emerged between Perceval and Gauvain.[37] However, one can surmise that the author or authors of the prose cycle understood the central importance of ensuring the mastery of time and configuring its course, from the obscure beginnings (Perceval) to the 'time regained' of the Château des Reines [Castle of the Queens] (Gauvain).

However, the authors of the *Lancelot-Graal*, and of *Lancelot* in particular, were not content merely to link Lancelot to the Grail, the theme of wandering to that of the quest, and human love and the feats that it inspired to the elucidations of the mysteries. These authors systematically borrowed from Chrétien – along with the places, the characters and the situations that are now associated with them – the motifs and paths that, for the most part, were reworked in light of the primary goal of fashioning and filling out Arthurian time. For instance, Chrétien's rapid mention in the *Charrette* of the fairy that 'nurtured' Lancelot in infancy and gave him a magical ring inspired the important character of the Dame du Lac [Lady of the Lake], the motif of young Lancelot's concealed childhood or, on another level, the often disrupted circulation of magical rings in the romance as a whole. Moreover, on many levels, a given motif could be multiplied, appearing in two, three or more forms. Thus, the hero's numerous raptures, when he is thinking too intently about the queen, are associated (or not) with the motif of the fall from a horse, more or less serious in nature, with the fight at a ford defended by some hostile knight or with a tournament taking place under the lady's gaze. Ladies and maidens in love, devoted or cruelly disappointed, play an important role in the hero's eventful career and are inherited from Chrétien's figures of the 'demoiselle entreprenante' [enterprising maiden], the seneschal's wife and Méléagant's sister, while other examples of particularly prolific narrative motifs include the 'don contraignant' [blind promise] or the unusual custom, invented by Chrétien in the *Chevalier de la Charrette*, of the 'conduit' [safe- conduct] of the maidens.

The rewritings of the 'Conte de la Charrette' in the prose *Lancelot*, of which there are at least three different versions, predictably constitute a privileged area for measuring the impact and resonance of Chrétien's romance.[38] Three manuscripts (BNF fr. 119, BNF fr. 122 and Paris, Ars. 3480) offer a 'de-rhymed' version of the *Chevalier de la Charrette*, attesting to direct contact with the original work. The long version, the only one we are considering here, inserted Chrétien's autonomous 'conte' [tale] into a broader context that tended to elucidate (or

---

[37] This complementarity is already textually visible through the device of alternation, which can be viewed as an early version of the device of 'entrelacement' [interlace] characteristic of the *Lancelot-Graal*.

[38] Alexandre Micha established the existence of two main versions, a long and a short one (which is no doubt an abridged version). An intermediary version also exists, with three manuscripts containing 'de-rhymed' versions of Chrétien's romance. Regarding these different versions, see Annie Combes, *Les Voies de l'aventure: réécriture et composition romanesque dans le 'Lancelot' en prose* (Paris, 2001), pp. 201–48. Combes is preparing an edition of the 'de-rhymed' versions.

justify) that which remained immanent in Chrétien's work, such as the causes of the imprisonment of Arthur's subjects in the kingdom of Gorre or the hatred between Meleaguant and Lancelot. However, the connecting thread that runs through the entire episode, the recent death and burial of Galehaut, Lancelot's companion, is a truly original invention of the prose writer. Another characteristic trait of the new text – and of prose romances in general – is the recasting of a given motif. A revealing example is the qualifying trial of the tomb, in which the chosen one must lift the slab and whose prototype is, of course, the episode of the 'Cimetière futur' [future cemetery] in the *Charrette*. In the prose text, at the Douloureuse Garde, Lancelot, by (initially) completing the trial successfully, frees the prisoners of the castle and learns his name and that of his father. He can then liberate the castle from its spells and change its name to 'Joyeuse Garde', venturing into the underground passages of a place besieged by the devil, to the very heart of the adventure.[39] In the recasting of the *Charrette*, at the 'Cimetière aux deux tombes' [cemetery of the two tombs],[40] it is through his success at the trial associated with the tomb of his ancestor Galaad that Lancelot becomes known as the liberator of the prisoners of the kingdom of Gorre. Yet he also receives revelations about his ancestors and makes possible the burial – the deliverance – of Galaad in his land of origin, Wales. He cannot, however, descend as liberator as far as the tomb of Symeu, which is a later adventure reserved for Galaad. Presented by Chrétien in its mysterious immanence, the repeated motif of the Cemetery (which no longer has anything to do with a 'cimetière futur') thus enables the prose writer to offer a gradual progression and initiation of his hero, to invent the past and the future of his lineage and to introduce the distinction, which the *Queste du saint Graal* would systematize, between 'social' knighthood (Lancelot) and 'celestial' knighthood (Galaad). On a no doubt more anecdotic level, the status of the *charrette* associated in Chrétien with a very strange custom, is also determined as the text progresses. Once Bohort succeeds in getting all of Arthur's court to climb into it, it loses any infamous connotation and will thereafter be replaced by an old horse in its function of itinerant pillory.[41]

If one studied the recastings and shifts carried out on the motifs inherited from Chrétien, the conclusion would doubtless be the same. The author of the *Lancelot* did not seek to assert himself over Chrétien, to shift the lines, or to play with motifs, as did the more inventive of the verse romance authors. Rather, it seems that he sought to exhaust the resources of the text by projecting them into the time of the narrative and by using them to forge a chain of causes and consequences that generated and gave its apparent truth to fictional time. If all great romance is about time, one can say that despite its refusal or inability to project itself into time – in essence to progress from fragment to cycle – Chrétien's

---

[39] See *Lancelot du Lac*, ed. and trans. François Mosès, et al., I, ed. Elspeth Kennedy, trans. François Mosès, p. 528.
[40] See *Lancelot du Lac*, ed. and trans. François Mosès, et al., V, pp 126–38.
[41] *Lancelot du Lac*, ed. Lepage and Ollier, p. 234.

oeuvre from the *Chevalier de la Charrette* to the *Conte du Graal*, contained the seed that would bear fruit a hundredfold in the prose.[42]

By inventing the motifs of the Grail and its quest and leaving them unfinished, Chrétien again provided for his successors an attractive and treacherous path. As the authors of the Continuations understood, the motif, as it appeared, of questions to be asked became obsolete after Perceval's visit to the hermit. It was thus imperative to shift the motif and to establish, through further questioning, the Grail's past, its origin and that of the Lance, the broken sword and the wound of the Fisher King. *Perlesvaus* and the *Queste du saint Graal* chose another path. Both revisited some episodes taken from Chrétien by charging them with an allegorical *senefiance*. In the *Queste*, for instance, the struggle between a lion and a serpent in which Perceval intervened[43] is reused from the *Chevalier au Lion*, but it henceforth 'signifies' the battle between the Old and the New Law. The device, often reused in the text, shows how one can create an allegorical discourse from anything, unless it also signifies the new power of the fable, the Arthurian fiction, to provide access to the *senefiance*. Yet, never did Chrétien thus freeze the meaning of a motif or a character. Nonetheless, a much more radical change, shared by *Perlesvaus* and the *Queste*, is to substitute the motif of the vision for the motif of questions to be asked. In the prose texts, the Grail quest is defined and developed as the quest for a total vision (the *veraie semblance*) of the secrets of God and for access to the foundation of knowledge – *l'acomençaille*, as the *Queste* says – which could not, at that time, be revealed anywhere other than through God. It is impossible to say whether Chrétien had considered such a reuse (such a deviation?) of the motif. Soon after, in fact, the Grail quest in the prose romances lost, for the most part, its religious and even mythic dimension to become, as in the Prose *Tristan*, for instance, and even more so in the *Post-Vulgate Queste*, a machine for the production of new knightly adventures, all the while serving as prelude, with its numerous deaths, to the final massacre of the *Mort Artu*. Need one look elsewhere to find Chrétien's vital legacy?

As diverse as it was, Chrétien's entire work was organized, it seems, around the quest for 'joy'. To affirm and construct oneself as a hero in this universe, ideal yet full of risk – as each romance starts the battle again from scratch – is it not equivalent to the noble struggle to achieve 'joy' for oneself which is then dispensed to the world with 'largesse', this joy that permeates Erec in the orchard of King Evrain, fascinates Yvain at the edge of the Fontaine au Pin and intoxicates Lancelot in the arms of the Queen? But is it not also this quest for joy, for an ever-threatened equilibrium between individual and collective happiness, that was the real backbone of the prose romances, that set the descendants of Chrétien's heroes again on the path of adventures and that signalled the fulfilment of their destiny? Galaad dies ravished by the vision of the Grail. Lancelot, the son of the 'la reine aux grandes douleurs' [the queen of great sorrows]

---

[42] Chrétien had forseen this influence in the prologue of the *Conte du Graal* (vs. 8): 'Chrestïen semme et fait semence' [sows and casts the seed], etc.

[43] *La Queste del saint Graal*, ed. Albert Pauphilet (Paris, 1921), pp. 94–104.

remains, from Chrétien to the prose romance, the 'chevalier desiré' [the desired knight] and *'fin'amant'* [courtly lover] – the one who, in the footsteps of Erec, of the Chevalier au Lion, of the Chevalier de la Charrette and of the Gauvain of the Château des Reines, undertakes the quest and restores his joy/Joy, taking it with him to his kingdom, this 'Joyeuse Garde' that is his dearest conquest and his grave.[44]

---

[44] It should be recalled that the *Mort le roi Artu* ends with the burial of Lancelot at Joyeuse Garde, in the tomb where Galehaut already lies.

Select Bibliography

BIBLIOGRAPHIES

Bibliographical Bulletin of the International Arthurian Society / Bulletin bibliographique de la Société internationale arthurienne. Published annually since 1949.
Kelly, Douglas. *Chrétien de Troyes. An Analytic Bibliography*. London, 1976.
Kelly, Douglas, et al. *Chrétien de Troyes: An Analytical Bibliography, Supplement 1*. London, 2002.

SELECTED EDITIONS

Chrétien de Troyes. *Cligés*, ed. Claude Luttrell and Stewart Gregory. Cambridge, 1993.
Chrétien de Troyes. *Œuvres complètes*. Paris, 1994. Genl ed. Daniel Poirion: Introduction (Daniel Poirion); ed. Peter F. Dembowski for *Erec et Enide*; ed. Philippe Walter for *Cligès*; ed. Karl D. Uitti, and trans. Philippe Walter for *Yvain ou le Chevalier au Lion*; ed. Daniel Poirion for *Lancelot ou le Chevalier de la Charrette* and *Perceval ou le Conte du Graal*; ed. and trans. Anne Berthelot for *Philomena, Guillaume d'Angleterre, Chansons courtoises*.
Chrétien de Troyes. *Philomena, conte raconté d'après Ovide*, ed. Cornelis De Boer. Paris, 1909.
Chrétien de Troyes. *Le Roman de Perceval, ou Le Conte du Graal*, ed. Keith Busby. Tübingen, 1993.
Chrétien de Troyes. *Le Roman de Perceval, ou le Conte du Graal, publié d'après le MS fr. 12.576 de la Bibliothèque nationale*, ed. William Roach (Geneva-Paris 1956, 1958², revised and enlarged).
Chrétien de Troyes. *Les Romans de Chrétien de Troyes édités d'après la copie de Guiot (Bibl. nat. fr. 794)*, ed. Mario Roques [unless otherwise indicated]. Paris, 1952–75: vol. I, *Erec et Enide* (1952); vol. II, *Cligés*, ed. Alexandre Micha (1957); vol. III, *Le Chevalier de la charrete* (1958); vol. IV, *Le Chevalier au lion (Yvain)* (1960); vols V–VI, *Le Conte du Graal (Perceval)*, ed. Félix Lecoy (1973 and 1975).
Chrétien de Troyes. *Romans suivis des Chansons, avec, en appendice, Philomena*. Genl ed. Michel Zink. Paris, 1994: ed. and trans. Jean-Marie Fritz for *Erec et Enide*; Charles Méla and Olivier Collet for *Cligès*; David Hult for *Le Chevalier au lion (Yvain)*; Charles Méla for *Le Chevalier de la Charrette ou Le Roman de Lancelot* and *Le Conte du Graal*; Marie-Claire Zai for the *Chansons*; Olivier Collet for the translation of *Philomena* [using the text of De Boer].
Chrétien de Troyes. *Sämtliche erhaltene Werke*, ed, Wendelin Foerster. Halle, 1884–32: vol. I, *Cligés* (1884); vol. II, *Der Löwenritter (Yvain)* (1887); vol. III, *Erec und Enide* (1890); vol. IV, *Der Karrenritter und das Wilhelmsleben* (1899); vol. V, *Der Percevalroman (Li Contes del graal)*, ed. A. Hilka, Halle, 1932.
Pyrame et Thisbé, Narcisse, Philomena: trois contes du XIIe siècle français imités d'Ovide, ed. Emmanuèle Baumgartner. Paris, 2000.

Three Ovidian Tales of Love ('Piramus et Tisbé', 'Narcisus et Dane', and 'Philomena et Procné'), ed. and trans. Raymond J. Cormier. New York, 1986.

SELECTED BILINGUAL (OLD FRENCH/ENGLISH) EDITIONS

Chrétien de Troyes. *Erec and Enide*, ed. and trans. Carleton W. Carroll. New York, 1987.
Chrétien de Troyes. *The Knight with the Lion or Yvain (Le Chevalier au lion)*, ed. and trans. William W. Kibler. New York, 1985.
Chrétien de Troyes. *Lancelot, or the Knight of the Cart (Le Chevalier de la Charrette)*, ed. and trans. William W. Kibler. New York, 1981.
Chrétien de Troyes. *The Story of the Grail (Li Contes del Graal, or Perceval)*, ed. Rupert T. Pickens; trans. William W. Kibler. New York, 1990.

SELECTED TRANSLATIONS

Chrétien de Troyes. *Arthurian Romances*, trans. William W. Kibler [*Cligés, Lancelot, Yvain* and *Perceval*] and Carleton W. Carroll [*Erec and Enide*]. London, 1991.
The Complete Romances of Chrétien de Troyes, trans. David Staines. Bloomington, 1990.
Chrétien de Troyes, trans. Ruth Harwood Cline. Athens, GA: *Yvain; or The Knight with the Lion* (1975); *Perceval; or The Story of the Grail* (New York, 1983; Athens, 1985); *Lancelot; or The Knight of the Cart* (1990); *Erec et Enide* (2000); *Cligès* (2000).

CRITICAL STUDIES

Allen, Peter L. *The Art of Love: Amatory Fiction from Ovid to the 'Romance of the Rose'*. Philadelphia, 1992.
Baldwin, John W. *The Government of Philip Augustus: Foundations of French Royal Power in the Middle Ages*. Berkeley, 1986.
Baumgartner, Emmanuèle. *Chrétien de Troyes: Yvain, Lancelot, la charrette et le lion*. Paris, 1992.
———. *Romans de Chrétien de Troyes*. Paris, 2003.
Benton, John, 'The Court of Champagne', *Speculum*, 36 (1961), 551–91.
Bezzola, Reto R. *Le Sens de l'aventure et de l'amour: Chrétien de Troyes*. Paris, 1947.
Bloch, R. Howard. *Medieval French Literature and Law*. Berkeley, 1977.
———. *Medieval Misogyny and the Invention of Western Romantic Love*. Chicago, 1991.
Boase, Roger. *The Origin and Meaning of Courtly Love: A Critical Study of European Scholarship*. Manchester, 1977.
Bruckner, Matilda Tomaryn. '*Le Chevalier de la Charrette (Lancelot)*', in Kelly, *Romances*, pp. 132–81.
———. *Narrative Invention in Twelfth-Century French Romance: The Convention of Hospitality (1160–1200)*. Lexington, KY, 1980.
———. *Shaping Romance: Interpretation, Truth, and Closure in Twelfth-Century French Fictions*. Philadelphia, 1993.
Buckbee, Edward J. '*Erec et Enide*'. In Kelly, *Romances*, pp. 48–88.
Burns, E. Jane. *Bodytalk: When Women Speak in Old French Literature*. Philadelphia, 1993.
———. 'Courtly Love : Who Needs It? Recent Feminist Work in the Medieval French Tradition', *Signs*, 27 (2001), 23–57.

Burgess, Glyn S. *Chrétien de Troyes: Erec et Enide*. Critical Guides to French Texts. London, 1984.

Burgess, Glyn S., and Karen Pratt, eds. *The Arthur of the French*. Cardiff. Forthcoming.

Busby, Keith. *Chrétien de Troyes: Perceval (Le Conte du Graal)*. Critical Guides to French Texts. London, 1993.

──────. *Codex and Context: Reading Old French Verse Narrative in Manuscript*. 2 vols. Amsterdam, 2002.

Busby, Keith, Terry Nixon, Alison Stones and Lori Walters. *Les Manuscrits de Chrétien de Troyes / The Manuscripts of Chrétien de Troyes*. 2 vols. Amsterdam, 1993.

Chandès, Gérard. *Le Serpent, la femme et l'épée. Recherches sur l'imaginaire symbolique d'un romancier médiéval*. Amsterdam, 1986.

Chênerie, Marie-Luce. *Le Chevalier errant dans les romans arthuriens en vers des XIIe et XIIIe siècles*. Geneva, 1986.

Cline, Ruth H. 'Heart and Eyes', *Romance Philology*, 25 (1971–72), 263–97.

Colby, Alice M. *The Portrait in Twelfth-Century Literature: An Example of the Stylistic Originality of Chrétien de Troyes*. Geneva, 1965.

Combes, Annie. *Les Voies de l'aventure: réécriture et composition romanesque dans le 'Lancelot' en prose*. Paris, 2001.

Doutrepont, Georges. *Les Mises en prose des épopées et des romans chevaleresques du XIVe au XVIe siècle*. Bruxelles, 1939.

Duby, Georges. *Le Chevalier, la femme et le prêtre*. Paris, 1981. Trans. Barbara Bray as *The Knight, the Lady and the Priest: The Making of Marriage in Medieval France*. New York, 1983.

Dufournet, Jean, ed. *'Le Chevalier au lion' de Chrétien de Troyes: approches d'un chef-d'œuvre*. Paris, 1988.

Duggan, Joseph J. *The Romances of Chrétien de Troyes*. New Haven, 2001.

Faral, Edmond. *Les Arts poétiques du XIIe et du XIIIe siècle: recherches et documents sur la technique littéraire du moyen âge*. Paris, 1924.

Fenster, Thelma S., ed. *Arthurian Women: A Casebook*. New York, 1996; repr. 2000.

Fourrier, Anthime. *Le Courant réaliste dans le roman courtois, en France, au moyen âge. I: Les Débuts (XIIe siècle)*. Paris, 1960.

Fourquet, Jean. 'Le Rapport entre l'œuvre et la source chez Chrétien de Troyes et le problème des sources bretonnes', *Romance Philology*, 9 (1955–56), 298–312.

Frappier, Jean. *Etude sur 'Yvain' ou 'le Chevalier au Lion'*. Paris, 1969.

──────. *Chrétien de Troyes et le mythe du graal: étude sur 'Perceval' ou 'le conte du graal'*. Paris, 1979.

──────. *Chrétien de Troyes: l'homme et l'œuvre*. Paris, 1957; rev. 1968. Trans. Raymond J. Cormier as *Chrétien de Troyes: The Man and His Work*. Athens, OH, 1982.

Freeman, Michelle A. 'Cligés'. In Kelly, *Romances*, pp. 89–131.

──────. *The Poetics of 'Translatio studii' and 'Conjointure': Chrétien de Troyes's Cligés*. Lexington, KY, 1979.

Gallais, Pierre. 'Recherches sur la mentalité des romanciers français du moyen âge', *Cahiers de civilisation médiévale*, 7 (1964), 479–93; and 13 (1970), 333–47.

Gravdal, Kathryn. *Ravishing Maidens: Writing Rape in Medieval French Literature and Law*. Philadelphia, 1991.

Green, D.H. *The Beginnings of Medieval Romance: Fact and Fiction, 1150–1220*. Cambridge, 2002.

Grimbert, Joan Tasker. *'Yvain' dans le miroir: une poétique de la réflexion dans le 'Chevalier au lion' de Chrétien de Troyes*. Amsterdam, 1988.

──────, ed. *Tristan and Isolde: A Casebook*. New York, 1995; repr. 2001.

Groos, Arthur, and Norris J. Lacy. *Perceval / Parzival: A Casebook*. New York, 2002.

Guerreau-Jalabert, Anita. 'Romans de Chrétien de Troyes et contes folkloriques: rapprochements et observations de méthode'. *Romania*, 104 (1993), 1–48.

Haidu, Peter. *Aesthetic Distance in Chrétien de Troyes: Irony and Comedy in 'Cligés' and 'Perceval'*. Geneva, 1968.

———. *Lion-queue-coupée: l'écart symbolique chez Chrétien de Troyes*. Geneva, 1968.

———. 'Au début du roman, l'ironie'. *Poétique*, 36 (1978), 443–66.

———. 'Text and History: The Semiosis of Twelfth-Century Lyric as Sociohistorical Phenomenon (Chrétien de Troyes: "D'amors qui m'a tolu")'. *Semiotica*, 33 (1981), 1–62.

Harf-Lancner, Laurence. *Les Fées au Moyen Age*. Paris, 1984; 1991.

———. *Le Monde des fées dans l'Occident médiéval*. Paris, 2003.

Holmes, Urban T., Jr., *Chrétien de Troyes* (New York, 1970).

Hult, David F. 'Author/Narrator/Speaker: The Voice of Authority in Chrétien's Charrete'. In *Discourses of Authority in Medieval and Renaissance Literature*, ed. Kevin Brownlee and Walter Stephens. Hanover, NH, 1989, pp. 76–96.

Hunt, Tony. 'Tradition and Originality in the Prologues of Crestien de Troyes'. *Forum for Modern Language Studies*, 8 (1972), 320–44.

———. 'Aristotle, Dialectic, and Courtly Literature', *Viator*, 10 (1979), 95–129.

———. 'The Emergence of the Knight in France and England 1000–1200'. *Forum for Modern Language Studies*, 17 (1981), 93–114.

———. *Chrétien de Troyes, Yvain*. Critical Guides to French Texts. London, 1986.

———. 'Chrétien's Prologues Reconsidered'. In *Conjunctures: Medieval Studies in Honor of Douglas Kelly*, ed. Keith Busby and Norris J. Lacy. Amsterdam, 1994, pp. 153–68.

Kay, Sarah. 'Who was Chrétien de Troyes?' *Arthurian Literature*, 15 (1997), 1–35.

Kellermann, Wilhelm. *Aufbaustil und Weltbild Chrestiens von Troyes im Percevalroman*. Halle, 1936.

Kelly, Douglas. *'Sens' et 'Conjointure' in the 'Chevalier de la Charrette'*. The Hague, 1966.

———, ed. *The Romances of Chrétien de Troyes: A Symposium*. Lexington, KY, 1985.

———. *The Art of Medieval French Romance*. Madison, 1992.

———. *Medieval French Romance*. New York, 1993.

———. *The Conspiracy of Allusion: Description, Rewriting, and Authorship from Macrobius to Medieval Romance*. Leiden, 1999.

Kennedy, Edward Donald. *King Arthur: A Casebook*. New York, 1996; repr. 2001.

Köhler, Erich. *Ideal und Wirklichkeit in der höfischen Epik: Studien zur Form der frühen Artus- und Graldichtung*. Tübingen, 1956. French trans. as *L'Aventure chevaleresque: idéal et réalité dans le roman courtois* by Eliane Kaufholz. Paris, 1974.

Krueger, Roberta L. *Women Readers and the Ideology of Gender in Old French Verse Romance*. Cambridge, 1993.

Lachet, Claude, ed. *L'Œuvre de Chrétien de Troyes dans la littérature française: réminiscences, résurgences, et réécritures*. Lyon, 1997.

Lacy, Norris J. *The Craft of Chrétien de Troyes: An Essay on Narrative Art*. Leiden, 1980.

———, Douglas Kelly and Keith Busby, eds. *The Legacy of Chrétien de Troyes*. 2 vols. Amsterdam, 1987–88.

———. *Medieval Arthurian Literature: A Guide to Recent Research*. New York, 1996.

———, et al., eds. *The New Arthurian Encyclopedia*. New York, 1991; rev. 1996.

———, and Geoffrey Ashe, with Debra Mancoff, *The Arthurian Handbook*, 2nd ed. New York: 1997.

Lazar, Moshé. *Amour courtois et 'fin'amors' dans la littérature du XIIe siècle*. Paris, 1964.

Le Goff, Jacques, and Pierre Vidal-Naquet. 'Lévi-Strauss en Brocéliande: esquisse pour une analyse d'un roman courtois'. *Critique*, 325 (1974), 541–71.

Loomis, Roger Sherman, and Laura Hibbard Loomis. *Arthurian Legends in Medieval Art*. London, 1938.

————. *Arthurian Tradition and Chrétien de Troyes*. New York, 1949.

————, ed. *Arthurian Literature in the Middle Ages*. Oxford, 1959.

Luttrell, Claude. *The Creation of the First Arthurian Romance: A Quest*. Evanston, 1974.

Maddox, Donald. *The Arthurian Romances of Chrétien de Troyes: Once and Future Fictions*. Cambridge, 1991.

————. *Structure and Sacring: The Systematic Kingdom in Chrétien's 'Erec'*. Lexington, KY, 1978.

Mahoney, Dhira B., ed. *The Grail: A Casebook*. New York, 2000.

Marx, Jean. *La Légende arthurienne et le graal*. Paris, 1952.

McCash, June Hall Martin. 'Eleanor of Aquitaine and Marie de Champagne: A Relationship Revisited'. *Speculum*, 54 (1979), 698–711.

McCracken, Peggy. *The Romance of Adultery: Queenship and Sexual Transgression in Old French Literature*. Philadelphia, 1998.

Méla, Charles. *La Reine et le graal: la 'conjointure' dans les romans du Graal, de Chrétien de Troyes au 'Tristan' en prose*. Paris, 1979.

Ménard, Philippe. *De Chrétien de Troyes au 'Tristan en prose': études sur les romans de la Table Ronde*. Geneva, 1999.

Mullally, Evelyn. *The Artist at Work: Narrative Technique in Chrétien de Troyes*. Philadelphia, 1988.

Nykrog, Per. *Chrétien de Troyes, romancier discutable*. Geneva, 1996.

Ollier, Marie-Louise, 'The Author in the Text: The Prologues of Chrétien de Troyes'. *Yales French Studies*, 51 (1974), 26–41.

————. 'Proverbe et sentence: le discours d'autorité chez Chrétien de Troyes'. *Revue des sciences humaines*, 41 (1976), 329–57.

————. *Lexique et concordance de Chrétien de Troyes d'après la copie de Guiot, avec introduction, index et rimaire*. Montreal, 1986.

Paris, Gaston. 'Etudes sur les romans de la Table Ronde: Lancelot du Lac, I. Le *Lanzelet* d'Ulrich de Zatzikhoven; Lancelot du Lac, II. *Le Conte de la Charrette'*, *Romania*, 10 (1881), 465–96; *Romania*, 12 (1883), 459–534.

————. 'Romans en vers du cycle de la Table Ronde'. *Histoire littéraire de la France*, 30 (1888), 1–270.

Paterson, Lee. *Negotiating the Past: The Historical Understanding of Medieval Literature*. Madison, WI, 1987.

Payen, Jean-Charles. *Le Motif du repentir dans la littérature française médiévale (des origines à 1230)*. Geneva, 1967.

————. 'Lancelot contre Tristan, ou la conjuration d'un mythe subversif (réflexions sur l'idéologie romanesque au moyen âge). In *Mélanges Pierre Le Gentil*. Paris, 1973, pp. 617–32.

Pickens, Rupert T. *The Welsh Knight: Paradoxicality in Chrétien's Conte du Graal*. Lexington, 1977.

————. 'Historical Consciousness in Old French Narrative'. *French Forum*, 4 (1979), 268–84.

————, ed. *The Sower and the Seed: Essays on Chrétien de Troyes*. Lexingon, KY, 1983.

————. 'Le Conte du Graal (Perceval)'. In Kelly, *Romances*, pp. 232–86.

Poirion, Daniel. *Le Merveilleux dans la littérature française du moyen âge*. Paris, 1982.

Polak, Lucie. *Chrétien de Troyes: Cligés*. Critical Guides to French Texts. London, 1982.

Pollman, Leo. *Chrétien de Troyes und der Conte del Graal*. Tübingen, 1965.

Quéruel, Danielle, ed. *Amour et chevalerie dans les romans de Chrétien de Troyes*. Paris, 1995.

Ribard, Jacques. *Chrétien de Troyes, Le Chevalier de la Charrette: essai d'interprétation symbolique*. Paris, 1972.

Sargent-Baur, Barbara N. *La Destre et la senestre: Etude sur le 'Conte du Graal' de Chrétien de Troyes*. Amsterdam, 2000.

Schmolke-Hasselmann, Beate. *Der arthurische Versroman von Chrestien bis Froissart: zur Geschichte einer Gattung* (Tübingen, 1980), pp. 178–248. Trans. Margaret and Roger Middleton as *The Evolution of Arthurian Romance: The Verse Tradition from Chrétien to Froissart*. Cambridge, 1998.

Snyder, Christopher. *The World of King Arthur*. London, 2000.

Topsfield, Leslie T. *Chrétien de Troyes: A Study of the Arthurian Romances*. Cambridge, 1981.

Trachsler, Richard. *Les Romans arthuriens en vers après Chrétien de Troyes*. Paris, 1997.

Uitti, Karl D. *'Le Chevalier au lion (Yvain)'*. In Kelly, *Romances*, pp. 182–231.

——, and Michelle A. Freeman. *Chrétien de Troyes Revisited*. New York, 1995.

Vinaver, Eugène. *A la recherche d'une poétique médiévale*. Paris, 1970.

——. *The Rise of Romance*. Oxford, 1971.

Vitz, Evelyn Birge. *Orality and Performance in Early French Romance*. Cambridge, 1999.

Walter, Philippe. *Canicule: essai de mythologie sur 'Yvain' de Chrétien de Troyes*. Paris, 1988.

Walters, Lori J., ed. *Lancelot and Guinevere: A Casebook*. New York, 1996; repr. 2002.

——. 'Le Rôle du scribe dans l'organisation des manuscrits des romans de Chrétien de Troyes'. *Romania*, 106 (1985), 303–25.

Wetherbee, Winthrop. *Platonism and Poetry in the Twelfth Century: The Literary Influence of the School of Chartres*. Princeton, 1972.

Whitaker, Muriel. *The Legends of King Arthur in Art*. Cambridge, 1990.

Zaddy, Z.P. *Chrétien Studies: Problems of Form and Meaning in 'Erec', 'Yvain', 'Cligés', and the Charrete'*. Glasgow, 1973.

Zink, Michel. 'Une Mutation de la conscience littéraire: le langage romanesque à travers des exemples français du XIIe siècle'. *Cahiers de civilisation médiévale*, 24 (1981), 3–27.

Index

ARTHURIAN STUDIES

Lightning Source UK Ltd.
Milton Keynes UK
UKHW021517070121
376603UK00003B/167